Practical Bookkeeping and Accounts

Seventh Edition

by A. J. Favell, B.Sc. (Econ.), A.C.I.S.
Late Principal of the Hammersmith Commercial Institute

Available:
Complete Course.
Part 1 (Elementary Course).
A KEY to the book.

University Tutorial Press Ltd
842 Yeovil Road, Slough, SL1 4JQ

Published by University Tutorial Press Ltd.
842 Yeovil Road, Slough, SL1 4JQ

Published 1935
Sixth Edition (Decimal) 1969
Seventh Edition 1980, Reprinted 1981

ISBN: Complete Course 0 7231 0801 3
Part 1 0 7231 0802 1

Printed in Great Britain by
Richard Clay (The Chaucer Press) Ltd.,
Bungay, Suffolk

Preface to the Seventh Edition
(Parts 1 & 2)

Practical Bookkeeping and Accounts describes the methods and principles on which accounts are based. The book is not restricted to the requirements of any particular examining body. It covers the requirements at Ordinary Level of the various Boards for the General Certificate in Education and of the elementary and intermediate examinations of the Royal Society of Arts and the London Chamber of Commerce. It also takes note of the requirements of the Business Education Council.

In the seventh edition a number of changes have been made, whilst retaining the general style and content of earlier editions, in order to improve the coverage of some topics and their sequence. The main changes are as follows:

(*a*) the chapter on Control Accounts (Ch. 13) has been brought forward to follow the initial treatment of sales, purchases and related matters;

(*b*) the chapters on partnership accounting (Ch. 33–36) have been brought together;

(*c*) the chapters on depreciation (Ch. 22), manufacturing accounts (Ch. 29) and mechanised accounting (Ch. 31) have been completely rewritten;

(*d*) new chapters have been added on accounting systems, flow charts and internal control (Ch. 16); funds flow statements (Ch. 30) and standard accounting practices (Ch. 43);

(*e*) recent examination papers or questions drawn from them have been included in the Appendices; these include several complete papers from the *Royal Society of Arts* (Stages 1 and 2) and selected questions from the *West African Examinations Council* School certificate papers.

(*f*) the sequence of some other chapters has been altered and some sections of the text have been moved to different chapters to improve the flow and development of ideas in the book;

(*g*) relevant changes in the law affecting accounts and in good accounting practice have been included up to the date of revision.

(*h*) monetary values have been increased in recognition of inflation, although even the revised figures may not long reflect reality;

(*i*) among other material, the vertical method of presenting final accounts has been used, some new terminology has been introduced, and the accounts are set out in a modern layout.

Acknowledgements

The publishers are particularly grateful to the following for undertaking the revision of the text: Professor A. M. Bourn (Department of Business Studies, University of Liverpool), and Mr. M. Chahin (formerly Lecturer at Ealing College). Thanks are due to all those who gave advice on the revision, particularly Mr. R. P. Jones (South Downs College of Further Education), Professor C. C. Magee (University College, Cardiff), Mr. R. C. Brown (Basildon College of Further Education) and Mr. J. I. Jacobson (Yaba College of Technology, Nigeria).

Thanks are due to the following for permission to reproduce material: John Wiley & Sons Inc., New York, for material on pp. 138 and 140–1; The Institute of Chartered Accountants (England & Wales) for material on pp. 191–2, 229 and 464–5.

The publishers would particularly like to thank the following examining bodies for permission to use past examination papers and questions: the Royal Society of Arts, and the West African Examinations Council. Thanks are due also to the following for permission to reprint past questions: The University of Cambridge Local Examinations Syndicate, the Northern Universities Joint Matriculation Board, the Oxford Delegacy of Local Examinations, the Associated Examining Board, the College of Preceptors, the London Chamber of Commerce, the Northern Counties Technical Examinations Council, the Union of Educational Institutions, the North Western Regional Examinations Board (formerly the Union of Lancashire and Cheshire Institutes). Where changes have been made to the amounts or wording of questions, this is indicated by the word *adapted*.

Contents

Part 1

Part 2 (only in the Complete Course)

1

Introduction

Bookkeeping is the recording of the financial transactions of a business in a methodical manner so that information on any point relating to them may be quickly obtained. The method of procedure is based upon definite principles which are discussed and illustrated in the chapters that follow. The kind of information which a trader may desire to have and which is readily available is summarised below.

The trader may discover:

(*a*) The value of his purchases.

(*b*) The value of his sales.

(*c*) His expenses.

(*d*) The amount of cash in the office or at the bank.

(*e*) The sums owing to him by customers.

(*f*) The sums owing by the business to creditors and lenders.

(*g*) The recorded value of the property and other possessions of the business.

(*h*) The profit or loss made during a particular period.

(*i*) The financial position of the business on any given day.

The ultimate purpose of business is to make a profit, by providing goods, services or employment. As every transaction plays its part in determining the final profit or loss for a trading period, accuracy in recording is essential. Such accuracy is also essential for the smooth running of a business as customers may be irritated and custom and money lost through inaccurate records of transactions. A bookkeeper, therefore, should cultivate accuracy and carefulness, should be able to write legibly, and to understand fully how to operate any equipment under his control.

The Business and the Owner

The first important point in the study of the principles of bookkeeping is to distinguish and separate the business from the owner. The bookkeeper records the transactions from the point of view of their effects on the business. The owner may personally attend to the buying and selling, but he must be regarded in such a case as acting on behalf of the business and not in his personal capacity. The sales and purchases must be recorded as sales and purchases by the business. This distinction should be borne in mind as the following chapters are studied.

Accounts as an Aid to Management

The owner of a business naturally wishes to run his business as efficiently as possible. One of the main purposes of keeping accounts is to enable him to do this. His accounts should tell him, so far as possible, the exact cost of what he is selling, the exact amount of each expense which is involved, and the exact revenue of the business. With such information the owner of the business can make comparisons from year to year, comparing the profit this year with that of preceding years and investigating the cause of any difference by making comparisons of the amount of each cost and each expense. These comparisons are much more difficult to make when prices are changing frequently by substantial amounts. By studying his accounts in this way the business man is helped to formulate a business policy. He may, for example, decide to raise or to lower prices, to advertise more, to change the method of delivery of his goods, or to change the organisation of the office work.

EXERCISES 1

1. Why is it necessary for a business to keep accounts? Give as many reasons as you can.

2. Why is it necessary to distinguish and separate the business from the owner?

3. What information is given in the accounts of a business?

2

The Ledger

The book required for a proper record of the transactions of a business is called the *Ledger*. It will be shown later how the recording is assisted, in certain circumstances, by the use of other books. A suitable Ledger may be purchased from a stationer who usually has a stock of Ledgers of various sizes and thicknesses. The Ledger may be recognised by the ruling of its pages, and an unused specimen page is shown below.

Specimen Page from the Ledger:

DATE	PARTICULARS	FOLIO	£	p	DATE	PARTICULARS	FOLIO	£	p

Ledgers are not always ruled in this way. With the growth of mechanised accounting, Ledger cards are increasingly used and are usually ruled as follows (the terms 'debit' and 'credit' are explained later in this chapter):

DATE	PARTICULARS	DEBIT	CREDIT	BALANCE

A sheet of paper ruled like this is called Ledger paper. Note that there are eight columns on a Ledger page, four of which fill half the width of the paper and are repeated again on the other half. A page in a Ledger is called a *folio*. The folios are numbered consecutively for reference purposes.

A Business Transaction

To show the particular use made of the columns and to make a start in the actual use of the Ledger, let us deal with the following example:

Example 1. M. Redman begins to deal in second-hand motor bikes, starting with £2 000 in cash.

On 1st January he buys 10 bikes for £1 200, paying cash down.

He sells 2 bikes on 8th January for cash at £250 each, and the remainder on 10th January for £200 each.

He pays £100 for advertising.

This example comprises several transactions which will have to be recorded in the Ledger, and they may be summarised as below:

(1) Redman separates from his private funds the sum of £2 000 for business purposes.
(2) The purchases of bikes on 1st January and the payment for them in cash.
(3) The sale of bikes on 8th January and the receipt of cash.
(4) The sale of bikes on 10th January and the receipt of cash.
(5) The payment of the advertising charges.

These transactions are entered in the Ledger by the bookkeeper as they occur, and the page in the Ledger will then appear as below. Reference numbers, as above, have been inserted to enable the student to trace the respective entries.

Cash Account

19..			£	19..			£
Jan. 1	Capital (1)		2 000	Jan. 1	Purchases (2)		1 200
Jan. 8	Sales (3)		500	Jan. 3	Advertising charges (5)		100
Jan. 10	Sales (4)		1 600				

Capital Account (M. Redman)

19..			£	19..			£
				Jan. 1	Cash (1)		2 000

Purchases Account

Jan. 1	Cash (2)		1 200				

Sales Account

				Jan. 8	Cash (3)		500
				Jan. 10	Cash (4)		1 600

Expenses Account

Jan. 3	Cash (Advertising (5)		100				

The student should have this completed Ledger page before him as he reads the following explanations of its use.

(*a*) it will be seen that the respective columns have special uses – the first column for the date of the transaction, the second for the particulars of the transaction, and the fourth for the money value. The sub-division for pence has been omitted in this example. The third column is called the folio column and its use is explained later. The four columns repeated on the right-hand half of the Ledger page have similar uses.

(*b*) five cross-headings have been inserted on the Ledger page – Cash Account, Capital Account, Purchases Account, Sales Account, and Expenses Account. Each of these gives a statement of a particular group of transactions. For example, records of transactions involving the movement of cash have been grouped into a statement or account called the Cash Account, and the records of sales have been grouped under the heading Sales Account. It is obvious that each item was first classified and then entered in its appropriate group or account. Further accounts are opened as may be necessary according to the range of transactions to be entered.

(*c*) there are ten entries in the Ledger, though the list on page 4 shows five transactions only. It should be apparent that there are two entries for each transaction, and it should be further apparent that one of the two entries is on the left-hand side of an account, and the other, or *corresponding*, entry is on the right-hand side of an account. There is one *debit* entry and one *credit* entry for each transaction.

This brings us to the basic principle of the system of *double entry bookkeeping* with which this book is concerned. Every transaction may be viewed from two aspects and both aspects of each transaction are recorded in the accounts. This fact becomes clearer as the transactions are analysed in more detail below.

(*d*) debit entries (i.e. those in the left-hand columns) used to be prefaced by the word 'To' and credit entries (i.e. those in the right-hand columns) by the word 'By'. This is no longer considered to be necessary. Similarly, the Ledger used to have the abbreviations 'Dr' and 'Cr' above the debit and credit sides. This is no longer considered necessary.

It is now appropriate to discuss the basis of classification of the items in the example and the respective entries in the accounts. The student is advised to have before him a properly ruled sheet of Ledger paper, and to make the entries as each transaction is dealt with.

Transaction 1. Redman starts the business with £2 000 in cash. His private means are diminished by this amount. Though he manages the business and appears to have no separate premises in which to work, this sum of £2 000 must be regarded as no longer available for his personal needs.

What the trader invests in the business is termed its *capital.* It may be money, as in this example, or money's worth in goods or other form of property, or both money and money's worth. Whatever form it takes, that is the original capital of the business and remains as a claim against the business by the proprietor.

In our example, the cash now belongs to the business, and as a check against the actual coins and notes wherever they are kept, a record must be made of the receipt of cash, of its expenditure, and of further receipts as business operations take place. All dealings with the cash are recorded in the Cash Account, and whenever cash is received or paid away the amount must be entered in this account.

The first entry, therefore, is to record that the business receives £2 000 from Redman, and it is made in the Cash Account – 'Jan. 1. Capital, £2 000' – on the left-hand or *debit* side of the account.

The left-hand side of all accounts is called the debit side, and an account is *debited* – that is, the entry is made on the debit side – with all value that comes into that account, whatever form the value takes. 'Debit' is often abbreviated to *Dr.*

One aspect of the transaction has now been entered, but there is the other aspect to be recorded. The receipt of anything implies a giver. The business receives £2 000 from Redman, but this implies that Redman gives £2 000 to the business, and this second aspect of the transaction must be entered so that the financial relationship of Redman to the business is on record.

Reference to the Ledger page will show that this entry is on the right-hand, or *credit*, side of the Capital Account – 'Jan. 1. Cash, £2 000'.

The right-hand side of every account is called the credit side, and the account is *credited* – that is, an entry is made on the credit side – with all value that goes out from that account. 'Credit' is often abbreviated to *Cr.*

If the Capital Account had been headed 'M. Redman's Account' it would doubtless have been more obvious to the student that this account contains all entries affecting M. Redman. The *Capital Account* is the name given to the personal account of the owner of the business, and it shows how he stands financially with the business. By making the credit entry of £2 000 it is recorded that he has parted with that sum and to that extent has a claim against the business. He is a person to whom a debt is owing, although his claim ranks after those of all other claimants such as trade creditors.

The two-fold aspect, therefore, of the first transaction in the example involves a debit entry in the Cash Account (cash in) and a corresponding credit entry in the Capital Account (capital invested).

Transaction 2. This is the purchase for cash of ten motor bikes for £1 200. The two aspects of this transaction are (a) that cash to the amount of £1 200 leaves the business, and (b) that motor bikes to the value of £1 200 come into the business.

Remembering what has been explained about the first transaction, it is obvious that the first entry must be in the Cash Account, and on the credit side, as the sum of £1 200 is paid away. The credit entry is 'Jan. 1. Purchases, £1 200'.

The second entry is to record the receipt of goods costing £1 200. As the goods are received it must be a debit entry. A special account is kept in which to record purchases made to provide a stock of goods for sale. This is called the *Purchases Account*, and the second entry of Transaction 2 is to debit this account – 'Jan. 1. Cash, £1 200'.

The record of the two-fold aspect of cash purchases of goods for sale is made by a credit entry in the Cash Account (cash out) and a corresponding debit entry in the Purchases Account (goods in).

Transaction 3. This is the sale of bikes for £500 in cash on 8th January. The two aspects are (a) that £500 in cash was received by the business, and (b) that the business parted with bikes to the value of £500.

The receipt of cash is entered on the debit side of the Cash Account – 'Jan. 8. Sales, £500'.

The sale involved parting with goods from stock to the value of £500. All such sales in the ordinary course of business are grouped in the Sales Account. As the goods go out from the business a credit entry in that account is required – 'Jan. 8. Cash, £500'.

In this case the two aspects involve a debit entry to the Cash Account (*cash in*) *and a credit entry to the Sales Account* (*goods out*).

Transaction 4. This is the sale of bikes for £1 600 in cash on 10th January. It is similar to Transaction 3 and similar entries are made. See the Ledger page.

Transaction 5. This is the payment of £100 for advertising. It is evident that one aspect of this transaction is the payment out of £100 in cash, and that the entry required is to credit the Cash Account – 'Jan. 3. Advertising charges, £100'.

The other aspect is what the payment was for, namely, £100 worth of advertising services. This demands a debit entry. It will be seen on the Ledger page in the Expenses Account. This account contains a record of all expenses incurred by the business. The £100 worth of services received for publicity, looked at from a profit-making point of view, is a loss, since the profit it is hoped to make from the sale of the bikes will be less by £100 paid for advertising.

Debit the amount to the Expenses Account – 'Jan. 3. Cash (Advertising Charges), £100'.

The entries, summarised, are a credit entry to Cash Account (*cash out*), *and a debit entry to Expenses Account* (*services in*).

All such expenses or losses are debited to the Expenses Account.

Double Entry

The two aspects of each transaction have been entered in the accounts. The student will have observed that the recording of the two aspects has involved a debit entry and a corresponding credit entry, but not in the same account. An essential point, therefore, to bear in mind is that every transaction must be entered in its two-fold aspect, and that this results in a debit entry and a corresponding credit entry in the accounts. The particulars of each entry identify the account in which the corresponding entry is made. This system is known as *double entry bookkeeping*. It is universal in its application to business transactions. The principles remain the same, whether the entries are made by hand in a bound ledger, or by the most up-to-date computers.

The bookkeeping record is made for reference purposes. It derives its value from the fact that it is a classified record and that the information it contains is readily available at any time. As the above simple example shows, it is possible to ascertain at once the total sales or the total purchases for the period, whichever is desired, by reference to the Sales Account or Purchases Account. The Cash Account gives full particulars of the cash received and the cash paid out and, by simple subtraction, it is possible to ascertain the amount of cash that should be in hand, i.e. in the till. This provides a check against the actual cash and makes known the amount available without the necessity of counting up the coins and notes every time – although it is vital to make such a count regularly and frequently as a check, for the purpose of control.

Double Entry – an Alternative Explanation

Double entry can also be understood in terms of the *sources and uses of funds*.

Funds are any arrangement which enables goods and services to be bought. It therefore usually means money (i.e. cash or bank balances) or credit (i.e. lending or borrowing). Every transaction which a business makes can be interpreted in terms of a *source of funds* and a *use of funds*, which must be equal in total. Since the double entry bookkeeping system analyses the activities of the business taking the transactions one at a time (as shown in the example earlier in this chapter), this analysis can be explained by referring to the sources and the uses of funds which are involved.

The main possible sources of funds for any transaction are:

(*a*) the owner's capital.

(*b*) borrowing from the bank or other lenders.

(*c*) taking trade credit, i.e. paying for goods or services some time after they have been received.

(*d*) revenues from sales or other commercial activities (e.g. renting-out properties).

In the ledger accounts sources of funds are always entered as credit entries.

The main possible uses of funds for any transactions are:

(*a*) to buy assets which are used repeatedly, e.g. property, equipment and vehicles.

(*b*) to buy finished goods or components or raw materials which will eventually be resold in some form.

(*c*) to incur expenses, i.e. to purchase other goods or services.

(*d*) to lend, or to repay borrowing.

(*e*) to give trade credit, i.e. allowing customers to pay for goods or services some time after delivery.

(*f*) to pay back owners.

(*g*) to hold as cash or bank balances.

In the ledger accounts uses of funds are always entered as debit entries. For every transaction there must be equal and opposite sources and use of funds. Therefore there must be equal and opposite credit entries in the books.

When a business is trading regularly some of its transactions will involve cash (or bank) receipts or payments. The holding of a cash (or bank) balance is a use of funds, since funds held in this way are not being used for anything else. When a transaction occurs which involves making a payment from cash (or bank), then the cash (or bank) will be the source of funds.

If cash is paid into the bank, then the source of funds is 'cash' and the use of funds is 'bank'. Therefore, 'cash' is credited and 'bank' is debited in the Ledger. Such transactions are fully explained in Chapter 7.

The two explanations which have been given of the basis of double entry bookkeeping tally in this way:

'Sources of funds' equal 'value given', and are entered in the Ledger as credit entries.

'Uses of funds' equal 'value received', and are entered in the Ledger as debit entries.

It is important to understand the basis of double entry bookkeeping. An early understanding will make it much easier to follow the detailed explanations of particular types of transaction in the rest of the book.

Checking the Entries

One benefit the bookkeeper derives from the principle of double entry is that it enables him to check the arithmetical accuracy of his work. As every debit entry has a corresponding credit entry it follows that the total of all the debit entries should equal the total of all the credit entries. This is not a complete check since it will not disclose, for example, that an item has been omitted altogether, if such is the case, or that the same wrong sum has been entered on both sides. Further, though the totals agree, an amount may have been entered to a wrong account. The value, however, is to the careful worker who usually avoids such mistakes.

The checking of the entries for the example given above is as below:

	Debit Entries	Credit Entries	Balance	
	£	£		
Cash Account	4 100	1 300	2 800	(debit)
Capital Account		2 000	2 000	(credit)
Purchases Account	1 200		1 200	(debit)
Sales Account		2 100	2 100	(credit)
Expenses Account	100		100	(debit)
Totals	£5 400	£5 400	0	

As the totals of the debit and credit entries agree, it may be assumed that, given careful work on the part of the bookkeeper, the entries have been made correctly.

It can be seen also that, since the totals entered as debits and credits are equal, so will the balances left in the accounts offset each other exactly.

EXERCISES 2

1. F. Watson begins to deal in clocks, starting with a capital of £140 in cash.

Jan. 10. He buys four clocks at £18 each, paying cash down.
" 14. He sells one clock for £27 in cash.
" 16. He sells two more clocks for cash at £30 each.
" 17. He buys another clock for cash, £20.
" 20. He sells the two remaining clocks for £50 the two, for cash.
" 21. He pays £15 cash for advertising and other sundry expenses.

Make the necessary entries to record these transactions in F. Watson's Ledger.

2. T. Williams started to sell transistors, putting aside £1 000 in cash for the business. On 1st October he purchased for cash 16 transistors, at £10 each and sold them at £16 each, the customers paying cash. He sold four on 3rd October, two on 4th October, four on 5th October, and the remainder on 7th October. His advertising expenses amounted to £10 which he paid in cash on 10th October. He intends to continue his business, but meanwhile, you are asked to show how he should have recorded the above transactions in his Ledger.

3. J. Dunbar starts to trade in radios with £900 in cash. Make the appropriate entries in his Ledger for the following transactions:

On 1st June he paid £200 for portable sets, and on 5th June he purchased battery sets for cash £480. His cash sales amounted to £1 500 by 8th June and the following day he sold the remainder of his stock for £1 600. He paid sundry expenses amounting to £40 on 10th June.

4. J. Bennett began to deal in handbags and wallets with £700 in cash as his capital. The following transactions took place:

			£
Dec.	1.	Bought for cash, handbags costing	550
,,	6.	Sold four handbags for cash	200
,,	8.	Sold four more handbags for cash	240
,,	12.	Paid carriage expenses	20
,,	14.	Sold remainder of handbags for cash	250
,,	15.	Paid man for help rendered	50

Show the record of these transactions in Bennett's Ledger.

5. Open the Ledger Accounts to record the following transactions.

H. W. Harrod started a business as a haberdasher with £560 cash as his capital. On 1st April he bought sundry articles for cash, £400. On 3rd April he paid £50 in cash for a further quantity. He paid £20 for expenses and £30 for carriage on 4th April. His sales for cash were: 8th April, £60; 10th April, £80; 14th April, £220; and for the remainder of his goods, on 19th April, £240.

6. Explain double entry bookkeeping in terms of value received and value given.

7. What are the main sources of funds of a business?

8. What are the main uses of funds of a business?

9. Explain double entry bookkeeping in terms of the sources and uses of funds.

3

The Question of Profit: Trading and Profit and Loss Accounts, and Balance Sheet

In practice it is usual for a trader to find the profit he has made in a definite period of trading, taking up to a year's trading as the basis. It is increasingly common to find that profit is calculated every quarter, or even monthly, and even shorter periods are not unknown.

In the example given in Chapter 2, M. Redman may be anxious to know his profit from that particular group of transactions. It is a simple matter arithmetically, and this is a suitable example to illustrate the bookkeeping method of ascertaining and recording the profit.

Gross Profit

The practice is first to find the *gross profit*, which is the amount by which the selling price exceeds the buying price (in the case of a wholesaler or retailer) or the manufacturing cost (in the case of a manufacturer). The information from which this may be ascertained is contained in the Purchases Account and the Sales Account. The Sales Account shows that the sales, in total, brought in £2 100, and the Purchases Account discloses that the Purchases, in total, cost £1 200. The difference, £900, is the gross profit.

The bookkeeping method is to transfer the information from the Purchases Account and Sales Account to a new account, called the *Trading Account*, used specifically for the purpose of finding the gross profit.

Once the information has been transferred from the Purchases Account and Sales Account these two accounts have served their purpose and are closed, new accounts being opened for the purchases and sales of the next trading period. The procedure to follow if some of the goods remain in stock is shown in Chapter 4. The transfers and the closing of the accounts are shown below:

Purchases Account

19..		£	19..		£
Jan. 1	Cash	1 200	Jan. 10	Transfer to Trading A/c.	1 200

Sales Account

19..		£	19..		£
Jan. 10	Transfer to Trading A/c.		Jan. 8	Cash	500
		2 100	Jan. 10	Cash	1 600
		2 100			2 100

Trading Account

19..		£	19..		£
Jan. 10	Purchases	1 200	Jan. 10	Sales	2 100
" "	Gross Profit	900			
		2 100			2 100

The double entry principle is carried out as follows. The credit entry of the transfer of the total purchases is in the Purchases Account and the corresponding debit entry is made in the Trading Account. The debit entry of the transfer of the total sales is in the Sales Account, and the corresponding credit entry is in the Trading Account.

The difference between the totals of the two sides of the Trading Account is the gross profit – provided, of course, that the selling price exceeds the buying price. Had the goods been sold for less than was paid for them then a trading loss would have resulted, being shown by the debit side of the Trading Account being greater in amount than the credit side.

The gross profit having been calculated, it is entered in the Trading Account as shown. Both sides of the account then add up to the same amount and the totals are inserted and the account ruled off. Ruling off an account is done with double lines.

The cash columns of the Purchases Accounts and the Sales Account are added and ruled off. As there is one amount only in this instance on each side of the Purchases Account it is not necessary to do more to close the account than to rule double lines.

Net Profit

The corresponding entry for the debit of gross profit (£900) in the Trading Account has not yet been made. It is made in the Profit and Loss Account which appears as below:

Profit and Loss Account

		£			£
19..			19..		
Jan. 10	Expenses (Advertising)	100	Jan. 10	Gross Profit from Trading A/c.	900

The Profit and Loss Account collects together the profits or gains on the credit side and the losses or expenses on the debit side. The main item of profits (which are credited) is gross profit. The corresponding debit for Gross Profit is the Trading Account. Losses (which are debited) consist of the various expenses of the business. The corresponding credit for expenses is in the Expenses Account.

The Profit and Loss Account is then balanced. The balance is the difference between the two sides of the account. It is entered on the debit side and the account is closed.

The entry of the balance in the Profit and Loss Account is one entry of the net profit and is on the debit side of the account. It remains to make the corresponding credit entry. First, however, consider the question of profit. It arises from the manufacturing and trading activities exercised by the owner in the business. His capital and his efforts, together with the work of his employees, have met with financial reward in the form of profit, and such profit belongs to the owner.

The Capital Account is the owner's account, showing his financial relationship with the business. It already contains an entry showing the owner as a potential claimant against the business for the initial capital invested. The credit entry of the net profit is made to the Capital Account as a record that the business holds £800 *net profit* on the owner's behalf in addition to the original capital.

The Profit and Loss Account and the Capital Account will appear as on page 16.

It is possible for expenses to exceed the gross profit, that is for the costs of selling to be greater than the profits on sales. In that case a *net loss* is made and will appear as the balance on the credit side of the Profit and Loss Account.

Had a loss and not a profit resulted from these dealings, the owner's claim against the business would be for the amount of the original capital less the amount of the loss. As the net loss would appear on the credit side of the Profit and Loss Account, the corresponding second entry would be on the debit side of the Capital Account. When balanced, it would show a smaller sum due to the owner.

Profit and Loss Account

			£				£
19..				19..			
Jan. 10	Expenses (Advertising)		100	Jan. 10	Gross Profit from Trading A/c.		900
	Net Profit transferred to Capital A/c		800				
			£900				£900

Capital Account

			£				£
19..				19..			
Jan. 10	Balance carried down		2 800	Jan. 1	Cash		2 000
				Jan. 10	Net Profit from Profit and Loss A/c.		800
			£2 800				£2 800
				Jan. 11	Balance brought down		2 800

The transfer of the net profit from the Profit and Loss Account to the Capital Account is the concluding double entry for the trading period under review. It remains for the Cash Account to be balanced and closed, and the balance representing the cash in hand to be carried down to the opposite side to start the new Cash Account for the next trading period.

The Ledger page is now given with all the accounts, including the Cash Account, completed on the lines discussed in this chapter. It will be seen that it contains a record of all the transactions and the entries required to record the financial results of the trading for the period.

Cash Account

		£			£
19..			19..		
Jan. 1	Capital	2 000	Jan. 1	Purchases	1 200
Jan. 8	Sales	500	Jan. 3	Advertising expenses	100
Jan. 10	Sales	1 600	Jan. 10	Balance carried down	2 800
		£4 100			£4 100
Jan. 11	Balance brought down	2 800			

Capital Account (M. Redman)

		£			£
19..			19..		
Jan. 10	Balance carried down	2 800	Jan. 1	Cash	2 000
			Jan. 10	Net Profit from Profit and Loss A/c.	800
		£2 800			£2 800
			Jan. 11	Balance b/d	2 800

Purchases Account

		£			£
19..			19..		
Jan. 1	Cash	1 200	Jan. 10	Transfer to Trading A/c.	1 200

Sales Account

		£			£
19..			19..		
Jan. 10	Transfer to Trading A/c.	2 100	Jan. 8	Cash	500
			Jan. 10	Cash	1 600
		£2 100			£2 100

Expenses Account

		£			£
19..			19..		
Jan. 3	Cash (Advertising)	100	Jan. 10	Transfer to Profit & Loss A/c.	100

Trading Account

19..		£	19..		£
Jan. 10	Purchases	1 200	Jan. 10	Sales	2 100
	Gross Profit	900			
		£2 100			£2 100

Profit and Loss Account

19..		£	19..		£
Jan. 10	Expenses (Advertising)	100	Jan. 10	Gross Profit from Trading A/c.	900
	Net Profit to Capital A/c.	800			
		£900			£900

The Balance Sheet

It will be observed that most of the above accounts have been closed by the transfer of the balance to another account. The balances of the Cash Account and the Capital Account, however, have been carried down to commence the new accounts for the next period. There will be a Purchases Account and a Sales Account for the next trading period, but they will be new accounts without any starting balance from the last period.

The balance of the Cash Account brought down represents the amount of cash in hand at the date of balancing the account and available for subsequent trading. The balance of the Capital Account is carried down as it indicates the amount to the owner's credit at the date of balancing and at the beginning of the new trading period. From the point of view of the business the cash balance of £2 800 in hand represents a valuable possession, whereas the balance of the Capital Account is the amount for which the owner has a residual claim against the business. In short, the cash is an *asset*, and the balance of the Capital Account is a *claim* against the business. The term 'asset' is applied to all forms of property and possessions which the business holds, including all debts due to the business, and the term 'Claim' to all sums owing by the business. When claims are due to third parties (e.g. trade creditors or lenders) they are called *liabilities*. Assets and claims may take forms of other than those shown in the above example, but these are discussed in succeeding chapters. It is very important that the student understands the distinction between 'claims' and 'liabilities'. Previous editions of this book have used the word 'liabilities' for all the claims on a business (i.e. (i) the owner's capital and (ii) the liabilities to parties outside the business). It is more exact to use the distinction that this edition makes (i.e. the word 'liabilities' is here only used for liabilities to parties outside the business).

If Redman wishes to know the financial position of the business at the date of balancing the accounts, all that is necessary is to trace the assets and claims and to set them down in customary form. The statement is called the *Balance Sheet* and comprises the balances of all of the accounts in the Ledger after the appropriate transfers have been made in the preparation of the Trading and Profit and Loss Accounts. All such remaining balances are either assets or claims, and the statement is compiled by placing the claims on the left-hand side and the assets on the right-hand side:

Balance Sheet

as at 10th January, 19..

CLAIMS	£	£	ASSETS	£
Capital 1st Jan.	2 000		Cash in hand	2 800
Add Net Profit	800			
		2 800		

This is the simplest form a Balance Sheet can take, but it illustrates the principles underlying its compilation. *The Balance Sheet is not a Ledger account*; it is a summary listing the outstanding balances. It is equally valuable as a statement of the financial position if the sides are reversed, but it conforms to the traditional practice in England to have the claims on the left-hand side and the assets on the right. In some countries, including the U.S.A., these listings are reversed, i.e. the assets are on the left and the claims on the right. There are historical reasons for this, which it is not necessary to explain at this stage.

Many balance sheets now list the claims and assets vertically one under the other.

It happens that the items in the above Balance Sheet do not differ, except in the amount, from the items which would have appeared in a

Balance Sheet prepared immediately after the business was started and before trading commenced.

This would have been as below:

Balance Sheet

as at 1st January, 19. .

CLAIMS	£	ASSETS	£
Capital	2 000	Cash in hand	2 000

A comparison of the two Balance Sheets shows that one of the results of trading has been an increase in the value of the business assets but, at the same time, the amount claimed against the business, in this case by the proprietor, has been increased by a similar sum.

The two sides of the Balance Sheet agree in total. The fact that they should do so provides a further arithmetical check on the accuracy of the entries in the accounts and on the preparation of the Trading and Profit and Loss Accounts.

The equality of the two sides of the balance sheet is derived from the equality of sources and uses of funds, which was explained in Chapter 2. The assets side lists the past uses made of funds, insofar as they still affect the future at the time of preparing the Balance Sheet. The claims side shows the sources of past funds, which still hold a claim against the business that will have to be settled at some time in the future. These two totals must be equal. The balancing figure is the profit or loss. The balance sheet can thus be represented by the so-called 'Balance Sheet equation' as follows:

ASSETS = CLAIMS [where CLAIMS = (OWNER'S CAPITAL + PROFITS) + LIABILITIES]

The Trader's Drawings

The profit from the series of transactions remains at present in the business. There is now the sum of £2 800, as against the original £2 000 as capital invested in the business. The owner may decide to leave the profit in the business as additional capital to finance further transactions. Or he may require money for personal needs and decide to withdraw all or part of the profit. Should he draw out £50 in cash on account, the business will, in that case, be indebted to him to an amount less by the £50 so drawn, and the cash balance will be £50 less.

The two aspects of the withdrawal of profit are that cash is paid out and that Redman receives the cash. It follows that a credit entry would be made in the Cash Account, 'Capital-Drawings, £50', and a debit entry in the Capital Account, 'Cash, £50'.

The reasons for these entries should now be apparent. The Capital Account would appear as below, showing £2 750 only as due to the proprietor.

Capital Account

19..		£	19..		£
Jan. 10	Cash (Drawings)	50	Jan. 1	Cash	2 000
,, ,,	Balance carried down	2 750	,, 10	Net Profit from Profit and Loss A/c.	800
		£2 800			£2 800
			Jan. 11	Balance brought down	2 750

The entries are made on the assumption that the withdrawal took place before the Cash and Capital Accounts were closed. The withdrawal would affect the balances on these accounts and, consequently, the figures in the Balance Sheet would vary from those given in the first Balance Sheet above, as that was prepared when no drawings had been made.

Profit and Valuation

The Profit and Loss Account and the Balance Sheet are complementary. This can be seen by considering another way of measuring profit.

M. Redman's profit was calculated by finding the difference between sales and costs. It worked out as £2 100 − (1 200 + 100) = £800. However, the credit balance of his capital account also increased by £800, from £2 000 to £2 800, over the same period, before allowing for drawings. It is thus possible to measure profit by comparing the owner's capital at two points of time, although this does not give the full analysis, shown in the Profit and Loss Account.

It is not necessary to prepare the Profit and Loss Account in order to measure the owner's capital. This can be done, as it was when the business was opened, by finding the value of the assets in the business (less any liabilities owed by the business to third parties). M. Redman's business held cash of £2 800 and had no liabilities. It can be seen that, if profit can be calculated by comparing the owner's capital, and if the owner's capital can be measured by listing the assets and liabilities, the figure for profit ultimately depends on the valuations placed on the various assets and liabilities.

In Redman's case, this was easy because the business held only cash, and had no liabilities, at the relevant times. Traditionally, other assets, such as property and inventory, have been valued on the basis of their *historic cost*, i.e. what was paid for them.

However, in the last few years there has been extensive discussion in many countries about this. If prices are rising fast there is doubt about whether valuations, and therefore profit, measured by using historic cost are really useful. A new system, known as *current cost accounting*, has been proposed. It replaces historic costs by more up-to-date figures, called *current costs*. This system is outlined in the last chapter of this book. It utilises double entry bookkeeping in the way explained in this book, but then develops the measurements further. Current cost accounting is potentially very important, but a full description of it is beyond the scope of this book.

EXERCISES 3

Enter the transactions in Exercises 1–5 in the Ledger and check the double entry. Prepare the Trading Account and complete the Profit and Loss Account in each case to find the gross profit and net profit or loss for the trading period. Prepare also the Balance Sheet as at the day after the last transaction in each example.

1.

			£
Oct.	1.	G. Pearce commenced to trade in second-hand radios with capital in cash of	840
Oct.	2.	He bought six radios and paid cash	78
,,	4.	Sold three radios for cash	56
,,	6.	Paid advertising charges in cash	30
,,	8.	Paid out cash expenses	10
,,	9.	Bought for cash three more radios	37
,,	10.	Sold remaining six radios for cash	113

2. On Dec. 15th J. Leatherhead set aside £1 700 from his private means as capital for a business deal in leather goods.

			£
Dec.	15.	He bought a job line of leather goods for cash	1 400
,,	17.	Paid for stationery	110
,,	18.	Sold a quantity of the goods for cash	1 250
,,	20.	Sold the remainder for cash	500
,,	20.	Paid travelling expenses	20
,,	20.	He withdrew cash for private use	150

3. On 10th January John Watt began business with £300 cash in hand. The same day he purchased a quantity of electrical equipment for £270.

			£
Jan.	12.	He sold part of the goods for cash	120
,,	14.	He made a further purchase for cash	100
,,	18.	He sold the whole of his remaining stock of goods for cash	300
,,	19.	He paid carriage and other expenses in cash	50

4. On April 10th J. Steering set aside £900 in cash from his private means as capital for a business deal in second-hand furniture.

			£
Apr.	12.	He paid in cash for second-hand furniture	290
,,	12.	He sold the furniture the same day for cash	350
,,	15.	He bought two pieces of furniture	400
,,	17.	He sold one piece of furniture	260
,,	18.	Paid haulage charges in cash in respect of purchases	45
,,	20.	He bought more furniture for cash	140
,,	22.	He sold the remaining pieces of furniture	460
,,	23.	He withdrew in cash all profit for private use	

5. J. Taylor began business as a dealer in used furniture on 1st May with capital in cash of £1 000. On 2nd May he purchased a quantity of goods at auction rooms for cash, £100, and a further quantity privately the next day for £35. His general expenses amounted to £4, which he paid on 4th May in cash. He made the following cash sales: 8th May, £30; 10th May, £26; 14th May, £35; 17th May, £31. On 21st May he sold the remainder of his goods for £72, paid wages to a part-time assistant, £15, and withdrew cash for private purposes, £30.

6. Explain two methods by which profit can be measured.

4

The Question of Stock

In the example in the preceding chapter the trader disposed of all his goods. This may happen occasionally in practice, but it is more usual to find that a quantity of goods remains in stock at the date to which the accounts are made up. Unsold goods must be taken into account when finding the gross profit for a trading period as the following example illustrates.

Example 2. M. Redman continues his business for a further period, from 11th January, his position on that date being shown in the Balance Sheet on page 19.

The following transactions take place: all purchases and sales being for cash:

Jan. 12. Bought six second-hand bikes at £80 each.
,, 15. Sold two bikes for £160 each.
,, 24. Bought two more bikes at £100 each.
,, ,, Paid £20 for lighting.
,, 26. Sold three bikes from his first purchase for £500 the lot.
,, ,, Paid charges for delivery to customers, £20.
,, ,, Redman withdrew £30.

Trading and Profit and Loss Accounts are to be prepared for the period ending 26th January, and a Balance Sheet as at that date. Redman values the stock of goods on hand at 26th January at cost, £280.

The financial position of the business is known from the state of the Ledger at the close of business on 10th January. This appears on page 17 and discloses that there is a cash balance in hand of £2 800. The Capital Account on that page shows that the sum of £2 800 is due to Redman as proprietor. It is assumed that Redman decided to make no drawings. The same accounts continue in use for the further period, and sufficient space would be allowed in practice between the accounts to allow for this – at least one page of the Ledger being allotted to each account. The balance brought down – in this case on the Cash Account and Capital Account – provide the first items for the accounts for the new trading period. Where no balances are brought down, as in the case of the Purchases and Sales Accounts, the account for the new period will begin immediately below the account for the old period, the original heading to the account being sufficient in each case.

For exercise purposes, if insufficient room has been left to continue the accounts, new accounts may be opened for fresh transactions, but the balances brought down must not be omitted.

The transactions set out in the example should be entered in the manner already explained, and the arithmetical accuracy should be checked when the last entry has been made for the period.

The new point is that of the stock of goods on hand. In Example 1, Redman sold all the goods, and the gross profit was easily calculated as the difference between cost and selling prices. In the present example the Purchases Account shows the total purchases as £680 and the Sales Account shows the total sales as £820 but bikes to the value of £280 at cost price have not been sold.

The value at cost of all the bikes is £680. The value at cost price of the bikes not sold is £280. It follows that the value at cost price of the bikes sold is £400 and that as these bikes costing £400 were sold for £820 the gross profit is £420.

This calculation is made in another form in the bookkeeping records.

The trader finds the value at cost price of the stock of goods on hand at the close of business on the last day of the trading period. In the example the value at cost is £280.

A double entry is made in the accounts for the value of the stock on hand; the debit entry is made in a new account – the *Stock Account* – and the credit entry in the Trading Account, as below. The sales and purchases are shown as already transferred to the Trading Account.

Stock Account

19..			£	19..			£
Jan. 26	Trading A/c. (Stock on hand)		280				

Trading Account

for the period 11th to 26th January, 19..

19..			£	19..			£
Jan. 26	Purchases		680	Jan. 26	Sales		820
	Gross Profit		420		Stock at close		280
			£1 100				£1 100

The arithmetical solution proceeded by subtracting the value at cost of the unsold goods from the value at cost of all purchases. The result was the value at cost of the goods sold. The gross profit was found by subtracting this figure from the value of the total sales.

The Purchases Account shows the value at cost of all the purchases. It would be more on the lines of the arithmetical method if an entry were made which had the effect of reducing the full value of the purchases in the Purchases Account to the value of that part which was sold. The entry would be to credit the value at cost of the stock on hand to the Purchases Account instead of to the Trading Account. For example:

Purchases Account

19..			£	19..		£
Jan. 12	Cash		480	Jan. 26	Transfer to Stock A/c. being value at cost of unsold stock	280
Jan. 24	Cash		200		Transfer to Trading A/c. being cost of goods sold	400
			£680			£680

Stock Account

19..			£	19..		£
Jan. 26	Transfer from Purchases A/c. being cost of unsold stock		280			

Trading Account

for the period 11th to 26th January 19..

19..			£	19..		£
Jan. 26	Purchases		400	Jan. 26	Sales	820
	Gross Profit		420			
			£820			£820

The opening of a special Stock Account separates the unsold portion from the full total of purchases and sets it down clearly for future reference and use.

The only objection to the credit entry for the value of the unsold stock being in the Purchases Account is that the balance of the Purchases Account then transferred to the Trading Account is not a record of the total purchases made during the period. The owner probably sees the Trading and Profit and Loss Accounts separate from the other records, and it is preferable for purposes of comparison that the full total of purchases made should be evident in the final accounts. The practice, therefore, is to place the credit entry for the stock at close to the Trading Account. The arithmetical result is, of course, the same. This is illustrated in the completed Ledger Accounts for Example 2 which are:

Cash Account

19..			£	19..			£
Jan. 11	Balance	b/d	2 800	Jan. 12	Purchases		480
„ 15	Sales		320	„ 24	Purchases		200
„ 26	Sales		500	„ „	Expenses		20
				„ 26	Expenses		20
				„ „	Drawings		30
					Balance	c/d	2 870
			£3 620				£3 620
„ 27	Balance	b/d	2 870				

Capital Account (M. Redman)

19..			£	19..			£
Jan. 26	Cash (Drawings)		30	Jan. 11	Balance	b/d	2 800
	Balance	c/d	3 150		Net Profit		380
			£3 180				£3 180
				Jan. 27	Balance	b/d	3 150

Purchases Account

19..			£	19..			£
Jan. 12	Cash		480	Jan. 26	Transfer to Trading A/c.		680
Jan. 24	Cash		200				
			£680				£680

Sales Account

		£			£
19..			19..		
Jan. 26	Transfer to Trading A/c.	820	Jan. 15	Cash	320
			„ 26	Cash	500
		£820			£820

Expenses Account

Jan. 20	Cash (Lighting)	20	Jan. 26	Transfer to Profit and Loss A/c.	40
„ 26	Cash (Delivery costs)	20			
		£40			£40

Stock Account

		£			£
19..			19..		
Jan. 26	Trading Account (Stock on hand)	280			

Trading Account

for the period 11th to 26th January, 19..

		£			£
19..			19..		
Jan. 26	Purchases	680	Jan. 26	Sales	820
„ „	Gross Profit	420	„ „	Stock	280
		£1 100			£1 100

Profit and Loss Account

for period 11th to 26th January, 19..

		£			£
19..			19..		
Jan. 26	Expenses	40	Jan 26	Gross Profit	420
	Net Profit	380			
		£420			£420

Tracing through the Ledger Accounts it is found that the Cash, Capital and Stock Accounts remain open. The other accounts have been closed in the preparation of the Trading and Profit and Loss

Accounts. The balance of each of these open accounts represents either an asset or a claim, and is an item for the Balance Sheet.

Balance Sheet

as at 26th January, 19..

CLAIMS	£	£	ASSETS	£
Capital 11th Jan.	2 800		Stock	280
Add Net Profit	380		Cash	2 870
	3 180			
Less Drawings	30	3 150		
		£3 150		£3 150

Stock at Start of Business

If the trader, M. Redman, continues his business, the books will show that the new trading period opens with assets in cash, £2 870 and in goods, £280, with the capital of the proprietor of £3 150.

Example 3. Redman continues his business for a further period, the following cash transactions taking place:

Feb. 10. Sold two second-hand bikes for £400.
,, 20. Bought four new bikes for £1 500.
,, 24. Sold one second-hand and two new bikes for £1 450.
,, 28. Paid sundry expenses, £200.

Trading and Profit and Loss Accounts are to be prepared for the period ending 28th February, and Balance Sheet as at that date. The stock of bicycles on hand on 28th February is valued at cost at £750.

As with Example 2, it is assumed that Redman has left sufficient room in his Ledger to continue his accounts for the further period so that on the balances being carried down the initial entries in the Cash, Capital, and Stock Accounts are already made.

The point of difference from the preceding period is that the stock at start must be taken into account as well as the stock at close. Where there is a stock of goods in hand at the start of a trading period it is more than probable that some, if not all, of this stock will be sold during the period. The stock of goods at start and the subsequent purchases are all available for sale. The total cost of the goods sold can be found only by deducting the cost price of the goods remaining on hand at the close of the period from the combined value at cost of the stock at start and the purchases – unless, of course, a record is kept as sales take place of the original cost of the articles sold.

	£
Stock at start	280
add Purchases	1 500
	1 780
less Stock at close	750
Cost price of goods sold =	£1 030

These goods were sold for £1 850. The gross profit is, therefore £820. The entries in the Trading Account may appear exactly as in the arithmetical example above. This method is usually adopted as it shows clearly the cost price of goods sold.

In the bookkeeping record the stock at *start* is added to the Purchases by transfer from the Stock Account to the Trading Account as shown below. The Stock Account is thereby closed and a new account is opened for the stock at close. The latter is treated as explained under Example 2.

Cash Account

19..			£	19..			£
Jan. 27	Balance	b/d	2 870	Feb. 20	Purchases		1 500
Feb. 10	Sales		400	„ 28	Expenses		200
„ 24	Sales		1 450	„ „	Balance	c/d	3 020
			£4 720				£4 720
Mar. 1	Balance	b/d	£3 020				

Capital Account

19..			£	19..			£
Feb. 28	Balance	c/d	3 770	Jan. 27	Balance	b/d	3 150
				Feb. 28	Net Profit		620
			£3 770				£3 770
				Mar. 1	Balance	b/d	£3 770

Purchases Account

19..		£	19..		£
Feb. 20	Cash	1 500	Feb. 28	Transfer to Trading A/c.	1 500

Sales Account

19..		£	19..		£
Feb. 28	Transfer to Trading A/c.	1 850	Feb. 10	Cash	400
			Feb. 24	Cash	1 450
		£1 850			£1 850

Stock Account

19..		£	19..		£
Jan. 28	Trading Account (Stock on hand)	280	Feb. 28	Transfer to Trading A/c.	280
Mar. 1	Trading Account (Stock on hand)	750			

Expenses Account

19..		£	19..		£
Feb. 28	Cash	200	Feb. 28	Transfer to Profit and Loss A/c.	200

Trading Account

for month ending 28th February, 19..

19..		£	19..		£
	Stock at start	280		Sales	1 850
	Add purchases	1 500		Stock at close	750
		£1 780			
	Gross Profit to Profit and Loss A/c.	820			
		£2 600			£2 600

Profit and Loss Account

for month ending 28th February, 19..

19..		£	19..		£
	Expenses	200		Gross Profit from Trading A/c.	820
	Net Profit to Capital A/c.	620			
		£820			£820

Balance Sheet

as at 28th February, 19..

CLAIMS	£	£	ASSETS	£
Capital 2nd Feb.	3 150		Stock	750
Add Net Profit	620	3 770	Cash	3 020
		£3 770		£3 770

Alternative Vertical form of the Final Accounts:

Trading and Profit and Loss Account

for month ended 28th February, 19..

	£	£
Sales		1 850
Opening Stock	280	
Purchases	1 500	
	1 780	
Less Closing Stock	750	
Cost of Goods Sold		1 030
Gross Profit		820
Deduct Expenses		200
Net Profit transferred to Capital Account		£620

Balance Sheet
as at 28th February, 19. .

	£
ASSETS	
Stock	750
Cash	3 020
	£3 770
CLAIMS	
Capital:	
at 2nd February	3 150
Add net profit for February	620
	£3 770

Valuation of Stock

The valuation of the stock on hand at the close of a trading period must be carefully made, as undervaluation or overvaluation materially affects the accounts. It is usual to value the stock at cost price. If, however, market conditions are such that the current prices for similar goods have fallen considerably, then the value should be the current market price, that is the price at which the stock could be sold at that date. On the other hand, a rise in market value does not warrant a marking-up of stock values, except under exceptional circumstances. The rise may be only temporary, and it is financially unwise to overstate profits and to allow inflated values to appear in the Balance Sheet. The general practice under historic cost accounting is thus to value stocks at the lower of their historic cost or their current selling price.

The value placed upon the stock affects the profits of a business, and one aim of sound bookkeeping and accounting is to give a true and fair view of profits, assets and claims. It would provide a useful exercise for the student to work again the above two examples with the stocks at close at lower values and again at higher values and to study the effect on the Final Accounts, i.e. the Trading and Profit and Loss Account and the Balance Sheet.

EXERCISES 4

Open the appropriate Ledger Accounts and record the transactions given in the following exercises, checking the accuracy of the double entry in each case. Find the gross profit and net profit, and prepare a Balance Sheet as at the closing date of each exercise.

Note: For Exercises 3, 4 and 5 leave sufficient space between accounts to continue them for a second period of trading.

1.

March	16.	J. Filmer began to deal in cameras with capital in cash	2 000
,,	16.	Bought cameras for cash	1 350
,,	17.	Bought tripods for cash	130
,,	17.	Paid sundry expenses	10
,,	19.	Sold tripods for cash	750
,,	20.	Sold cameras for cash	1 030
,,	20.	Paid messenger	10

Stock on hand at 20th March valued at cost, £220

2.

			£
April	16.	J. Ribbon commenced to deal in new and second-hand books with capital in cash	1 500
,,	16.	He bought new books for cash	1 260
,,	16.	Bought second-hand books for cash	150
,,	17.	Paid for advertisements	60
,,	19.	Sold new books for cash	1 260
,,	20.	Sold second-hand books for cash	160

Stock on hand at 20th April valued at cost, £360.

3.

			£
Sept.	2.	J. Sharp began to deal in cutlery with capital in cash	1 000
,,	2.	Purchased quantity of cutlery for cash	800
,,	2.	Purchased further quantity	80
,,	2.	Paid carriage	10
,,	3.	Bought packing materials	20
,,	8.	Sold cutlery for cash	500
,,	10.	Sold further quantity for cash	400

Find the gross and net profit for the period and prepare the Balance sheet as at 10th September. Value at cost of stock on and at that date, £360.

Continue the accounts for a second period:

Sept.	11.	Bought more cutlery for cash	700
,,	12.	Paid carriage	20
,,	15.	Sold cutlery for cash	520
,,	16.	Sold further quantity for cash	600
,,	16.	Withdrew cash for private purposes	200

Stock on hand at 16th September at cost, £260. Find the gross and net profit for this period, and prepare a Balance Sheet as at 16th September.

4.

			£
Oct.	1.	J. Plater began business in hardware with capital in cash	10 000
,,	2.	Bought quantity of goods for cash	6 000

Oct.	3.	Bought further quantity for cash	3 200
„	6.	Paid carriage	200
„	12.	Sold goods for cash	3 600
„	18.	Sold further quantity for cash	4 000

Find his gross and net profit (if any), and prepare Balance Sheet as at 18th October. Stock on hand at cost, £1 700.

Continue his accounts for a further period:

			£
Oct.	22.	Bought quantity of hardware for cash	5 000
„	24.	Paid carriage	100
„	29.	Sold goods for cash	3 900
„	30.	Of goods sold on 29th October customer returned quantity as defective. Refunded cash, £500 (credit Cash, debit Sales Account).	
			£
Oct.	31.	Sold goods for cash	3 800
„	31.	Withdraw for private use, cash	2 000

Find the gross and net profit for the period, and prepare Balance Sheet as at 31st October. Stock on hand at cost, £3 000.

5.

Nov.	1.	J. Preston began to deal in clearance lines of motor car tyres with cash capital of £2 000.	£
Nov.	1.	Bought quantity of tyres for cash	600
„	2.	Bought further quantity for cash	750
„	3.	Bought further quantity for cash	450
„	6.	Paid advertising	130
„	8.	Sold tyres for cash	2 160
„	8.	Withdrew cash for private use	150

Find his gross and net profit for the period and prepare a Balance Sheet as at 8th November. Stock of tyres on hand at cost, £300.

Continue the accounts for a further period:

Nov.	10.	Bought tyres for cash	1 560
„	12.	Paid advertising charges	120
„	15.	Sold tyres for cash	900
„	30.	Sold tyres for cash	1 050
„	30.	Paid carriage expenses	60

Prepare Trading and Profit and Loss Accounts for the period, and Balance Sheet as at 30th November. Stock of tyres on hand at cost, £480.

5
The Question of Credit

The transactions in the earlier examples have been cash transactions, the cash passing at once in exchange for the goods. Business transactions may be either for cash or on *credit*. In credit transactions the goods are taken but payment is made later, after an interval of days, weeks, or months, according to the arrangements between buyer and seller. Most transactions in the retail trade are cash transactions, but between wholesaler and manufacturer and between wholesaler and retailer credit transactions are more usual than cash transactions.

Credit transactions create debts, and a record must be kept of the debts owing by or to another person or firm as a result of such credit transactions.

If Redman sells to Brown goods for cash, Redman records the sale of the goods and the receipt of cash. If, however, Redman sells to Brown goods valued £100 on credit, Redman parts with the goods but no cash passes at the time of sale. Payment is to be made later. Meanwhile Redman must record that £100 is due from Brown.

Similarly, Redman may purchase goods on credit, receiving the goods at once and being trusted to pay at a later date. He records the value of the goods coming in, and, also, he must record that he owes the supplier for the goods.

Credit transactions, therefore, involve the opening of *personal accounts*. A personal account is an account in the name of a customer or a supplier. Cash transactions, as a general rule, require no personal accounts to be opened as each transaction is completed on the immediate payment of cash in exchange for goods.

Example 4. Redman continued his business from 1st March, the capital of the business then being £3 770, comprising Stock, £750 and Cash, £3 020.

The following transactions took place:

March	5.	Bought on credit from Smith's Motor Cycle Company, bikes value £1 680.
,,	12.	Sold one bike for cash, £480.
,,	19.	Sold bikes on credit to J. Dunbar, value £1 200.
,,	26.	J. Dunbar paid £500 cash on account.
,,	28.	Paid for packing materials, £60.

Prepare Trading and Profit and Loss Accounts for the month of March, and Balance Sheet as at 31st March.

Value of stock on hand at 31st March, at cost price, £1 070.

Only the transactions occurring on the 5th, 19th and 26th March require illustration.

The purchase on the 5th March is entered to the debit of the Purchases Account in the usual manner. The credit entry is in a new account:

Smith's Motor Cycle Company Account

19..			£	19..			£
				Mar. 5	Purchases		1 680

This follows the rule to credit an account with the value that leaves it and records that Smith's Company parted with these goods. In short, the company is Redman's *creditor* (i.e. one to whom money is owed).

Later, when Redman decides to pay for the goods, the payment will be credited to the Cash Account and *debited* to Smith's Motor Cycle Company's Account. The latter entry will have the effect of cancelling the debt on record in Smith's Account.

The sale on 19th March to Dunbar is entered in the usual way to the credit of the Sales Account. The corresponding debit entry is in a new account, to record the receipt of the goods by Dunbar.

J. Dunbar's Account

19..			£	19..			£
Mar. 19	Sales		1 200				

When, on 26th March, Dunbar pays £500 on account of the amount due from him, the Cash Account will be debited and Dunbar's Account will be credited with that sum. He remains a *debtor* (i.e. one who owes) for the balance of £700 as is shown by his account on page 38.

Redman's Ledger will appear as below, the accounts in practice following on those from the preceding period:

Cash Account

19..			£	19..			£
Mar. 1	Balance	b/d	3 020	Mar. 28	Packing materials		60
,, 12	Sales	b/d	480	,, 31	Balance	c/d	3 940
,, 26	J. Dunbar		500				
			£4 000				£4 000
Apr. 1	Balance	b/d	3 940				

Capital Account

19..			£	19..			£
Mar. 31	Balance	c/d	4 030	Mar. 1	Balance	b/d	3 770
				,, 31	Net Profit		260
			£4 030				£4 030
				Apr. 1	Balance	b/d	4 030

Stock Account

19..			£	19..			£
Mar. 1	Trading A/c. (Stock on hand)		750	Mar. 31	Transfer to Trading A/c.		750
Apr. 1	Trading A/c. (Stock on hand)		1 070				

Purchases Account

19..			£	19..			£
Mar. 5	Smith's Motor Cycle Co.		1 680	Mar. 31	Transfer to Trading A/c.		1 680

Sales Account

19..			£	19..			£
Mar. 31	Transfer to Trading A/c.		1 680	Mar. 12	Cash		480
				Mar. 19	J. Dunbar		1 200
			£1 680				£1 680

Smith's Motor Cycle Company Account

19..			£	19..			£
				Mar. 5	Purchases		1 680

J. Dunbar's Account

19..			£	19..			£
Mar. 19	Sales		1 200	Mar. 26	Cash		500
				Mar. 31	Balance	c/d	700
			£1 200				£1 200
Apr. 1	Balance	b/d	700				

Expenses Account

		£			£
19..			19..		
Mar. 28	Cash: Packing materials	60	Mar. 31	Transfer to Profit and Loss A/c.	60

Trading Account
for month of March, 19..

		£			£
19..			19..		
	Stock at start	750		Sales	1 680
	add Purchases	1 680			
		2 430			
	less Stock at close	1 070			
	Cost of goods sold	1 360			
	Gross Profit	320			
		£1 680			£1 680

Profit and Loss Account
for month of March, 19..

		£			£
19..			19..		
	Expenses	60		Gross Profit	320
	Net Profit to Capital A/c.	260			
		£320			£320

Balance Sheet
as at 31st March, 19..

CLAIMS	£	£	ASSETS	£
Capital at 1st March	3 770		Stock	1 070
Add Net Profit	260	4 030	Debtors	700
Creditors		1 680	Cash	3 940
		£5 710		£5 710

An additional point to be observed is the effect on the Balance Sheet of the outstanding amounts on the personal accounts. There are two more open accounts in this example than in the preceding examples. The accounts remaining open after the preparation of the Trading and Profit and Loss Accounts are either real or personal accounts. *Real Accounts* are records of property – such as the Stock Account. *Personal Accounts* are records of dealing with persons. The balances of personal accounts are either assets or claims and are therefore listed in the Balance Sheet.

The balance on Dunbar's Account is called a *debit balance*: the debit side is greater in amount than the credit side. The difference, or balance, is placed on the credit side to make the two sides equal in amount, and is brought down to the debit side for the next period. Smith's Motor Cycle Company Account shows a *credit balance*, as does the Capital Account: the credit side exceeds the debit side in total and the balance is inserted on the debit side, being brought down to the credit side of the account for the new period.

Debit balances of both real and personal accounts are always assets. Credit balances are always claims. The accounts of creditors – those to whom debts are owing – normally show a credit balance, whereas the accounts of debtors – those who owe debts to the business – show a debit balance.

The financial position of Redman's business at 31st March has altered from the position at the commencement of the new trading period. There is a new liability, the amount due to Smith's Motor Cycle Company, and a new asset, the balance due from J. Dunbar.

The proprietor's capital is now £4 030 but it is not now so simple a matter to show how that amount is invested in the business. On 1st March it was invested in cash and stock. Now, at the close of the month, it is invested in cash, stock, and a book debt, less the amount due to a creditor.

The proprietor's capital can thus be expressed as the excess of the value of the assets over the liabilities of the business. This is another way of expressing the Balance Sheet equation set out in Chapter 3.

EXERCISES 5

Enter the transactions given in the following exercises in their appropriate Ledger Accounts, and check the double entry. Find the gross and net profit or loss for the period, and prepare a Balance Sheet in each case as at the date of the last transaction. Transactions are on credit unless otherwise stated.

1. Jan. 1, J. White commenced business in motor car accessories with capital in cash, £10 000.

			£
Jan.	1.	Bought accessories for cash	6 000
,,	2.	Sold accessories on credit to F. Lawson	5 000
,,	6.	Paid carriage charges	300
,,	16.	Bought goods on credit from Motor Equipment Company	9 000
,,	19.	F. Lawson paid his account in cash	5 000
,,	23.	Sold goods on credit to B. Coombes	7 000
,,	27.	Sold goods on credit to F. Lawson	7 200
,,	31.	Paid sundry expenses	500

Stock on hand at 31st January, £300.

2. May 1, J. Cade began to deal in tennis equipment with capital in cash, £1 200.

			£
May	1.	He bought rackets for cash	600
,,	2.	Bought sundry equipment for cash	260
,,	3.	Bought equipment and rackets from Lazenby & Sons	600
,,	8.	Paid cash for advertising and fares	80
,,	12.	Sold goods to L. White & Co.	1 000
,,	17.	Sold goods to B. Blackburn	150
,,	24.	Cash sales	400
,,	27.	Paid Lazenby & Sons their account in cash	
,,	31.	Received cash from L. White & Co. on account	500

Stock on hand at 31st May, £300.

3. June 1, J. Shaw began to deal in camp stores with capital in cash, £1 700.

June	1.	He bought tents and sundries from Camp Supplies Ltd.	1 500
,,	2.	He bought further equipment for cash	1 200
,,	4.	Paid for transport by rail	70
,,	10.	Sold tents to Smith's Stores Ltd.	1 400
,,	15.	Sold equipment for cash	1 190

Find his gross and net profit for this period, and prepare Balance Sheet at this date. Stock on hand, £840.

Continue accounts for a further period:

,,	16.	Sold equipment to Smith's Stores Ltd.	1 000
,,	21.	Paid Camp Supplies Ltd., cash	1 500
,,	22.	Bought tents from Camp Supplies Ltd.	1 200
,,	28.	Received cash from Smith's Stores for their account to date	2 400
,,	30.	Paid sundry expenses	40
,,	30.	Drew cash for private use	400

Find the gross and net profit for the period, and prepare a Balance Sheet as at 30th June. Stock on hand, £1 400.

4. Sept. 4, J. Wright began as a used furniture dealer with capital in cash, £2 640.

			£
Sept.	4.	He expended £2 400 on sundry articles for stock	
,,	7.	Bought furniture from Shaw & Wood	3 000
,,	9.	Paid sundry expenses in cash	150
,,	12.	Sold furniture for cash	1 800
,,	14.	Sold furniture to B. Burns	1 980

Find his profit or loss for the period and prepare Balance Sheet as at 14th September. Stock on hand, £2 100. Continue his accounts for a further period:

Sept.	15.	Bought furniture from Shaw & Wood	1 500
,,	20.	Paid Shaw & Wood cash on account	1 800
,,	20.	Cash sales	1 300
,,	27.	B. Burns paid cash	1 980
,,	30.	Sold furniture to P. Hastings	2 400
,,	30.	Paid sundry expenses	330
,,	30.	Withdrew for private use	450

Find the profit or loss for the period, and prepare Balance Sheet as at 30th September. Stock on hand at that date, £1 200.

6

The Trial Balance

The entries for the transactions in the examples already considered have been few so that the check upon the double entry has been simple. The possibility of error increases with the number of entries, and it is necessary to prevent the carrying of errors into the Final Accounts. A check by means of a *Trial Balance* is therefore made on the arithmetical accuracy of the entries after the last transaction of the trading period has been entered and before the preparation of the Trading Account.

The transactions from Example 4 in Chapter 5 are taken for illustration. The accounts are shown as they stood after the last transaction was entered.

Cash Account

19..			£	19..			£
Mar. 1	Balance	b/d	3 020	Mar. 28	Packing materials		60
„ 12	Sales		480				
„ 26	J. Dunbar		500				

Capital Account

19..			£	19..			£
				Mar. 1	Balance	b/d	3 770

Stock Account

19..			£	19..			£
Mar. 1	Stock		750				

Purchases Account

19..			£	19..			
Mar. 5	Smith's Motor Cycle Company		1 680				

Sales Account

19..			£	19..			£
				Mar. 12	Cash		480
				,, 19	J. Dunbar		1 200

Smith's Motor Cycle Company Account

19..			£	19..			£
				Mar. 5	Purchases		1 680

J. Dunbar's Account

19..			£	19..			£
Mar. 19	Sales		1 220	Mar. 26	Cash		500

Expenses Account

19..			£	19..			£
Mar. 28	Cash: Packing materials		60				

The fact that the double entry principles lead to a debit and a credit entry for each transaction and that this permits the accuracy of the entries to be checked has already been referred to. A debit entry has a corresponding credit entry somewhere in the accounts for the trading period. A complete list of all the debit entries in all the accounts should therefore equal in total a similar list of all the credit entries. Again, for the same reason, if the debit entries in each single account are added and a list made of their totals, this should equal in amount a similar list of the totals of the credit entries in each account.

The Trial Balance, as its name implies, is, however, a trial of the balances of the accounts to check the accuracy of the entries. The use of the balances and not of the totals of the debit and credit entries saves much clerical work, and is valuable as a check.

In preparing the Trial Balance the balance of each account is ascertained. If the debit side of the account is the greater, then the balance is a debit balance, and it is placed in the column for debit balances in the Trial Balance. If the credit side is the greater, then the balance of the account is a credit balance and it is entered in the credit balances column of the Trial Balance. When all the balances are entered, the columns are added and the totals should agree.

Below is the Trial Balance extracted from the above accounts.

Trial Balance

	Dr.	*Cr.*
	£	£
Cash	3 940	
Capital		3 770
Stock	750	
Purchases	1 680	
Sales		1 680
Smith's Motor Cycle Company		1 680
J. Dunbar	700	
Expenses	60	
	£7 130	£7 130

Sometimes the totals do not agree: the debit column may be greater than the credit, or the other way round. In either case there must be an error or errors in the Ledger or in extracting balances from the Ledger.

The errors, of course, must be found, and students would be well advised to follow the routine described below when they find a Trial Balance disagreeing. If (*a*) does not reveal the error then (*b*) should be tried, and so on. The difference between the two sides may, of course, be the result of more than one error.

(*a*) Re-add the totals in order to be sure that the difference is not a matter of simple addition.

(*b*) Check all figures from the Ledger to the Trial Balance in order to be certain that figures have not been overlooked when the Trial Balance was compiled.

(*c*) If the amount by which the two sides of the Trial Balance differs is, say £14, look for amounts of £14 in the Ledger and be sure that the double entry for each amount has been completed.

(*d*) If an amount of £7 was entered twice on the debit side in the Ledger, or twice on the credit side, then the amount of difference will be doubled, in this case £14. So halve the difference between the two sides of the Trial Balance and look in the Ledger for entries of this amount and check the double entry to see that they have been carried out properly.

(*e*) If the error or errors still cannot be found, then go through the

Ledger and check all totals and balances to make sure of the accuracy of the arithmetic.

(*f*) Finally, check the double entry throughout the Ledger.

The preparation of the Final Accounts should not be proceeded with until any error or errors indicated by the non-agreement of the Trial Balance have been discovered and corrected. If, however, it is necessary to prepare Final Accounts quickly while there is still a difference in the Trial Balance, this difference is placed to a *Suspense Account*. The Balance of the Suspense Account is shown in the Balance Sheet on the claims or assets side according to whether the balance is a credit or a debit entry.

The agreement of the Trial Balance does not prove that no errors have been made in the books.

Here is a list of types of error which a Trial Balance does not disclose:

(i) Errors of Omission.
(ii) Errors of Commission.
(iii) Errors of Principle.
(iv) Errors in the Original Entry.
(v) Compensating Errors.

(i) Errors of Omission: In the event of an invoice for goods purchased being lost, no entry would have been made on the debit side of the Purchases Account nor would there be an entry on the credit side of the Supplier's Account. The missing debit equals the missing credit so the Trial Balance would agree. This is an example of an Error of Omission.

(ii) Errors of Commission: Making an entry of a transaction in a wrong account of the same class. (In this context 'commission' is derived from the word 'commit'. It is not a form of payment.)

If money were received from B. Jones the entries would be debit Cash or Bank Account and credit B. Jones's Account. But it is possible we may also have dealings with a W. Jones & Co. and if the credit were entered in W. Jones & Co.'s Account instead of in the account of B. Jones, this would of course be an error. The Trial Balance would not show it up because a debit (in the Cash Book) has a credit (in W. Jones & Co.'s Account). This is an example of an Error of Commission.

(iii) Error of Principle: Entry of transactions in the wrong class of account.

T. Edwards purchased some machinery for use in his business. His bookkeeper, seeing it as a purchase, made the debit entry in the Purchases Account. The only entries in the Purchases Account should be goods bought for resale, so the debit in this case is wrong; it should have been made in an Asset Account, e.g. Machinery. This is an example of an Error of Principle. This will be better understood after Chapters 12 and 14 have been studied.

(iv) Error in Original Entry: Where an incorrect entry is made in a book of prime (or original) entry and the incorrect entry is posted to the debit and the credit sides of the Ledger.

This type of error can be understood only after the student has studied the use of books of prime entry in Chapters 9 and 12.

(v) Compensating Error: Incorrect entries on the debit side are compensated for by incorrect entries of an equal value on the credit side.

Suppose the purchases were over-added by £15, then the debit side of the Trial Balance would be £15 too great. Suppose that the Sales Account by some coincidence had also been over-added by £15. This would mean that the credit side of the Trial Balance was also too great. Thus, although two errors have been made, the Trial Balance agrees. This is an example of a Compensating Error.

These classes of error could naturally be corrected only when they were discovered, and the method of correction will be found in Chapter 12.

EXERCISES 6

Enter the transactions in the following exercises into their appropriate Ledger Accounts. Take out a Trial Balance for each exercise as on the date of the last transaction.

Find the gross and net profit for the period, and prepare a Balance Sheet.

1. Dec. 1, J. Bentham began to deal in picture frames, with capital in cash, £900.

Dec. 1. Bought six frames for cash at £60 each.
,, 3. Bought six frames at £30 each from J. Tobin & Co.
,, 7. Bought a quantity of frames at auction for cash, £450.
,, 8. Paid for packing materials, £10.
,, 10. Sold to J. Smith, frames, £780.
,, 12. Sold to W. Wilkins, frames, £360.
,, 17. J. Smith paid his account in cash.
,, 31. Paid sundry expenses in cash, £50.
,, 31. Stock on hand, £300.

2. N. Chambers began business on 1st July with £162 as capital in cash.

			£
July	1.	Bought quantity of goods for cash	97
,,	3.	Sold goods for cash	54
,,	7.	Bought further quantity of goods from Silk Weavers Ltd.	180
,,	10.	Paid Silk Weavers Ltd. on account	90
,,	15.	Sold goods to the following customers:	
		J. Wesley & Sons	30
		H. Boyce	112
,,	17.	Paid for parcel post	2
,,	19.	H. Boyce paid £45 on account	
,,	19.	Stock of goods on hand valued at £126.	

3.

			£
May	1.	J. Summer began to deal in sports goods with capital in cash	4 200
,,	1.	Bought quantity of goods from Sportsman & Sons	5 200
,,	3.	Bought goods for cash	1 600
,,	7.	Bought goods from Fielding & Co.	1 700
,,	8.	Paid for postages in cash	20
,,	12.	Sold sports goods on credit to:	
		J. Park	3 150
		M. Meadow	14 750
		L. Field	2 125
,,	15.	Sold goods for cash	330
,,	17.	Received cash from J. Park	1 000
,,	18.	Received cash from L. Field	1 075
,,	18.	Paid for postage in cash	20

Stock on hand, 18th May, valued at £2 000.

4. The following Trial Balance shows all the balances of the accounts in J. Thorburn's Ledger. From the Trial Balance prepare the Trading Account, Profit and Loss Account, and Balance Sheet.

Trial Balance

31st December

	Dr. £	*Cr.* £
Cash Account	210	
Purchases Account	840	
Sales Account		1 000
Expenses	50	
J. Wilson's Account	620	
M. Dover's Account	530	
T. Kent's Account		150
Capital Account		1 100
	£2 250	£2 250

The stock on hand at 31st December was valued at £240.

5. H. Williamson's Trial Balance shows the following balances on his Ledger Accounts as at 31st December. From the Trial Balance prepare his Trading Account, Profit and Loss Account, and a Balance Sheet as at 31st December.

Trial Balance

	Dr.	*Cr.*
	£	£
Cash Account	480	
Capital Account		570
Purchases	1 040	
Sales		1 060
Expenses	80	
B. Watson's Account	260	
F. Morgan's Account	190	
T. Young's Account		420
	£2 050	£2 050

Stock on hand at 31st December was valued at £300.

6. Give one example of each of the following kinds of error. State whether each may cause a Trial Balance to disagree, giving reasons for your answer:

(*a*) Error of principle.
(*b*) Error of omission.
(*c*) Compensating error.

7. The following balances were extracted from the books of S. Martin on 31st December, 19... You are required to prepare a Trial Balance therefrom, inserting the amount required to balance it as 'Capital':

	£
Purchases	8 280
Cash at bank	1 278
Drawings	612
Loan from J. Haylock	500
Loan to J. Smith	100
Stock in hand at 1st January, 19..	335
Returns inwards	63
Sales	13 122
Furniture	80
Freehold property	2 000
Sundry debtors	1 316
General expenses	495
Discount received	41
Sundry creditors	1 042
Carriage outwards	68
Plant and machinery	1 412

R.S.A.

8. If a Trial Balance failed to agree, what steps would you take in order to find the difference?

9. What are the different types of error which are not thrown up by a Trial Balance? Give an example under each heading.

10. A Trial Balance was extracted from the books of V. Baker, and it was found that the debit side exceeded the credit side by £40. This amount was entered in the Suspense Account. Subsequently the following errors were discovered and corrected:

(i) The Purchases were over-added by £20.

(ii) An amount paid to B. Simpkins was debited to his account as £98 instead of £89.

(iii) The Sales were under-added by £11.

Write up and rule off the Suspense Account as it would appear in Baker's Ledger.

11. The Trial Balance of B. Clandon failed to agree because the credit side exceeded the debit by £19. The difference was placed to Suspense Account. Later, the following errors were discovered and corrected:

(i) An amount received from T. Black was credited to his account as £52 instead of £25.

(ii) An amount for Cash Sales £18 was entered in the Cash Account but was omitted from the Sales Account.

(iii) The Sales had been over-added by £10.

Write up and rule off the Suspense Account as it would appear in Clandon's Ledger.

7

The Trader's Bank Account and the Cash Book

Few traders find it either safe or convenient to use only coin and notes to settle their transactions. If only for safe keeping of cash a trader will open a bank account and, having such an account, he is able to make use of the other facilities that banks offer to their customers. An account is opened by the payment in of an initial sum of money. When the trader has to pay an account, he may do so by *cheque*, which is a written order to a banker to pay a stated sum of money to a named person on demand. The payment of this sum by the banker depletes the trader's bank account. On the other hand, if the trader receives cheques from his customers in payment of their accounts, his bank will collect the sums due on the cheques and place them to the credit of his account.

By means of the cheque system the holder of a bank account has a simple yet safe means of making payments and of receiving payment. Cash which is surplus to immediate requirements may be paid into the bank account, and many traders pay their *takings* daily into the bank whatever form the takings are in: whether coin, notes, postal orders, or cheques. Payments out are then made by cheque.

The bank keeps an account in its Ledger of the money received and paid out for each customer and periodically sends a copy of the account to the customer. This copy is called a *Bank Statement*, i.e. it is a statement of the entries which have been made in the customer's account.

The trader also keeps a Ledger Account showing his transactions affecting his bank balance, as a record and as a check upon the bank. Periodically he compares the bank's account, as disclosed by the Bank Statement, with his own account to satisfy himself that both are in order and complete.

It follows that the trader should now have two accounts in his own books to record his cash, one relating to the cash in the office and the other to the cash at the bank.

Example 5. M. Redman continues his business during April, the position on 1st April being:

Cash in hand	£3 940
Stock	£1 070
Owing *by* J. Dunbar	£700
Owing *to* Smith's Motor Cycle Company	£1 680
Capital	£4 030

The following transactions take place:

April	1.	Redman opens an account with the Counties Bank, paying in cash £3 500.
„	3.	Received from J. Dunbar, cheque £700 in settlement of his account.
„	8.	Bought from Smith's Motor Cycle Company bikes value £3 000.
„	15.	Sold bikes to J. Dunbar, value £3 600.
„	20.	Paid sundry expenses in cash, £60.
„	24.	J. Dunbar paid his account by cheque, in full.
„	27.	Sold one bike for cash, £450, which was not banked.
„	29.	Paid Smith's Motor Cycle Company £4 680 by cheque.
„	30.	Paid assistant's wages in cash, £360. Stock at close at cost, £1 920.

Note that the items dated 8th and 15th April are on credit. As credit transactions are more frequent in practice than cash transactions it is assumed that a transaction is on credit unless it is otherwise indicated. Compare the transaction dated 27th April.

The entering of the above transactions requires the continuation of the Cash Account and the opening of a Bank Account in Redman's books.

It is the usual practice of traders to pay in all takings in to the bank daily. Cheques received should be debited direct to the Bank Account.

What the bank receives is entered on the debit side of the Bank Account. The sums it pays away are entered on the credit side of the account. If this is borne in mind no difficulty should be experienced with the first transaction. Redman takes £3 500 from the office cash and pays it in to the bank. The double entry is in the Cash and Bank Accounts – credit Cash Account, debit Bank Account, to record the change in location. The procedure is the same whenever he makes payments in to the bank.

On the other hand, the trader may find himself short of office cash and may cash a cheque to replenish his supply. 'Drew cheque for £20 for office cash', as it is often worded, would involve a credit entry in the Bank Account, since the bank parts with £20, and a debit entry in the Cash Account as the trader receives the cash.

Below are the Cash and Bank Accounts as they would appear for the month of April. The corresponding entries are not shown – except for the first item for which they come within the two accounts – as these should now present no difficulty.

Cash Account

19..			£	19..			£
Apr. 1	Balance	b/d	3 940	Apr. 1	Bank		3 500
„ 27	Cash Sales		450	„ 20	Expenses		60
				„ 30	Wages		360
				„ „	Balance	c/d	470
			£4 390				£4 390
May 1	Balance	b/d	470				

Bank Account

19..			£	19..			£
Apr. 1	Cash		3 500	Apr. 29	Smith's Motor Cycle Co.		4 680
„ „	J. Dunbar		700	„ 30	Balance	c/d	3 120
„ 24	J. Dunbar		3 600				
			£7 800				£7 800
May 1	Balance	b/d	3 120				

The balance of the Bank Account will appear among the assets in the Balance Sheet when that is drawn up. An exception to this is referred to in Chapter 19, and occurs when the bank allows a customer to draw out more than he has paid in to his account at the bank.

Balance Sheet

CLAIMS	£	ASSETS	£
Capital (including net profit for April)	5 510	Stock	1 920
		Cash at bank	3 120
		Cash in hand	470
	£5 510		£5 510

The student will find it a useful exercise to complete the full double entry for Redman's transactions for April.

The Cash Book

As the business grows in volume and the transactions increase in number a greater demand is made on the bookkeeper to keep the accounts entered day by day. Care must also be taken to limit the opportunities for theft or embezzlement. Some suitable scheme must be devised to sub-divide the work, but the use of one Ledger only for all accounts sets a limit to any scheme, as the Ledger cannot be used by more than one person at a time. A step in the direction of sub-division of duties is to place one person in charge of the cash and the Cash and Bank Accounts, and to separate these two accounts from the other accounts in the main Ledger. The Cash and the Bank Accounts, in such circumstances, are kept in the *Cash Book* – a book bound separately from the Ledger purely as a matter of convenience in the internal organisation of the business. The Cash Book is placed in the keeping of the *cashier*. The accounts are still Ledger Accounts and the separation does not affect the double entry principles already discussed.

A second convenience is achieved by adapting the Ledger ruling contained in the Cash Book. Instead of the Cash Account and the Bank Account being opened in different parts of the book, the account columns are placed together, enabling the cash and bank balances to be found on the same page. To do this, the Cash Book is ruled as on page 55. The debit column of the Cash Account is placed alongside the debit column of the Bank Account, and the credit columns of the two accounts are similarly placed together. The transactions affecting the accounts are entered chronologically, but care is taken that the amounts are entered in the right money columns according to whether they affect the office cash or the banked cash. Though the accounts appear in conjunction they are balanced in the usual way.

The Cash Book should be compared with the Cash Account and Bank Account on page 53. It will be observed that there is no departure from the bookkeeping principles. The change is only in the ruling of the accounts and their separation from the Ledger. Should a customer pay or be paid his account, as the case may be, partly in cash and partly by cheque, the particulars have to be entered once only and the amounts paid must be entered side by side in the cash and bank columns on the appropriate side of the Cash Book.

Cash Book

Dr. | *Cr.*

Date				CASH	BANK	Date				CASH	BANK
19..				£	£	19..				£	£
April	1	Balance	b/d	3 940		April	1	Bank		3 500	
,,	1	Cash			3 500	,,	20	Expenses		60	
,,	3	J. Dunbar			700	,,	29	Smith's Motor Cycle Co.			4 680
,,	24	J. Dunbar			3 600	,,	30	Wages		360	
,,	27	Cash Sales		450		,,	30	Balance	c/d	470	3 120
				£4 390	£7 800					£4 390	£7 800
May	1	Balance	b/d	470	3 120						

EXERCISES 7

Enter the transactions in the following exercises in their appropriate accounts, using a two-column Cash Book. Extract a Trial Balance, and prepare the final accounts to show the profit or loss for the trading period. Prepare also a Balance Sheet in each case as at the date of the last transaction.

1. April 1, M. Rafter commenced business with capital in cash, £2 500.

			£
April	1.	Paid cash into bank	2 200
,,	3.	Bought goods from B. Croydon	1 600
,,	8.	Bought goods from T. Brighton	1 300
,,	12.	Cash sales	520
,,	13.	Paid cash into bank	500
,,	15.	Paid expenses by cheque	70
,,	21.	Sold goods to L. Sussex	100
,,	22.	Sold goods to J. Worthing	2 000
,,	24.	Paid cash for stationery	30
,,	27.	Paid B. Croydon by cheque	1 600
,,	28.	Received cheque from L. Sussex	100
,,	30.	Paid expenses by cheque	80
,,	30.	Paid carriage in cash	100

Stock of goods on hand, 30th April, £1 200.

2.

			£
Oct.	1.	J. Pearce commenced business with capital:	
		Cash at bank	4 000
		Cash in hand	200
,,	2.	He bought goods from R. Southwark	3 000
,,	3.	Bought goods for cash	180
,,	4.	Cashed cheque for office cash	200
,,	7.	Cash sales	570
,,	7.	Paid cash into bank	600
,,	12.	Sold goods to J. Fulham	1 500
,,	17.	Paid sundry expenses in cash	40
,,	24.	J. Fulham paid his account by cheque	1 500
,,	27.	Paid R. Southwark by cheque	3 000
,,	28.	Bought goods from R. Southwark	2 000
,,	30.	Cash sales	350
,,	30.	Paid for stationery by cheque	200
,,	30.	Withdrew cash for personal use	300

Stock on hand, 30th October, £3 100.

3. Dec. 1, J. Mackintosh began business in fancy goods, with capital of £500 consisting of: Cash at bank, £475; Cash in hand, £25.

			£
Dec.	2.	Bought job line of goods and paid by cheque	200
,,	3.	Bought leather goods from Farmer & Co.	250
,,	7.	Cash sales paid into bank	70
,,	8.	Paid Farmer & Co. by cheque	250
,,	10.	Paid sundry expenses in cash	12
,,	12.	Sold goods to H. Benson	340
,,	14.	Paid sundry expenses in cash	6

Prepare Final Accounts and Balance Sheet as at 14th December. Stock on hand, £170.

Continue the accounts for a further period:

Dec.	15.	Bought goods from Farmer & Co.	300
,,	20.	Sold goods for cash	53
,,	22.	Sold goods to J. Wilson	200
,,	22.	Paid postage in cash	2
,,	22.	H. Benson paid on account by cheque	200
,,	24.	Sold goods to J. Wilson	136
,,	28.	Paid assistant cash	6
,,	31.	Paid expenses by cheque	8

Stock on hand, £90.

4.

			£
Feb.	1.	J. Harding began business in hardware with:	
		Cash in hand	200
		Cash at bank	6 000
,,	2.	Bought goods from M. Cromwell	3 250
,,	3.	Sold goods to B. Ward	500
,,	6.	Paid M. Cromwell by cheque	3 250
,,	6.	Paid wages in cash	150
,,	8.	B. Ward paid in cash on account	250
,,	10.	Bought goods from P. Pitt	1 500
,,	12.	Cash sales	750
,,	13.	Paid wages in cash	150
,,	14.	Paid sundry expenses by cheque	100
,,	18.	Sold goods to B. Burton	2 000
,,	20.	Paid wages in cash	155
,,	21.	Cash sales	207
,,	22.	Paid all cash, except £50, into bank.	

Stock on hand, 22nd February, £2 250.

8

The Classification of Expenditures

The written record of financial transactions is of the utmost value, but the scheme of classification by accounts is of equal importance. Any information that is required is readily accessible, and time is saved and the possibility of error is lessened by grouping related transactions under their appropriate headings. Moreover, as the system of bookkeeping is adaptable to special needs, accounts may be opened to record the information that a trader may wish to be available at any time. The *Expenses Account*, for example contains the record of all the expenses or losses of a business, and that is the account to which the proprietor would refer if he wished to know the various expenses incurred in conducting the business. Such expenses would take the form of wages and salaries, postage, stationery, rent, rates and taxes, lighting and heating.

Usually as trade increases expenses also increase, so that the proprietor would find the Expenses Account becoming a lengthy account and containing many repetitive items. Anxious to know his expenditure in any particular direction the trader would have to analyse the items in the account to find the total expenditure for the period. Wages, paid weekly, would, for example, occur about fifty times during the year. To save the trouble of analysis and to have the information available at any time, accounts are opened in the Ledger for each form of expense, loss or gain. Expenses and losses are debited and gains are credited to their respective accounts. At the end of the trading period the balances of these accounts are transferred to the Profit and Loss Account which then contains all the expenses and gains as hitherto shown, but in summarised form. Such accounts for the expenses, gains and losses of the business are known as *Nominal Accounts.*

Instead, therefore, of all items of expenditure being posted to the Expenses Account items belonging to a definite class are posted to a separate account for that class, while the Expenses Account, now called *General Expenses*, is used only for minor items of expenditure which cannot be easily classified or which individually are likely to be only very small in amount.

Example 6. The following transactions took place during June:

June 4. Paid assistant's wages, £60.
,, 10. Bought for cash envelopes and other office stationery, £30.
,, 11. Paid assistant's wages, £60.
,, 18. Paid assistant's wages, £60.
,, 25. Paid rent by cheque, £200.
,, 25. Paid assistant's wages, £60.
,, 27. Paid Fire Insurance Premium, £30.
,, 30. Received from J. Whiteman cheque for £220 as commission on arranging the sale of certain goods for him.

The above transactions are entered in their appropriate accounts as follows. The transfer entry as at 30th June, the closing date of the period of trading, is also given in each case and is shown in the Profit and Loss Account that would then be prepared. The Cash Book entries are now shown.

Wages

19..			£	19..			£
June 4	Cash		60	June 30	Transfer to Profit & Loss A/c.		240
,, 11	,,		60				
,, 18	,,		60				
,, 25	,,		60				
			£240				£240

Stationery Account

19..			£	19..			£
June 10	Cash		30	June 30	Transfer to Profit & Loss A/c.		30

Rent Account

19..			£	19..			£
June 25	Cash		200	June 30	Transfer to Profit & Loss A/c.		200

Insurance Premiums Account

19..			£	19..			£
June 27	Cash		30	June 30	Transfer to Profit & Loss A/c.		30

Commission Account

19..			£	19..			£
June 30	Transfer to Profit & Loss A/c.		220	June 30	Cash: J. Whiteman		220

Profit and Loss Account

19..			£	19..			£
June 30	Wages		240	June 30	Commission		220
,, ,,	Stationery		30		Gross Profit (when ascertained)		
,, ,,	Rent		200				
,, ,,	Insurance		30				

It is not practicable to give numerous items of expense as examples, but the above should be sufficient to indicate the use of specified accounts for expenses and how the Profit and Loss Account is built up from these details. In practice, there are likely to be several dozen such nominal accounts for expenses in a business. It is also necessary to have extensive systems to calculate the amount of some expenses, e.g. a payroll system to calculate wages and all related matters.

Purchases Not for Resale

A trader buys goods for his stock and continues to buy from time to time as he finds his stock needs to be replenished. These are the kinds of purchases which have been considered in earlier chapters. They may be purchases for cash or on credit, but in every case the intention is to sell all such purchases in the ordinary course of business. It is not long, however, before a trader finds he must buy certain things to keep for *use* and not for his stock to sell in the ordinary course of business. He may require shop fittings, such as counters and show-cases, and office furniture, typewriters and motor vans. He may consider it desirable to purchase the business premises. All such things are kept permanently in the business for use, and for that reason are differentiated from the goods bought for the purpose of selling again at a profit.

All payments made on behalf of the business are included in the term *expenditures*. The term expenses excludes those expenditures which are purchases not for resale; it includes those expenditures which are goods that are resold (i.e. purchases) and those which are for services used up in a short period of time (e.g. wages, fuel, rent etc.)

It has been shown that the entries of purchases for stock and eventual sale are made in the Purchases Account. This account is reserved for such purchases and should not be used to record the purchase of things to be kept for permanent use.

The business premises, shop fittings, office furniture, and similar purchases made with the view of keeping them for use are counted among the valuable possessions, or assets, of the business, and, as it will be necessary to keep a record of their value, a special account is opened in the Ledger for each of such assets.

Example 7. On Dec. 1, M. Redman buys his shop premises, freehold, for £14 500, paying by cheque.

The credit entry for this transaction is in the Bank Account in the Cash Book. The corresponding debit entry is made to a new account to record the asset of the value of £14 500 that the business has acquired and which takes the place of the cash asset to that amount.

Shop Premises

19..			£	19..			£
Dec. 1	Cash		14 500				

On closing the books and preparing the Final Accounts, the accounts for such assets will remain open and their balances will be included among the items in the Balance Sheet. In the above example, Shop Premises, £14 500, will appear as an asset in the Balance Sheet. The total value of the firm's assets have not been increased by the purchase: there is only a change in the form of the assets.

The trader may, of course, purchase such assets on credit. That will involve no immediate change in the Cash Account, but the fact that an asset has been acquired must be recorded and, at the same time, a record must be made of the debt created.

Example 8. On Jan. 10 M. Redman bought one showcase, £60, on credit from Mint & Company, Ltd.

Shop Fittings

19..			£	19..			£
Dec. 10	Mint & Co.		60				

Mint & Company

19..				19..			£
				Dec. 10	Shop fittings		60

Shop fittings will appear among the assets in the Balance Sheet. If payment is not made before the Balance Sheet is prepared, the debt due to Mint & Co. must be included in the item Sundry Creditors on the claims side. Notice that in this case the assets have increased in total, but the liabilities show a similar increase in amount. The payment of the account would extinguish the liability to Mint & Co., and at the same time the total assets would be diminished as £60 would be paid out from the office or bank cash.

Consumable Stores

From time to time purchases will be made differing from either of the kinds discussed above, such as office stationery, typewriter ribbons, envelopes, packing materials and postage stamps. These are consumable goods, being used up in the ordinary routine of business, and as such, must be treated as part of the expense of conducting the business.

Accounts will be kept for these forms of expense, for example, Office Stationery and Sundries Account, Packing Materials Account, and Postage Account. The balances of these accounts will be transferred to the Profit and Loss Account at the close of a trading period. The expenses will be debited to their respective accounts, the credit entries being to Cash Account, if bought for cash, or if bought on credit, to the personal accounts of the firms from whom they are obtained.

Thus it will seem that a business purchases three different kinds of goods which should not be confused:

(1) Goods bought for resale (or for manufacture for resale): debit Purchases Account.
(2) Consumable stores: debit appropriate Expenses Account.
(3) Assets: debit appropriate Asset Account.

In addition to the above, a business will find that it must spend money for which no return in goods is to be obtained. This fourth classification of out-goings will include expenditure on wages, insurance, advertising, etc.

At the end of the Trading Period the expenditure on goods bought for resale is transferred to the Trading Account together with such items of consumable stores and expenses such as wages, etc., which directly affect the Gross Profit. At the same time the expenditure on consumable stores and expenses such as wages etc. (other than those items referred to above which directly affect the Gross Profit) are transferred to the Profit and Loss Account. The expenditure on assets is left in the Asset Accounts concerned as balances which consequently appear on the Balance Sheet.

EXERCISES 8

1. J. Whitehouse began business with capital of £2 000 cash at bank. Enter his capital and the following transactions in his Ledger and Cash Book, using separate accounts for his expenses.

			£
Jan.	1.	Drew from bank for office cash	200
,,	2.	Bought goods from R. Nunn	600
,,	3.	Bought goods and paid by cheque	1 300
,,	7.	Paid wages in cash	60
,,	12.	Sold goods to J. Dunn	750
,,	12.	Cash sales, paid into bank	380
,,	14.	Paid wages in cash	60
,,	16.	Paid postage and delivery charges	15
,,	20.	Cash sales	400
,,	21.	Paid wages in cash	60
,,	22.	Paid for packing paper	25
,,	24.	Paid R. Nunn his account, in cash £200, by cheque £400	
,,	28.	Paid wages in cash	60
,,	31.	Paid rent by cheque	125
,,	31.	Paid lighting account in cash	50

Take out Trial Balance, prepare Trading and Profit and Loss Accounts, and draw up a Balance Sheet as at 31st January. Stock on hand, £900.

2. Enter the following transactions of J. R. West, who is dealing in tape recorders and gramophone records, in his accounts, including a two-column Cash Book, and using separate Expense Accounts:

			£
Dec.	7.	Cash in hand	240
,,	7.	Cash at bank	1 200
,,	9.	Bought tape recorders from Electricity Ltd.	840
,,	11.	Bought records by cheque	1 000
,,	15.	Sold records for cash	420
,,	16.	Paid advertising charges in cash	40
,,	18.	Sold tape recorders for cash	780
,,	19.	Paid delivery charges in cash	20
,,	19.	Paid cash into bank	1 100
,,	24.	Cash sales, paid direct to bank	800
,,	24.	Paid delivery charges in cash	20
,,	31.	Drew cheque for personal use	200

Take out a Trial Balance. Prepare Trading and Profit and Loss Accounts, and draw up a Balance Sheet as at 31st December. Stock on hand at that date, £440.

3. R.B. Agarwal began business as a stationer on 1st October. Enter the following transactions in his books, using separate expense accounts:

			£
Oct.	1.	Cash at bank: Capital	220
,,	3.	Bought stationery from Johnson & Co. Ltd.	150
,,	5.	Bought notebooks and pens and pencils from Wetherby & Co.	25
,,	7.	Cash takings, paid into bank	42
,,	14.	Cash sales	38
,,	18.	Bought further goods from Johnson & Co. Ltd.	130
,,	21.	Cash sales, paid into bank	61
,,	25.	Paid rent by cheque	30
,,	28.	Bought packing paper and string for cash	5
,,	31.	Cash sales, paid into bank	54

Take out a Trial Balance. Prepare Trading and Profit and Loss Accounts and a Balance Sheet as at 31st October. Stock on hand at that date, £140.

4. The balances of the accounts of N. Shepherd at 31st December are shown in the following Trial Balance. From it prepare Trading Account and Profit and Loss Accounts and a Balance Sheet as at 31st December.

Trial Balance 31st December

	Dr.	*Cr.*
	£	£
Capital Account		2 500
Cash balance	120	
Bank balance	2 120	
Stock at start	2 000	
Purchases	12 000	
Sales		17 200
Wages Account	1 000	
Lighting Account	100	
Telephone Account	210	
Debtors: J. White	1 040	
J. Smith	1 370	
Creditor: B. Burt		260
	£19 960	£19 960

The stock on hand at 31st December was valued at £1 800.

5. At 31st December, 19.., J. Spalding's Ledger showed the following balances. You are required to prepare from them a Trial Balance in proper form, and from the Trial Balance a Trading Account and Profit and Loss Account for the month and a Balance Sheet as at 31st December.

The balances were: Capital Account (*Cr.*), £800; Sales, £3 000; Purchases, £2 250; Cash in hand, £18; Cash at bank, £542; Carriage Account, £10; Rent and Rates Account, £135; Insurance Premiums Account, £4; Wages Account, £150; Stock Account, 1st Dec., £460; S. Kemp (Debtor), £299; L. Lacey (Creditor), £68.

The stock on hand at 31st December was valued at cost at £500.

6. The following Trial Balance was extracted from the books of R. Heather. Prepare his Trading and Profit and Loss Accounts for the period, and a Balance Sheet as at 31st December.

Trial Balance 31st December

	Dr.	*Cr.*
	£	£
Capital Account		5 005
Cash in hand	101	
Cash at bank	3 502	
Stock at start	2 500	
Sales		11 003
Purchases	7 004	
Wages Account	1 500	
Rent Account	1 000	
Rates Account	450	
B. Rivers	742	
J. Hills		791
	£16 799	£16 799

Stock on hand, 31st December, £2 600.

9

Records of Sales, Purchases, and Returns

The growth of a business is usually growth in the number of its transactions. The most numerous of these transactions are usually sales on credit. Purchases will have to be made in correspondingly larger quantities to meet the increased demand, but as these purchases will usually be in bulk the entries necessary are not so numerous as for sales.

The increase in sale and purchase transactions give rise to the use of numerous *invoices*. An invoice is a document which gives details and prices of the goods sold and shows the customer how much he owes. These documents are used as the original material for the purpose of recording sale and purchase transactions. With a large number of such documents it would be most cumbersome to make an entry for each separate invoice in the Sales Account or in the Purchases Account, as these accounts would be hopelessly overloaded with entries. It is necessary, therefore, to organise the material in such a way as to economise the number of entries which must be made. In order to do this a system of *books of prime* (or original) *entry* has been developed. This was mentioned briefly in Chapter 6. It provides for items relating to certain classes of transaction to be grouped together and summarised before entries are made in the Ledger. These entries can then be simplified. This chapter describes the *Sales Book* and the *Purchases Book*. Chapter 12 describes the *Journal*. These are the main books of prime entry.

Sales Records

When a sale on credit is made, an invoice is sent to the customer. A copy of this invoice is retained by the firm supplying the goods and forms the basis of bookkeeping entries relating to the transaction. To deal with the numerous invoices arising from sale transactions they may be listed day by day on a Sales Record. An example of a handwritten sales record, known as a *Sales Book* or *Sales Day Book*, showing the amount of invoices sent to three customers might be as follows.

Sales Book

19..	NAME	INVOICE NUMBER	LEDGER FOLIO	£
Sept. 1	M. Tyburn	214	47	128
8	J. Laxton	220	33	80
20	T. Rose	221	40	87
30	Cr. to Sales A/c.		14	£295

The copy invoices, containing details of the goods sold are filed and can be referred to if necessary.

The entries from the copy invoices would continue day by day for a definite period, usually one month. During the month each sale is debited to the customer's account and to indicate that this has been done the number of the Ledger page on which the customer's account appears is placed in the *folio column*. Note the numbers 47, 33 and 40 in the example. At the end of the month the Sales Book is totalled. This total is credited to the Sales Account and represents perhaps hundreds of individual items which have been debited to the personal accounts of customers. At the end of a year there will be twelve monthly totals in the Sales Account which gives, easily, the total sales for the year for transfer to the Trading Account.

It will be noticed that in the above Sales Book there is a column headed 'Invoice No.' This is a useful addition to any Sales Book. The copy invoices containing details of the goods sold to the customer bear numbers corresponding to the numbers on the original invoices. The copy invoices are filed and should they be required they are easily located by the reference number shown in the Sales Book. The same method may be adopted in the Purchases Book (described below) by numbering the invoices received from creditors before filing them.

The Sales Book above contains only three entries, but can be used for illustration purposes. In practice there would be many more entries and for a much longer period. The *posting*, as it is called, of this Sales Book would be as follows.

47 **M. Tyburn** 47

19..			£	19..			£
Sept. 1	Sales	S.B.7	128				

33 **J. Laxton** 33

19..			£	19..			£
Sept. 8	Sales	S.B.7	80				

40 **T. Rose** 40

19..			£	19..			£
Sept. 20	Sales	S.B.7	87				

Sales Account

19..			£	19..			£
				Sept. 30	Sundries	S.B.7	295

The reference S.B.7 in the folio column refers to page 7 of the Sales Book, which was illustrated above.

The method of assembling sales transactions illustrated above, while useful for small business and for use in exercises and examination work by students, is being increasingly superseded by methods which save labour and time by the use of mechanical aids.

With the aid of a simple adding machine or *calculator*, the copy invoices may be totalled thus giving the total to be credited to the Sales Account. The entries to the personal accounts may be made direct from the copy invoices. A further development was the use of a simple *accounting machine* which makes the debit entry in the Personal Account on a Ledger card similar to that shown on page 3, and prints the new balance on the account. The machine, at the same time, accumulates the amount of the individual entries to give the total of postings to be credited to the Sales Account. More recently, the application of first, *punched card machines*, and now *electronic computers*, has brought about further changes. This is more fully explained in Chapter 31 on mechanised accounts. However, the basic principles remain the same. The Sales Account must be credited, and the personal accounts of customers who buy on credit terms must be debited, with the amounts sold.

The method of dealing with numerous sale transactions will also vary with the type of business. A retail business dealing mainly in *cash* sales may use a cash register which adds up the amount of cash sales to all customers and at the end of the day gives the total cash sales for the day, which should agree with the amount of cash in the till of the cash register. This amount may be debited to the Cash Book in a special column, the total amount paid into bank being recorded in the bank column. At the end of a specified period, say a week or a month, the sales column in the Cash Book may be totalled, thus giving the amount to be credited to the Sales Account. Many cash registers can now be used also to automatically analyse the cash sales according to which type of goods have been sold, or which sales assistant made the sales.

Where a retailer makes sales on *credit*, each assistant may be supplied with a 'bill' book. The customer is given the 'bill' and a carbon copy remains in the assistant's book. These carbon copies may be used to post the amount to the debit of customers' accounts and the credit to the Sales Account by totalling the carbon bill copies on an adding machine.

In practice students may find a variety of methods in use for dealing with the multiplicity of sale transactions in various types of businesses, but *all will result eventually in the same Ledger entries: a debit to the account of a customer for a sale on credit or to the cash record for a cash sale, and in each case an accumulated total to be credited to the Sales Account.*

Purchases Records

When a purchase is made from a supplier an invoice will be received. The amount of each invoice will be credited to the account of the supplier either direct from the invoice or from an entry made in a *Purchases Book*, or *Purchases Day Book*, which is similar in form to a Sales Book. The total of individual credit postings will be debited periodically to the Purchases Account thus completing the double entry. This total may be obtained from the Purchases Book where it is in use or from an adding machine, calculator, accounting machine, or computer.

4 **Purchases Book** 4

19..			£	
Sept. 1	Speedway Cycle Co.	15	126	
	Cycles Ltd.	22	36	
	Cycles Supplies Ltd.	27	13	
	Dr. to Purchases A/c.	13	£175	

15			**Speedway Cycle Co.**				15
19..			£	19.. Sept. 1	Purchases	P.B.4	£ 126

2			**Cycles Ltd.**				22
19..			£	19.. Sept. 1	Purchases	P.B.4	£ 36

27			**Cycle Supplies Ltd.**				27
19..			£	19.. Sept. 1	Purchases	P.B.4	£ 13

			Purchases Account				
19.. Sept. 1	Sundries	P.B.4	£ 175	19..			£

Folio numbers to indicate the posting of items are used in the same way as in the Sales Book.

Returns and Allowances Records: Sales Returns and Allowances

After a sale has been made, a customer may return goods as damaged or unsuitable, or it may be necessary to make an allowance to the customer because the goods are damaged, have been wrongly priced, or for some other reason. In such cases it will be necessary to reduce the amount of the invoice already sent to the customer. The amount of this invoice will have been debited to the customer's account. It will, therefore, be necessary to credit the account to reduce the amount already debited. A *credit note* is sent to the customer to show that this has been done. This credit note shows details of the allowance made and it is printed in red to distinguish it from an invoice.

The firm sending the credit note retains a carbon copy. The amount of each credit note may be credited direct to the customer's account, and the total of all credit notes so credited is then debited to a *Sales Returns and Allowances Account*. Alternatively the carbon copies may be entered into a *Sales Returns and Allowances Book*, in the same form as a Sales Book, and the Ledger entries made from that book. The total of the Sales Returns and Allowances Account will be transferred, at the end of the trading period, to the Trading Account and shown in that account as a deduction from sales.

Purchases Returns and Allowances

When a business returns goods or, for some reason, receives an allowance on goods it has already purchased it will expect to receive a credit note from the supplier of the goods. Suppose a number of such credit notes are received. These credit notes may be entered into a *Purchases Returns and Allowances Book* and the necessary Ledger postings made from that book: i.e. a debit to the personal account of each supplier (the amount of the goods purchased will have been credited to his account) and the total credited to a *Purchases Returns and Allowances Account*. Alternatively the debit entries may be made direct from the credit notes and the total, ascertained by adding machine, credited to the Purchases Returns and Allowances Account. At the end of the trading period the total amount credited to this account will be transferred to the Trading Account and shown as a deduction from purchases.

Undercharges on Invoices

If, for any reason, goods have been undercharged, a *debit note* will be sent to the customer. This will be treated as an additional invoice and passed through the Sales Book, or will be debited direct to the customer's account.

Value Added Tax

Value added tax, or V.A.T., is becoming widely used. It is a system whereby a tax is added to the selling price of certain goods and services at a percentage rate set by the Government. The business making the sale must collect the tax from the customer. Periodically, say once a quarter, it must then pay over to the Government all of the tax which has arisen in respect of its sales.

However, the business will also have to pay V.A.T. to its suppliers at the same percentage rate on the purchase price of many of its goods and services. When it pays over the V.A.T. arising on its own sales it may offset the tax payable to its own suppliers on its purchases. It therefore pays over only the net amount. There are sometimes cases in which the tax on the purchases is greater than the tax on the sales; the business can then claim the net amount as a refund.

V.A.T. should be separately identified on all invoices, as in the following example:

THE LAGUNA MOTOR CO., P.O. Box 88, Laguna
V.A.T. Registration no. 879456312

Dr. C. Charles,
The Surgery,
High Street,
Laguna.

Invoice no.: 876
Vehicle: Rover 2600
BQS 973T

V.A.T. Rate: 10%

	TOTAL	PRICE	V.A.T.
12 July, 19..	£ p	£ p	£ p
12,000 mile service.	38·50	35·00	3·50
Air and oil filters.	8·35	7·59	0·76
Plugs, contacts, etc.	4·59	4·17	0·42
Light unit.	5·50	5·00	0·50
9 pints oil.	4·05	4·05	—
	£60·99	£55·81	£5·18

In the books, accounts are opened for V.A.T. on Sales and for V.A.T. on Purchases. A separate column for V.A.T. is kept in both the Sales Book and the Purchases Book to record the V.A.T. on credit transactions. Postings are made to the V.A.T. accounts in the same way as the postings to the Sales and Purchases Accounts. The inclusive amount of the price of the goods (i.e. the price plus the V.A.T.) is recorded in the personal account of the customer or supplier.

V.A.T. on cash transactions must be recorded separately for each transaction, or calculated at the appropriate percentages of the total cash sales and cash purchases. For example, if cash sales are £110, including V.A.T. at 10 per cent of the sales price, then the bookkeeping entries would be to debit Cash Account £110, credit Sales Account £100, and credit V.A.T. Account £10.

EXERCISES 9

1. Sales transactions may be entered in a Sales Book from copy invoices and then posted to the personal account of debtors. Explain any alternative method of dealing with sales transactions.

2. Explain how a retailer may deal with a multiplicity of small cash sale transactions for bookkeeping purposes.

3. In working the following exercise use a two-column Cash Book and a Sales Book and Ledger. Extract a Trial Balance.

John Purvis began business with capital of £2 960 of which £400 was Cash in hand and £2 560 Cash at bank.

			£
Jan.	1.	Bought quantity of cutlery from Cutlery Manufacturers Ltd.	2 000
,,	7.	Bought six canteens of cutlery and paid by cheque	1 200
,,	10.	Paid special advertising expenses in cash	100
,,	14.	Sold to J. Beaumont:	
,,		2 canteens of cutlery at £310 each.	
		6 sets of carvers at £40 a set.	
,,	21.	Sold to W. Bishop & Sons:	
		3 canteens of cutlery at £310 each	
,,	22.	J. Beaumont paid his account by cheque	
,,	27.	Sold to A. M. Godfrey:	
		6 doz. table knives at £30 a dozen.	
		6 doz. table forks at £20 a dozen.	
,,	31.	Cash sales for the month	240
,,	31.	Paid rent by cheque	160
,,	31.	Paid delivery and packing charges in cash	30

Prepare Trading and Profit and Loss Accounts and a Balance Sheet as at 31st January. Stock on hand, £1 500.

4. Using a two-column Cash Book, Sales Day Book, and Ledger, enter the following transactions of M. Sinclair:

			£
		M. Sinclair's capital at 1st June consisted of:	
		Cash in hand	160
		Cash at bank	840
June	2.	Bought record players, paying by cheque	600
,,	4.	Bought record players and records from the Star Recording Company	1 020
,,	10.	Sold to J. Welch portable record players	270
,,	17.	Cash sales	150
,,	23.	Sold to T. Palmer & Sons 1 console record player for £250	
,,	25.	J. Welch paid his account by cheque	
,,	27.	Sold to B. Fogg 2 table record players at £150 each	
,,	28.	Paid sundry expenses by cheque	50
,,	29.	Paid stationery and printing charges in cash	30
,,	30.	Withdrew cash for private use	100

Take out a Trial Balance. Prepare Trading and Profit and Loss Accounts and a Balance Sheet as at 30th June. Stock on hand, £820.

5. Enter the following transactions of B. Luscombe in his Cash Book, Sales Day Book, and Ledger:

			£
Dec.	3.	B. Luscombe began business with capital:	
		Cash in hand	150
		Cash at bank	1 600
,,	3.	Bought fancy leather goods and paid by cheque	630
,,	7.	Bought further supply from Hounsditch & Co.	1 500
,,	7.	Paid fares in cash	10
,,	8.	Paid postage and cost of circulars in cash	10
,,	12.	Sold to J. Platt & Co. 1 dozen handbags at £10 each and 1 dozen manicure sets at £10 each.	
,,	15.	Cash sales	550
,,	16.	Paid cash into Bank	550
,,	17.	Sold to B. Newton brush and comb sets	720
,,	18.	J. Platt & Co. paid their account by cheque	
,,	20.	Paid Hounsditch & Co their account by cheque.	
,,	24.	Cash sales	320
,,	30.	Paid transport charges in cash	20
,,	31.	Withdrew cash for private use	300

Take out Trial Balance at 31st December. Prepare Trading and Profit and Loss Accounts for the month, and Balance Sheet as at 31st December. Stock on hand, £420.

6. Enter the following transactions in B. Bertram's books, using a two-column Cash Book, Sales Book, and Sales Returns Book, and Ledger Accounts:

B. Bertram began business with capital of £4 000 in the bank.

			£
Nov.	1.	Drew cheque for office cash	200
,,	3.	Bought quantity of electrical equipment, paying by cheque	3 200
,,	4.	Bought further quantity from Electrical Supplies Ltd.	1 000
,,	10.	Paid cash for circulars	150
,,	15.	Cash sales paid into bank	1 750
,,	20.	Sold to B. Johnson 6 lacquered case electric clocks at £100 each	600
,,	23.	B. Johnson returned one clock sold on 20th instant as defective.	
,,	25.	Sold to B. Beamish & Sons:	
		6 fancy dial electric clocks at £50 each.	
		6 electric kettles at £20 each.	
,,	27.	B. Beamish & Sons returned two electric clocks as not of kind ordered.	
,,	30.	Paid rent by cheque	160
,,	30.	B. Johnson paid his account by cheque.	

Take out a Trial Balance as at 30th November.

Prepare Trading and Profit and Loss Accounts for the month, and a Balance Sheet as at 30th November. Stock on hand, £2 370.

7. J. Riley began business on 1st January with capital, in cash £400, at bank £4 000, and transacted the following business during the month:

			£
Jan.	3.	Bought from Lynch & Co., stock of photographic goods	1 200
,,	3.	Bought from Barnet & Hurst:	
		24 pocket cameras at £40 each	
		12 ,, ,, ,, £60 ,,	
		6 folding tripods at £10 each	
,,	6.	Bought from Essex Camera Company 3 reflex cameras at £100 each.	
,,	12.	Cash sales paid direct to bank	2 000
,,	19.	Cash sales paid direct to bank	1 000
,,	26.	Paid Lynch & Co., Barnet & Hurst, and the Essex Camera Company their accounts by cheque.	
,,	27.	Customer returned goods purchased on 19th Jan., refunded cash	60
,,	28.	Cash sales	750
,,	31.	Paid delivery expenses in cash	50
,,	31.	Paid rent by cheque	300
,,	31.	Drew cheque for personal use	750

Draw out a Trial Balance as at 31st January. Prepare Final Accounts, including Balance Sheet as at 31st January. Stock at close, £900.

Note: In working Exercises 8–10 bring into use as required a two-column Cash Book, Sales Day Book, Sales Returns Book, Purchases Book, and Purchases Returns Book.

8. J. M. Biggs began to deal in household furniture on 1st December with capital of £750 cash at bank.

			£
Dec.	2.	He bought from J. Townsend & Sons: 3 beds at £75 each; 3 armchairs at £60 each; 3 chairs at £12 each	441
,,	2.	Bought sundry articles, paying by cheque	560
,,	2.	Paid carriage by cheque	36
,,	7.	Cash sales	90
,,	10.	Sold to J. Burton: 2 beds at £96 each; 3 chairs at £9 each	219
,,	12.	Cash sales, paid direct to bank	264
,,	12.	J. Burton returned one chair as faulty	9
,,	17.	J. Burton paid his account by cheque	
,,	19.	Paid J. Townsend & Sons their account by cheque.	
,,	21.	Bought from J. Townsend & Sons: 2 coffee tables at £36 each; 6 rugs at £15 each	162
,,	23.	Returned to J. Townsend & Sons one defective rug	15
,,	28.	Cash sales, paid to bank	231
,,	31.	Sundry expenses paid in cash	26

Take out Trial Balance as at 31st December. Prepare Trading and Profit and Loss Account for the month, and a Balance Sheet as at 31st December. Value of stock on hand, £510.

9. R. B. Thornton began to trade in silverware on 12th October. His capital consisted of:

		£
	Cash at bank	6 000
	Cash in hand	450
Oct. 12.	Bought from Silversmiths Ltd.: 3 dozen hand-wrought silver tablespoons at £240 a dozen; 3 dozen similar table forks at £240 a dozen	1 440
,, 13.	Bought quantity of silverware including teaspoons and forks, paying by cheque	3 000
,, 13.	Bought further quantity for cash	240
,, 15.	Returned to Silversmiths Ltd. as of wrong design, 6 table spoons and 6 table forks	240
,, 18.	Sold to Webb & Warings: 1 dozen silver table spoons at £360 a dozen. 1 dozen silver table forks at £360 a dozen. 2 silver soup ladles at £100 each	920
,, 20.	Paid sundry expenses in cash	40
,, 20.	Webb & Warings returned the 2 silver soup ladles, style not as ordered. Allowed them	200
,, 21.	Paid Silversmiths Ltd. their account by cheque.	
,, 24.	Bought from Silversmiths Ltd: 2 dozen hand-wrought silver coffee spoons at £130 a dozen	260
,, 27.	Sold to Swan & Lacy 1 dozen tea spoons at £160 a dozen	160
,, 31.	Cash sales for the month paid into bank	3 750
,, 31.	Paid sundry expenses by cheque	300

Take out Trial Balance and prepare Trading and Profit and Loss Accounts for the month, and a Balance Sheet as at 31st October. Stock on hand, £1 500.

10. Allow sufficient space to continue the accounts for a further period.

J.B. Freeman began business on 1st May with capital of £300, consisting of £200 Cash at bank and £100 Cash in hand.

		£
May 1.	Paid cash into bank	60
,, 1.	Bought from Firestoves Ltd goods value	100
,, 2.	Bought from Electric Supplies Ltd. goods value	36
,, 5.	Bought from Firestoves Ltd. goods value	96
,, 7.	Returned to Electric Supplies Ltd., 4 items at £6 each and exchanged them for 4 other items at £5 each.	
,, 14.	Paid Firestoves Ltd. their account by cheque.	
,, 24.	Sold to Baring & Lee goods value	70
,, 31.	Cash sales for the month	40
,, 31.	Paid carriage by cheque	16
,, 31.	Paid sundry expenses in cash	1

Prepare Trial Balance and Trading and Profit and Loss Account for the month and Balance Sheet as at 31st May. Stock on hand, £145. Balance the Ledger Accounts at 31st May, and record the following transactions:

			£
June	10.	Sold to Warner & Sons goods value	18
,,	12.	Warner & Sons returned one item as defective. Forwarded credit note for	2
,,	30.	Paid stationery in cash	1
,,	30.	Paid Carriage by cheque	16
,,	30.	Received cheque from Baring & Lee for their account	70
,,	30.	Cash takings paid into bank	183
,,	30.	Drew cheque for private use	40

Prepare Trial Balance and Trading and Profit and Loss Accounts for the month of June, and a Balance Sheet as at 30th June. Stock on hand valued at £14.

10

The Columnar System of Bookkeeping

A trader may be satisfied with the information provided by his accounts that the year's trading has yielded certain sums of gross profit and net profit. Other traders whose businesses are of a different nature or are organised on different lines may require further information. One business may deal in several distinct commodities. Another business may be divided into departments. The proprietors may wish to have the trading results relating to each commodity or department in order to determine future policy. Without *analysis* in some form it is impossible to discover whether each department is contributing its share to the general profits or whether the expenses and management costs of one department are disproportionate to the total costs and stand in need of revision.

In order that the accounts may yield the required information all the items from which the Trading Account is built up must be analysed and the analysis should be in continuous form throughout the trading period. This will involve analysis of the purchases, sales, returns inwards and outwards, and it may be done by suitable alterations in the rulings of the subsidiary books to provide *analysis columns*.

The trader who deals, for example, in three distinct commodities may use subsidiary books ruled as below. The three commodities are analysed on the right.

Sales Book

DATE	PARTICULARS		SOLD LEDGER FOLIO	TOTALS	RADIOS	MUSIC CENTRES	TAPES AND RECORDS
	NAME	INVOICE NO.					
				£	£	£	£
19..							
July 9	J.W. Jackson	277	36	240	240		
„ 10	P.W. Jones	278	39	80		60	20
„ 12	L. Palmer	279	56	250	150	100	

The Purchases Book and the Returns Books will be ruled on similar lines.

The amount entered in the Totals column is posted to the personal account of the customer, and the Totals column also permits of the cross checking of the totals of the analysis columns. The personal accounts in the Bought and Sold Ledgers are not affected by the analysis, but in order to make full use of the information given in the analysed subsidiary books it is necessary to extend the analysis to the accounts in the General Ledger. (For an explanation of Bought and Sold Ledgers and the General Ledger, see Chapter 13.) The Stock Account, the Sales Account, the Purchases Account, the Sales Returns Account, and the Purchases Returns Account, will accordingly be given similar analysis columns, and the periodical totals of the analysis columns of the subsidiary books will be posted to the appropriate columns in the Ledger Accounts. The Sales Account for the above example of a Sales Day Book will appear as shown on page 80, the entries in the example being treated for the purpose of illustration as the total sales for the month.

The illustration refers to different commodities. If the business is departmental and the purpose of the analysis is to ascertain the trading results of each department, the rulings will be as shown but the headings of the columns will refer to the departments and not to commodities. Where there are many departments it may be impossible to have sufficient additional columns in the Ledger Accounts without causing the Ledger to be unwieldly in size. The alternative method is to open separate accounts for each department, for example, 'Dept. A. Stock Account,' and 'Dept. A. Purchases Account,' and similarly for each other department.

To obtain the trading results for each department or commodity there must be separate Trading Accounts or one Trading Account with analysis columns. The separate Trading Accounts will be combined to form the general Trading Account for the business. Where an analysed Trading Account is used the totals column is the general Trading Account. For a business with three departments as illustrated on page 80, the analysed Trading Account would have the same form of ruling as the Sales Account there shown. The purchases, sales, and stocks of each department would be entered in the appropriate columns, yielding a department gross profit or loss as the case might be. The totals column would contain the combined figures and would show the gross profit or loss for the business as a whole.

The analysis will yield the *turnover* and gross profit of each depart-

Sales Account

DATE		FOLIO	RADIOS	MUSIC CENTRES	TAPES AND RECORDS	TOTAL	DATE		FOLIO	RADIOS	MUSIC CENTRES	TAPES AND RECORDS	TOTAL
19..			£	£	£	£	19..			£	£	£	£
							July 31	Total sales for July		390	160	20	570

ment or each commodity as the case may be. Turnover is equal to net sales (i.e. sales less sales returns), normally omitting V.A.T. In many cases the analysis is carried far enough when this point is reached. In other cases it may be necessary to ascertain the net profit earned by each department, as, for example, when the department manager is entitled to a percentage commission based on the net profit. This will involve the analysis of the expenditure shown in the Profit and Loss Account. Separate Profit and Loss Accounts or a Profit and Loss Account with analysis columns may be used, but the apportionment of the expense items needs careful consideration.

Advertising, general administrative costs, and similar expenses may be apportioned on the basis of the turnover of each department. Special advertising or other charges for a particular department would be charged to that department. The items for rent and rates may be similarly apportioned or, as in some cases, apportioned on the basis of the floor space occupied by each department, but no one method of apportioning the expenses is applicable to all cases.

Such allocations of costs which are only indirectly related to the sales of particular products or departments, are essentially arbitrary. They may lead to misleading views as to the contribution which each product or department makes to the profit of the business. The practice of allocating indirect or joint costs is undoubtedly widespread. In any particular case it should be viewed critically in relation to the decision for which the information is being used.

The portions of the various expenses to be carried to the respective sections of the Profit and Loss Account may be obtained from analysed expense accounts, or the ordinary form of expense accounts may be used and the analysis made on separate sheets of analysis paper.

Brief reference may be made to another form of analysed day book, namely, the Purchases Day Book with analysis rulings to provide for the usual entries of purchases of stock for resale and also for purchases of fixed assets and of sundries. The use of such a book simplifies the postings to the assets and expense accounts in the same way that it simplifies the postings to the sales and purchases accounts.

The purpose of the additional columns in the accounts and the subsidiary books is to provide information by continuous analysis that would involve much labour to obtain by other means. The method does not abrogate the principles of double entry; it is only an adaptation of procedure to meet special requirements as may be seen from the above examples, and in the analysed Petty Cash Book and Bill Books described in later chapters.

The illustrations given above have been concerned with the application of the columnar system to find the trading results for each of several departments or commodities. In some kinds of businesses the ordinary day to day records of transactions involve a system of tabulation to simplify the work of recording. Water, gas and electricity companies, hotels, dairies, bakers, and similar business dealing in a few regular commodities or services for a large number of customers, find it convenient to keep their records on a tabular system of bookkeeping and to carry periodical totals only to the appropriate Ledger Accounts. A dairyman's record may take the form of large sheets in a loose-leaf Ledger, and a customer's account for a week may occupy one line across the page. With thirty horizontal lines the page would accommodate the weekly account of thirty customers. Vertical lines divide the page into the days of the week, and each vertical column for a day is subdivided to record the commodities sold. Vertical cash columns are ruled for each day to contain the sums payable by the customers, and additional cash columns are included in which the balance brought forward and the balance due at the end of the week are shown.

The Visitors' Ledger used in hotels usually shows each visitor's account in a vertical column. The page is divided vertically into columns for each visitor and room number and the items are shown horizontally. The total at the foot of each column is the balance due from the visitor at the close of the day. The cross totals are carried forward from day to day, and at the end of the month the accounts brought forward are posted in the General Ledger.

The tabular system is applicable only to the kinds of business having uniformity from day to day in the services rendered or the commodities dealt in.

EXERCISES 10

1. Rule a suitable Sales Book for three departments, (*a*) radios, (*b*) record players, (*c*) bicycles, and enter the following sales:

Jan. 2. To M. Keston, 3 'Trevor' radios at £31 each.
" 6. To G. Elton, 2 portable record players at £20 each, and 1 'Trevor' radio at £31.
" 7. To T. Edwards, 2 'Speedway' bicycles at £32 each, and 1 portable record player at £28.

2. D. Krishnan & Co. are provision importers. They divide their business into three departments: (1) butter and eggs, (2) poultry and bacon, and (3) tinned or bottled goods. Rule a suitable Purchase Book and enter the following invoices:

Nov. 12. M. Peterson:
A quantity of eggs for £500.
A quantity of bacon for £900.
A quantity of condensed milk for £200.
„ 13. A. Merrick:
A quantity of 'Amber' peaches in syrup for £700.

R.S.A. (adapted)

3. A trader opens a shop dealing in cigarettes, sweets and stationery. In order to ascertain separately the trading profit realised by each of these commodities he adopts, as far as may be necessary, the columnar system of bookkeeping.

Give suitable rulings for the Purchases Day Book and the Nominal Account(s) affected, and insert sufficient entries to make clear the working of the system.

R.S.A.

4. J. Whitehouse is in business dealing in cutlery and tools and gardening supplies and equipment. He maintains separate departments, (1) for the cutlery and tools, and (2) for the gardening sundries. His financial position on 31st May was as follows:

	£
Capital	17 400
Shop fittings	1 200
Cash in hand	190
Cash at bank	2 600
Stock: Cutlery and tools	6 000
Garden sundries	8 000
Creditors: J. Smith	590

Open his books and enter the following transactions for June, using analysed subsidiary books and separate Stock Accounts:

			£
June	2.	Bought cutlery from J. Smith	780
„	8.	Cash sales paid to bank:	
		Cutlery	340
		Garden sundries	630
„	10.	Sold to C. Welchman:	
		Cutlery	160
		Garden sundries	260
„	12.	Paid carriage on sales in cash	10
„	15.	Sold to B. Wells garden sundries	240

		£
June 20.	Paid advertising charges by cheque	50
,, 21.	Paid J. Smith his account by cheque	
,, 21.	Paid for stationery, cash £10, packing materials, cash £20	
,, 24.	Bought from J. Smith:	
	Cutlery	300
	Garden sundries	450
,, 30.	Cash sales to date, paid to bank:	
	Cutlery	860
	Garden Sundries	1 500
,, 30.	Paid rent by cheque	300

Take out a Trial Balance. Prepare departmental Trading and Profit and Loss Accounts, and a Balance Sheet as at 30th June. Stock on hand at 30th June was valued, cutlery £6 100, gardening sundries £6 650. Expenses to be apportioned, one-third to cutlery and tools, two-thirds to garden sundries.

5. A business is carried on in two departments, A and B. From the following Trial Balance prepare Trading and Profit and Loss Accounts in departmental form, and prepare also a Balance Sheet as at 31st December.

Trial Balance

31st December

	Dr. £	*Cr.* £
Cash at bank	35 260	
Capital		120 000
Stock: Dept. A	48 000	
Dept. B	26 000	
Debtors	67 240	
Creditors		28 510
Purchases: Dept. A	52 000	
Dept. B	48 600	
Sales: Dept. A		96 000
Dept. B		64 000
Salaries	12 560	
Rent, rates and taxes	4 710	
Water and electricity	1 040	
Discounts	760	1 040
Postage and telephone	520	
General Expenses	2 560	
Printing and stationery	1 440	
Carriage on sales	360	
Advertising	8 500	
	£309 550	£309 550

Value of stock on hand at 31st December, Dept. A £46 200, Dept B £39 500. The expenses are to be apportioned between the departments on the basis of the sales.

6. Smith's Stores are owned by S. Smith. The stores are divided into three departments, A, B, and C. From the following Trial Balance prepare Trading and Profit and Loss Accounts for the year in departmental form, and prepare a Balance Sheet as at 31st December. The expenses are to be apportioned between the departments on the basis of their sales.

Trial Balance 31st December

		Dr.	*Cr.*
		£	£
Capital Account:			
	S. Smith		40 000
Drawings		6 000	
Stock, 1st January:			
	Dept. A	11 000	
	,, B	5 000	
	,, C	24 000	
Purchases:			
	Dept. A		32 000
	,, B	22 000	
	,, C	54 000	
Sales:			
	Dept. A		48 000
	,, B		32 000
	,, C		80 000
Cash at bank		12 500	
Wages and salaries		8 500	
Advertising		2 200	
Printing and stationery		200	
Postage and telephone		420	
Fixtures and fitings		3 500	
Rent and rates		5 000	
Insurance		250	
General expenses		970	
Discounts			1 500
Sundry creditors			2 040
Sundry debtors		16 000	
		£203 540	£203 540

The stock on hand at 31st December was valued at, Dept. A £12 000, Dept. B £6 300, Dept. C £25 400.

Note: Fixtures and fittings is an asset and will appear in the Balance Sheet.

11

Trade and Cash Discounts: The Cash Book

Trade Discounts

Traders who buy in large quantities from a manufacturer or wholesaler are generally given an allowance on the list price of the goods. This is known as *trade discount.* In some cases manufacturers recommend a retail selling price, invoice the goods at that price and allow the retailer a trade discount to cover his expenses and margin of profit. In the United Kingdom the manufacturer can not normally enforce his recommended retail selling price, except in rare cases such as books.

The amount charged to the trader is the invoice price, i.e. the list price less trade discount and it is the *net* amount which is entered in both the subsidiary sales and purchases records and in the Ledger Accounts. When allowances are made on such goods the amount of the allowance will be the invoice price, i.e. the list price *less* trade discount.

Some wholesale houses provide catalogues of goods from which the retailer may order his supplies and which he may keep by him for reference purposes. The catalogue or trade list may be a costly production and, to avoid frequent reprints being required on any change in price levels, the price against each article is purposely placed at a high figure bearing little relation to current prices. The retailer is notified that present wholesale prices are the list prices less, say, 40 per cent trade discount. At any change in the price level owing to changes in the cost of materials or labour or other cause, the percentage deduction may be altered and the retailers are informed of the fact.

The price to be paid to the wholesale house is the net amount after the deduction has been made. *The trade discount is a means only of arriving at the price to be paid. It is never entered on the Ledger Accounts, as it forms no part of the value of the goods or of the debts due for them.*

Cash Discounts and the Cash Book

In the sale of goods on credit the advantage is with the purchaser, as he may sell the goods and may realise sufficient cash to meet his account and to yield a profit before the expiration of the credit period. In such circumstances his own capital requirements for buying stock are reduced, as he is making use of the capital of his wholesale supplier. The wholesaler realises this and is willing, in many instances, to forgo something from the account if the purchaser will pay promptly and not take advantage of a longer period of credit. What he offers to a purchaser as an inducement to pay promptly is a specified percentage reduction called *Cash Discount*. To firms having sufficient capital resources to pay their accounts promptly the discount offers an additional profit and, in the course of a year's trading, may amount to a considerable sum. However, if the resources need not be used to pay accounts promptly but could be put to some other profitable use, or could be used to repay loans, then the gain from taking advantage of the cash discounts is in practice largely offset.

The amount of cash discount offered for prompt payment is usually notified on the trade lists and on the invoices. For example, the terms may be stated as $2\frac{1}{2}\%$ discount on monthly credit accounts; $1\frac{1}{4}\%$ extra for prompt cash. Whatever the terms of payment may be, the discount is granted only on payment within the specified period; thereafter the amount is payable without deduction.

Prompt Cash is payment within seven to ten days from the date of the invoice.

Trade Discount and Cash Discount must not be confused. The treatment of cash discount can never arise until payment is made as, until such time, it is not known whether payment is being made within the period during which the allowance may be claimed.

Discounts Received

The following example illustrates the treatment of discounts received:

Example 8. M. Redman buys motor-cycle accessories to the value of £400 from Cycles Supplies Limited, on 1st November. Terms of payment: $2\frac{1}{2}\%$, one month. He pays the account by cheque on 28th November.

The amount of the cheque is £390, being £400 less $2\frac{1}{2}\%$ cash discount. The sum of £390 will be credited by Redman in his Bank

Account and debited to the account of Cycle Supplies Limited. A that moment the latter account will appear as below:

Cycle Supplies Ltd. 79

19..			£	19..			£
Nov. 28	Cash	C.B.	390	Nov. 1	Purchases	P.B.	400

Cycle Supplies Ltd., by their terms of payment, indicate that in this case £390 settles the debt of £400 but the above account, as it stands, shows £10 outstanding. The entry of the amount of the discount on the debit side would close the account. The corresponding credit entry for the discount is made to a new account opened in the Ledger and called the *Discounts Received Account*. The discount received is regarded by Redman as a gain, and at the close of the trading period the balance of the Discounts Received Account is transferred to the *credit* of the Profit and Loss Account.

The Account for Cycle Supplies Ltd. and the Discounts Received Account will now appear as below:

Cycle Supplies Ltd.

19..			£	19..			£
Nov. 28	Cash	C.B.	390	Nov. 1	Purchases	P.B.	400
„ 28	Discount Received	14	10				

Discounts Received Account

19..			£	19..			£
				Nov. 28	Cycle Supplies Ltd.	79	10

Discounts Allowed

Similarly Redman may allow cash discount to his customers to encourage prompt payment.

> ***Example 9.*** On Dec. 1, Redman sold bike accessories to the value of £200 to J.S. Smith on terms 5%, one month.
> Dec. 17 Smith paid his account by cheque.

When Smith paid his account the cheque received was for £190, being £200 less 5% cash discount, as he paid within the credit period of one month.

The amount of the discount must be credited to his account as otherwise the entry of £190 only will make it appear that he still owes £10. The corresponding entry for the discount will be to the debit of a new account called the *Discounts Allowed Account*, as the amount of the discount is of the nature of a loss to M. Redman.

The balance of the Discounts Allowed Account will be transferred at the close of the trading period to the *debit* side of the Profit and Loss Account.

J. S. Smith 84

19..			£	19..			£
Dec. 1	Goods	S.B.	200	Dec. 17	Cash	C.B.	190
					Discount	16	10

Discounts Allowed Account 16

19..			£	19..			£
Dec. 17	J.S. Smith	84	10				

The Three-Column Cash Book

Cash discount occurs frequently in business, and the number of entries relating to discount is correspondingly large. The method of recording discounts to be described in this section yields the same advantages as the subsidiary books, in that periodical totals are posted to the discount accounts instead of individual items. The system is still much used in some Commonwealth, or former Commonwealth countries.

The deduction for cash discount is made at the time of payment. It saves time and labour if, instead of turning at once to the appropriate Discount Account, a note of the discount is made alongside the entry in the Cash Book, and only periodical totals of the discounts allowed and of discounts received are posted to the respective Discount Accounts. To do this another cash column is added to each side of the Cash Book, making three cash columns on each side. The use of two of each of the three columns is already known. The third column on each side is to be regarded as a memorandum column only, wherein a note is made of the discount as it occurs. In this way the additional columns serve the same purpose of grouping like things for eventual posting to the Ledger as the subsidiary books do.

Cash Book

Dr. | *Cr.*

			DISCOUNT ALLOWED	CASH	BANK				DISCOUNT RECEIVED	CASH	BANK
19..			£	£	£	19..			£	£	£
Jan. 1	Balance			50	840	Jan. 2	J. Jones		20		780
,, 4	R. Roberts		10		390	,, 5	B. Brown		10		190
,, 7	Bank			100		,, 7	Cash				100
,, 8	G. Green		10		110	,, 10	Balance	c/d		150	460
,, 9	S. Smith		10		190						
			£30	£150	£1 530				£30	£150	£1 530
,, 10	Balance	b/d		150	460						

Example 10. The following transactions took place during the first two weeks of January:

Jan. 1. Balance at bank £840.
Cash in hand, £50.
„ 2. Paid J. Jones his account for £800 by cheque, less $2\frac{1}{2}$% cash discount.
„ 4. Received cheque from R. Roberts for £390 being in payment of account for £400, less $2\frac{1}{2}$% discount.
„ 5. Paid B. Brown by cheque his account for £200, deducting 5% discount.
„ 7. Drew from bank for office cash, £100.
„ 8. Received cheque from G. Green for £110 in full settlement of account rendered for £120.
„ 9. S. Smith paid his account for £200 by cheque, deducting 5% discount.

The above are typical transactions affecting the firm's cash, and would be entered in the Cash Book as shown. The personal accounts are not given.

On page 90 is a simplified example of a three-column Cash Book. The Cash and Bank columns are added and balanced in the usual way. The Discount columns are added but not balanced, as they are not account columns but memorandum columns only. The addition is made at the time the Cash and Bank Accounts are balanced, usually weekly or monthly. The details of cash and discount are posted from the Cash Book to the respective personal accounts. The weekly or monthly totals of the discount columns are taken to the Discounts Allowed Account and Discounts Received Account. The double entry for the discount items in the personal accounts is then to be found in the appropriate Discount Account. The entries to the Discount Accounts are placed on the same side of those accounts as the side on which the totals are found to be in the memorandum columns in the Cash Book.

Discounts Allowed Account

			£				£
19..				19..			
Jan. 10	Total discounts allowed		30				

Discounts Received Account

			£				£
19..				19..			
				Jan. 10	Total discounts received		30

Dr. **Bank Cash Book** *Cr.*

DATE	PARTICULARS	FOLIO	DISCOUNT ALLOWED	DETAILS	BANK	DATE	PARTICULARS	FOLIO	DISCOUNT RECEIVED	DETAILS	BANK
19..			£	£	£	19..			£	£	£
July 1	Balance	b/d			370	July 3	Brown & Co.		4		76
,, 2	R. Lloyd			57		,, 5	Rent				50
	B. Ward & Co.			10		,, 6	B. James		1		16
	Cash sales			14	81	,, 6	Sundries:				
							Carriage			36	
,, 3	Tanner & Sons			5			Petty cash			5	41
	J. Thompson		1	19			Balance	c/d			493
	Cash sales			21	45						
,, 4	Lawson & Co.		2	38							
	Cash sales			12	50						
,, 5	W. Jackson			67							
	W. Greenfield			11	78						
,, 6	Buxton & Co. Ltd.			37							
	Cash sales			15	52						
			£3		£676				£5		£676
,, 7	Balance	b/d			493						

The balances of these accounts will be transferred at the close of the trading period to the Profit and Loss Account.

There should be no difficulty in understanding the use of the three-column Cash Book if it is borne in mind that it is simpler in practice for the cashier to make a note of the discount when he enters the cash items, and for those notes of the discounts to be entered in total in the Discount Accounts in the Ledger.

The Bank Cash Book

This form of Cash Book is now widely used in business, as it is a means of preventing the occurrence of errors and discrepancies in the cash. The book is illustrated on page 92, and its use follows the rule that all money received, whether coins, notes, drafts, or cheques, is to be paid intact into the bank, and that all payments are to be made by cheque. Certain small payments in cash, such as messengers' fares and telegrams, are necessary in any business, but where these occur they are reserved for payment out of petty cash, as described in Chapter 17, a cheque being drawn weekly or monthly to cover such payments. These are recorded separately from the Cash Book.

Each day the cash and cheques received are entered in the Bank Paying-in Book and are paid into the bank. The details of the cash received are entered in the Cash Book in the details column on the debit side. These details are added up, and the total is carried to the bank column on the debit side. This amount should agree with the total shown in the Paying-in Book. The credit side of the Cash Book shows a bank column for the entry of the cheques drawn, and a details column for use if one cheque is drawn to cover two or more payments which have to be debited separately to the Ledger Accounts.

There is no actual cash column as no cash is kept in the office. The petty cash is treated separately. It follows that there will be no cross entries of cash withdrawn from the bank for office use or for surplus cash paid into the bank.

The above points are illustrated on page 92.

EXERCISES 11

1. (*a*) What are the advantages to business people of the practice of allowing cash discount?

(*b*) Record the following transactions in the Cash Book. Balance the Cash Book as on 6th Feb., 19...

			£
Feb.	1.	Cash in hand	270
,,	1.	Cash at bank	1 100
,,	2.	Received from F. Johnson in cash £230, allowing him discount £20. Total:	250
,,	3.	Received from A. Bowman in cash	20
,,	3.	Paid to R. Shipley, cash	30
,,	4.	Paid by cheque to L. Patterson his account of £200, less $2\frac{1}{2}\%$ discount. Total:	200
,,	4.	Received cheque from W. Winter and paid it into bank	350
,,	4.	Paid in cash sundry expenses	30
,,	5.	Received payment in cash of A. Crowe's account £50, from which he deducted 5% discount. Total:	50
,,	5.	Paid for postage stamps, cash	10
,,	6.	Sold goods for cash	120
,,	6.	Paid cheque to J. Williams, £300, having deducted discount £20 from his account. Total:	320
,,	6.	Paid into bank	300

U.L.C.I. (adapted)

2. On 1st July, 19. ., G. Triptree commenced business as a gardening tools dealer with £400 in the bank. He paid into the bank a further sum of £300 borrowed at 5 per cent interest from his father, T. Triptree.

Prepare a Cash Book with three columns recording the above and the following transactions. In writing up your Cash Book, show quite clearly the Ledger Account to which you would post each item.

July	1.	Bought a used motor van for £450, which was paid for by cheque.
,,	1.	Drew cash from bank £30, bought for cash postage stamps, £7.
,,	5.	Cash sales, £39.
,,	5.	Paid to W. Johnson & Sons by cheque the balance of their account, £89, less a discount of 5%.
,,	7.	Bought by cheque 3 sets of tools at £16 per set.
,,	9.	Paid in cash wages, £13, to part-time handyman.
,,	11.	Received a cheque for £35 from S. Holmes, and accepted this in settlement of his account of £36. The cheque was paid into bank.
,,	12.	Cash sales, £66.
,,	14.	Paid into Bank, £50.
,,	16.	Paid wages in cash, £13, and drew £10 in cash for personal expenses.
,,	16.	S. Slater, who owed £18, deducted £1 from the amount due and sent a cheque for the balance. Paid the cheque into bank, and wrote to Slater saying the deduction could not be allowed.
,,	16.	Bought for cash job lot of tools, £30.

Balance the Cash Book as on 16th July, 19. ., and bring down the balance. No posting to the Ledger is required.

3. On 1st February, 19.., A. Ralph commenced business as a bookseller. He had £700 in the bank, stock of books worth £250, and his fixtures and fittings were worth £72. He owed P. Gelling £31 and R. Lee £50.

Open accounts for these entries, and from the following transactions enter up a three-column Cash Book, Purchases Book, Sales Book and Returns Book. Post all the items into the Ledger and take out a Trial Balance, and prepare a Trading Account, Profit and Loss Account, and a Balance Sheet. The exercise should be folioed:

Feb. 2. Sold on credit books value £30 to L. Peacock.
,, 3. Bought on credit from P. Gelling books value £90, less 10% trade discount.
,, 4. Drew cheque for office use £8.
,, 5. Paid sundry expenses in cash £4.
,, 6. Paid R. Lee the amount owing to him, less 5% cash discount.
,, 8. Sold to L. Peacock books value £300.
,, 9. L. Peacock paid cheque £28 and was allowed discount £2.
,, 10. Drew cheque for private use £30.
,, 11. Paid postages in cash £6.
,, 12. Returned to P. Gelling books purchased on February 3, being defective, £36.
,, 15. Bought on credit from Austins Ltd. a used motor van, value £375.
,, 16. Paid into bank £3.
,, 16. Sold for cash to R. Felton, books value £22.

The stock of books on 16th February was £46.

U.E.I. (*adapted*)

4. R. Seymour carries on business as a retail hosier. On the 1st October, 19.., his assets were: Shop fixtures and fittings, £1 250; Cash in hand, £72; Trade debtors, S. Silver, £54; Stock, £863. His liabilities were: Loan from J. Robinson, £200; Trade creditor, H. Sorter, £74; Bank overdraft on Current Account, £19.

You are required to open the necessary accounts to record the above position in the books, and to post thereto through the proper subsidiary books the following transactions:

Oct. 2. Purchased from H. Black, on credit, goods value £86.
,, 4. Borrowed a further £700 from J. Robinson.
,, 4. Paid H. Sorter by cheque £71 which, with discount receivable, cleared his account.
,, 6. Paid wages, £35, and bought postage stamps £2 and stationery £1 from Cash.
,, 8. Received £20 cash on account from S. Silver.
,, 9. Purchased additional shop fittings for £450, and paid for them by cheque.

Oct. 19. Sold goods for cash, £28.
,, 20. Sold goods on credit to S. Silver, £31.
,, 24. Goods returned by S. Silver, valued at £12.
,, 24. Paid £50 of the cash in hand into the bank.

Balance the Ledger Accounts and Cash Book, bring down the balances and extract a Trial Balance as on 24th October, 19. . .

Note: No Trading Account, Profit and Loss Account, or Balance Sheet is to be prepared.

R.S.A.

5. On 1st February, 19. ., Albert Spence had the following assets and claims: Cash in hand, £150; Cash at bank, £670; Sundry debtors: D. Dowty, £150, E. Evans, £720; Stock on hand, £2 500; Motor car, £750; Fixtures, £250; *Claims:* Sundry creditors: W. Mix, £220, H. Harris, £50, M. Mason, £500, J. Johnson, £300; Capital Account, £4 120. During the month of February he transacted the following business:

Feb. 2. Sold goods on credit to D. Dowty, £500.
,, 2. Paid H. Harris by cash, £50.
,, 4. Bought goods on credit from W. Mix, £240.
,, 6. Received from D. Dowty, cash £140, and allowed him discount, £10.
,, 8. Paid cash into bank, £100.
,, 8. Paid wages in cash, £110.
,, 9. Paid sundry expenses in cash, £20.
,, 9. Drew for personal expenses by cheque, £150.
,, 11. Sold goods on credit to M. Jones, £400.
,, 13. Received cheque from E. Evans, £720 and paid same into bank.
,, 15. Paid M. Mason by cheque, £500.
,, 17. Bought goods on credit from J. Johnson, £300.
,, 19. Returned part of the goods supplied by J. Johnson on the 17th, and received credit note, £100.
,, 19. Drew from the bank for office purposes, £200.
,, 21. Paid wages in cash, £110.
,, 24. Paid rent by cheque, £50.
,, 26. Paid rates in cash, £40.
,, 26. Drew cheque for private purposes, £150.

Stock in hand at the end of the month, £2 380.

Enter the above transactions in the appropriate books, then extract a Trial Balance and prepare a set of accounts for the above, showing the profit or loss made during the period, and a Balance Sheet at the end of the month.

N.C.T.E.C. (adapted)

6. The following account is in the books of T. Jones:

K. Brown

19..		£	19..		£
Jan. 15	Returns	20	Jan. 1	Balance	120
„ 20	Cash	100	„ 10	Goods	340
Feb. 10	Cash	323			
„ 10	Discount	17			
		£460			£460

Explain what is recorded by each entry in this account, from what subsidiary books the postings are made, and where the corresponding double entry would be found.

12

The Journal

Books of Original or Prime Entry

It has been shown how the pressure of work and the need to subdivide duties among a larger staff led to the use of the subsidiary books known as the *Purchase Day Book*, the *Sales Day Book*, and *Sales Returns* and *Purchases Returns Books*. They are of proven worth as aids to efficiency in the accounts department, but they do not diminish the importance of the Ledger, nor do they act as a substitute for any part of the actual double entry record the Ledger should contain. The subsidiary books are useful channels only, directing the flow of entries to their appropriate places in the Ledger Accounts. *However, their usefulness is so great as adjuncts to the Ledger that, in businesses that use them, it is made an imperative rule that no entry shall be made in the Ledger unless the data has first been entered in its appropriate subsidiary book.* The carrying out of this rule ensures that the information contained in the respective subsidiary book is complete and leads also to accuracy in the Ledger record, since the rule provides for an orderly system of posting to the Ledger. Interruptions cannot be avoided in practice, and to post to the Ledger from what are virtually lists of transactions avoids omissions in posting, as it is an easy matter to note on the list the last item dealt with before the interruption and to resume again from that point. The entry of the Ledger folios against the items in the subsidiary books is in itself an excellent method of indicating which items have been posted.

Because of the rule that transactions must be passed through the subsidiary books before being entered in the Ledger, the subsidiary books are known collectively as *books of original* (or *prime*) *entry*. The term is also applied to the *Cash Book*. The four books referred to above contain classified records of transactions and provide chronological lists for posting to the Ledger. The Cash Book, though part of the Ledger and containing Ledger Accounts, is a separate book and contains entries of a particular kind, namely those affecting the firm's cash. It provides, therefore, a suitable record from which the entries may be posted to their respective Ledger Accounts. The Cash

Book differs from the four subsidiary books as it is a substitute for the Cash and Bank Accounts in the Ledger and is an integral part of the double entry record, whereas the other books of prime entry are not. The Cash Book contains, however, a record only of one aspect of each transaction, except in the case of transfers between office cash and bank cash.

The cashier enters in the Cash Book each transaction affecting the firm's cash, ignoring the other aspect, so that the Cash Book contains a specialised list of transactions from which the double entry may be completed by posting therefrom to the Ledger.

As the rule above referred to is extended to cover the Cash Book, the Cash Book is regarded as one of the books of original entry, but it cannot be classed with the others as a subsidiary book as it contains actual Ledger Accounts.

The Journal

The books of prime entry mentioned above are limited to certain transactions, namely:

(*a*) Purchases on credit and any purchases returns.
(*b*) Sales on credit and any sales returns.
(*c*) Transactions affecting the firm's cash.

Transactions other than those mentioned above do occur, but they are usually not so numerous as to warrant special books for each class. A single book is brought into use as a book of prime entry for these items. This book is called the *Journal.* It has two value columns on the right-hand side of the page, but the form in which the entries are made differs from the form taken in the other subsidiary books. Both aspects of each transaction are recorded, and, since the items relate to several kinds of transactions and the Journal is not reserved for any one kind, an explanatory note, called the *narration*, is made immediately below each entry. The making of this note ensures that the nature of and reason for the entry are not forgotten.

As a Journal entry is the setting down of the two-fold aspect of a transaction, it follows that all transactions may be journalised. It was once the practice to pass every transaction through the Journal, but the use of subsidiary books renders this unnecessary.

Some of the present uses of the Journal are discussed below.

Fixed Assets

The purchase on credit of fixed assets, such as machinery, furniture and fittings is one of the kinds of transaction passed through the Journal.

Example 11. On Dec. 1, M. Redman purchased two office desks at £81 each on credit from the Hoxton Furnishing Co.

Journal

			Dr.	*Cr.*
19..			£	£
Dec. 1	Office Furniture Account	29	162	
	Hoxton Furniture Co.	77		162
	being the purchase of two office desks.			

Examination of the above entry will show that the debit and credit aspects of the transaction were first determined, and the appropriate entries made in a particular form. The name of the account to be debited is entered first. The amount is entered in the first cash column. The account to be credited is entered on the next line, usually starting a short space to the right. The amount is entered in the second cash column. On the next line is the narration, and below this is ruled a line to separate this journal entry from the next. The line is not continued across the cash columns. Sometimes these are totalised at the foot as a simple check to find that the two columns agree.

The following is the form the entry takes if the transaction affects two or more accounts:

Example 12. On Dec. 2, M. Redman purchased on credit from the Hoxton Furniture Company one office desk at £81 and showcase for shop at £60.

Journal

			Dr.	*Cr.*
19..			£	£
Dec. 2	Office Furniture Account	29	81	
	Shop Fittings Account	31	60	
	Hoxton Furnishing Co.	77		141
	being purchase of office desk and showcase.			

It must be stressed that the Journal entries, though recording both aspects of a transaction, are not part of the double entry record proper. They are entries in the Journal as a book of *prime* entry, and are posted from there to the appropriate accounts in the Ledger. The fact that the two-fold aspect is recorded in the Journal makes the posting a simple task. Note that, when the postings are done, the Ledger folios are entered against the items in the Journal. A similar entry of the Journal page is made in the folio column of the Ledger Account.

No entry, of course, would have been made in the Journal had Redman bought these goods for cash and not on credit. In that case, the transaction would have been entered in the Cash or Bank Account. Also, the Journal and not the Purchase Day Book is used, as the Purchase Day Book is reserved for the purchase on credit of goods bought to sell again in the ordinary course of business. These goods were bought to keep for regular use.

Correction of Errors

Another use for the Journal is for the *preliminary record of entries to correct wrong postings in the Ledger.*

> ***Example 13.*** June 4. Under this date goods, £10, were sold to J. Brown. The amount was debited in error to A. Brown.

The wrong entry made in A. Brown's account is not erased or struck through, as the reason for the alteration would not be apparent. A double entry is made. £10 is credited to A. Brown's account, as a set off to the wrong debit of £10, and a corresponding debit entry is made to J. Brown's account. This is the usual method of correcting all similar errors in posting. The usefulness of the Journal explanation of the entries is obvious.

Journal

			Dr.	*Cr.*
19..			£	£
June 4	J. Brown	65	10	
	A. Brown	69		10
	being correction of error in posting to A. Brown for J. Brown.			

On those few occasions when the Trial Balance does not agree and a Suspense Account is opened, the error or errors when subsequently discovered are also corrected by means of a Journal entry (see Example 14 below).

Example 14. July 21st. M. Redman finds that the credit balance of £75 in the Suspense Account is accounted for as follows:

Cash £35 received from S.K. Green on 6th June was not credited to his account.

Purchases Returns £20 for the month of June were posted to the debit side of the Sales Returns Account.

	Journal		*Dr.*	*Cr.*
19..			£	£
July 21	Suspense Account		35	
	S.K. Green			35
	being cash received from S.K. Green on June 6th not previously credited to his account.			
„ 21	Suspense Account		40	
	Sales Returns			20
	Purchases Returns			20
	being correction of error in posting £20 Purchases Returns for June to the debit side of Sales Returns Account.			

The first entry, which is really completing the double entry of the debit in the Cash Book on 6th June by crediting S.K. Green's account, must, however, be debited to the Suspense Account, as in that account appears the £35 credit entry (part of the £75) which was made to agree the Trial Balance. The entry may be regarded as transferring the £35 from the Suspense Account to S.K. Green's account.

The second entry is not only a question of posting to the wrong account but also posting to the wrong side of the Ledger. A debit entry, or (remembering that Purchases Returns are posted individually to the debit side of the creditor accounts) a total of debit entries, is posted to the debit side of the Sales Returns Account.

It will be seen that a credit is necessary in the Sales Returns Account to correct the debit entry of £20 and a further credit in the Purchases Returns Account is necessary to make the correct posting to that account. The original error in the Suspense Account was in this case £40, twice the amount which was incorrectly posted.

The two entries could have been corrected as one Journal entry, but the matter is more clearly shown as two entries.

Opening Entries

The opening of a new set of books involves the entry of assets and claims existing at the time. The financial position is summarised and *a preliminary entry is made in the Journal from which the various asset and claim accounts may be posted.*

Example 15. Hugh Hurd, whose financial position on 1st January 19.. is as below, decides to open a set of books on double entry principles:

	£
Cash in hand	100
Cash at bank	1 040
Shop fittings	500
Office furniture	600
Stock of goods	5 000
Debtors: B. Beaver	350
R. Weaver	240
Creditor: L. C. Smith	760

The trader's capital is the excess in value of the assets over the liabilities, and a simple calculation gives H. Hurd's capital at 1st January as £7 070.

Journal

			Dr.	*Cr.*
19..			£	£
Jan. 1	Sundry Debtors: B. Beaver		350	
	R. Weaver		240	
	Shop fittings		500	
	Office furniture		600	
	Stock		5 000	
	Cash at bank		1 040	
	Cash in hand		100	
,, 1	Sundry Creditors: L.C. Smith			760
	Capital (Hugh Hurd)			7 070
	being assets and claims at this date		£7 830	£7 830

A Journal entry is made, as above, summarising the position and separating the assets and claims. In the journalising of the opening entries, an exception appears to the rule that no cash entries should be made in the Journal. If they were omitted in this case the summary would not represent the true financial position.

This summary of the financial position is on record in the Journal for reference at any time. The Ledger is opened by posting from this summary to the appropriate accounts, the assets being debited and the claims being credited respectively. The summary is useful in two ways: it is a preliminary classification of the items, and it lessens the risk of omissions in the Ledger postings.

Closing Entries

Modern practice does not require the journalising of closing entries, such as those in Example 4, pp. 37–39, in the preparation of the Final Accounts at the end of the trading period.

A letter T in the folio columns of the accounts indicates that a transfer has been made (see chapter 15). The balances of *personal* and *real* accounts are not transferred, such balances being carried down on the accounts for the new period; they are shown in the Balance Sheet. All *nominal* accounts are closed by the transfer of their balances to the Trading and Profit and Loss Account, *after* the extraction of the Trial Balance.

EXERCISES 12

1. Record the following transactions by Journal entries:

Jan. 14. The purchase of a delivery van on credit from the London Motor Company for £6 750.
„ 17. The purchase of an office desk on credit from Shoreditch Cabinet Co. for £45.
„ 25. The purchase of an electric typewriter on credit from the British Typewriter Co., for £400.
„ 30. The purchase on credit of shop fittings from Mint & Co. for £165.

2. Record the following transactions of A. Bentley, funiture dealer, in Journal form.

Feb. 2. The purchases of a lease on a warehouse and showroom for £10 000 from the Freehold Properties Company.
„ 6. The sale of a second-hand delivery van for £150 to Car Mart Auction Company.
„ 8. A. Bentley took for his private use a coffee table which cost £20.
„ 10. The purchase of a calculator for office use for £50, from the Office Furniture Supplies Company.
„ 12. The purchase of a delivery van for £5 000 from the City Motor Company.

3. A. Burton's financial position on 1st January was as follows:

		£
Cash in hand		27
Cash at bank		230
Stock on hand		750
Creditors:	J. Bones	130
	T. Smith	150
Debtors:	Williams & Co.	20
	Wilson & Sons	35
Capital		782

Make the appropriate Journal entries to open his books.

4. The following are the liabilities and assets of R.B. Graham, excepting his capital. Find his capital, make the appropriate Journal entries preparatory to opening a new set of accounts, and post the items to the respective Ledger Accounts.

		£
Cash		10
Bank		321
Stock		800
Office furniture		50
Delivery bicycle		10
Shop fittings		60
Debtor:	Brown & Co.	204
Creditors:	J. Westerby	87
	R. Easter	31
	B. Groombridge	8

5. The following Balance Sheet represents L. Chamber's financial position as at 31st December. Make the appropriate opening entries for the next year in the Journal from which the Ledger and Cash Book may be posted.

Balance Sheet

31st December

CLAIMS		£	ASSETS		£
Capital		1 180	Cash in hand		30
Creditors:	R. Jones	240	Cash at bank		320
	T. Lewis	120	Stock		530
			Furniture and fittings		110
			Debtors:	J. Neill	150
				R. Firth	380
				N. Tyson	20
		£1 540			£1 540

6. Ascertain M. T. Green's capital as at 1st January from the following list of his liabilities and assets, and prepare the appropriate Journal entry to open a set of books on that date. Post the items to the Ledger Accounts.

LIABILITIES	£	ASSETS	£
Creditors: B. Smith	44	Cash in hand	20
B. Brown	33	Cash at bank	169
B. Robinson	22	Stock on hand	750
		Shop premises	1 200
		Delivery van	120
		Shop fittings	52
		Debtor: J. Winder	18

Enter Green's transactions:

			£
Jan.	3.	Sold goods to J. Winder	130
,,	6.	Bought goods by cheque	50
,,	9.	Bought petrol for van in cash	7
,,	12.	Paid B. Smith his account by cheque	
,,	14.	J. Winder paid his account by cheque	
,,	15.	Paid B. Robinson his account by cheque	
,,	17.	Bought new showcase on credit from Cabinetmakers Company Ltd.	100
,,	17.	Stock on hand valued at	770

Take out a Trial Balance and prepare Trading and Profit and Loss Accounts for the period. Draw up a Balance Sheet as at 17th January.

7. The financial position of L. J. Lewis, a dealer in furniture, was as follows on 1st July, 19..:

	£
Cash in hand	100
Cash at bank	8 000
Stock on hand	3 500
Shop furniture and fittings	1 500
He owed R. Jones	800
His debtors were:	
Smith's Stores	1 200
Benson & Co.	330

Journalise these items and his capital preparatory to opening L. J. Lewis's books. Post the items to the Ledger and Cash Book, and enter the following transactions:

			£
July	2.	Sold goods to Smith's Stores	750
,,	6.	Bought furniture from R. Jones	1 800
,,	8.	Drew cheque for personal use	250
,,	10.	Paid rent for quarter ending 30th June by cheque	300
,,	12.	Benson & Co. paid their account by cheque	330
,,	14.	Paid R. Jones his account	2 600

Take out a Trial Balance as at 14th July. Prepare Trading and Profit and Loss Account for the period, and a Balance Sheet as at 14th July. Stock on hand, £4 800.

8. Show the Journal entries to correct the following errors in J. Sullivan's books:

Sept. 2. Goods to the value of £20 were returned to B. Clark, but the item had been posted to J. B. Clarkson's account.
" 10. The sale of one of the office desks for £10 in cash was wrongly posted to the Sales Account.
" 13. The purchase of an office desk for £36 cash to replace the one sold was posted to the Purchases Account.
" 17. A purchase of goods for £75 from R. Wilkinson & Co. was credited in error to R. Williamson & Sons.

9. Show in Journal form the entries required to correct the following errors made in R. Benson's books:

July 3. £50 paid by R. Lewis was credited to R. Levy's account.
July 28. A sale of goods for £25 to R. Jones on credit was debited to R. B. Jones & Co's account.
" 31. The purchase of a stapling machine for the office for cash, £15, posted to the Purchases Account.
Aug. 6. The payment of £10 by cheque to B. Watson was debited to B. Watkinson's account.

10. Journalise the closing entries on the transfer of the following balances to the Trading and Profit and Loss Accounts on the 31st December:

	£
Purchases	1 600
Sales	2 590
Stock at start	300
Wages	120
Expenses	47
Rent	150
Stock at close	400

11. There was a difference in the Trial Balance of A. Spencer at 31st August, 19.., which was transferred to the Suspense Account. Subsequently the difference was found to be due to the following errors:

£10 cash received from A. Brown was correctly entered in the Cash Book but was debited to his account.

Sales Day Book for August was undercast by £10. The total sales should have been £2 060 not £2 050.

£25 paid to the landlord for rent on 28th August was entered in the Cash Book but not in any other account.

Correct the errors by means of Journal entries and state the nature and amount of the balance on the Suspense Account.

12. Give entries in the Journal proper to correct the following errors:

(*a*) Feb. 1 A cheque received for £18 was posted to the credit of P. Dawson. In fact it came from F. Dawson & Co. and should have been credited to them.

(*b*) „ 1 An entry for £10 goods returned was, in error, made in the Sales Book instead of the Purchases Returns Book.

(*c*) „ 1 A cheque for £5 paid to G. Law was debited to a personal account in his name. It should have been charged to Legal Expenses Account.

13. Prepare Journal entries to show the effect of the following transactions in the books of Peter Grimes.

Dec. 1. Sold to A. Butt for £100 goods belonging to G. Sykes. Commission £5.

„ 31. £56 has been included in the Wages Account and £63 in the Purchases Account which sums represent expenditure on an extension of the business premises.

Purchases Returns £5 had been posted in error to the debit of Sales Returns and the resulting difference in the books has been placed temporarily in a Suspense Account. The matter is now to be corrected.

One of the branch shops makes a net profit of £1 100 and it is decided to give the manager a commission of 10% of the amount of profit that will remain after the commission has been granted.

13

Control Accounts

Sales Ledger Control Accounts

The *Sales Ledger* contains the personal accounts of debtors. These are kept together in their own Ledger as a matter of convenience, in view of the similarity of the nature of the entries made in them. If there are a great many personal accounts the Sales Ledger may be divided up, for example on an alphabetic basis by name of customer or a geographic basis by location of customer. The Sales Books will then be similarly subdivided. An analysis of the items in such accounts would show that they are of the following kinds.

(i) Opening debit balance brought down from the previous period.
(ii) Debit entries for goods sold to customers (sales).
(iii) Credit entries for cash received from debtors.
(iv) Credit entries for allowances made and discounts allowed.
(v) Credit entries for bad debts.
(vi) Closing credit entries for balances carried down for the next period.

When a large number of *Sales* (or *Sold*) *Ledgers* and *Purchases* (or *Bought*) *Ledgers* are in use it is necessary to devise a system whereby the accuracy of the personal accounts *in each ledger* may be checked. This is done by constructing a *Control Account* for each Sales or Purchases Ledger, e.g. Sales Ledger No. 4 Control Account.

This account is constructed entirely apart from the system of double entry and is no part of that system. It is simply a means of checking the accuracy of the entries.

1. If there are, say, 200 accounts in Sales Ledger No. 1, then the Sales Ledger No. 1 Control Account would open with the total of all the debit balances in that Ledger checked as correct by listing all of the balances at the end of the previous period of trading.

2. The total of individual sales items debited to the personal

accounts in Sales Ledger No. 1 for the month can be ascertained from Sales Book No. 1 or other subsidiary records.

3. By incorporating analysis columns in the debit side of the Cash Book, corresponding to each Sales Ledger, the total of cash received from debtors and posted to the credit side of debtors accounts in Sales Ledger No. 1 can be ascertained.

4. Analysis of the discount column of the Cash Book will give the total of discounts posted to the credit side of the debtors' accounts in each Sales Ledger including Sales Ledger No. 1.

5. Totals of amounts credited to the accounts in Sales Ledger No. 1 in respect of Returns can be ascertained by analysis of the Sales Returns Books or appropriate subsidiary records.

6. *Bad debts* (i.e. debts which are not yet paid, and seem unlikely ever to be) and any other extraneous items affecting the accounts of debtors in Sales Ledger No. 1 will have been journalised and by analysing the Journal entries the total of such items either debited or credited to the accounts in any Sales Ledger can be ascertained. The method of recording bad or doubtful debts is described in Chapter 20.

We can now construct an account *in total* of all the individual items which have been entered in the debtors' accounts contained in any particular Sales Ledger during a particular period, usually one month.

Sales Ledger Control Account

19..			£	19..			£
June 1	Balance, total debtors at this date		12 000	June 30	Cash		55 000
				,, 30	Discounts		1 000
				,, 30	Bad debts		200
				,, 30	Returns inwards		300
,, 30	Sales		75 000	,, 30	Balance carried down		30 500
			£87 000				£87 000
July 1	Balance brought down		30 500				

Purchases Ledger Control Account

In the same way as above, the personal accounts of trade creditors are segregated into one or more *Purchases* (or *Bought*) *Ledgers*. The totals of the individual items posted to creditors' accounts in a particular Purchases Ledger can be ascertained: the total of creditors' opening balances from the previous month's Trial Balance or Control Account, the total of purchases from the relevant Purchases Book or other record, the total of cash paid and discounts received from the analysis of the credit side of the Cash Book, the total of returns and allowances from the Purchases Returns Book and any other items from an analysis of the Journal.

When complete a Purchases (or Bought) Ledger Control Account might appear as on page 112.

These Control Accounts are prepared by a supervisor working independently of the Ledger clerks. It is clear that the final balance of the Control Account for a particular Sales or Purchases Ledger should agree with the total of the balances in the individual accounts in that Ledger at the end of the period covered. The clerk in charge of each Ledger will extract and total the balances on the accounts in his Ledger at the end of each month. This total should agree with the balance on the Control Account for that Ledger constructed independently by the supervisor. If it disagrees then any discrepancy must be investigated and rectified in the same way as with a Trial Balance, as described in Chapter 6. Unlike a Trial Balance, however, it is possible, by using Control Accounts to isolate an error to a particular Ledger.

When all the Sales and Purchases Ledgers have been agreed with their respective Control Accounts then the total balances on all the Sales Ledger Control Accounts will give the total of sundry debtors at the end of any particular month, and the total of balances on the Purchases Ledger Control Accounts will give the total of sundry creditors.

When comparatively few Sales and Purchases Ledgers are in use the Cash Book and subsidiary records may be adapted to facilitate analysis of entries for the construction of Control Accounts. Rulings of subsidiary books are illustrated on page 112. Where columns become too numerous then a separate Sales Book corresponding to each Sales Ledger may be used. Special analysis sheets may be used for the analysis of cash, discount, and journalised transactions.

One of the great advantages of mechanised accounts is the economy

Sales Book

DATE	PARTI-CULARS	LEDGER FOLIOS	TOTAL	SALES LEDGER A—K	SALES LEDGER L—R	SALES LEDGER S—Z	DEPT. A	DEPT. B	DEPT. C
			£	£	£	£	£	£	£

Cash Book

Dr. (Debit side)

DATE	PARTI-CULARS	FOLIO	DISCOUNT	DETAILS	BANK	SALES LEDGER A—K	SALES LEDGER L—R	SALES LEDGER S—Z	GENERAL LEDGER
			£	£	£	£	£	£	£

Cash Book

(Credit side) *Cr.*

DATE	PARTI-CULARS	FOLIO	DISCOUNT	DETAILS	BANK	BOUGHT LEDGER A—M	BOUGHT LEDGER N—Z	GENERAL LEDGER
			£	£	£	£	£	£

in time and labour. Machines accumulate the amount of individual postings as they are made. These totals are posted by machine to a Control Account so that the total balances in any Sales Ledger may

Bought Ledger Control Account

19..			£	19..			£
June 30	Cash		35 000	June 1	Balance being total creditors at this date		10 000
,, 30	Discounts		700	,, 30	Purchases		40 000
,, 30	Returns and allowances		140				
,, 30	Balance carried down		14 160				
			£50 000				£50 000
				July 1	Balance brought down		14 160

be ascertained day by day. This is more fully explained in the chapter on mechanised accounts.

Control Accounts are particularly useful as instruments of management control, since the *total* figures are always available, and decision-making is not hindered by the time that would otherwise be required to collect and compute figures from the various sources. Control Accounts also help to minimise the incidence of fraud, by providing a basic system of internal control.

EXERCISES 13

1. What is the purpose of Sales Ledger and Purchases Ledger Control Accounts? How are they constructed and from what sources are the entries in them derived?

2. From the following particulars relating to a particular Sales Ledger construct a Sales Ledger Control Account for the month of May, 19..

	£
Total debtors' balances in Sales Ledger at 1st May, agreeing with balance of Sales Ledger Control Account at 30th April	4 607
Sales for month	5 291
Returns and allowances for month	342
Cash received from debtors during the month	3 996
Discounts allowed to debtors during the month	197
Bad debts during the month	47

3. From the following particulars relating to a particular Purchases Ledger construct a Purchases Ledger Control Account for the month of May, 19..

	£
Total of creditors' balances in Purchases Ledger at 1st May, agreeing with balance of Purchases Ledger Control Account at 30th April	8 409
Purchases for month	7 308
Returns and allowances for month	243
Cash paid to creditors during the month	6 504
Discounts received during the month	292

4. Complete the Bought Ledger and Sales Ledger Control Accounts, from the following details:

19..			£
Jan.	1.	Debit balances in Sales Ledger	3 694
,,	1.	Credit balances in Sales Ledger	149
,,	1.	Debit balances in Bought Ledger	58
,,	1.	Credit balances in Bought Ledger	983
,,	31.	Sales	8 523
,,	31.	Purchases	2 938

		£
Jan. 31.	Cash received from customers	6 954
,, 31.	Discount received	56
,, 31.	Discount allowed	80
,, 31.	Sales returns	193
,, 31.	Purchases returns	100
,, 31.	Sales Ledger debits transferred to Bought Ledger	50
,, 31.	Customers' balances transferred to Bad Debts Account	25
,, 31.	Cash paid to creditors	2 659
,, 31.	Credit balances in Sales Ledger	49
,, 31.	Debit balances in Bought Ledger	83

R.S.A.

5. F. Kay both sells goods to R. Tyler and buys goods from him. He keeps one account for Tyler in his Sales Ledger and another in his Purchases Ledger.

On 31st May, 19.., the debit balance on Tyler's account in the Sales Ledger was £137. This was transferred to Tyler's account in the Purchases Ledger which had a credit balance of £207. Make a Journal entry to show this transfer.

Where would the entries for this transfer appear in the Control Accounts for (i) the Sales Ledger and (ii) the Purchases Ledger?

6. Johnson & Son keep a Sales Ledger. At the end of each month a Sales Ledger Control Account is prepared.

(*a*) From the following particulars construct the Control Account for the month of October, 19..:

19..		£
Oct. 1.	Debit balance	10 461
	Credit balance	81
,, 31.	Sales for month	12 484
	Sales returns for month	140
	Cash received from debtors during month	11 058
	Discounts allowed to debtors during month	582
	Transfers of debit balances in the Sales Ledger to debit of Purchases Ledger during month	104
Oct. 31.	Credit balances in Sales Ledger at end of month	131

(*b*) The debit balance on the Control Account did not agree with the total of debit balances in the Sales Ledger. On investigation the following errors were discovered:

(i) A total in the Sales Book had been carried forward as £2 749 instead of £2 479.

(ii) A discount allowed £6 to F. Ames had been entered in the Cash Book but not posted to Ames' account.

(iii) The total of the discount allowed column in the Cash Book for October had been undercast by £10.

(iv) A sale to J. Bragg had been entered correctly in the Sales Book as £195 but had been posted to Bragg's account as £95.

(v) A credit note for £21 sent to W. Carr had been entered in the Sales Returns Book and posted to Carr's account as £12.

State what corrections you would make in:

1. The Sales Ledger, and
2. The Sales Ledger Control Account

to rectify the above errors.

A.E.B., G.C.E. 'O' Level

14

Capital and Revenue Expenditure: Types of Capital

Capital and Revenue Expenditure

All expenditure by a business is either ultimately transferred to the Trading and Profit and Loss Account or retained in other separate accounts as assets. Those items which are transferable to Trading and Profit and Loss Accounts are called *Revenue Expenditure* and those retained in the Accounts as assets are called *Capital Expenditure*.

Sometimes there is some doubt as to which category an item of expenditure belongs. If, for example, extra machinery is bought, then clearly the value of the machinery in the business has risen and the extra machinery is a Capital Expenditure. But when the existing machinery is repaired in order to maintain it at its present book value, then the asset has not risen in value, and so the expenditure on repairs is Revenue Expenditure chargeable to Trading and Profit and Loss Account. The distinction between capital and revenue expenditure cannot be easily described in terms of a single principle. However, expenditures of a capital nature will be listed in the Balance Sheet. Revenue expenditures are those which are paid out in order to gain revenue, directly or indirectly, during the accounting period. Capital expenditures may be converted gradually into revenue expenditures over several years, as is explained in the chapter on depreciation.

Capital

When a man starts a business he usually begins with a sum of money, which, let us say, is £5 000. He will probably open a Business Bank Account and place this sum, called his capital, to it. If we were asked to produce his Balance Sheet at the commencement of business, it would appear as follows:

Balance Sheet,

as at 1 Jan. 19..

	£		£
Capital	5 000	Cash at bank	5 000

This position, of course, would not last long. We know that he would spend money on the purchase of various assets. Before he began trading, his financial position might be as follows:

Balance Sheet,

as at 15 Jan. 19..

	£		£
Capital	5 000	Machinery	1 500
		Furniture and fittings	500
		Stock	2 000
		Cash at bank	1 000
	£5 000		£5 000

From this second Balance Sheet we can see that capital may be not simply money, but the total of assets which can be converted into money. The owner has a claim of £5 000 against the business: it can pay him £5 000 in cash only if the machinery, furniture, fittings and stock can be converted into sufficient money, and provided that all of the debts of the business due to other persons or firms have been paid off.

The assets which he purchases are of two kinds. Machinery and furniture and fittings are acquired for use in the business over a prolonged period. They are known as *Fixed Assets.* Assets such as stock, sundry debtors, and cash in hand and at bank are known as *Current Assets* as they are acquired for disposal and conversion into cash in the course of trade, and will quickly be renewed again. Hence they are sometimes known as *circulating assets.*

The liabilities of a firm may be of two types. *Current Liabilities* are those such as trade creditors or a bank overdraft which will have to be met within a comparatively short period of time. *Long Term Liabilities* may consist of loans made to the firm for a fairly long period of time, at least more than one year.

When the trader has been in business for some time his balance sheet might be as follows:

Balance Sheet,

as at 15 Jan. 19..

CLAIMS	£	ASSETS	£	£
Capital:	6 400	*Fixed assets:*		
Long Term Liabilities:		Machinery	3 300	
Loan (7 years) S. Gee	2 000	Furniture and fittings	700	
				4 000
Current Liabilities:				
Trade creditors	2 100	*Current assets:*		
		Stock	3 750	
		Trade debtors	950	
		Cash in hand and balance at bank	1 800	6 500
	£10 500			£10 500

The total of fixed assets is £4 000, the total of current assets is £6 500 and of current liabilities £2 100. The total of assets in the business is £10 500 but, of this amount, £2 100 must be easily available to pay the trade creditors. The difference, £8 400, is known as the *net value of the assets* (or alternatively as the *value of the net assets*). This net value is equal to the *capital employed* in the business. This 'capital employed' may consist partly of funds contributed by the owner of the business known simply as 'capital', and also of funds borrowed from other sources which will be available for a prolonged period. This is known as *Loan Capital.* In the above balance sheet the capital employed is £8 400 consisting of £6 400 contributed by the owner of the business and £2 000 due to S. Gee.

Alternatively the Balance Sheet may be set out as on page 119. An important item in this Balance Sheet is the *Working Capital*, which is equal to the amount of current assets *less* the amount of current liabilities. (In this example the working capital is £4 400.) It is important because it is essential that a business should have a sufficient margin of current assets over current liabilities not only to meet its immediate liabilities but to carry on and expand its trading activities. If the working capital was inadequate the business might not be able to meet its immediate liabilities and even if it could do so the margin might not be sufficient to enable it to quickly renew its stocks or to take advantage of trading opportunities. It is clear that a business would be in a very serious position indeed if it were compelled to sell any of the fixed assets to meet pressing and immediate liabilities. If a business has been buying large amounts on credit and has, perhaps, acquired a large bank overdraft it may get into difficulties if it is unable to collect cash quickly from its debtors. This is known as *overtrading*. It is a frequent reason for financial failures.

Balance Sheet

	£				£	£
Capital:	6 400	*Fixed assets:*				
Long Term Liabilities:		Machinery			3 300	
Loan (7 years): S. Gee	2 000	Furniture and fittings			700	
						4 000
		Current assets:				
		Stock		£3 750		
		Trade debtors		£950		
		Cash in hand and balance at bank		£1 800		
					6 500	
		Less current liabilities:				
		Trade creditors			2 100	
		Working Capital:				4 400
Capital employed:	£8 400	**Net value of assets:**				£8 400

The style of balance sheet above, which shows working capital, is now widely used. Another development is the presentation of the information in *vertical* form, as was illustrated in Chapter 4. The above Balance Sheet can be set vertically as follows:

Balance Sheet,
as at 15 Jan. 19. .

Capital Employed:		£
Owner's Capital:		6 400
Long-Term Liabilities:		
Loan (7 years): S. Gee		2 000
		£8 400
Net Value of Assets:	£	£
Fixed Assets:		
Machinery	3 300	
Furniture and fittings	700	
		4 000
Current Assets:		
Stock	3 750	
Trade debtors	950	
Cash and bank	1 800	
	6 500	
Current Liabilities		
Trade creditors	2 100	
Working Capital		4 400
		£8 400

Note that the words 'Claims' and 'Assets' do not normally appear as main headings on the Balance Sheet.

The student is advised to show the amount of the working capital when setting out balance sheets, whether using either the traditional or the vertical form.

EXERCISES 14

1. Enter the following transactions of J. Herbertson in his books. Take out a Trial Balance and prepare Trading and Profit and Loss Accounts for the period, and a Balance Sheet as at 17th March.

			£
Mar.	3.	J. Herbertson began business with cash at bank	6 000
,,	3.	He bought business premises and paid by cheque	3 600
,,	5.	Paid by cheque for shop fittings and fixtures	186

			£
Mar.	7.	Paid by cheque for automatic scales and cash register	72
,,	7.	Cashed cheque for till money	30
,,	7.	Paid by cheque for paper bags, string, and packing papers	13
,,	9.	Bought from National Stores: provisions, £450; groceries, £750	1 200
,,	10.	Bought from Hudson & Co.: goods	300
,,	17.	Cash Sales to date	258
,,	17.	Paid boy's wages in cash (one day's work)	3
,,	17.	Paid cash into bank	240
,,	17.	Stock on hand valued at	1 305

2. B. W. Ward began business on 10th April with the following capital:

			£
Cash in hand			10
Cash at bank			680
April	10.	Bought from J. Birmingham:	
		Cutlery	100
		Fancy silver goods	350
,,	10.	Bought at auction old silver, and paid by cheque	300
,,	12.	Bought showcase for shop, paying by cheque	80
,,	12.	Paid cash for stationery	3
,,	15.	Sold to J. Bentley: cutlery	50
,,	16.	Paid cash for polishing materials	2
,,	18.	J. Bentley returned part of cutlery order; allowed him	6
,,	23.	Cash sales to date, paid direct to bank	370
,,	30.	Paid by cheque for rent of premises	25
,,	30.	Paid J. Birmingham his account by cheque	450
,,	30.	Drew cheque for personal use	50

Take out Trial Balance and prepare Trading and Profit and Loss Accounts for the period, and a Balance Sheet as at 30th April. Stock on hand, £500.

3. The following balances were extracted at 31st December from J. Wetherby's books. From them prepare a Trial Balance and from the Trial Balance prepare Trading and Profit and Loss Accounts for the year and a Balance Sheet as at 31st December: Purchases, £17 000; Sales, £27 000; Salaries and Wages, £4 000; Carriage on Sales, £100; Office expenses, £750; Office furniture, £1 500; Rent Account, £1 000; Sundry debtors, £8 000; Sundry creditors, £2 770; Cash in hand, £100; Cash at bank, £1 820; Stock, 1st Jan., £5 000; Stock, 31st Dec., £4 800; Capital Account (credit balance), £9 500.

4. From the following Trial Balance from B. Downing's books, prepare Trading and Profit and Loss Accounts, and a Balance Sheet as at 31st December:

Trial Balance

31st December

	Dr.	Cr.
	£	£
Stock at start of year	3 500	
Purchases	11 000	
Sales		21 000
Wages	2 500	
Office expenses	900	
Carriage on sales	810	
Rent and rates	1 600	
Capital account		7 910
Sundry creditors		3 600
Sundry debtors	7 500	
Cash at bank	3 500	
Office furniture	1 200	
	£32 510	£32 510

The stock on hand at the close of the year was valued at £3 200.

5. From the following Trial Balance, you are required to prepare Trading and Profit and Loss Accounts, and a Balance Sheet.

Trial Balance

31st December

	Dr.	Cr.
	£	£
Stock on hand at beginning of year	3 260	
Purchases	8 790	
Sales		22 480
Salaries and wages	5 960	
Office expenses	980	
Carriage on sales	870	
Rent and rates	1 570	
Capital Account (H. Dickson)		6 000
Creditors		3 210
Debtors	7 770	
Cash at bank	2 490	
	£31 690	£31 690

The stock in hand at the end of the year was valued at £2 950.

R.S.A. (adapted)

6. Distinguish carefully between Capital Expenditure and Revenue Expenditure.

7. Give a list under the two headings Capital and Revenue, of items of expenditure which might be made by (*a*) a driving school, (*b*) a bus operator, (*c*) a wholesale grocery and provision merchant.

8. Say, with reasons, whether the following transactions of a catering business should be classified as capital or revenue expenditure:

(i) Bought a new refrigerator to replace old one which both faulty and too small.
(ii) Ordered and received 2 cans of detergent.
(iii) Purchased on credit 12 doz. sets of cutlery for new dining room.
(iv) Paid for hire of new coffee-making machine.
(v) Bought and paid for 5 000 cigarettes.

9. T. S. Appleby gave you the following figures and asked you to prepare from them his Balance Sheet as at 31st May, 19.. In addition, he wishes you to state the total capital employed in the business, the total borrowed capital, the working capital and the total capital due to himself. Cash in hand, £24; Loan from his uncle V. Appleby, £750; Motor vans, £1 200; Sundry debtors, £2 376; Sundry creditors, £1 850; Bank overdraft, £90; Machinery, £2 000; Loan from T. Garth and Sons, £600; Furniture and fittings, £350; Stock in hand, £1 340.

10. The following balances remained in J. Ashworth's Ledger *after* he had prepared his Trading and Profit and Loss Account for the year ended 31st December 19..

	Dr.	*Cr.*
	£	£
Capital		6 000
Profit and Loss Account		2 950
Drawings	2 500	
Trade debtors	3 210	
Creditors: Trade		4 170
Expense		140
X.L. Loan Co. (10 year loan)		1 000
Stock	4 670	
Furniture and fittings	690	
Motor vans	1 320	
Cash in hand and balance at bank	1 870	
	£14 260	£14 260

Prepare Ashworth's Balance Sheet in such a way as to show *within the Balance Sheet:*

(i) The total of fixed assets.
(ii) The total of current assets.
(iii) The total of current liabilities.
(iv) The working capital.
(v) The net value of the assets.
(vi) The capital employed.

15

A Worked Example

This chapter is concerned with the working of an exercise appropriate to this stage of the subject. The example should prove of value to the student in that it indicates the method of setting out the work for class use and for examinations.

For practice purposes the student should usually have two exercise books – one with Ledger ruling and the other with Journal ruling. In some cases a third book, ruled as a Cash Book, is available. Where only two are in use the Cash Book, subsidiary books, and Journal for an exercise are usually grouped together on a double page of the Journal exercise book. With the appropriate headings in bold writing it is possible for the student to consider each section of the page as a separate book. The upper halves of two facing Journal pages are suitable for the Cash Book, but if a three-column Cash Book is required, an additional cash column should be ruled on each side. The left-hand lower half-page is usually sufficient for the Purchases Day Book and Sales Day Book, leaving the right-hand lower half for the Returns Books and the Journal proper. The Trial Balance should, if possible, be included, but if space is insufficient the Trial Balances of all the exercises may, as some teachers prefer, be grouped together at the end of the Journal exercise book.

The student should arrange the Ledger Accounts in a definite order, and should keep to the arrangement for all exercises. In the worked example the real and nominal accounts are grouped together, and likewise the creditors' accounts and the debtors' accounts. The Trading Account, Profit and Loss Account, and Balance Sheet bring the exercise to its conclusion. As explained in Chapter 12, closing entries are no longer journalised; instead they are made direct between the Ledger Accounts. The student should however be conversant with the full use of the Journal, and full Journal entries are therefore shown.

In considering the example given overleaf, each transaction should be traced through the books of original entry to the Ledger Accounts. The student would find it profitable to work the example and then to compare his working with the printed key, and differences being corrected and the reasons for the corrections being sought for and fully understood. Note that the letter T in the folio column of an account indicates that a transfer has been made.

Example 16. R. Blackwell runs a small business. His financial position on 1st December, 19. . was as follows: Cash in hand, £5; cash at bank, £340; stock value, £480. He owed Smith's Tools Company, £20; and T. Lawrence, £10; and was owed £40 by M. Lewis.

Journalise these items, and open Blackwell's books at 1st December. Enter the following transactions, extract a Trial Balance, and prepare Trading and Profit and Loss Accounts and a Balance Sheet as at 31st December.

Dec. 1. Arranged a loan from bankers for £2 800, which was credited to current account this day.
,, 2. Bought Leasehold premises – paid by cheque £3 000.
,, 2. Paid by cheque, £30, for fixtures and fittings.
,, 3. Paid expenses of removal to new premises by cheque, £18.
,, 3. Cashed cheque for office cash, £10, and paid cash for stationery, £3.
,, 8. Cash sales to date, paid direct to bank, £60.
,, 10. Bought from Smith's Tools Co., sundry goods value £96, less 25% trade discount.
,, 12. Returned to Smith's Tools Co., goods which were faulty, £16 at cost.
,, 16. Cash sales, paid to bank, £32.
,, 16. Sold to F. Logan, goods value £160.
,, 17. Paid Smith's Tools Co. their account by cheque, less 5% cash discount.
,, 18. Bought from T. Lawrence, goods value £180, less 25% trade discount, and accessories and sundries, £120.
,, 20. Sold to M. Lewis, accessories, £200.
,, 20. Bought office furniture from Roland Furniture Co., £36.
,, 24. Cash sales to date £68, paid £40 direct to bank.
,, 24. Drew cash for private use, £30.
,, 28. M. Lewis paid his account by cheque, less 2½ cash discount.
,, 31. Repaid £100 of loan from bank.
,, 31. Bank charged interest on loan, £11.
,, 31. Stock on hand valued at £390.

Journal

			Dr.	Cr.
19..			£	£
Dec. 1	Cash in hand	C.B.	5	
	Cash at bank	C.B.	340	
	Stock	3	480	
	M. Lewis	17	40	
	Smith's Tools Co.	14		20
	T. Lawrence	15		10
	Capital, R. Blackwell	1		835
			£865	£865
	being assets and claims at this date			
Dec. 20	Furniture and Fittings Account	5	36	
	Roland Furniture Co.	16		36
	for shelves purchased for office			

Purchases Day Book

19..			£
Dec. 10	Smith's Tools Co.	14	72
,, 18	T. Lawrence	15	255
		6	£327

Purchases Returns Book

19..			£	£
Dec. 12	Smith's Tools Co.:			
	Faulty goods		16	
	less 25% trade discount – faulty	14	4	12
		6		£12

Sales Day Book

19..			£
Dec. 16	F. Logan	18	160
,, 20	M. Lewis	17	200
		7	£360

Trial Balance

19..			£	£
Dec. 31	Cash in hand		10	
	Cash at bank		261	
	Capital			835
	Drawings		30	
	Stock		480	
	Leasehold Premises		3 000	
	Furniture and fittings		66	
	Purchases		315	
	Sales			520
	General expenses		18	
	Stationery and printing		3	
	Loan Account			2 700
	Interest		11	
	Discount received			4
	Discount allowed		6	
	T. Lawrence			265
	Roland Furniture Co.			36
	F. Logan		160	
			£4 360	£4 360

Cash Book

Dr.											*Cr.*
DATE	PARTICULARS	FO.	DISCOUNT	CASH	BANK	DATE	PARTICULARS	FO.	DISCOUNT	CASH	BANK
19..			£	£	£	19..			£	£	£
Dec. 1	Balance	J.		5	340	Dec. 2	Leasehold Premises	4			3 000
,, 1	Loan from bank	10			2 800	,, 2	Fixtures and fittings	5			30
,, 3	Bank	√		10		,, 3	Removal expenses	8			18
,, 8	Cash sales	7			60	,, 3	Office cash	√			10
,, 16	,,	7			32	,, 3	Stationery and printing	9		3	
,, 24	,,	7		28	40	,, 17	Smith's Tools Co.	4	4		76
,, 28	M. Lewis	17	6		234	,, 24	Drawings	2		30	
						,, 31	Bank, part loan repaid	10			100
						,, 31	Interest on loan	11			11
			£6						£4		
			L13			,, 31	Balances carried down			10	261
									L12		
				£43	£3 506					£43	£3 506
19.. Jan. 1	Balances brought down	√		10	261						

Capital Account

19..			£	19..			£
Dec. 31	Drawings	J.	30	Dec. 1	Balance	J.	835
,, 31	Balance	c/d	886	,, 31	Net Profit	T	81
			£916				£916
				Jan. 1	Balance	b/d	886

Drawings 2

19..			£	19..			£
Dec. 24	Cash	C.B.	30	Dec. 31	Transfer to Capital A/c.	T	30

Stock Account 3

19..			£	19..			£
Dec. 1	Balance	J.	480	Dec. 31	Transfer to Trading A/c.	T	480
Jan. 1	Trading A/c.	J.	390				

Leasehold Premises 4

19..			£	19..			£
Dec. 2	Cash	C.B.	3 000				

Furniture, Fixtures, and Fittings 5

19..			£	19..			£
Dec. 2	Cash	C.B.	30	Dec. 31	Balance		66
,, 20	Typewriter Co.	J.	36				
			£66				£66
Jan. 1	Balance	b/d	66				

Purchases Account 6

19..			£	19..			£
Dec. 31	Sundries – to Purchase Day Book	P.B.	327	Dec. 31	Returns	R.B.	12
				,, 31	Transfer to Trading A/c.	T	315
			£327				£327

Sales Account 7

19..			£	19..			£
Dec. 31	Transfer to Trading A/c.	T	520	Dec. 8	Cash sales	C.B.	60
				,, 8	,, ,,	C.B.	32
				,, 24	,, ,,	C.B.	68
				,, 31	Sundries – by Sales DayBook	S.B.	360
			£520				£520

General Expenses 8

19..			£	19..			£
Dec. 3	Cash – removal expenses	C.B.	18	Dec. 31	Transfer to Profit & Loss A/c.	T	18

Stationery and Printing 9

19..			£	19..			£
Dec. 3	Cash	C.B.	3	Dec. 31	Transfer to Profit & Loss A/c.	T	3

Bank Loan Account 10

19..			£	19..			£
Dec. 31	Cash	C.B.	100	Dec. 1	Bank	C.B.	2 800
,, 31	Balance	c/d	2 700				
			£2 800				£2 800
				Jan. 1	Balance	b/d	2 700

Interest on Loan 11

19..			£	19..			£
Dec. 31	Cash	C.B.	11	Dec. 31	Transfer to Profit & Loss A/c.	J.	11

Discounts Received 12

19..			£	19..			£
Dec. 31	Transfer to Profit & Loss A/c.	T	4	Dec. 31	Sundries	C.B.	4

Discounts Allowed 13

19..			£	19..			£
Dec. 31	Sundries	C.B.	6		Transfer to Profit & Loss A/c.	T	6

Smith's Tools Company 14

19..			£	19..			£
Dec. 12	Returns	PRB.	12	Dec. 1	Balance	J.	20
,, 17	Cash	C.B.	76	,, 10	Goods	P.B.	72
,, 17	Discount	C.B.	4				
			£92				£92

T. Lawrence 15

19..			£	19..			£
Dec. 31	Balance	c/d	265	Dec. 1	Balance	J.	10
				,, 18	Goods	P.B.	255
			£265				£265
				Jan. 1	Balance	b/d	265

Roland Furniture Company 16

19..			£	19..			£
				Dec. 20	Furniture and Fittings	J.	36

M. Lewis 17

			£	19..			£
Dec. 1	Balance	J.	40	Dec. 28	Cash	C.B.	234
,, 20	Goods	S.B.	200	,, 28	Discount	C.B.	6
			£240				£240

F. Logan 18

19..			£	19..			
Dec. 16	Goods	S.B.	160				

Trading Account

for the month ending 31st December, 19.. 19

	£	£		£
Stock at start	480		Sales	520
Purchases	315			
	£795			
less Stock at close	390			
		405		
Gross Profit		115		
		£520		£520

Profit and Loss Account 20

for the month ending 31st December, 19..

	£		£
General expenses	18	Gross Profit	115
Stationery	3	Discount received	4
Interest	11		
Discount allowed	6		
Net Profit to Capital A/c.	81		
	£119		£119

Balance Sheet

as at 31st December 19..

	£	£		£	£
Capital:			*Fixed Assets:*		
Balance at 1st December	835		Leasehold Premises	3 000	
Add Net Profit	81		Furniture and Fittings	66	
	916				3 066
Less Drawings	30		*Current Assets:*		
		886	Stock	390	
Long Term Liabilities			Debtors	160	
			Bank	261	
Bank Loan		2 700	Cash	10	
				821	
			Less Current Liabilities:		
			Creditors	301	
					520
Capital Employed:		£3 586	*Net Assets:*		£3 586

The following vertical form of the final accounts is also shown. In this context, the examples in chapters 4 and 14 should be carefully studied.

Trading and Profit and Loss Account

for month ended 31st December 19..

Sales		520
Opening Stock	480	
Purchases	315	
	795	
Less Closing stock	390	
Cost of sales		405
Gross Profit		115
Discounts Received		4
		119
General Expenses	18	
Stationery	3	
Interest	11	
Discounts Allowed	6	38
Net Profit transferred to Capital		81

Balance Sheet

as at 31st December 19. .

Fixed Assets:		
Leasehold Premises	3 000	
Furniture and Fittings	66	3 066
Current Assets:		
Stock	390	
Debtors	160	
Cash at bank	261	
Cash in hand	10	
	821	
Less Current Liabilities:		
Creditors	301	
Working Capital		520
Net value of assets		3 586
Financed by:		
Capital 1st December	835	
Add Net Profit	81	
	916	
Less Drawings	30	886
Long Term Liabilities:		
Bank Loan		2 700
Capital employed		3 586

16

Accounting Systems; Flowcharts; Internal Control

Accounting Systems

Before entries can be made in the ledger accounts there may have to be a considerable amount of detailed work in order to provide the information, which is the subject of the entries. For example, before entering payments for wages and salaries it is necessary to work out the amounts payable by using a *payroll system*. Before recording a credit sale it is necessary to complete an *invoicing system*. All sales and purchases transactions affect stock, which must be recorded in a *system of stock records*.

In essence, a *payroll system* is based on periodic calculations of *gross pay* for each employee, based on records of their time at work or production achieved. It is necessary also to calculate overtime and other additional payments. The gross pay calculations are followed by calculations of the various *deductions* that have to be made from each employee's pay. These usually include income tax, national insurance, pension contributions, union dues, and any other individual deduction. Following this, there must be a calculation of *net pay*. All of this information for each employee has to be set out on a payslip to be given to the individual. The net pay must also be printed out on a bank giro credit, or on a cheque to be given direct to the employee, or in a form suitable for the cashier's department to use in making up pay packets.

The payroll system must also produce totals of each type of deduction. Furthermore, it is necessary to devise a system to check as far as possible that the detailed calculations have been made correctly, that every employee has been paid (including those who have just joined), that no-one who is not an employee (such as those who have just left), has been paid, and that the detailed calculations tally with the totals.

Another important system is that for *materials and purchase transactions*. This will often be linked into *systems for stock recording and control*, and *cost analysis*, and probably also to the *system of personal accounts in the purchases ledger*. The system must provide for the placing of orders for goods, checking that they are received in conformity with the terms of the order, and that the supplier's invoice is correct. It must record the receipt of each type of goods in the appropriate *inventory record*, which must include information about the main suppliers of that type of goods, its location in the warehouse, the minimum and maximum levels of stock which should normally be held, and other matters, as well as a record of the quantity and value of the inventory held. It is necessary to be able to check that all goods received have actually been ordered, and to know which of the goods which have been ordered have been received so far.

Similarly, *when goods are sold*, or removed from the warehouse for any other reason, it is necessary to know this, to be able to check that the transaction was authorised, and to know what action (such as re-ordering) needs to be taken. This knowledge is valuable in all types of business. For example, consider a supermarket store. Developments are now taking place in electronic point-of-sale systems, in which cash registers are linked to a mini-computer in the store. All the products on sale in the store carry labels bearing individual codes (which are likely soon to be printed on by the manufacturers). At the cash desk these details are keyed into the cash register for each item sold. This leads to the production of a detailed, itemised receipt for the customer, utilising price information stored in the computer. At the same time, a record of the number of each product sold is entered into the computer, which automatically updates the number of items which should be left on the shelves, indicating automatically when stocks are running lower than is desired. It can also produce summary listings of the sales made, analysed by product, or size of customer's purchase, or in other ways, as desired.

Sales on credit also require an extensive supporting system. The receipt of an order leads to several activities. The potential customer's credit-worthiness must be checked, as must the availability of the goods ordered. If they are not in the store or warehouse, arrangements must be made to buy or make them and to advise the customer. When they are available, they must be picked out, packed, and despatched from the warehouse to the customer, who must also be invoiced. The *invoicing system* requires that information about the goods, the order, and the customer is brought together.

There are many other possible illustrations of systems. For example, the need for *asset registers* is described in Chapter 22.

The need for these systems has been outlined in order to emphasise that the information which the bookkeeping entries record in the Ledger Accounts, and which is passed first through the books of original entry, had even earlier to be developed to reflect the activities of the business. In terms of the work involved, the operation of the necessary systems is far more than that of making the bookkeeping entries. The over-riding importance of the bookkeeping entries is that they establish a complete self-checking record which summarises the detailed records, and can in turn be further summarised and condensed to enable final accounts to be prepared, presenting the firm's performance and position in financial terms.

Flowcharts

A *flowchart* is a diagrammatic representation of the flow of data within the firm. One flowchart can replace extensive and complex verbal descriptions; it helps the understanding of the systems by showing them in diagram form; it is succinct; it provides a permanent record of how the system works, yet can be adapted easily. There are two main types of flowchart. These are the *systems flowchart*, and the *document flowchart*.

A *systems flowchart* gives an outline of the flow of data through a system, with little detail. It can be supplemented by more detailed *programme flowcharts*, particularly in the case of mechanised accounting systems. A very simple system flowchart for a payroll might look as follows on p. 139.

Each subsection of the system flowchart can be elaborated on a separate programme flowchart.

A *document flowchart* shows the routes followed by documents or reports from person to person or department to department. It gives an oversight of the paper flow involved in any system.

Consider the following illustration of the purchase of raw materials, based on an example given by Robert J. Thierauf in his book *Data Processing for Business and Management* (Wiley). This shows the flowchart of a large industrial business, involved in purchasing stocks of raw materials.

> ***Raw Material Purchases Illustration.*** Requisitions for raw material purchases are forwarded from the manufacturing departments by the respective plant foremen to the purchasing department (1). These form the basis for typing a six-part purchase order (2). One copy of the purchase order is sent to each of the following depart-

PAYROLL FLOWCHART

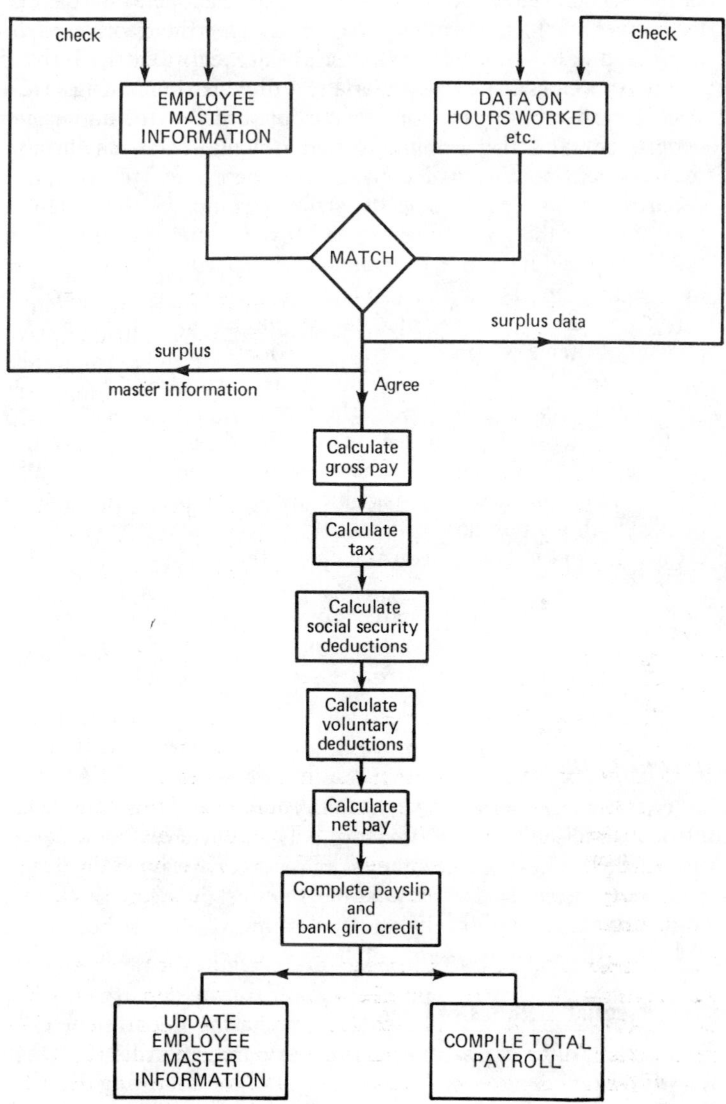

ments: manufacturing, receiving, and accounting (accounts payable section), while one copy is retained by the purchasing department. The original and duplicate orders are mailed directly to the outside vendor. One copy of the purchase order is returned by the vendor to the firm in order to acknowledge receipt of the order and date of future raw material shipments (3).

Upon receipt of the raw materials, a three-part receiving report form is prepared (4). One copy each is forwarded to the purchasing department and the accounting departments (accounts payable section), leaving the final copy as a file copy for the receiving department. The purchasing department compares the purchase order against the goods received as shown in the receiving report (5). The procedure allows the purchasing department to control all outstanding goods on order. Once the vendor invoices are received (6), both are forwarded to the purchasing department for review of items shipped, terms, discounts, discrepancies, and similar items with the corresponding purchase order and receiving report. After making changes on the invoice if applicable, one copy of the invoice is sent to the accounting department (accounts payable section) for auditing the work of the purchasing department. Here, the accounts payable clerk compares the vendor invoice with the purchase order and the receiving report (7). Next, the invoice amount is typed on a cheque authorisation (8). Two of the three copies are sent to the cashier's section. Periodically, cheques or bank giro credits are prepared from the accumulated authorisations (9). A copy of the authorisation, detailing the items purchased and now being paid for, is sent to the supplier, with the cheque if appropriate. (See p. 141.)

Internal Control

The term *internal control* refers to the system of financial and other controls established by the directors and management in order to carry on the business of the company in an orderly way, safeguard its assets, and ensure as far as possible that its financial and other records are accurate and reliable. It is a control against both error and fraud. It includes systems of both *internal check* and *internal audit*.

The essential methods of internal control are:

(*a*) a plan of organisation, particularly the allocation of staff duties;

RAW MATERIALS PURCHASES: DOCUMENT FLOWCHART

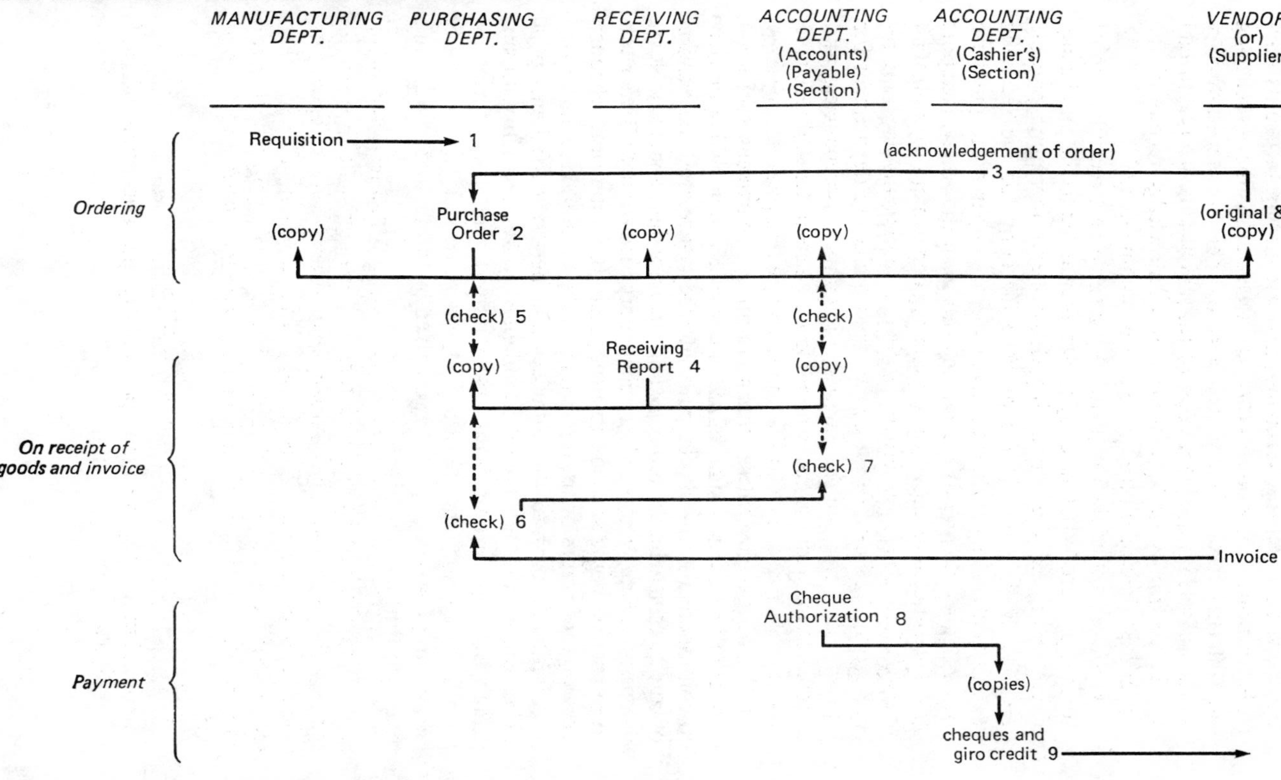

Based on material from *Data Processing for Business Management*, by J. Thierauf (Wiley).

(*b*) control procedures for the authorisation, recording, and custody of the objects of expenditure, including automatic internal check;
(*c*) managerial supervision and reviews, including internal audit.

The internal control aspects of *organisational planning* must provide for the subdivision of the firm's activities, the appointment of responsible employees, and the establishment of clear lines of responsibility.

Financial and accounting *control procedures* have three main purposes:

(*a*) to ensure that the firm's assets are kept under proper custody, and cannot be misapplied, whether deliberately or by mistake;
(*b*) to ensure that expenditures are properly authorised and accounted for;
(*c*) to ensure that all revenues receivable are collected and accounted for.

To help to achieve these aims there must be a suitable *division of duties*, and a proper system of *internal check*. This is the name given to continuous routine checks built into the system, so that the work of any person who is authorised to spend or receive resources is independently proved, or is complementary to somebody else's work. Such checks should lead towards the prevention, or at least the early detection, of errors or fraud.

A basic approach to internal check is to design all systems so that no one individual has complete independent responsibility for any transaction. For example, the calculation of wages, and their payment in cash, should not be done by the same person; there should be a division of the responsibilities involved in authorising, conducting, and recording a transaction. A complementary approach is to arrange for prompt and regular independent verification of a person's work, either by requiring reconciliation with independently ascertained control totals (as in using the control accounts described in Chapter 13), or by directly examining that particular person's records.

Managerial reviews, using monthly accounts, or special reports on matters such as inventory or cash balances, are also important. *Internal audit* is an extension of this review principle, by which independent staff examine the operations and records of the firm. In relation to accounting matters the main purpose of internal audit is to test whether the accounting system and the system of internal check are effectively designed and operated, and to recommend changes if necessary.

The system of internal control may be formally set out in larger companies, and may be quite informal in small businesses where the owner is continually and directly involved. Its practical extent and implementation depends on the risks caused by not having a system, matched against the cost of running one.

Cash is the most likely asset to be misappropriated, and it must be given special consideration. However, errors may occur anywhere and other forms of asset, such as stocks or tools or office equipment may also be liable to be misappropriated. There have been many instances also of payments being made to fictitious employees or suppliers, the proceeds being misappropriated. Care must therefore be exercised generally.

Summary

This chapter has suggested:

(1) that before bookkeeping entries can be made, extensive systems of data processing must be operated;
(2) that flowcharts are practical and convenient ways of describing these systems;
(3) that, in order to guard against fraud and error, it is necessary to develop systems of internal control.

EXERCISES 16

1. What is a flowchart?

2. Draw a system flowchart for a payroll system.

3. Describe in words any accounting system which you know and draw a document flowchart of it.

4. Distinguish between internal check and internal audit.

5. What are the aims of internal control?

6. What are the main methods of internal control?

7. Explain how control accounts contribute to a system of internal control.

17

The Columnar Petty Cash Book and the Imprest System

The growth of business may increase the pressure of work on the cashier so much that it may become necessary to relieve him of the duty of attending to the expenditure on small items that frequently occur in the ordinary routine of business. Minor expenses such as the cost of telegrams, parcel post, local rail and bus fares, small purchases of stationery, and similar items of minor expenditure, may be placed in the care of a clerk called the *petty cashier*. The petty cashier is given a cheque by the general cashier for a sum of money estimated to cover the normal expenditure of this nature during a week or a month. The general cashier posts the amount of the cheque to the credit column of the Bank Account in his Cash Book. The petty cashier enters the same sum on the debit side of the account he keeps in his *Petty Cash Book*. The Petty Cash Book thus contains a Ledger Account of petty (i.e. minor) expenses separated from the Ledger in a similar way that the main Cash Book is separated from the Ledger.

The expenditure of the petty cash is recorded on the credit side of the Petty Cash Account. Periodically, usually weekly or monthly, the debits corresponding to these credit entries are posted to the respective expense accounts in the Ledger to complete the double entry. The Petty Cash Account is balanced at the same time, and the balance indicates the amount of cash the petty cashier should have in hand.

The Petty Cash Book contains, therefore, a cash account in simple form, but relating only to the petty expenses occurring in the business or department.

The Columnar Petty Cash Book

If certain items of expenditure on the credit side of the Petty Cash Book recur frequently many repetitive postings have to be made to the Ledger Expense Accounts. There may be, for example, twelve instances during a week of the payment of local fares. It is quicker to

Petty Cash Book

RECEIPTS		CASH BOOK FOLIO	DATE	PARTICULARS	VOUCHER NO.	TOTAL PAYMENT		POSTAGES AND TELEGRAMS		CLEANING		STATIONERY		TRAVELLING EXPENSES		SUNDRIES		LEDGER		LEDGER FOLIO
£	p		19..			£	p	£	p	£	p	£	p	£	p	£	p	£	p	
20		24	Jan. 1	Cheque																
			,, 1	Postage stamps	1	5		5												
			,, 2	Travelling expenses: S. Smith	2	4								4						
			,, 3	String	3	1						1								
			,, 3	Coffee	4	1										1				
			,, 5	Cleaners	5	2				2										
			,, 6	Parcel post	6	2												2		72
				Total		15		5		2		1		4		1		2		
				Balance, c/d		5														
20						£20		L.	67	L.	84	L.	73	L.	77	L.	89	L.	89	
5			,, 8	Balance, b/d																

post the week's *total* for this item to the Travelling Expenses Account in the Ledger, as eleven entries will be saved. To do this requires that the credit side of the Petty Cash Book is analysed to find the totals of like expenses. A simple method is to make the analysis progressively as each item is entered.

On page 145 is a specimen page of a Petty Cash Book. It shows on the debit side the entry of the petty cash received, and on the credit side the expenditure, the amount of each item being entered in the column headed 'Total.' These two columns provide the ordinary debit and credit columns of any Ledger Account. There are, however, additional money columns on the credit side. These are added to provide space for a continuous analysis of the entries as they are made, but these additional columns are for memorandum purposes only. Each column carries its heading, and the headings correspond to the expense accounts in the Ledger. As an entry is made in the credit column it is repeated in the appropriate analysis column. The weekly, or monthly, totals of these analysis columns provide the amounts for posting to the expense accounts in the Ledger. The Ledger folio is entered below each total for reference and as an indication that the posting has been made. The ordinary debit and credit columns are balanced in the usual way, and the balance carried down to begin the new period.

The analysis columns are, of course, adaptable to the special needs of a business. How many columns and what the particular headings should be is for experience to decide. One column headed 'Ledger' is useful for the items that are of infrequent occurrence, the appropriate Ledger Account being posted from that column.

The Imprest System

A common procedure is to hand to the petty cashier a cheque for the first sum sufficient to cover the usual petty cash expenditure for a week or a month. When the Petty Cash Book is checked and posted, the petty cashier is given a cheque to reimburse him for the amount expended during the period. He therefore starts the next period with the same sum as he started the last. The procedure is followed week by week, or month by month, as the case may be. This is called the *Imprest system* of petty cash, and may be combined with the columnar method of recording the petty expenditure. In the specimen page (page 145) the starting balance, called the *Imprest* (or *float*) is £20. During the week the sum of £15 is expended and at the beginning of the next week the cashier refunds that amount. The balance brought down to begin the next period is again £20. Whether the refund takes place at the end or at the beginning of the week is a matter for individual convenience, so long as the method chosen is consistently adhered to. In this example the *Petty Cash Account* would appear as below. The analysis columns have been omitted in this illustration as they would be the same as on page 145.

Petty Cash Account

RECEIPTS	CASH BOOK FOLIO	DATE	PARTICULARS	VOUCHER NO.	TOTAL PAYMENT
£ p		19..			£ p
20	24	Jan. 1	Cheque		
		,, 1	Postage stamps	1	5
		,, 2	Travelling expenses: S. Smith	2	4
		,, 3	String	3	1
		,, 3	Coffee	4	1
		,, 5	Cleaners	5	2
		,, 6	Parcel post	6	2
			Total		15
15	26	,, 8	Cheque		
			Balance carried down		20
35					35
20		,, 8	Balance brought down		

An alternative method of treating petty cash is to regard the Petty Cash Book as a memorandum book only, and not as a Ledger Account or part of the double entry system. It would then be kept by the petty cashier to record his expenditure for information purposes and as a check on his expenditure. Under this method the Petty Cash Book for the example given above would show no change. What would occur is that the original sum of £20 for Petty Cash would be credited in the Cash Book as usual, but the debit entry would be in a Petty Cash Account in the General Ledger. The expenditure for the week as shown by the Petty Cash Book, would be credited to this account and debited to the respective expense accounts. Then the amount of the 'imprest' to reimburse the petty cashier would be credited in the Cash Book and debited to the Petty Cash Account.

This account is then closed and the balance carried down for the next weekly period.

In either case the balance of petty cash in hand should not be overlooked when a Trial Balance is extracted.

Vouchers

The petty cashier should be instructed that bills must be obtained for all payments and, if bills are not available, as in the case of travelling expenses, the member of staff who receives the money should sign a petty cash *voucher* or slip acknowledging receipt of the sum. The Petty Cash Book is usually checked against the vouchers, and the balance in hand inspected at the end of each week or month at the time of reimbursement of the amount expended.

EXERCISES 17

1. Write up a Petty Cash Book from the following particulars, and balance the book so that it will be ready for the cashier:

Jan. 16. Cash in hand, £10.
„ 17. Postage stamps, £2.
„ 18. Bus fares, £1·19.
„ 19. Labels, £1·05.
„ 20. Window cleaning, £1·02.

2. (*a*) What is the use of the Petty Cash Book?
(*b*) Enter the following in the Petty Cash Book, using separate columns for: (1) Postages and telegrams; (2) Carriage; (3) Stationery.
Balance the book as at 10th January.

			£
Jan.	4.	Balance in hand	15·00
„	4.	Paid for postage stamps	1·50
„	5.	Paid for stationery	3·50
„	5.	Paid for carriage	0·85
„	6.	Paid for postage stamps	1·25
„	8.	Paid for stationery	1·50
„	8.	Received from the chief cashier	8·60

U.L.C.I. (adapted)

3. Rule a suitable Petty Cash Book with analyis columns for Postage and Telegrams, Stationery, Travelling Expenses, Carriage, and Sundry Office Expenses, and enter the following transactions:

July	1.	Petty cash balance in hand, £3.
		Received £3 cash to make Imprest up to £6.
,,	2.	Paid bus fare, £0·24; Postages, £0·32; ink, £0·22.
,,	3.	Paid postages, £0·70; bus fares, £0·75.
,,	4.	Paid window cleaner, £0·75.
,,	5.	Office cleaner's wages, £2·15.
,,	6.	Bus fares, £0·85.

Show the balance in hand on 6th July.

4. Explain briefly the working of the Imprest Petty Cash System. Give as an illustration a ruling (with three analysis columns), and enter therein the following items:

			£
Jan.	1.	Balance in hand (float)	20·00
,,	5.	Paid for postage stamps	1·50
,,	7.	,, ,, telegrams	0·53
,,	10.	Paid for office tea, etc.	0·95
,,	14.	,, ,, sundry cash purchases of goods for resale	8·37
,,	20.	Paid for stationery	1·12
,,	23.	,, ,, postages	0·20
,,	30.	,, ,, subscription to trade periodical	2·10
,,	31.	Received reimbursement for the month's expenditure to restore the float.	

R.S.A.

5. On 21st February, 19.., you are given a petty cash Imprest of £15 out of which to pay small expenses during the week. Write up a Petty Cash Book (no analysis columns required) showing (*a*) the Imprest received on 21st February, (*b*) four items of expenditure made during the week, amounting in all to £8·60, and (*c*) the amount added to the petty cash balance on 28th February 19... Rule off and bring down the balance.

R.S.A.

6. Rule a Petty Cash Book with four analysis columns for Postages and Stationery, Travelling Expenses, Carriage, and Office Expenses, and enter up the following transactions. The book is kept on the Imprest system, the amount of the Imprest being £50.

Jan.	4.	Petty cash in hand, £7·50.
		Received cash to make up the Imprest.
		Bought stamps, £7·50.

Jan. 5. Paid railway fare, £0·95, bus fares, £0·50, telegrams, £4·50. Bought shorthand notebooks for office, £2·50.
„ 6. Paid carriage on small parcels, £4·38; railway fares, £4·25; bought envelopes, £1·12.
„ 8. Paid for repairs to typewriter, £2·62; paid carrier's account for December, £6·40.
„ 8. Paid office cleaner, £6.

Balance the Petty Cash Book as on 9th January, 19.., and bring down the balance.

18

Checking the Bank Balance: Bank Reconciliation Statements

Usually most, if not all, of a firm's cash is held at the bank. The amount of cash there may be ascertained from two sources; either from the balance of the Bank Account in the Cash Book or from the Bank Statement. The one is the office record from the firm's point of view of dealings with the bank cash; the other is the bank's own record. These records should correspond, or if they do not, it should be a simple matter to account for the disagreement. The *Bank Statement* is obtained from the bank at regular intervals for checking purposes to ensure that no error has crept into either the Cash Book or the Bank Statement, but it is not unusual for the Cash Book and Bank Statement balances to disagree. The disagreement arises from a difference in procedure. The firm's Cash Book is entered up daily, so the entries will be made the same day that either a cheque is despatched to pay an account, or receipts are paid into the firm's bank. The bank, however, does not necessarily enter these payments and receipts immediately in their books. It has to wait until the firm's cheque is presented for payment by the person who received it. Similarly some of the firm's receipts (if they are in the form of cheques) may take some days to clear. The entries in the bank's books are therefore usually made some days later than those in the firm's books.

The Bank Statement may, therefore, sometimes not agree with the balance in the firm's Cash Book for the following reasons:

(1) Cheques drawn and entered in the Cash Book may not have been presented to the bank for payment.

(2) Cheques paid into the bank and entered to the debit of the Bank Account in the Cash Book have not been entered into the account in the Bank's Ledger and, therefore, are not shown in the Bank Statement.

The following illustration should make these points clear.

Example 17. At 31st December the balance at bank as shown by S. Morgan's Cash Book was £207, whereas his Bank Statement showed a balance of £217.

The items in the Bank Statement are usually checked against the Cash Book, and the items not ticked in the Cash Book are those which do not appear in the Bank Statement. The latter items appear in the Cash Book as below:

Cash Book

(Bank Columns Only)

19..			£	19..			£
Dec. 31	P. Johnson		10	Dec. 29	P. Jackson		15
				,, 30	P. Thompson		5

Jackson's and Thompson's cheques, entered in Morgan's Cash Book as paid to them, have not yet been presented by their bankers to Morgan's bank for payment. The bank, therefore, has at the moment £20 more in Morgan's account than is shown by his Cash Book.

Johnson's cheque was paid into the bank by Morgan but had not yet been entered in the account in the banker's Ledger by the date to which the Bank Statement is made up. The bank balance as shown by the Bank Statement is therefore £10 less than the Cash Book shows.

Within a day or so the two cheques may be presented for payment, and the bank will be able to record in the Bank Statement the payments to Thompson and Jackson, as well as the deposit of Johnson's cheque.

At any time it may be necessary to reconcile the Cash Book and Bank Statement balances. It is especially necessary at the close of a trading period. As a record of the reasons for the apparent discrepancy between the balances, a statement showing the reasons is made in the Cash Book similar to the one following.

Sometimes the difference between the balances is partly attributable to items appearing in the Bank Statement, such as bank charges for certain services, which have not been entered in the Cash Book. These points are discussed in the next chapter.

There may be items such as bank charges, receipt by the bank of dividends, and payments by the bank on standing orders, in the Bank Statement but not in the Cash Book. (A *standing order* is an instruction by the firm to the banker to pay a stated amount to a stated person on stated dates, e.g. monthly or annually.) Such discrepancies

Reconciliation Statement
of Cash Book and Bank Statement Balances

31st December, 19. .

		£
Bank Statement balance		217
Deduct Cheques not yet presented		
P. Jackson	£15	
P. Thompson	£ 5	
	—	20
		197
Add Cheque not yet credited:		
P. Johnson	£10	
	—	10
Cash Book balance		£207

can be dealt with by adding back the bank charges and payments on standing orders to the balance as shown by the Bank Statement and deducting any dividends received by the bank and not yet entered in the Cash Book. It is, however, a better and more practical procedure to correct the Cash Book balance by entering these items in the Cash Book and ascertaining a corrected balance. A Bank Reconciliation Statement can then be made reconciling the corrected balance with the balance as shown on the Bank Statement. This is illustrated in the following example.

Example 18. On 31st December 19. ., the balance at bank as shown by Boyd's Cash Book was £517, whereas the Bank Statement showed a credit balance of £567. Comparison of the Cash Book with the Bank Statement showed the following discrepancies.

		£
(i)	Cheques drawn and not yet presented for payment	214
(ii)	Cheques paid into bank on 31st December and not appearing in the Bank Statement	196
(iii)	Items shown in the Bank Statement but not yet entered in the Cash Book:	
	Bank charges	4
	Payment of insurance premium on 2nd December on bank standing order	26
	Dividends collected by the bank	62

Enter the items shown under (iii) in the Cash Book to show a correct cash book balance and then prepare a Bank Reconciliation Statement.

Cash Book

			£				£
Dec. 31	Balance		517	Dec. 1	Insurance		26
	Dividends		62		Bank charges		4
					Balance	c/d	549
			£579				£579
,, 31	Balance	b/d	549				

Bank Reconciliation Statement

31st December 19..

	£	£	£
Balance as Bank Statement	567		
Add cheques paid in and not yet credited	196	763	
Less cheques drawn and not yet presented for payment		214	549

The student must always remember that, although a balance in a business's favour at the bank will be recorded as a *debit* balance in its books, on the Bank Statements the balance will appear as a *credit* balance. This is because the Bank Statement shows the business's position in relation to the bank from the *bank's* point of view. Therefore the business's bank account shows the bank as a debtor and the Bank Statement shows the business as a creditor.

EXERCISES 18

1. Draw up a Bank Reconciliation Statement from the following particulars:

	£
Cash at bank as shown by the Bank Statement on June 30th	293
Cheques drawn and entered in the Cash Book, but not yet presented for payment	54
Cheques paid into bank, but not entered in the Bank Statement	72
The debit balance of the Bank Account in the Cash Book was	311

2. From the following particulars draw up a Bank Reconciliation Statement:

		£
Dec. 31.	Bank Statement balance at bank	142
,, ,,	Cash Book balance at bank	214
	Cheques drawn and entered in the Cash Book, but not presented for payment	32
	Cheques received and paid into bank, but not yet entered in the Bank Statement	104

3. F. Smith's Cash Book showed a balance of cash at bank of £327·95 on December 31st. His Bank Statement showed an overdraft of £267·89 on that date. The difference arose as follows:

A cheque for £32·94, drawn by F. Smith, had not been presented for payment; £616·40 received on December 31st, was not credited by the bank until January 1st; the bank had charged him £12·38 interest, which was not entered in the Cash Book.

Prepare the Reconciliation Statement.

R.S.A.

4. On 30th June, 19. ., D.L.'s Cash Book showed a debit balance of £393·40 in the Bank Account. The Bank Statement of the same date showed a credit balance of £689·55.

On comparing the Cash Book with the Bank Statement the following differences were found:

(i) Cheques £76·45 had been paid into bank on 30th June but were not credited by the bank until the following day.
(ii) Cheques £284·35 had been drawn but not yet presented for payment.
(iii) Bank charges £5·50 appeared on the Bank Statement but not in the Cash Book.
(iv) A standing order £5 to Trade Protection Society, payable on 24th June had been paid by the bank but not entered in the Cash Book.
(v) Dividends £98·75 collected and credited by the bank did not appear in the Cash Book.

(*a*) Make additional entries in the Cash Book to show the balance which it should have shown on 30th June 1963.

(*b*) Prepare a Bank Reconciliation Statement as on 30th June, 19. .

A.E.B., G.C.E. 'O' Level

5. On 31st May, 19. ., the debit balance in J. Carr & Sons Bank Account as shown in the Cash Book was £370·40. The Bank Statement at that date showed a credit balance of £409·50.

On checking the Bank Statement against the Cash Book the following differences were found:

(*a*) Interest due on Westshire County Council Loan £36·75 had been collected by the bank during the month but not entered in the Cash Book.
(*b*) A standing order £12·85 payable each 20th May for fire insurance premiums had been paid by the bank but not entered in the Cash Book.
(*c*) Two cheques drawn on 30th May and entered in the Cash Book, one for £16·35 and one for £84·22 had not yet been presented for payment.
(*d*) On 31st May a cheque for £85·37 had been entered in the Cash Book and paid into bank after the Bank Statement had been collected from the bank.

Show your calculation of the balance that should appear in the Cash Book and then prepare a Bank Reconciliation Statement.

A.E.B., G.C.E. 'O' Level

19

Various Banking Matters

References to a bank account usually mean the trader's *current account* with a bank. The bank accepts the deposit of money from its customer, but is liable to be called upon to repay all or part on demand. The cheque is the form that the demand takes, and the bank may be ordered by cheque to repay the owner or to pay a sum to a third party. Because of this liability for repayment on demand, banks do not as a rule allow interest on the balances on current accounts. If they do allow interest, then a charge is made for the services rendered in connection with the account. A customer may, however, have a balance at the bank larger than he is likely to need for use in the immediate future. To withdraw this temporary excess and to invest it in shares or other securities might be more profitable from an interest-bearing point of view, but the sum is not then immediately available should it be required. In such cases the customer may ask the bank to transfer a certain sum from the current account to a *deposit account*. The sum so placed 'on deposit' cannot be withdrawn on demand but only after the expiration of an agreed length of notice. The bank is willing to grant interest for sums placed in deposit accounts, as it has the use of the customer's money for a definite period. The usual length of notice of withdrawal is seven days, but the customer may agree to give longer notice, say one month, in which case the bank may grant a slightly higher rate of interest. If immediate withdrawal, without notice is necessary, then the bank may charge the current deposit rate of interest for seven days on the amount withdrawn.

The Bank Account in the Cash Book is the trader's current account at the bank. If he asks for a sum to be transferred from his current account to a deposit account an entry must be made in the Cash Book as his current account is affected, and a new account, the *Deposit Account*, must be opened in the Ledger to keep a record of the dealings with the amounts placed on deposit.

Example 19. M. Tomkin's balance on current account at the bank at 1st January, 19 . . , is £800. He arranges for £500 to be placed on deposit.

Cash Book

Dr. (Bank columns only) *Cr.*

			£				£
19..				19..			
Jan. 1	Balance	b/d	800	Jan. 1	Deposit Account	34	500

In the Ledger the record will appear as follows:

Deposit Account

(London Bank Limited)

			£				£
19..				19..			
Jan. 1	Cash	C.B.	500				

Example 20. M. Tomkin gives notice of withdrawal of £500 on deposit to expire 1st July.

The entries for this will be the reverse of those shown above. Credit the Deposit Account in the Ledger, and debit the Bank Account in the Cash Book, as the bank will place that sum again in the current account where it will be available to be drawn on by cheque.

Interest on Deposit

The interest rate on deposits varies from time to time as long-term interest rates fluctuate in accordance with general economic conditions. Assuming that it is 6 per cent per annum, and interest is payable half-yearly, Tomkin, in the above example, becomes entitled to £15 for interest on £500 for six months.

The bank pays this to Tomkin by crediting £15 to his deposit account, thereby increasing his balance on deposit account by that amount. It will be noted by the bank in the Bank Statement for the deposit account, and that will be the first intimation to Tomkin of it.

Entries must be made in respect of it in Tomkin's books, so on finding the entry in the Bank Statement, it is entered to the debit of the Deposit Account and credited to a new account, headed *Interest on Deposit Account* as a gain. The balance of the Interest on Deposit Account is transferred at the close of the trading period to the credit of Profit and Loss Account.

Alternatively, the bank may have been instructed by Tomkin to credit the Deposit account interest to his current account. In that case it will first appear on the current account bank statement. In his own books Tomkin would debit the Cash Book, and credit Interest on Deposit Account. Interest on deposit account being entered in the Bank Statement and not being shown in the Cash Book may be one of the reasons for non-agreement of the Bank Statement and Cash Book bank balances. If so, it will be shown in the Reconciliation Statement, but it is seldom that the necessity arises, as the Cash Book is usually kept open until the amount of interest is known.

Bank Loans and Overdrafts

Traders sometimes require larger sums of money than they at the moment possess to finance business deals or to tide them over difficult periods of trading. They may, in such circumstances, have to ask their bankers for the financial assistance that they require. As the banker makes his profits largely from the interest on advances made to customers, he is usually willing to help, provided adequate security is given for repayment. Bankers' advances take the form of *loans* or *overdrafts*. A loan is the advance of a fixed sum to a customer for a definite period. The banker's procedure is to credit the amount of the loan to the customer's current account and to debit a Loan Account for the customer in the bank's Ledger. The customer's current account balance is thereby increased by the amount of the loan, and can be drawn upon by cheque. The trader will record the loan in his own books by debiting the Cash Book with the amount, and by crediting a *Bank Loan Account* in his Ledger; the entries on repayment being the reverse of these. The Bank Loan Account is shown as a liability in the Balance Sheet. If it is for not more than one year's duration it is shown as a current liability.

Interest is charged on the full amount of the loan whether all or only part is withdrawn from the current account. Such interest is a bank charge, and the bank recoups itself by debiting the amount of the interest in the customer's current account, thereby reducing the bank balance by that sum. The trader credits his Bank Account in the Cash Book with the interest, and debits the amount to an *Interest on Loan Account* or *Bank Charges Account* for transfer eventually to the Profit and Loss Account.

In other cases a trader may prefer to obtain permission to *overdraw* his account as a temporary expedient. This means that he is allowed to draw out more money than he has in his bank account. A limit is fixed by the bank to the amount by which the account may be overdrawn. This is known as an *overdraft limit*.

Every business has certain weekly and monthly outgoings such as wages and salaries to meet. The income may come irregularly though the total over the year is enough to cover all commitments. In such cases a standing permission to overdraw up to a certain limit is a definite advantage for which interest is willingly paid by the trader.

No special entries are required to record an overdraft – it happens as and when more is paid out by the bank than is to the customer's credit.

In the illustration below, there is on 1st Jan. a bank balance in hand of £100. Payment by cheque of £300 to J. Jones immediately puts the trader in debt to the bank for £200. This is the overdraft. Note that the balance representing the overdraft appears on the opposite side of the account to that on which the normal bank balance appears. The overdraft is shown as a current liability in the Balance Sheet, and there is then no bank balance among the assets unless the trader has another bank account.

Cash Book

(Bank columns only)

19..			£	19..			£
Jan. 1	Balance	b/d	100	Jan. 3	J. Jones		300
,, 4	Balance (Overdraft)	c/d	200				
			£300				£300
				,, 4	Balance	b/d	200

The trader having an overdraft at the time of balancing his books, starts the new period with a credit entry in the bank columns. Any cash or cheques received and paid into the bank will automatically reduce the overdraft, and any further cheques paid out will increase it.

The bank charges interest on the varying balance only, debiting it in the current account as in the case of interest on loans. The trader makes the entries for the interest charged by a credit entry in his Cash Book, and a debit entry in the Bank Charges or Interest on Overdraft Account.

When a bank makes an advance by loan or overdraft it usually requires from its customers some form of *security* for repayment. The bank may be satisfied with the guarantee of a third person, or the customer may assign a life assurance policy, or he may deposit share or stock certificates or debentures with the bank. In other cases the customer may deposit the title deeds to land, or shipping documents of title to goods, such as Bills of Lading. Securities so deposited are termed *collateral security* for the overdraft or loan. The bank takes no action to realise their value except in the event of the customer being unable to either pay interest or repay the loan. Even then the bank may prefer to extend the period of the loan.

Bank Charges

Banks make charges for certain services, some of which are referred to in later chapters. The bank usually pays itself by debiting the charge against the customer's account, and shows the amount in the customer's Bank Statement. In addition, therefore, to the need to examine the Bank Statement periodically to check its accuracy, there is the need to ensure that all entries of this nature appearing in the Bank Statement are duly entered in the accounts.

Bank Giro Credit System

Instead of drawing individual cheques for each creditor a trader may supply his banker with a list of creditors to be paid, and the name and branch of the bank at which each creditor keeps his account. *Bank Giro Credit Slips* (or *Schedules*) will be supplied by the banker for this purpose. The banker will then arrange to transfer the appropriate amounts to the banks named, to be credited to the accounts of the creditors and will inform the trader when this is done. The trader gives the bank one cheque to cover the total amount. The banker makes a charge for his services which will be included in the bank charges appearing on the trader's Bank Statement.

This system is a great convenience to traders who, instead of drawing and posting numerous cheques, simply supply the bank with a list of payments to be made. It is, of course, necessary for the trader to know the bank at which his creditor keeps his account, but it is becoming increasingly the custom to give this information on

Invoices and Statements of Account to facilitate payment by this method. Bank Giro Credit Slips for the use of debtors may be incorporated as a detachable part of an invoice. The system is also particularly appropriate for the payment of wages and salaries.

When a trader adopts this method of payment the total amount transferred by the bank will appear as a single item on the Bank Statement. The trader may enter it also in his Cash Book as a single total, keeping a separate list of amounts paid to each creditor, and post the relevant amounts from this list to the debit side of each creditor's account. Alternatively, the trader may enter in his Cash Book the names of all creditors who have been paid, with the amounts paid to each creditor, in the 'Details' column of his Cash Book and the total amount paid, corresponding to the amount on the Bank Statement, in the 'Bank' column. Similarly, the total wage and salary payment will be credited in the Cash Book and debited to the Wages Account, the details in respect of each employee being produced by the payroll system and kept in the Wages and Salaries records.

Direct Debits

A recent development of the standing order system is the system of *direct debiting*. A trader may authorise a supplier to claim sums from the trader's bank which will definitely become due to the supplier, but the amounts of which are not known at the time of making the arrangement. For example, a trader may agree to pay his annual bill for rates in this way. The rating authority will advise him of the amount which it proposes to charge him in the particular year. He will then pick up the entry on his bank statement in due course, and will make the appropriate entries in his own books, i.e. debit rates account, credit bank account.

The trader can cancel a direct debit arrangement and change to payment by cheque at any time, as he can also in the case of standing orders.

Layout of the Bank Statement

Bank statements are normally presented with the debit and credit column adjacent, as in the Journal. In addition a third column is added immediately to the right of the credit column. It is used to show the running balance on the account at the end of each day. For example, Bonaparte has an overdraft of £10 000 on 1st June 19... During June he pays in cheques from Cole, Smith & Moore, and pays out cheques to Fuel Supply Ltd. and M. Patel. His bank statement would appear as follows:

Bank Statement—J. Bonaparte

	Particulars	*Dr.*	*Cr.*	*Balance*
19..		£	£	£
June 1.	Balance			10 000 *Dr.*
5.	R. Cole		3 000	7 000 *Dr.*
10.	Fuel Supply Ltd.	700		7 700 *Dr.*
20.	P. Smith		800	6 900 *Dr.*
25.	M. Patel	1 200		8 100 *Dr.*
29.	M. Moore		3 500	4 600 *Dr.*

The clarity of the presentation is self-evident.

This form of layout is also entirely suitable for a cash book, and indeed for Ledger Accounts generally. It is particularly appropriate when the accounting system is mechanised; the earliest forms of bookkeeping machines, described in Chapter 31, used it. The principles of double entry bookkeeping remain exactly the same. It is only the appearance of the Ledger Accounts which changes.

As banks have increasingly mechanised their procedures they have given less detail in the Particulars column, giving the numbers of the cheques paid out instead of the names of the payees.

EXERCISES 19

1. M. F. Ford is in business trading in china and glassware. On 1st June his financial position was as follows:

	£
Cash in hand	15
Bank overdraft	250
Stock	1 400
Debtors:	
J. Austin	70
T. Rover	78
Creditors:	
K. Lanchester	90
M. Riley	80
Fixtures and fittings	200

Open Ford's books to record his position and enter the following transactions:

June 1. Sold glassware for cash, £40, and paid takings into bank.
" 3. Paid in cash, sundry expenses, £12.
" 5. Sold to W. Morris, china, £50.
" 7. Bought from M. Riley, china and glass invoiced at £50, less 10% trade discount.
" 8. J. Austin paid his account by cheque, deducting 5% cash discount.
" 10. Cashed cheque for £25 and paid sundry expenses in cash, £10.
" 15. Sold for cash, £12, unwanted shop fittings.
" 17. Paid K. Lanchester's account by cheque less 5% cash discount.
" 19. Cash sales paid into bank, £84.

Take out Trial Balance.

Prepare Trading and Profit and Loss Accounts and a Balance Sheet as at 19th June. Stock on hand at that date was valued at £1 325.

2. M. Gardiner's position on 14th June was as below:

	£
Cash in hand	25
Cash at bank	1 050
Stock	1 500
Debtors:	
C. Smart	50
R. Sharp	40
Creditor:	
J. Cutler	70
Capital	2 595

Open M. Gardiner's books to record his position, and enter the following transactions:

June 15. Obtained loan from bank of £3 000 at 6% per annum to assist purchase of machinery.
" 18. Purchased new machinery, paying by cheque £3 800.
" 20. Bought fittings on credit from Mint & Co., £150.
" 21. Paid sundry expenses by cheque, £20.
" 30. Paid carriage in cash, £10.
" 30. Cash takings, paid to bank, £133.
" 30. Bank charged interest on loan, £7.

Take out Trial Balance. Prepare Trading and Profit and Loss Accounts, and a Balance Sheet as at 30th June. Stock on hand at that date, £1 400.

3. From the following Trial Balance of A. Dealer, prepare Trading and Profit and Loss Accounts for the year ended 31st December, 19. ., and Balance Sheet as at that date.

The stock on hand at 31st December was valued at £5 700.

Trial Balance.

31st December, 19. .

	£	£
Purchases	55 850	
Stock (1st January)	6 500	
Carriage on sales	400	
Discounts allowed	1 450	
Bank interest and charges	150	
Sales		70 000
Returns outwards		1 380
Discounts received		1 620
Returns inwards	1 370	
Bank overdraft		3 440
Rent and rates	1 930	
Sundry debtors and creditors	6 800	3 660
A. Dealer: Capital		4 150
A. Dealer: Drawings	4 500	
Cash in hand	550	
Salaries	4 750	
	£84 250	£84 250

U.L.C.I. (adapted)

4. State, very briefly, the object of preparing:

(*a*) A Trial Balance.
(*b*) A Trading Account.
(*c*) A Profit and Loss Account.
(*d*) A Balance Sheet

R.S.A.

5. The Balance Sheet of J. Abbots, a radio dealer, was:

Balance Sheet.

31st December, 19..

	£	£		£	£
Capital:			*Fixed Assets:*		
At 1st Jan. 19..	3 400		Leasehold Premises		5 950
Add Profit for 19..	3 167		Fixtures and fittings		517
		6 567			6 467
Loan from S. Roberts		4 200			
Current Liabilities:			*Current Assets:*	£	
Creditors:			Stock	4 120	
J. Gibbs	500		Debtors:		
T. Orrett	96		R. Wright	190	
		596	T. Tomkins	270	
				460	
			Bank	275	
			Cash	41	
					4 896
		£11 363			£11 363

His order book shows that during January 19.. he ordered and received delivery on credit of the following goods for resale:

Jan. 3. From A. Robbins, 5 'Excel' speakers at £40 each, less 10% trade discount.
,, 12. From B. Fearn & Co. Ltd., batteries, value £220.
,, 26. From Music Centres Ltd., 2 music centres at £480 each.

His other transactions during January were:

Jan. 18. Sold for cash, £60, one of the speakers received on 3rd January. Found one of the remaining four speakers faulty, and returned it to Robbins.
,, 19. R. Wright paid by cheque the mount owing by him, less 5% cash discount, which was allowed.
,, 20. Paid by cheque to S. Roberts, a half-year's interest at 6% on the loan from him.
,, 28. Purchased new fixtures for use in shop and paid for them by cheque, £240.
,, 31. Received an account £14 by cheque from Tomkins. Paid sundry expenses in cash, £50.

You are required to open a set of books for Abbots, and record therein his position on 1st January, 19.., and his transactions for January, using proper subsidiary books to enter the transactions and posting from these to the Ledger. Balance the accounts, and draw up a Trial Balance on 31st January.

20

Reserves and Provisions

A matter for consideration in preparing the Final Accounts of a business is the extent to which the trading profits disclosed are to be treated as available for distribution to the proprietors and, as an act of financial prudence, what portion of the profits should be retained in the business. To retain or to set aside profits is to create a *reserve*, and the purpose of such action may be *general* or *specific*.

Reserves

Reserves for *general* purposes are voluntary appropriations of profit. The motive may be to strengthen the financial position of the business by increasing the working capital or it may be, for example, to institute and maintain pension or provident funds for the benefit of employees. These reserves are dealt with further in Chapter 23 on the Final Accounts. The profits retained may be invested in many different kinds of asset. Except in cases such as the pension fund mentioned above, reserves are not normally held in the form of cash. Reserves are not emergency supplies of cash put aside for a rainy day. They are the past profits which have been ploughed back into the business to promote growth.

Provisions

Where there is a definite charge against profits to meet known liabilities, the exact amount of which may nevertheless be uncertain, or to meet expenses already incurred, such as outstanding wages, rent, and travellers' commission, the requirement is *specific* and is now known as a *provision*. Provisions, therefore represent charges against profits for expenses incurred and not yet paid, while reserves represent allocation or appropriations of profit for general or particular purposes.

Bad Debts

Provisions may be made to meet certain contingencies (such as *bad debts*) which may arise but the actual amount of which is in doubt.

In order to ensure that the Balance Sheet presents a true and fair view of the financial position it is necessary to review the item 'Sundry Debtors'. Examination of the debtors' accounts included in this total may disclose that certain debts are actually 'bad debts' which are irrecoverable, and that others are *doubtful debts*. To include these in the item 'Sundry Debtors' in the Balance Sheet as if all were equally good debts would give a false value to the asset.

Bad debts must be written off the books either during or at the end of the trading period in which they are recognised to be bad. As they represent actual losses, they must be charged against profits in the Profit and Loss Account. For example, a debtor may fail and, having no assets, the whole of his debt may be irrecoverable. Another debtor for, say £40, may compound with his creditors and offer £0·30 in the £. He would pay £12, and the remaining £28 would have to be written off as a bad debt. A debtor may be declared bankrupt and his debts paid by instalments as and when his assets are realised. If his debt is £100, there may be a payment of £25, representing a dividend in the bankruptcy of £0·25 in the £. A second and equal instalment may be received, to be followed by a third and final instalment of £0·25 in the £. As it is known that no further payment will be received, the remainder must be written off as bad and irrecoverable. If the debtor is a limited liability company it can not be declared bankrupt, but if it is unable to pay its debts it may be placed in receivership or liquidation. The effect is much the same as far as the purposes of this Chapter are concerned.

Example 21. On 1st November, J. Watson, who owes £100 for goods supplied on March 10th, is declared bankrupt. Received cheque for £75, being first and final dividend at £0·75 in the £.

J. Watson

19..			£	19..			£
Mar. 10	Goods	S.B.	100	No. 1	Cash	C.B.	75
				,, 1	Bad Debts A/c.	J.	25
			£100				£100

Received notice of the failure of B. Burton & Co., who owe £40 for goods supplied on June 20th. There being no assets, the whole of the debt is written off as bad.

B. Burton & Co.

19..			£	19..			£
June 70	Goods	S.B.	40	Nov. 1	Bad Debts A/c.	J.	40

Journal *Dr.* *Cr.*

			Dr.	Cr.
Nov. 1	Bad Debts Account J. Watson being balance of account written off as bad		25	25
	Bad Debts Account B. Burton & Co. being debt written off on their failure. No assets available.		40	40

Bad Debts Account

19..			£	19..			£
Nov. 1	J. Watson	J.	25	Dec. 31	Transfer to Profit and Loss A/c.		65
,, 1	B. Burton & Co.	J.	40				
			£65				£65

If payment is received later for a debt written off as bad, cash is debited and a corresponding credit entry is made to Bad Debts Account. The payment is treated in the books as an unexpected gain, and is ultimately transferred to the credit of the Profit and Loss Account.

Provisions for Doubtful Debts

Other debts may be doubtful, being considered so either from known facts about the debtor or from the debt being one of long standing. As doubt exists about some of the accounts it is prudent to adjust the item 'Sundry Debtors' accordingly. A provision is made for doubtful debts, which has the effect of reducing the profits available for distribution by the amount provided. The sum to be provided may be arrived at by a scrutiny of all the accounts to find the total of doubtful debts, or a sum calculated as a percentage of the total debtors is set aside. Past experience is a safe guide to the percentage advisable as a provision, or an estimate may be made for the current year and revised in subsequent years in the light of experience.

The action taken is to debit the amount decided upon to the Profit and Loss Account, and to make a corresponding credit entry in a Provision for Doubtful Debts Account. On closing the books a credit balance remains on the latter account. As a provision it resembles a liability, but instead of its being shown on the left-hand side of the Balance Sheet, it is brought into relation with the asset Sundry Debtors, and shown as a deduction from it.

Example 22. The Sundry Debtors amount to £5 000 at 31st December, and it is decided to create a provision for doubtful debts equal to 5% of this total. Show the entries required.

Journal

			Dr.	*Cr.*
19..			£	£
Dec. 31	Profit and Loss Account		250	
	Provision for Doubtful Debts Account			250
	being provision of 5% reserve on Sundry Debtors at this date.			

Provision for Doubtful Debts

			£	19..			£
				Dec. 31	Profit and Loss A/c.	J.	250

The debit entry is made to the Profit and Loss Account, and the item appears on the assets side of the Balance Sheet as below:

	£	£
Sundry Debtors	5 000	
less Provision for Doubtful Debts	250	4 750

Actual bad debts which occur are written off to a Bad Debts Account as shown earlier in this chapter. That is the common practice and is the simplest. As a provision exists they may, of course, be written off against it, the debit entry being to the Provision for Doubtful Debts Account instead of to a Bad Debts Account. It would then be necessary to restore the provision to its appropriate amount by charging a further sum, equal to the bad debts, against Profit and Loss Account.

The student may observe a debit item for 'Bad Debts' among the list of balances in a given Trial Balance. This refers to bad debts already written off, and is the balance of the Bad Debts Account as at the date of extraction of the Trial Balance. It should be debited to the Profit and Loss Account when this is prepared. Any instruction that is given *with* a Trial Balance to write off a sum for bad debts requires *different* treatment. This has not been passed through the books and therefore requires a two-fold entry as a deduction from the total of Sundry Debtors and a debit to the Profit and Loss Account. If a provision for doubtful debts has also to be made it should be calculated on the net figure for Sundry Debtors after deduction of the sum to be written off for bad debts.

To Increase the Provision

The provision carried forward to the next date of balancing may be insufficient as a provision on the Sundry Debtors on the books at that date. To carry on the above example, it may be found at the second date that the Sundry Debtors amount to £6 000. If 5 per cent is considered adequate, the provision for the ensuing year should be £300, involving an increase of £50 on the existing provision. Such increase is provided for by a debit entry to Profit and Loss Account, and a credit entry to the Provision for Doubtful Debts.

Journal

			Dr.	*Cr.*
19..			£	£
Dec. 31	Profit and Loss Account		50	
	Provision for Doubtful Debts Account			50
	being an increase to maintain Provision at 5% on Sundry Debtors.			

Provision for Doubtful Debts

			£	19..			£
				Jan. 1	Balance	b/d	250
				Dec. 31	Profit and Loss A/c.	J.	50

An instruction accompanying a Trial Balance to make a provision of a given sum, or to maintain a provision at a certain percentage, should not be acted upon until it is known from enquiry or observation whether or not a provision already exists. Any existing provision must be taken into account in calculating the new figure.

To Decrease the Provision

It may appear at the next balancing time that the existing provision is more than adequate owing to a fall in the total of Sundry Debtors. If the £6 000 in the above example had fallen to £4 000, and the provision is to be maintained at 5 per cent, £200 would be the new provision figure. As the existing provision is £300, £100 of that sum may be written back by a credit entry in the Profit and Loss Account, and a debit entry in the Provision Account as below:

Journal

			Dr.	*Cr.*
19..			£	£
Dec. 31	Provision for Doubtful Debts		100	
	Profit and Loss Account			100
	being excess written back to maintain Provision at 5% on Sundry Debtors.			

Provision for Doubtful Debts

19..			£	19..			£
Dec. 31	Balance	c/d	300	Jan. 1	Balance	b/d	250
				Dec. 31	Profit and Loss A/c.	J.	50
			£300				£300
19.1				19.1			
Dec. 31	Profit and Loss A/c.	J.	100	Jan. 1	Balance	b/d	300
Dec. 31	Balance	c/d	200				
			£300				£300
				19.2			
				Jan. 1	Balance	b/d	200

Provision for Discounts

Another example of provision for contingencies, though of much less frequent occurrence in practice, is that for discounts likely to be taken by the debtors included in the total of Sundry Debtors. If the debtors take advantage of discount terms, the sums received will be less than the full amount shown as an asset in the Balance Sheet. If provisions for discounts are required, the procedure is similar to that described for bad debt provision. The sum provided is usually calculated at a percentage of the Sundry Debtors, but care must be taken that it is calculated on the net figure only after deduction of the provision for bad and doubtful debts, as such debts cannot be subject to discount.

Example 23. Show the entries such as are necessary for a provision of 2½% discounts on Sundry Debtors which stand, at 31st December, at £4 000. A provision at 5% for bad and doubtful debts has also to be made.

Journal

		Dr.	*Cr.*
19..		£	£
Dec. 31	Profit and Loss Account	95	
	Provision for Discount on Debtors' Account		95
	being 2½% provision for discounts.		

Provision for Discounts on Debtors

19..			£	19..			£
				Dec. 31	Profit and Loss A/c.		95

The provision for discounts is calculated on £4 000 less 5 per cent provision for bad debts, and it should be shown in the Balance Sheet as a deduction from the item Sundry Debtors in addition to the deductions for a provision for doubtful debts.

	£	£	£
Sundry Debtors		4 000	
less Provision for Doubtful Debts	200		
Provision for Discounts	95	295	
	—	—	3 705

Still less frequent is the making of a provision on Sundry Creditors for discounts. A provision for discounts on creditors is created by converse entries. The sum is credited to Profit and Loss Account and is debited to a 'Reserve for Discounts on Creditors Account'. The balance of the latter account remains open on the books and is taken to the Balance Sheet, to appear there as a deduction from the Sundry Creditors.

Contingent Liabilities

A firm may have certain *contingent liabilities* which are not included in the accounts. For example, a trader may have guaranteed payment of a cheque drawn by another party. If the drawer of the cheque fails to meet it when presented for payment the payee may have recourse to the trader for reimbursement. Until such contingency arises no actual liability exists, but as a reminder of the existence of the contingency a note of it is usually made for information at the foot of the Balance Sheet.

EXERCISES 20

1. At the close of the year the Sundry Debtors of a firm stand at a total of £5 000. It is considered that two of the debts, amounting to £450, are doubtful, and it is desired to create a provision to the extent of the doubtful debts.

Give the Journal entries to create the provision, and show the appropriate Ledger Accounts. Show also how the item 'Sundry Debtors' should then appear in the firm's Balance Sheet.

2. The Trial Balance extracted from B. A. James & Co.'s books at 31st December shows the Sundry Debtors as at £2 750. It is decided to create a provision of 5% of the total debtors for doubtful debts.

Give the entries to effect this decision, and show how the item of Sundry Debtors should be set out in the firm's Balance Sheet.

3. Give the entries to carry into effect the decision to create a provision for doubtful debts of 5% of the total of Sundry Debtors which stand at £3 750 on 31st December. Show also the items of Sundry Debtors and the provision as they should appear in the Balance Sheet.

4. At 31st December the Sundry Debtors of the firm of Brown & Sons stand at £4 200. There is existing already a provision for doubtful debts of £150, but it is desired that the provision should amount to a sum equal to 5% of the present total of Sundry Debtors. Make the entries to carry this into effect.

5. It is decided to maintain the provision for doubtful debts on the books of B. Wilson & Co. at 5% of the Sundry Debtors. The present provision stands at £120, and at 31st December the Sundry Debtors amount to £3 100.

Give the Journal entries, and show the Ledger Accounts to carry out this decision.

6. The present provision for doubtful debts on the books of James Allen & Sons is £430. At 31st December the Sundry Debtors amount to £9 500. Give the entries required to increase the existing provision to £475, and show the item for Sundry Debtors as it should appear in the next Balance Sheet.

7. The existing provision for doubtful debts in the books of J. Scott stands at £360. The Sundry Debtors at 31st December amount to £6 000. Give the entries required to decrease the provision to £300.

8. The provision for doubtful debts of a company is to be maintained at 5% of the Sundry Debtors. The existing provision is £540. The Sundry Debtors amount to £8 200 at 31st December. Give the entries required to maintain the provision at 5% of the Sundry Debtors.

9. It was decided to reduce the provision for doubtful debts in the books of T. Layton from the present amount, £620, to £500. Show how this decision is carried into effect. At this date the Sundry Debtors stood at £10 020. Set down this item and the new provision as they should appear in the Balance Sheet.

10. The Sundry Debtors of W. Watson & Co. amount to £12 500. Provide for a provision for bad debts of 5% and a provision for discounts on debtors of 2½%, and show the item for Sundry Debtors as it should appear in the Balance Sheet.

11. In the books of Williams & Sons the Sundry Debtors stand at £8 000 at 31st December. It is proposed to create a Bad Debts Provision of 5%, and a Provision for Discounts on Debtors of 2½%. Show the entries required to carry this into effect, and the items as they should appear in the Balance Sheet.

12. The existing provision for bad debts on the books of Thompson & Co. is £560. On 31st December the Sundry Debtors stood at £9 800.

Give the entries required:

(*a*) To reduce the bad debts provision to £490.
(*b*) To create a provision of 2½% for discounts on debtors.

And show the items for Sundry Debtors and the provision as they should appear in the Balance Sheet.

13. Give the entries required to create a Provision for Discounts on Creditors of 2½%, the Sundry Creditors standing at £5 000 on 31st December.

14. The Sundry Creditors of B. Hallett amount to £5 000, and his Sundry Debtors to £7 000 on 31st December. He decides to create:

(*a*) A provision of 2½% for discounts on creditors.
(*b*) A provision of 5% on Sundry Debtors for bad debts.
(*c*) A provision of 2½% for discounts on debtors.

Show the entries required to carry this decision into effect, and how the items should appear in his Balance Sheet.

15. On 1st January, Arthur Sharp, who owes you £77, is adjudicated bankrupt. On 8th February the first dividened of £0·10 in the £ is paid, and on 23rd March the second and final dividend of £0·05 in the £ is paid. Give the entries in your books which are necessary to record the above transactions and to close the account. Show the Ledger Account of Arthur Sharp in its final form.

N.C.T.E.C.

21

Year-end Adjustments

Almost invariably it is found at the close of the financial year that certain expenses or liabilities properly belonging to the period just ended have been incurred, but payment has not been made. Business comprises a continuous series of operations unaffected by the arbitrary dates of the accounting periods, and some overlapping may be expected.

Wages may be paid, for example, on Friday in each week. If 31st December falls on, say, Wednesday, part of the total wages for the week (for Saturday to Wednesday) should be charged in the accounts as an expense for the year ending 31st December. The payment, however, is made on 2nd January in the next period.

Similarly, rent, salaries, commission, interest, and other expenses may be outstanding. Each financial year should bear its own charges if the profits are to be stated fairly, and, to this end, it is necessary to bring into account all outstanding expenses and to apportion others so that each period bears its proper proportion. Accordingly a provision is made for each outstanding liability by charging against profits the appropriate amount, as shown in the following examples:

Example 24. The rent of the firm's premises is £2 000 per annum, payable quarterly in arrear. For the year under review the March, June, and September payments have been made. The final quarter's rent has accrued due, but remains unpaid at 31st December. Show the entries involved in bringing the accrued rent into account.

It will be observed that the two-fold entry for the rent outstanding is within the Rent Account itself. A debit entry is made for the accrued sum due and a corresponding credit entry is made in the Rent Account for the ensuing period. Sufficient space must be left to allow for the balancing and ruling off of the account.

By making this debit entry the balance of the Rent Account to be transferred to Profit and Loss Account is £500 more than it would otherwise have been. The effect is to charge against profits both the rent paid and the rent accrued. The credit entry in the Rent Account is an open balance representing the provision of profit to meet

Rent Account

19..			£	19..			£
Apr. 2	Cash	C.B.	500	Dec. 31	Profit and Loss A/c.		2000
July 5	,,	C.B.	500				
Oct. 2	,,	C.B.	500				
Dec. 31	Provision for accrued rent	c/d	500				
			£2 000				£2 000
				Jan. 1	Provision for accrued rent	b/d	500

accrued rent, and when the Balance Sheet is prepared, it will be shown in it as a liability.

The effect of the payment eventually of the outstanding rent should be noted. The credit entry will be to Cash, and the debit entry to the Rent Account. The latter will counterbalance the credit entry for the provision, and the liability shown in the Balance Sheet is paid off.

Example 25. Wages paid during the year amounted to £61 200. Three days' wages, amounting to £600, had accrued due to 31st December. Show the entries necessary to bring this sum into account.

Wages Account

19..			£	19..			£
Jan. to Dec.	Cash	C.B.	61 200	Dec. 31	Manufacturing A/c.		61 800
Dec. 31	Provision for 3 days wages accrued due	c/d	600				
			£61 800				£61 800
				Jan. 1	Provision for accrued wages	b/d	600

The provision for accrued wages, £600, will be shown on the liability side of the Balance Sheet.

The method of providing for accrued liabilities illustrated in the above two examples is applicable in all similar cases. A complete list of the various outstanding liabilities that may be met with in accounts cannot be given, but their treatment should present little difficulty to the student if the above examples are carefully studied.

Occasionally, in a test or examination question, unfamiliarity with the details of a particular kind of business may cause some difficulty. Usually a comparison of the adjustment to be made with the item in the Trial Balance to which it relates will help towards a solution. The above examples show the Ledger Account and the effect of the entries in it on the Profit and Loss Account and Balance Sheet. In many such questions the Trial Balance, from which Trading and Profit and Loss Accounts and Balance Sheet are to be prepared, is accompanied by instructions to take certain adjustments into account, and many of such adjustments refer to outstanding liabilities. If no Ledger Accounts are required by the test, it is necessary to give only the effect of the appropriate Ledger entries on the Final Accounts. One aspect of the adjustment will be shown in the Trading Account or the Profit and Loss Account and the other aspect in the Balance Sheet. Take again the above example of outstanding rent (Example 24). The rent actually paid, £1 500, would appear in the Trial Balance, but the accrued but unpaid rent, £500, would be noted as an instruction to be taken into account. In preparing the Final Accounts from the Trial Balance the sum of £500 should be added to the £1 500 taken to the Profit and Loss Account, and should also be included among the liabilities in the Balance Sheet. Similarly, in the above example of an adjustment for accrued wages (Example 25), the sum of £600 should be added to the Wages, £61 200, taken to the Profit and Loss Account, and should also be shown as a liability in the Balance Sheet.

It is imperative that the student should remember that items in the Trial Balance have been passed through the books, and that they will appear once only in the Trading or Profit and Loss Accounts or the Balance Sheet. Items given as adjustments or instructions outside the actual Trial Balance have not been passed through the books, and a two-fold entry affecting both the Balance Sheet and the Trading or Profit and Loss Account is required for them.

In practice such adjustments are of course made in the appropriate accounts before the Trading and Profit and Loss Accounts and Balance Sheet are prepared.

Unexpired Values and Payments in Advance

Many items which have to be considered at the time of balancing are of a nature converse to the outstanding liabilities explained above. They are payments made *in advance*, for example for insurance premiums or rates. The periods covered by insurance premiums, rates, and other expenses do not always coincide with the accounting period, and part of the expenditure may be properly attributable to the next financial year. For example a firm may pay £1 000 in October for rates for the half-yearly period October–March. It will thus have paid *in advance* rates for the months January–March of the next accounting period. If each year's accounts should be charged with the expenses of that year then charges such as the above should be apportioned. In the Rates Account, the above £1 000 will appear as a debit entry. On closing the books £500 only, representing the rates for October to December, is transferred to the debit of the Profit and Loss Account, that being the portion properly chargeable against the current year's profits. The balance of £500 is, at 31st December, the value of the unexpired portion of the rates payment and is shown in the Balance Sheet as a temporary asset.

Example 26. The rates are paid in half-yearly instalments in advance for the period 1st April to 31st March; £1 000 on 30th April and £1 000 on 31st December. The financial year ends on 31st December. Show the Rates Account and the entries which are necessary to apportion the expenditure between the two accounting periods.

Rates Account

19..			£	19..			£
Apr. 30	Cash	C.B.	1 000	Dec. 31	Rates paid in advance	c/d	500
Oct. 31	Cash	C.B.	1 000	„ 31	Profit and Loss A/c.		1 500
			£2 000				£2 000
Jan. 1	Rates paid in advance	b/d	500				

Balance Sheet

as at 31st December, 19..

(Assets side only)

	£
CURRENT ASSETS	
Unexpired rates	500

The procedure is to credit this year's account with the value of the unexpired portion, and to make the corresponding debit entry in the account for the next accounting period. Sufficient room must be left to permit the account to be balanced and ruled off. The new account opens with a debit balance which, in due course, will be included in the account transferred to the Profit and Loss Account for the next year. Meanwhile, it appears in the Balance Sheet as an asset representing the unexpired value in hand.

This method applies to all similar examples of payments in advance, and is also suitable for the treatment of items requiring the carrying forward of expenditure, either wholly or in part, to subsequent years.

Example 27. A firm enters into an advertising contract for one year as from 1st September 19.0. Payment of £9 300 is made on September 10th. At 31st December, on closing the books, it is decided to spread the advertising cost over the year. Give the entries as are necessary to carry this decision into effect.

Advertising Account

19.0			£	19.0			£
Sept. 1	Cash	C.B.	9 300	Dec. 31	Proportion of expense carried forward	c/d	6 200
				„ 31	Transfer to Profit & Loss A/c.	T	3 100
			£9 300				£9 300
19.1							
Jan. 1	Proportion of expense brought forward	b/d	6 200				

As shown, one-third of the advertising cost is transferred to Profit and Loss Account. The remainder of the expenditure is held in suspense to be charged against the profits of the next year. Meanwhile, it is shown in the Balance Sheet as a temporary asset representing advertising value in hand at 31st December 19.0.

As with outstanding liabilities, the forms which the adjustments of payments in advance and the apportionment of expenses may take depend upon the nature of the business and the particular circumstances under which the accounts are prepared. In whatever form they are expressed the treatment should follow the lines described above. If such adjustments are given as instructions to be observed in the preparation of the Final Accounts from a given Trial Balance, only the effect on the Final Accounts need be shown. As already remarked, such items appearing outside the Trial Balance have not been passed through the books, and the double entry effect must be given. This will affect both the Balance Sheet and the Trading or Profit and Loss Account. If the above examples had been given as instructions, the actual expenditure on Rates, £2 000, and Advertising, £9 300, would be shown as items in the Trial Balance, and the adjusting entries would be made when the Profit and Loss Account is prepared, and would be shown on the debit side.

Profit and Loss Account

(Debit Side only)

		£	£
Rates		2 000	
less unexpired		500	1 500
Advertising		9 300	
less amount carried forward		6 200	3 100

The sum shown in the debit column of the Profit and Loss Account is the sum that would be transferred from the Ledger Account for the expense item after the adjustment had been made. This corresponds to the entry for £3 100 to the credit of the Advertising Account in Example 27. The other entry for the adjustment is the amount brought down in the expense account for the new period and, in the Final Accounts, appears in the Balance Sheet on the assets side.

Whilst most year-end adjustments deal with outstanding liabilities, and payments in advance, other forms are sometimes to be met, a few examples of which are mentioned below. One important type of adjustment is for the *depreciation of fixed assets*. It is explained in Chapter 22. Reserves and provisions, explained in Chapter 20, are also types of year-end adjustment.

Packing materials may also appear as an expense item in the Trial Balance. If no stock on hand is stated the whole item is treated as an expense, and is debited to Profit and Loss Account. If the value of the packing materials on hand is given, this sum should be credited to the Packing Materials Account and debited to the same account for the new period. Only the used amount is then transferred to Profit and Loss Account, and the stock of packing materials on hand is shown as an asset in the Balance Sheet.

Similarly, the value of catalogues on hand may be given, and should be treated in the Catalogues Account in like manner to the packing materials. The cost only of the catalogues distributed is then charged against the profits of the current year, and the stock of catalogues on hand is shown as an asset in the Balance Sheet.

The factory wages may include payments for work done on, say, patterns for future use in the firm. The amount of wages so expended should be deducted from the item for manufacturing wages and added to the value of the asset.

The owner of a business may take out goods from stock for his personal use. It is usual to debit the cost of such goods to the Proprietor's Drawing Account and to credit the Purchases Accounts.

As a final example, Goodwill may appear in an examination question as an asset, and the instructions may be to write down the value by a given sum.

Goodwill

Goodwill as an accounting item usually arises from the purchase of a business as a going concern. The assets of a business may be worth, say, £4 000 on valuation. The purchaser may pay £5 000, that is, £4 000 for the stock, fittings, and other assets, and £1 000 for the Goodwill. He believes that the custom, reputation, and other similar advantages attaching to the business will accrue to him on his taking over, and that this prospect is worth £1 000 over and above the value of the assets. If he founded a new business it would take time to create similar advantages, and during that time he could not expect his profits to be so great. The purchase of the Goodwill is capital expenditure on something of value, and for this reason it is placed among the assets, although it is not of a concrete nature. The Balance Sheet of the above purchaser, if drawn up on the day of purchase, would contain the following items:

	£		£
Capital	5 000	Goodwill	1 000
		Stock, fittings, and other assets	4 000

There will be a Goodwill Account in the Ledger to which the £1 000 will be debited.

The custom from which the Goodwill arises may be attracted by the personal service of the proprietor, or from that and the site of the premises. Trade is better, in some cases, on one side of a road than on the other, and, for some shops, proximity to a railway station or a marketing centre is an advantage. The advantage, however, may not prove permanent, and it may be prudent to write down the value of the Goodwill. In cases where there is no definite evidence of decline in value, it is often the practice to lower the figure at which the Goodwill stands to avoid possible overstatement of value, probably over a period of three to five years.

If instruction to write down the value of Goodwill is given, the amount to be written off should be credited to the Goodwill Account and debited to the Profit and Loss Account, the effect being a reduction in the value of the asset in the Balance Sheet as well as a reduction in the profit available for distribution to the proprietors.

Other adjustments of special application to the accounts of a partnership firm or a limited company are referred to in the chapters dealing with those accounts.

EXERCISES 21

1. The following items are taken from a Trial Balance extracted from B. Marchant's books on 31st December:

	£
Insurance Account (debit balance)	600
Rates Account	3 000

In each case three-quarters only of the expense is properly attributable to the year ending 31st December.

Show the Ledger Accounts for these items and the entries required to adjust the above amounts, taking into consideration that insurance, £150, and rates, £750, represent payments in advance. Show how such adjustments will affect the firm's Balance Sheet.

2. The Trial Balance extracted from the books of A. Macdonald at 31st December includes the following debit balances:

	£
Rent Account	7 500
Rates	5 000
Wages	360 000
Salaries	40 000
Interest on loan	1 000
Insurance	1 200
Advertising	20 000

The following adjustments have to be made before the preparation of the Final Accounts:

	£
Rent outstanding	2 500
Rates paid in advance	1 250
Wages accrued due	5 000
Salaries accrued due	450
Interest on loan unpaid	1 000
Insurance paid in advance	300
Advertising cost to be carried forward	10 000

Show the Ledger Accounts as from which the Trial Balance was prepared, and make the necessary entries to effect the above adjustments.

3. The Trial Balance extracted on 31st December contains the following debit balances:

	£
Rent Account	3 000
Wages Account	48 000

At 31st December one quarter's rent, £1 000, remained owing, and three days' wages, £500, had accrued to the factory workers. Show the Ledger Accounts for rent and wages, enter the above balances, and show the adjusting entries to bring the outstanding items into account.

State how these outstanding items affect the firm's Balance Sheet.

4. William Robinson sub-lets the flat over his shop at an annual rent of £480 payable quarterly. During 19. . the tenant of the flat pays the rent due from him on 25th March, 24th June, and 29th September, but at 31st December has not paid the quarter's rent due. Show the Rent Account in William Robinson's books after the preparation of his Profit and Loss Account for the year ending 31st December, 19. .

R.S.A.

5. Set out the Journal entries necessary to deal with the following matters:

(*a*) The writing off as bad debts of £550 due from A, £190 from B, and £270 from C.

(*b*) The allocation of £10 000 to General Reserve.

(*c*) The transfer to Furniture and Fittings of £450, originally posted to Office Expenses.

(*d*) The bringing into account of three months' interest accrued on a loan of £5 000 at 5% per annum, due from D.

R.S.A. (adapted)

6. A. Wholesaler carries on business in both home and export markets and requires his accounts to show the results separately. From the following

Trial Balance prepare departmental Trading and Profit and Loss Accounts for the year ending 31st December, 19.., and Balance Sheet at that date:

	£	£
A. Wholesaler, Capital Account		12 382
,, Drawings Account	840	
Advertising (Home, £512; Export, £415)	927	
Carriage (Home)	261	
Cash in hand	70	
Freight, insurance, etc. (Export)	598	
Freehold premises	3 500	
Lighting and heating (Home ½, Export, ½)	70	
Office expenses (Home ½, Export ½)	654	
Office furniture and fittings	600	
Purchases (Home £24 710; Export £22 583)	47 293	
Rates (Home ½, Export ½)	120	
Provision for bad debts		100
Sales (Home £28 027, Export £25 414)		53 441
Salaries (Home £726, Export £798)	1 524	
Stocks at 1st Jan., 19.. (Home £2 962, Export £2 629)	5 591	
Traveller's commission (Home)	520	
Sundry debtors	5 325	
Sundry creditors		3 756
Balance with bank	1 786	
	£69 679	£69 679

When preparing the accounts the following must be taken into consideration:

(1) The values of the stocks at 31st December, 19.., were Home £2 721 and Export £2 599.
(2) The traveller's commission due at 31st December, 19.., but not paid amounted to £40 (Home).
(3) An increase in the provision for bad debts of £173 is required (Home).

22

Provision for Depreciation

The necessity for careful scrutiny of the items of the Balance Sheet in order that it may present a true and fair view of the financial position has already been emphasised. One of the essential points to note is the value at which the fixed assets appear. Buildings (but not normally land), machinery, furniture, and fittings which are all acquired for use in the course of business are such that in the nature of things, wastage and wear occurs. Over a period of time these assets diminish in value. The *depreciation*, as the fall in value is termed, is caused by the asset being put to use for productive purposes, and is part of the cost of production. An effort is therefore made to estimate the proportion of the monetary value of the asset that has been used up, both for the purpose of valuing the asset and to take it into account in arriving at the profits for the period.

In every case the depreciation is charged against profits, and the asset is shown at the revised value in the Balance Sheet.

Depreciation may also arise as a result of the asset becoming *obsolete*. For instance, a machine may not physically be worn out and may still be capable of further use, but new machines may have been developed which reduce its *economic* working life by rendering it perhaps too slow, or too expensive in terms of, say, labour requirements to operate it, or too limited in its capacity to produce a range of products, or not sufficiently reliable for quality control purposes.

Other fixed assets, such as leases, patents, or copyrights, diminish in value as the date approaches of the expiration of the rights which they give.

To determine the depreciation the questions to be considered in most cases are:

(*a*) The original cost of the asset.
(*b*) The probable period of time it will last in use.
(*c*) Its anticipated disposal price at the end of its 'working life'.

The difference between the original cost and the approximate value at the close of its useful life is the decline in value of the asset that has to be apportioned over the period estimated to be its probable working life.

The question of depreciation is usually considered at the close of a trading period after the Trial Balance has been extracted and before the preparation of the Final Accounts. A credit entry is made in the *Provision for Depreciation Account* for the depreciation so that the balance of the account is the new figure at which the asset stands. The debit entry is made directly into the Profit and Loss Account. The customary practice is as described in this chapter. It has generally replaced the former practice of crediting depreciation in the fixed asset account and bringing down only a net balance on that account. The debit entry is in the Profit and Loss Account in both methods.

Various methods can be used to estimate the amount of depreciation to charge in any particular year. In some instances additions are made during the year to the machinery or other asset, and the instructions are to provide for depreciation at a given rate. Whichever method of depreciation is adopted the depreciation should be provided for on the final value of the asset after the additions are made. If the instructions refer specifically to the depreciation on the additions during the year such instructions should, of course, be followed.

The Straight-line or Equal Annual Instalment Method

This method is very widely used in many countries. It is so-called because the annual depreciation charge each year is constant until the asset's value is written down to its estimated scrap or disposal price, and if plotted on a graph would give a straight line.

Under this method, depreciation over the expected working life of the asset is estimated and the loss in value is spread by *equal* instalments over the probable working life of the asset.

Example 28. A machine, costing £10 000, is estimated to have a useful life of 10 years, and to be worth £1 000 at the end of that period. Depreciation is therefore £9 000 and is charged against profits by ten equal yearly instalments of £900.

In journal form only the entry in the books for each of the ten years would be as follows:

Journal

		Dr.	Cr.
19..		£	£
Dec. 31	Profit and Loss Account	900	
	Provision for Depreciation		900
	being depreciation of machine at £900 per annum		

By the end of the tenth year the Provision for Depreciation Account will show a credit balance of £9 000, offsetting the debit balance of £10 000 in the Machine Account. No further depreciation will be charged in respect of the machine as long as it continues to be kept by the business.

Some assets, such as patent rights, may have no value at the end of a term of years, and the value of the asset may be completely extinguished by charging against profits annual instalments of the original value as depreciation.

The Diminishing Balance Method

This method is also frequently used. It is also used in the United Kingdom in connection with the computation of taxation allowances, although the student should understand that such computations are entirely separate to the calculation of depreciation in the books of the firm.

Under this method depreciation is charged at a fixed percentage of the diminishing debit balance found by subtracting the credit balance on the Provision for Depreciation Account at the start of the particular year from the debit balance on the Asset Account. The fixed percentage rate is calculated such that the depreciation charged will offset the asset's value at the end of its expected working life, leaving as the net difference the anticipated scrap or disposal value.

In the U.S.A. this method is known as the 'double-declining balance' method.

Example 29. A new machine cost £10 000, and stands in the books at that figure. Provide for depreciation at 40% per annum by the diminishing balance method until the net book value is reduced to a nominal amount of £100. Make all calculations to the nearest pound.

The depreciation provided in the first year will be £4 000, which is 40% of £10 000. This leaves a net book value of £6 000. Therefore depreciation in the second year will be £2 400, which is 40% of £6 000. In the third and succeeding years it will be £1 440, £864, £518, £311, £187, £112, and in the ninth year £67 leaving a net book value of £100. The accounts for Machinery and Provision for Depreciation, together with extracts from the Balance Sheets, are shown below for the first three years:

Machinery

		£			£
19..					
Jan. 1	Bank	10 000			

Provision for Depreciation

		£			£
19..			19..		
Dec. 31	Balance c/d	4 000	Dec. 31	Profit & Loss A/c.	4 000
19.1			19.1		
Dec. 31	Balance c/d	6 400	Jan. 1	Balance b/d	4 000
			Dec. 31	Profit & Loss A/c.	2 400
		6 400			6 400
19.2			19.2		
Dec. 31	Balance d/d	7 840	Jan. 1	Balance b/d	6 400
			Dec. 31	Profit & Loss A/c.	1 440
		7 840			7 840

Extracts from Balance Sheets

(Fixed Assets Only)

	£	£
As at 31st December, 19..		
Machinery	10 000	
Less Provision for Depreciation	4 000	
		6 000
As at 31st December, 19.1		
Machinery	10 000	
Less Provision for Depreciation	6 400	
		3 600
As at 31st December, 19.2		
Machinery	10 000	
Less Provision for Depreciation	7 840	
		2 160

Usage Method

Under this method the expected working life of the asset is estimated in terms of its *output*. For example, the working life of a taxi-cab may be estimated at 200 000 miles. Depreciation is then charged each year on the basis of the output achieved, relative to the working-life output of the asset. Suppose the taxicab cost £8 000, and was used for 25 000 miles in 19. . . In 19. . , 12½% of the taxi's estimated working life has been used up, and depreciation for that year is therefore charged at 12½% (i.e. £1 000). Depreciation will be computed in a similar way for further years, until the 'working life' of the asset is completely used up. Thereafter, no depreciation is charged.

Periodical Re-valuation

With some assets, such as loose tools, patterns and dies, *re-valuation* is the only satisfactory method of arriving at the depreciation. A valuation is made of the asset as at the Balance Sheet date, and any diminution in value as compared with the cost or former valuation is treated as depreciation.

Loose tools, patterns, and dies are often made by a firm's own workmen and for particular jobs. The valuation of the stock of loose tools and patterns at the close of the trading period may show an increase over the value as at the commencement owing to the fact that a larger quantity has been made during the year. The cost of making has been included in the wages and materials, and the stock is continuously being used up and added to so that normal depreciation does not take place. For this reason, whether the value has increased or decreased, the usual practice is to debit the old value and credit the new value to the Profit and Loss Account, which will bring the increase or decrease into account.

Other Methods

The above methods are in common use, but brief reference may be made to the *Sinking Fund Method* and the *Insurance Policy Method.* In these cases the assets remain on the books at their original cost. Each year a fixed sum is debited to Profit and Loss Account, and a corresponding sum is paid out from cash. Under the Sinking Fund Method the cash is invested in gilt-edged securities. Under the Insurance Policy Method the cash is expended in meeting the premiums on an endowment insurance policy which is to mature at the expiration of the life of the asset. In both cases provision is made for replacement of the asset when it becomes necessary without affecting the working capital of the business.

Comparison of the Methods

It will be readily apparent that, although the various methods described here charge more or less the same total depreciation over the whole life of an asset, they charge widely varying amounts from year to year. This means that profits will vary in any year according to which method is adopted. It means also that the apparent trend of profits will vary over several years according to which method is adopted.

The views of the accounting profession on depreciation are contained in a document known as *Statement of Standard Accounting Practice (SSAP) no.* 12, issued in December 1977.

Amongst other things, the SSAP makes the following statements:

> The management of a business has a duty to allocate depreciation as fairly as possible to the periods expected to benefit from the use of the asset and should select the method regarded as most appropriate to the type of asset and its use in the business.
>
> The allocation of depreciation to accounting periods involves the exercise of judgement by management in the light of technical, commercial and accounting considerations and accordingly requires annual review. When, as the result of experience or of changed circumstances, it is considered that the original estimate of useful life of an asset requires to be revised, the unamortised (i.e. un-depreciated) cost of the asset should be charged to revenue over the revised remaining useful life. If at any time the unamortised cost is seen to be irrecoverable in full (perhaps as a result of obsolescence or a fall in demand for a product), it should be written down immediately to the estimated recoverable amount which should be charged over the remaining useful life.
>
> A change from one method of providing depreciation to another is permissible only on the grounds that the new method will give a fairer presentation of the results and of the financial position. In these circumstances the unamortised cost should be written off

over the remaining useful life commencing with the period in which the change is made.

Where fixed assets are disposed of for an amount which is greater or less than their book value, the surplus or deficiency should be reflected in the results of the year and disclosed separately if material.

The Disposal of Fixed Assets

When an asset is disposed of before the end of its anticipated economic working life the book entries are as follows:

(1) Credit the Asset Account with the cost of the asset, debiting a *Disposal of Fixed Asset Account.*
(2) Debit the Provision for Depreciation Account with the accumulated depreciation on the asset, crediting the Disposal of Fixed Asset Account.
(3) Debit Bank Account with the proceeds of the disposal, crediting the Disposal of Fixed Asset Account.
(4) Transfer the Balance of the Disposal of Fixed Asset Account to the Profit and Loss Account at the end of the accounting period.

If the balance on the Disposal Account is a credit balance, profit will be increased. If it is a debit balance, profit will be decreased.

Assume that on 1st October 19.5 a taxicab costing £8 000, with an expected life of 200 000 miles, is sold for £3 000 after it has been driven for 150 000 miles. The Disposal of Fixed Asset Account will appear as follows:

Disposal of Taxicab Account 68

19.5			£	19.5			£
Oct. 1	Taxicab	52	8 000	Oct. 1	Provision for depreciation	47	6 000
Dec. 31	Profit transferred to Profit & Loss Account	T	1 000	Oct. 1	Bank: sale proceeds	CB3	3 000
			£9 000				£9 000

The student should now set out the Disposal Account assuming that the sales proceeds were only £500. It will be necessary to transfer a loss of £1 500 to the Profit and Loss Account.

Asset Registers

It greatly assists the proper recording of asset and depreciation accounts if the business maintains *Asset Registers*. These should detail at least the location of the asset, its output capacity and characteristics, the date and cost of its purchase, the expected working-life and disposal value, the depreciation method used, and the maintenance requirements.

Current Cost Accounting and Depreciation

This chapter, like most of this book, utilises the historic cost approach to valuing assets. The recent developments in *current cost accounting* have particular effect on certain aspects of accounting. One of them is depreciation. These new ideas do not affect the mechanics of providing for depreciation, but they do alter the basic amount on which it is based, whichever method is used. Instead of the historic cost, or purchase price, of the asset, it is necessary to use the 'current cost'. This will often, but not always, be the *replacement cost* of a comparable new asset at the time when the particular accounts are being prepared. It may well vary, therefore, during the life of the asset. At the present time, in most cases, the effect is to increase the depreciation provision, sometimes very considerably.

Depreciation is charged as an expense and so reduces profits each year. Nevertheless it does not measure a cash outflow during the year in which it is charged. Even if all of the profits were distributed to the proprietors, there should therefore remain a balance of cash for re-investment. One of the aims of current cost accounting is to make that balance of cash approximately sufficient to allow for the replacement of assets as they reach the end of their life, without recourse to heavier borrowing.

EXERCISES 22

1. Among the Assets Accounts of a manufacturing business are the following, with the balances as shown:

			£
Dec.	31	Plant and machinery	40 000
„	31	Office furniture	4 000

Depreciation is to be provided for at the rate of 10% per annum on the plant and machinery, and at 5% per annum on the furniture.

Open the Ledger Accounts for the assets, and make the necessary entries for the depreciation for three years, using the diminishing balance method.

Show how the assets should appear in the firm's Balance Sheet in each year.

2. A firm bought a machine for £12 000. Its probably working life is estimated at 10 years, and its probable scrap value at the end of that time is estimated at £2 000. Depreciation is to be written off by equal instalments over the period of ten years. Show the Machinery Account for the first three years, including the provision for depreciation.

3. On what basis should 'Fixed Assets' be valued for the purpose of the Balance Sheet of a trading business?

Illustrate your answers by showing how you would deal with a motor lorry bought two years ago for £45 000 which, it is expected, will have to be disposed of in 5 years' time, when it will probably realise £2 500. Its current replacement cost is £50 000.

4. A business buys an electric generator plant on 1st January, 19. ., for the sum of £25 000. The generator is estimated to last 10 years, and to have a scrap value at the end of that time of £2 500. Show how you would deal with this asset in the books of the business at the end of the first year.

R.S.A. (adapted)

5. Explain what is meant by Depreciation and illustrate your answer by giving the account of a machine purchased on 1st January, 19. ., for £600 and estimated to be worth £150 at the end of a life of two years.

R.S.A.

6. An engineering firm has loose tools valued at 1st January at £1 425. At 31st December stock is taken of the loose tools, and their value is placed at £1 623. Show how you would deal with the matter in the firm's books and in the Balance Sheet.

7. The loose tools of an engineering firm were valued at the commencement of the year at £1 134. At 31st December, on stock being taken, the valuation of the loose tools stood at £921. Show how this matter should be dealt with in the firm's books, and the effect of the revaluation on the Balance Sheet.

8. (*a*) Enter the following transactions through their appropriate books.
(*b*) Post to Ledger.
(*c*) Take out Trial Balance.
(*d*) Prepare Trading and Profit and Loss Account and Balance Sheet.

The following Trial Balance was extracted from the books of K. Watts on 31st May, 19..

Trial Balance.

31st May, 19..

	Dr. £	*Cr.* £
Capital (1st July, 19..)		2 000
Drawings	220	
Stock (1st July, 19..)	1 345	
Machinery	1 500	
Furniture and fittings	125	
Purchases	4 624	
Sales		7 012
Returns inwards	126	
Office expenses	480	
Carriage inwards	97	
Cash	33	
Bank	100	
Discounts allowed	74	
Discounts received		118
F. Haynes	69	
C. Peace		132
Salaries	469	
	£9 262	£9 262

During June Watt's transactions were as follows:

Received from F. Haynes a cheque for the amount of his account, less 5% cash discount.
Sold goods, on credit, to G. Leach, £87.
Bought goods, and paid for by cheque, £63.
Bought goods on credit from F. Appleton, £44.
Received a credit note for £9 from F. Appleton for goods returned to him.
Paid by cheque Fire Insurance premium, £5.
Withdrew from bank £35 for office use.
Paid from cash: salaries, £30; office expenses, £12; and carriage on goods sold to G. Leach, £2.
Cash sales, £136, banked during month.
Cash sales, £14, not banked.
Drew cheque for £20 for private expenses.

Wrote off 10% of the furniture and fittings and 20% of the machinery for depreciation.
Paid cheque, £100, on account to C. Peace.
The stock on 30th June, 19.., was valued at £1 041.

N.B.: Unless otherwise stated, all moneys received were paid into Bank same day.

Oxford Local Examinations School Certificate

9. From the following list of balances draw up the Trial Balance of E. W. Rowcroft as at 31st December, 19.., and then prepare Trading Account, Profit and Loss Account, and Balance Sheet:

	£
E. W. Rowcroft, Capital Account	13 500
Purchases	4 080
Heating and lighting	20
Drawings	82
Sales	7 000
Returns outwards	70
Machinery and plant	1 300
Discounts received	27
Land and buildings	11 100
Returns inwards	116
Rent and rates	32
Fixtures and fittings	222
Repairs	118
Trade expenses	124
Motor vehicle	228
Sundry creditors	1 029
Wages	1 526
Commission received	90
Carriage outwards	39
Cash at bank	19
Sundry debtors	230
Carriage inwards	31
Stock, 1st July	2 389

The stock on 31st December was valued at £1 275.
When preparing the Trading Account, Profit and Loss Account, and Balance Sheet, you are required to depreciate the machinery and plant by 10% per annum.

U.E.I.

10. From the following Trial Balance prepare a Trading Account, Profit and Loss Account, and a Balance Sheet, as on 31st December, 19..:

Trial Balance

(D. Gerrard)

	Dr.	*Cr.*
	£	£
Stock (1st January)	452	
Plant and machinery	560	
Furniture and fittings	280	
Sundry debtors	295	
Sundry creditors		442
Drawings	50	
Purchases	1 675	
Sales		2 587
Returns outward		35
Returns inwards	73	
Manufacturing wages	381	
Carriage outwards	27	
Discount (balance)		58
Bad debts(*debit P. and L. A/c.*)	89	
Insurance	54	
Trade expenses	13	
Rate and taxes	107	
Commission	36	
Cash at bank	196	
Cash in hand	34	
Capital (D. Gerrard)		1 200
	£4 322	£4 322

10% depreciation to be written off plant and machinery, 7½% depreciation to be written off furniture and fittings. Stock on hand, 31st December, valued at £432.

U.E.I.

11. On 1st January, 1971, a company purchased four machines for £2 000 each. The balance on 'Machine Account' has been carried down at cost and the annual charge for depreciation, calculated at the rate of 10 per cent per annum on cost, has been credited to a 'Provision for Depreciation Account'.

On 1st January, 1972, one of the machines was sold for £1 722 and on the same day two additional machines were purchased at a cost of £2 400 each.

On 1st January, 1973, another of the original machines was sold for £1 625 but was not replaced.

You are required to show:

(*a*) the machinery account and the provision for depreciation account for the years 1971, 1972 and 1973, and

(*b*) how the machinery would appear in the balance sheet as on 31st December, 1973.

R.S.A. II (*adapted*)

12. John Baker carried on business as a manufacturer. On 30th June, 19.. the following Trial Balance was extracted from his books:

	Dr.	*Cr.*
	£	£
Machinery and plant	5 760	
Office salaries and expenses	6 100	
Bad debts	1 800	
Returns inwards and outwards	3 500	3 370
Carriage on purchases	2 280	
Carriage on sales	2 000	
Depreciation	750	
Manufacturing wages	12 730	
Discounts allowed and received	950	1 700
Fixtures and fittings	2 090	
Sundry debtors and creditors	16 270	12 240
Drawings	4 200	
Purchase and sales	67 270	105 800
Cash in hand	670	
Cash at bank	3 540	
Rent and rates	2 860	
Stock (1st July)	22 340	
Capital (1st July)		32 000
	£155 110	£155 110

You are required to prepare Trading and Profit and Loss Accounts for the year ended 30th June, and a Balance Sheet as on that date. The stock on hand on 30th June, 19.. was valued at £18 960.

R.S.A. (adapted)

13. The following Trial Balance was extracted from the books of J. Cooper, a trader, on 19th March, 19..:

	Dr.	*Cr.*
	£	£
Capital (1st April)		30 000
Drawings	3 300	
Freehold property	12 000	
Furniture and fittings	1 500	
Stock (1st April)	14 360	
Sales		80 410

Returns inwards	1 590	
Purchases	67 350	
Returns outwards		2 520
Rent and rates	5 100	
Bad debts	1 310	
Carriage outwards	1 590	
Carriage inwards	1 450	
Salaries and commission	4 550	
Discount		150
F. Drake	740	
W. Wright	330	
H. Nelson		3 180
C. Blake		1 520
Cash	370	
Bank	2 240	
	£117 780	£117 780

Post the above balances direct to the appropriate accounts in the Ledger, then pass thereto, through the proper subsidiary books, the following transactions:

Mar. 21. Received from F. Drake a cheque for the amount of his account. The cheque was paid into bank.
,, 22. Sold goods, on credit, to G. Cook, £940.
,, 23. Bought goods, by cheque, £820.
,, 23. Received a final payment of £0·67 in the £ from W. Wright, the balance being irrecoverable. The cheque was paid into bank.
,, 24. Sold goods on credit to F. Drake, £1 540, and paid £50 out of cash for carriage on these goods.
,, 24. Paid salaries and commission in cash, £230.
,, 29. Paid H. Nelson £1 000 on account by cheque.
,, 30. Drew and cashed a cheque for £500, and paid in cash Rent and Rates, £160, and private expenses, £300.
,, 30. Sent a Credit Note for £250 to F. Drake for goods returned.
,, 31. Cash sales, £360. (Not banked.)
,, 31. Write off 10% of the furniture and fittings for depreciation.

Extract a Trial Balance as on 31st March, and prepare Trading and Profit and Loss Accounts for the year ended 31st March 19... Balance the Ledger and draw up a Balance Sheet as on that date. The stock on 31st March was valued at £10 750.

N.B.: The Trial Balance given above need not be reproduced.

R.S.A. (*adapted*)

14. From the following Trial Balance prepare a Trading Account, Profit and Loss Account, and a Balance Sheet, as on 30th June, 19..:

Trial Balance

(F. T. Layton)

	Dr. £	*Cr.* £
Capital A/c. (F. T. Layton)		8 300
Purchases	12 000	
Sales		17 500
Returns inwards	550	
Returns outwards		640
Plant and machinery	2 400	
Furniture and fittings	750	
Sundry debtors	1 370	
Sundry creditors		860
Wages	2 280	
Bad debts	360	
Discount		270
Stock (1st Jan.)	5 000	
Insurance	160	
Commission		430
Trade expenses	220	
Cash in hand	170	
Cash at bank	2 740	
	£28 000	£28 000

7½% depreciation to be written off plant and machinery.
5% depreciation to be written off furniture and fittings.
Stock on hand, 30th June, valued at £6 300.

U.E.I. (*adapted*)

15. The following balances were extracted from the books of Walter Wilson, grocer and provision dealer, on the 31st December, 19..:

Dr.	£	*Cr.*	£
Cash in hand	130	Sales	25 650
Cash at bank	3 470	Returns outwards	140
Machinery	800	Discount	130
Motor lorry	1 800	Creditors	6 030
Fixtures and fittings	3 000	Capital Account	18 440
Returns inwards	570		
Purchases	21 280		
Stock, 1st Jan.	12 200		
Bad debts	430		
Wages	3 120		
Discount	260		
Drawings Account	240		
Heating and Lighting	670		
Sundry debtors	2 420		
	£50 390		£50 390

You are required to prepare the Final Accounts and a Balance Sheet as on the 31st December, 19... Before doing so, the following adjustments must be taken into account:

Write 5% depreciation off fixtures and fittings, and 10% off the motor lorry and machinery. Make a provision of $2\frac{1}{2}$% on debtors for doubtful debts. The value of the stock in hand at the end of the period was £13 800.

N.C.T.E.C. (*adapted*)

16. The following balances were extracted from the books of M. Robinson, ironmonger, on the 31st December, 19..:

Dr.	£	*Cr.*	£
Motor van	2 800	Sales	29 050
Shop fixtures	3 400	Returns outwards	240
Returns inwards	670	Discount	230
Purchases	24 280	Sundry Creditors	6 630
Stock in hand, 1st Jan.	12 300	Capital Account	18 590
Bad debts	530		
Wages	3 020		
Discount	60		
Drawings Account	480		
Rent and rates	880		
Sundry debtors	2 620		
Cash in hand	200		
Cash in bank	3 500		
	£54 740		£54 740

You are required to prepare the Final Accounts and a Balance Sheet as on the 31st December, 19... Before doing so, the following adjustments must be taken into account: (*a*) Write 5% depreciation off shop fixtures, and 15% off motor van; (b) make a provision of 2½% on sundry debtors for doubtful debts. The value of the stock in hand at the end of the period was £13 000.

N.C.T.E.C.

17. The figures of the following Trial Balance were extracted from the books of W. Walker, a wholesale provision merchant, on December 31st:

	£	£
Capital		17 874
Lease (to run 10 years from January 1st)	5 000	
Advertising	127	
Motor vans	927	
Purchases	68 485	
Postage	138	
Lighting and heating	91	
Wages	2 837	
Rates and water	101	
Telephone	34	
Furniture and fittings	1 104	
Sales		73 498
Returns inwards and outwards	56	392
Bad debts	26	
Insurance	192	
Debtors	4 882	
Creditors		8 405
Cash in hand	352	
Balance with bank	3 792	
Stock at January 1st	12 025	
	£100 169	£100 169

Prepare Trading and Profit and Loss Accounts for the year ending December 31st, 19.., and Balance Sheet at that date. In preparing the accounts, the following matters should be taken into consideration:

(*a*) The stock at December 31st was valued at £10 787.
(*b*) An appropriate amount of depreciation should be written off the lease.
(*c*) 20% per annum on cost (£1 250) should be written off motor vans.
(*d*) £100 is to be reserved for rates in arrear.
(*e*) Make a provision of bad debts for £300.
(*f*) 10% per annum should be written off furniture and fittings.

Indicate in the accounts the rate of gross profits earned on the sales.

R.S.A.

18. The following trial balance was extracted from the books of Essex, a trader, as at 31st December, 1972:

	£	£
Capital Account		22 000
Freehold Land and Building	11 000	
Furniture and Fittings	1 200	
Purchases	63 420	
Sales		78 880
Stock in trade 1st January 1972	8 300	
Trade Debtors	8 125	
Trade Creditors		5 426
Rates and Insurance	850	
General Expenses	2 165	
Wages and Salaries	7 155	
Balance at Bank	1 966	
Drawings	2 570	
Bad Debts	465	
Provision for Doubtful Debts		175
Rents received		735
	£107 216	£107 216

The following matters are to be taken into account:

(*a*) Stock in trade 1st December 1972, £9 420.
(*b*) Wages and salaries outstanding at 31st December 1972, £247.
(*c*) Rates and Insurance paid in advance at 31st December 1972, £105.
(*d*) Part of the building was let to a tenant who owed £85 for rent at 31st December 1972.
(*e*) The provision for doubtful debts is to be increased by £70.
(*f*) Essex took for his own use goods costing £52.

You are required to prepare a trading and profit and loss account for the 1972 and a balance sheet at 31st December 1972.

(*R.S.A.II*)

23

General Principles: The Ledger, Trial Balance, and Final Accounts

The student who has worked carefully through the preceding chapters should have, at this stage, a good grasp of the principles of double entry bookkeeping. The chapters have dealt with the basic principle of the two-fold aspect of all transactions and with the recording of the two aspects in the accounts. They have included reference to the principle of classification which underlies the Ledger Accounts and makes them of informative value to the proprietor of the business. The student should now concentrate not only on being able to make the entries correctly, but also on being able to understand quickly and clearly the meaning of the entries in an account and the *financial situation* disclosed.

The student should also appreciate the development of the books in which the record is made to adjust the methods to the pressure of business requirements. For a simple system of accounts the Ledger is sufficient. The growth in the number of transactions to be recorded and the consequent pressure on the bookkeepers has led to the separation of Ledger Accounts and the introduction of other books to ease the volume of work required on the Ledger. It will have been observed that the basic principles of double entry have been maintained, yet the system is flexible enough in form to permit its adaptation to meet special conditions arising from a growing business. Full appreciation of the adaptive nature of the system should prepare the student for further developments to meet the needs of the different types of business organisation and the different demands made upon the bookkeeping system.

The earlier chapters show the separation of the cash accounts from the Ledger, and the benefits derived from a separate Cash Book. Later, the subsidiary books, or books of prime (or original) entry, are introduced to provide a means of recording details from which summary totals may be posted to the Ledger. For the purpose of ascertaining the gross profit, for example, for a trading period it is necessary to know, among other things, the total sales for the period.

It is sufficient for this purpose to know the total only and not the details of which the total is composed. This being so, it is unnecessary to overload the Sales Account in the Ledger. Periodical totals are enough, and the details, as they are wanted for other purposes, can be recorded separately. The separate record thus reduces the number of entries in the Sales Account and at the same time provides a classified record readily available for reference. It also permits the division of duties among the staff, a crucial part of any system of internal control, as well as a necessity for efficient operation of the bookkeeping records. This method of grouping details into special books, and the using of totals only for the Ledger entries, is capable of indefinite extension as need arises, and renders the system adaptable without abrogation of basic principles.

Chapter 13 has dealt with the separation of the Ledger into parts. The growth of large-scale business involves the maintenance of large bookkeeping systems, and the work has to be subdivided to be properly carried on. Recognising that customers and suppliers are seldom identical in person, an easy division is possible – one Ledger for the accounts of customers, and another for the accounts of firms from whom purchases are made. The former, known as the Sales, or Sold, Ledger, contains the debtors' accounts, and the latter, the Purchases Ledger, or Bought Ledger, contains the creditors' accounts. A third Ledger, called the General Ledger – sometimes the Nominal Ledger – contains the real and nominal accounts relating to the assets and liabilities and the gains and expenses of the business. In sole trading and partnership concerns a fourth Ledger, known as the Private Ledger, may be used to contain the Capital Account, the Drawings Account, and the Trading and Profit and Loss Accounts and Balance Sheets for each period. It is also kept for the Final Accounts of limited companies. A discussion of this follows in later chapters.

Further growth may demand further subdivision of these Ledgers, so that in some businesses the Sold Ledgers and the Bought Ledgers are divided into sections. One firm may find that it is best to have separate Ledgers for Town, Country, and Foreign Accounts. Another may prefer to make an alphabetical division on customers' names, such as A-K, L-R, S-Z, or departmentally, according to the nature of the business, such as for example, China Dept., Glass Dept., Hardware Dept.

Brief reference has also been made to the extensive systems of records which must be maintained in order to develop the data which is entered into the subsidiary books and the Ledger Accounts. These include systems for invoicing, payroll, stock control, payment of expenses, asset registers, and cash handling, amongst many others.

In businesses still using mainly clerical systems of bookkeeping Loose Leaf Ledgers and Card Ledgers are now commonly substituted for bound books. A Loose Leaf Ledger consists of an expanding binder into which is inserted separate sheets printed in Ledger ruling. Card Ledgers consist of similarly printed cards which are kept in trays or drawers arranged in cabinets. Such systems are also common among firms using the simpler forms of mechanised accounts. The advantages of these forms over the ordinary bound book is that the 'dead' accounts may be removed and kept separately. The binder or drawer then contains only the 'live' accounts, and sheets or cards can be added as new accounts are wanted. This avoids the work of opening a new Ledger as the old bound Ledger is filled. Further, as the sheets or cards are loose the accounts may be arranged alphabetically, rendering a separate index unnecessary. In times of pressure, as for example, when the monthly statements of account have to be prepared, loose leaf or card systems make for faster and more convenient methods of work, as they may be used by a number of clerks each taking a number of accounts. Time is saved in ordinary posting, since the accounts are continuous. As one leaf or card is filled a new one is added next to it. In the bound Ledger an estimate has to be made of the space to be allotted to an account, and if this proves insufficient, the account is continued in another place.

The disadvantage of the Loose Leaf and Card Ledger has been that leaves or cards may be wilfully destroyed or substituted or fresh cards inserted for fraudulent purposes, but this can be largely overcome by the introduction of safety locking devices and by instituting control of the issue of blank leaves or cards, allied to a well-planned system of division of duties.

The development of systems using punched card machines (see Chapter 31) in which all the details of a particular transaction are kept in a punched card, led to yet different ways of maintaining records. Although Ledger Accounts are normally printed out in such systems this is not technically necessary, as long as the punched cards can be filed in appropriate categories and readily re-sorted into different categories.

Early computer systems also used punched cards, but these have now been replaced in many cases by the storage of information in other forms, such as on magnetic tapes and discs. With modern equipment it is possible to gain access to any desired item of information, regardless of the order in which the data is recorded in the system. This reduces the need for written records, and represents a significant advance in the ways of maintaining the Ledger Accounts. Nevertheless, the basic double-entry principles are unchanged.

All these variations in form have their uses. They are introduced to meet the needs of particular types of businesses, and in every case the purpose is to facilitate the recording in order that it may keep pace with the volume of the business. *The principles of bookkeeping remain constant – it is only the material form of the recording medium that is changed to meet new conditions.*

The Trial Balance

The Trial Balance is a list of all the debit and credit balances extracted from the Ledger Accounts, including the cash and bank balances from the Cash Book. Its use as a means of checking the arithmetical accuracy of the postings to the Ledger has already been referred to. It is also used as a list of Ledger balances from which to prepare the Trading and Profit and Loss Accounts and the Balance Sheet. It is important, therefore, that the Trial Balance should be accurately drawn up, and that any error disclosed should be traced and rectified.

Examination tests often take the form of a Trial Balance from which the Final Accounts are to be prepared. In some cases only a list of the Ledger balances is given, and it is necessary to draft the Trial Balance in its normal form from it, separating the debit and credit balances. If the capital is not shown in the list it is found by ascertaining the difference between the total of the debit and the total of the credit balances. Frequent practice in drawing up Final Accounts from given Trial Balances is apt to cause one to forget the existence of the Ledger Accounts from which the Trial Balance is prepared. It should be borne in mind that the Trading and Profit and Loss Accounts are part of the double entry system, and that the items contained in them must have their corresponding entries somewhere in the Ledger Accounts if the double entry for the trading period is to be complete. In other words, in the preparation of the Final Accounts from a given Trial Balance, one aspect only of each of the items is used, it being assumed that it is known that the other aspect must be entered in its appropriate Ledger Account if the double entry record is to be complete.

However, as has been explained in Chapters 20–22, where information is given about reserves, provisions, and other adjustments, both aspects must be taken into account in preparing the Trading and Profit and Loss Accounts and Balance Sheet. This applies also to information about closing stocks.

When preparing the Final Accounts from the Trial Balance the first step is the drafting of the Trading Account to find the gross profit, and the next is the preparation of the Profit and Loss Account. After these accounts have been prepared the items remaining in the Trial Balance are those which are necessary for compiling the Balance Sheet. The profit or loss for the period must also be recorded in the Balance Sheet.

Certain difficulties may arise in the drafting of Final Accounts as the items present many variations according to the nature of the business. It is possible, however, to give a few broad rules for guidance.

The Trading Account

The first purpose of the Trading Account is to discover the gross profit for the trading period under review, partly for the amount in itself and partly for the usefulness of knowing the ratio the gross profit bears to turnover. It is useful to compare this ratio with similar information from preceding trading years.

The typical percentage of gross profit on turnover varies considerably from industry to industry, and between different kinds of retail business, but in any one business it should be fairly constant from year to year. Fluctuations in the percentage indicate a need for enquiry into causes. The stock valuation may be at fault, or pilfering may cause loss and consequently a low figure for stock on hand. Over-stocking of goods followed by sales to clear at prices near or below cost may be another reason, or, on the other hand, the buying may have been done at unduly high prices.

As the value of the gross profit figure lies at least partly in its usefulness for purposes of comparison, it is essential that the basis of its calculation should be consistent. To this end the component items of the Trading Account should not vary from year to year, but should remain constant. What those component items are necessarily varies from business to business, but a general rule to apply to all businesses is to include in the Trading Account only those items which vary directly with the turnover. This will often mean confining it to purchases, stocks, and sales.

The business man will therefore not only call for a Trading Account showing the gross profit for the period under review, he will also require the percentage of gross profit on turnover to be shown with comparative figures and percentages for previous trading periods. A simple example is given below.

Comparative Trading Accounts

	19..	19.1	19.2
	£	£	£
Stock at 1st January	20 000	30 000	20 000
Purchase (less returns)	70 000	50 000	69 500
	90 000	80 000	89 500
Less stock at 31st December	30 000	20 000	30 500
Cost of Goods Sold	60 000	60 000	59 000
Sales (or Turnover)	138 000	130 000	139 000
Gross Profit	78 000	70 000	80 000
Percentage G/P on Turnover	56·52%	53·85%	57·55%

A study of the above figures will prove of great value; a comparison of the percentages in conjunction with the turnover figures and the cost of goods sold would be the most obvious things to look at first. Of course, comparative profit and loss figures could be added as well, as may other percentages found to assist comparison, e.g. percentage of net profit on capital employed; of various expenses on turnover, etc.

In the event of stock being destroyed by fire it is possible to work out the estimated loss so long as the percentage gross profit on turnover is known. Consider the following:

Example 29. The premises of S. James were damaged by fire on 5th November and all his stock was destroyed with the exception of £200 worth which was

Trading Account of S. James

for the period ended 5th November, 19..

	£		£	£
Stock, 1st Jan.	6 000	Sales		18 000
Purchases	13 800	Stock salvaged	200	
Gross profit (estimated 20% on turnover)	3 600	Stock (estimated lost in fire)	5 200	5 400
	£23 400			£23 400

salvaged. His stock on 1st January last was £6 000. Purchases to 5th November were £13 800, and sales £18 000. James was accustomed to making 20% gross profit on turnover.

A study of the above Trading Account will show that by putting in an estimated gross profit it becomes possible to total the debit side. The amount by which the debit side now exceeds the credit side, i.e. £5 200, must be the estimated value of the stock destroyed.

Stock in Relation to Trading

Stock is a quantity of physical material waiting to be sold. When goods are bought they are entered in the Purchases Account at cost price; when they are sold these same goods appear in the Sales Ac-Account at selling price. While waiting to be sold the goods are said to be 'in stock', and at the end of the trading period, if they are still unsold, they are valued at cost and entered in the Stock Account. So goods will appear in three different accounts and students should be quite sure that they understand the relationship between them, especially as all three accounts have transfers to Trading Account. The following example should help.

Example 30. A trader had in stock 1 000 articles valued at £0·15 each on 1st Jan. During the month he bought 6 000 more of these articles at the same price but returned 200 as useless. He sold 6 500 articles during the month for £0·25 each. Customers returned 400 as not suitable. His trading Account for the month would appear as follows:

Trading Account
for the month ended 31st January

	Articles	Price £	£		Articles	Price £	£
Stock	1 000	0.15	150	Sales	6 500	0.25	1 625
Purchases	6 000	0.15	900	*Less* Returns	400	0.25	100
	7 000		1 050		6 100		1 525
Less Returns	200	0.15	30	Stock	700	0.15	105
	6 800		1 020		6 800		
Gross profit c/d			610				
			£1 630				£1 630

In the information given, no mention is made of the closing stock, but it is evident that this must be the number of articles in hand at the end of the trading period and valued at cost price, viz. 700 articles at £0·15 each.

If the cost price of the goods were to alter during the trading period it would be necessary to determine the price at which to show the goods remaining in stock at the end of the period.

One of three methods is usually adopted. They are:

(*a*) First-in, first-out (known as FIFO)
(*b*) Last-in, first out (known as LIFO)
(*c*) Average price.

The *FIFO method* assumes that goods are sold in the same order that they are purchased. Therefore the closing stock is valued at the latest unit prices paid.

The *LIFO method* assumes that goods are sold in the reverse order to that in which they were purchased. Therefore the closing stock is valued at the earliest unit prices paid.

The *average price method* assumes that goods are sold without reference to the order in which they were purchased. Therefore the closing stock is valued at the weighted average cost of the goods handled during the period.

For example, assume that in Example 30 the opening stock was purchased at £0·15 each, but that the next 3 000 units purchased cost £0·17 each, and the other 3 000 cost £0·20 each. Assume also that the returns were made from the goods purchased at £0·20.

Under FIFO the units of closing stock will be valued at £0·20 each. Under LIFO each unit of closing stock will be valued at £0·15. Under the average price method each unit of closing stock will be valued at £0·179, which is the weighted average of (1 000 × £0·15) + (3 000 × £0·17) + (2 800 × £0·20).

The student should calculate the effect of these various methods on the gross profit.

Rate of Turnover

The gross profit of any business will naturally be affected by the *rate of stock turnover*; that is, the number of times in a trading period that any particular line of goods is bought and sold. Obviously, the more rapid this rate of turnover is the greater must be the total gross profit, whether the gross profit on the article be large or small.

The rate of turnover is computed by finding the average of stocks in the trading period in question and dividing it into the cost of goods sold, defined as the turnover less the gross profit.

Consider the figures in the Trading Account below showing 1 month's trading:

Trading Account for January 19. .

	£		£
Stock, 1st Jan.	1 000	Sales	12 000
Purchases	8 000	Stock, 31st Jan.	1 500
Gross Profit	4 500		
	£13 500		£13 500

The *cost of goods sold* is £1 000 + £8 000 − £1 500 = £ 7500.

The *average stock* is $\frac{£1\,000 + £1\,500}{2} = £1\,250.$

The *rate of turnover of stock* is $\frac{£7\,500}{£1\,250} = 6$ times per month.

By finding the rate of turnover on particular lines of goods in this way, it is possible to discard slow-moving lines (that is those on which the rate of turnover is considered too low) and to try to step up the sales of fast-moving lines (those on which the rate of turnover is high or at least adequate). However, it is necessary to check that the gross profit on the slow-moving stock is not so great as to make up for the slowness.

Before proceeding to some observations on the Profit and Loss Account it is as well to remind students at this point that a frequent examination question concerns the effect on the gross profit of errors found in the books. It is of the utmost importance for a student to be able to trace errors through to the Trading and Profit and Loss Accounts and practice should be had in answering the following type of question:

> If the Returns Inwards Journal was over-cast by £10, say what effect, if any, this would have on the gross profit for the period.

Profit and Loss Account

The gross profit as shown by the Trading Account is carried to the Profit and Loss Account, and against it are set all the expenses incurred in the course of the business other than those which have already been taken to the Trading Account. Any gains other than those arising from the sale of goods included in the Trading Account are added to the gross profit. The difference is the net profit or loss, as the case may be, for the trading period. This is of importance as, if price levels are not changing too much, it represents the amount available for distribution to the proprietors of the business. Because of this, it is also of importance that in the process of arriving at the net profit every form of expense should be taken into account. Certain adjustments may have to be made in the expenses in order that the true net profit may be shown. For example, account must be taken of any decline in value of the assets and of any outstanding expense properly attributable to the year under review. These and similar adjustments are considered more fully hereafter.

No particular form of Profit and Loss Account has to be used, but the modern tendency is (*a*) to use the vertical form as this facilitates the reading of accounts; (*b*) to group together like items. Broadly speaking, the expense items in the Profit and Loss Account may be placed in one of the three following categories.

	£	£
Gross Profit brought down		x
Add Receipts:		
Discounts Received		x
		x
Less Expenses:		
Administration:		
Office Salaries	x	
Directors' Fees	x	
Rent and Rates	x	
Heating and Lighting	x	
Insurance	x	
Postages and Telephone	x	
Selling and Distribution:		
Advertising	x	
Salesmen's Salaries and Commissions	x	
Carriage on sales	x	
Petrol and Oil (Delivery Vans)	x	
Finance		
Discounts Allowed	x	
Bank Interest and Charges	x	
Bad Debts	x	
Provision for Bad Debts	x	
Provision for Depreciation:		
Fixtures and Fittings	x	
		x
Net Profit (or Loss)		x

The disposal of the net profit varies according to the nature of the ownership of the business. It may be posted to the Capital Account of a sole trader, or, in the case of a partnership business, distributed among the partners. In company accounts the net profit is partly paid out as dividends, and partly retained in the business in the accounts for reserves. In the case of partnerships and companies this distribution of profit is entered in a second section of the Profit and Loss Account called the Appropriation Account.

The Balance Sheet

The purpose of a Balance Sheet is to present a true and fair view of the financial position of the business at a given date. It is prepared from the balances of the accounts that remain open on the books after the preparation of the Trading and Profit and Loss Accounts. Such balances are assets or claims, or are regarded temporarily as such for Balance Sheet purposes. The Balance Sheet is not a Ledger Account. It is simply a statement in a particular form, and may best be defined as a classified list of the debit and credit balances remaining on the books after the preparation of the Trading and Profit and Loss Accounts.

If the Balance Sheet is to present a true and fair view of the financial position, it is essential that its component items should be examined with the greatest care to ensure that each appears at its appropriate value. Much will depend upon the work done to ensure that all outstanding debts and all declines in value of the assets have been provided for. Provision for depreciation was dealt with in Chapter 22, where it was explained that normal wear and tear in use of, for example, plant and machinery, or furniture and fittings, must cause some loss of value, and that to ignore such a fall would give a false value for the asset in the Balance Sheet. Such valuations are necessarily only reasonable estimates of the value of the assets to the business as a going concern. Current cost accounting attempts to tackle this problem of asset valuation in a different way. It is, however, impossible to make an actual test unless the business is wound up, the assets are converted into cash and the liabilities paid off, or, alternatively, unless the business is sold as a going concern. Then, and then only, could it be said whether the valuations were fair estimates, and the Balance Sheet a true picture of the financial position. Failing such a test, the only action possible is to ensure that there is no serious mis-statement of value, and that all precautions are taken to make the

Balance Sheet a reasonable and honest statement, perhaps erring on the side of prudence and caution.

Comparison of a series of Balance Sheets may help in assessing correctly the position as disclosed by the last Balance Sheet of the series. Some idea can then be formed of the periodical treatment of the assets and whether sufficient allowance has been made for declines in value. Further, some insight is possible into the trading position of the firm. The fact that the assets exceed the liabilities (i.e. the claims other than capital), shows that the concern is solvent and could pay its debts in full provided that, if necessary, the assets can be converted into cash at approximately their balance sheet valuations. The soundness or otherwise of the trading position is also indicated. The current liabilities should be less than the current assets, such as cash, stock, sundry debtors, and investments, i.e. there should be sufficient working capital. If not, the firm is overtrading and disaster may follow on the contracting of debts without sufficient means of payment. It does not follow that there should be cash of an amount equivalent to the total trade creditors. Trade creditors do not all have to be paid at one time, and meanwhile trade continues and stock and debtors are converted into cash. The flow is continuous and may be ample to meet needs as they arise, but debts should not be created of a nature and to an extent that pressure for payment may jeopardise the continuance of the business through lack of ability to meet the demand.

There is no statutory compulsion regarding the form of a Balance Sheet except that in the case of limited companies certain information must be disclosed. All companies are subject to legislation in the Companies Acts, and to professional accounting guidelines in the form of Statements of Standard Accounting Practice. Companies with shares quoted on the Stock Exchange are subject to the Exchange's Listing requirements.

It is customary in England to summarise the credit balances on the left-hand side, and the debit balances on the right-hand side, of the Balance Sheet, and that the purpose of the statement may be fully served, it is advisable to give full information on all essential points, as, for example, the rate or amount of depreciation and the method of valuation of the assets. Companies now give a statement listing their main accounting policies. The component items should be presented in an orderly manner and in a sequence that should be adhered to year by year. The fixed assets are grouped together, followed by the current assets. In many commercial concerns the form adopted is to arrange the assets in the reverse order of their realisability or ease of conversion into cash, starting with the least easily convertible asset and ending with the cash balance itself. Somewhat similarly, the claims are arranged in the reverse order to that in which they must be met, starting with the proprietor's capital.

In these days the headings claims, liabilities and assets are usually omitted altogether from a Balance Sheet. In their place appear sub-headings to groups of items, e.g. sub-headings such as Capital, Loans, and Current Liabilities on the Left-hand side of the Balance Sheet and sub-headings such as Fixed Assets and Current Assets on the right-hand side of the Balance Sheet.

To reveal, at a glance, the total of fixed assets, the total of current assets, the working capital, the net book value of the assets and the amount of capital employed, a balance sheet may be set out as shown below.

The capital employed consists of funds contributed by the proprietor of the business and long-term funds (long-term loans) borrowed from other sources, and is equal to the book value of the net assets employed in operating the business.

Balance Sheet, as at 31st December, 19. .

	£		£ *Cost*	£ *Depreciation*	£ *Net Value*
CAPITAL	9 300	FIXED ASSETS			
LOAN (LONG TERM)	4 000	Machinery	10 000	4 000	6 000
		Fixtures and fittings	1 000	300	700
			11 000	4 300	6 700
		CURRENT ASSETS			
		Stock	5 500		
		Sundry debtors	3 600		
		Cash in hand and balance at bank	1 750	10 850	
		LESS CURRENT LIABILITIES			
		Trade creditors	4 150		
		Accrued Expenses	100	4 250	
		WORKING CAPITAL			6 600
Capital employed	£13 300	Net book value of assets			£13 300

The Fixed Assets have been set out in a form consistent with modern practice. It shows the cost, depreciation and net value of each category of Fixed Asset, and also of the Fixed Assets as a whole.

This form of layout can be incorporated in a vertical presentation of the Balance Sheet, which would otherwise be in the form illustrated in Chapter 14, page 120.

Layout of Ledger Accounts

An alternative to the normal T-shaped account was illustrated in Chapter 19. It uses three columns adjacent to each other to show respectively debits, credits, and the balance after each transaction. This involves a change of presentation but not of bookkeeping principle.

EXERCISES 23

1. A Reynolds commenced business as a dealer in machinery and spare parts with the following assets and liabilities:

	£
Stock on hand	8 320
Debtor: The Pulman Sawmills Ltd	5 350
Creditor: Torquay Machinery Co.	2 525
Premises	1 500
Balance at bank	1 762
Cash in hand	158

Open a set of books for the business as at July 1, 19.., and record the following transactions:

July 7. Received from the Pulman Sawmills Ltd. a cheque for the balance of the company's account, less $1\frac{1}{4}\%$ cash discount.
,, 20. Sold on credit, to the Wood & Lumber Co., machinery to the value of £2 500.
,, 31. Paid by cash, wages, £41.
Aug. 5. Purchased from the Torquay Machinery Co., machinery to the value of £1 750.
,, 19. Sold machinery, on credit, to the Pulman Sawmills Ltd., for £3 575.
,, 31. Paid by cash, wages £41.
Sept. 11. Paid by cheque, to the Torquay Machinery Co., the sum of £1 262 on account.
,, 30. Paid by cash, wages, £41.
,, 30. Cash takings paid into bank, £420.

Prepare Trial Balance and Trading and Profit and Loss Accounts for the three months ending September 30th. The stock on hand at September 30th was valued at £5 125.

Balance the Ledger Accounts at September 30th, and record the following transactions:

Oct.	5.	Purchased adjoining premises for the purpose of extending showrooms and stores, and paid by cheque, £3 500.
,,	30.	Sold machinery on credit, to the Export Co. for £2 205.
Nov.	17.	Paid by cheque, the balance of the Torquay Machinery Co.'s account.
Dec.	2.	Cashed a cheque for £200 and handed proceeds to the petty cashier.
,,	31.	Paid by cash, wages, £75.
,,	31.	Cashed a cheque for private use, £100.

Prepare Trial Balance and Trading and Profit and Loss Accounts for the three months ending December 31st, 19. ., and Balance Sheet at that date.

The stock on hand at December 31st was valued at £3 486.

R.S.A.

2. The Trial Balance given below was extracted from the books of G. Britton on December 31, 19. . . You are required to:

(1) Open Ledger Accounts showing the balances.
(2) Prepare Trading and Profit and Loss Accounts for the year ended December 31, 19. ., closing off the proper Ledger Accounts.

Note: (*a*) The Stock on December 31 was valued at £14 100. (*b*) Two-thirds of wages is to be charged to Trading Account, and one-third to Profit and Loss Account.

(3) Bring down the remaining balances of Ledger Accounts and prepare a Balance Sheet as in December 31, 19. . .

Trial Balance.

December 31, 19...

	Dr. £	*Cr.* £
Capital (fixed) January 1		30 000
Drawings during year	3 640	
Creditors (W. Miles & Co.)		4 280
Debtors (Lightwood Bros.)	8 780	
Stock (January 1)	12 340	
Investment	4 000	
Plant and machinery	9 600	
Purchases	37 020	
Sales		57 240
Carriage on purchases	580	
Returns inwards	720	
Rent and rates	2 080	
Travellers' salaries	3 260	
Discounts on sales	1 150	
Wages	8 490	
Interest on investment		140
	£91 660	£91 660

R.S.A. (adapted)

3. Explain in as detailed a way as you can the reasons why a business would use the following books:

(i) Sales Day Book.
(ii) Cash Book.
(iii) Returns Outwards Book.

4. From the following information prepare the account of S. Fane as it would appear in the Ledger of G. Mason.

(i) Fane owed Mason £20 on 1st Feb.
(ii) Mason sold goods to Fane, £126, on 12th Feb.
(iii) Fane returned goods, £14, to Mason on 17th Feb.
(iv) Fane bought goods from Mason, £49, on 20th Feb.
(v) Fane sent Mason a cheque for £150 on account, 25th Feb.
(iv) Balance off the account and bring down the balance as at 28th Feb.
(vii) Mason received notification of the bankruptcy of Fane and a cheque for a first and final dividend of £0·50 in the £. Rule off and close the account.

5. Define (*a*) Fixed Asset.
(*b*) Current Asset.
(*c*) Working Capital.

(*d*) Current Liability.
(*e*) Net book value of assets.
(*f*) Capital employed.

6. Explain why stock-taking is carried out periodically. What are the bases for valuing stock?

7. (*a*) State how each of the following errors would affect the gross profit of a business. (*b*) The gross profit before discovery of the errors was £3 000. Give the correct gross profit.

(i) The Sales Returns Book was over-added by £20.
(ii) An invoice for goods bought totalling £60 was omitted from the books.
(iii) The closing stock was under-valued by £649.
(iv) Carriage on purchases had been entered as £189 instead of £198.

(*c*) If the turnover was £6 000, state what difference the above errors would make to the percentage of gross profit on turnover.

8. The following is the Balance Sheet of V. Williams as at 29th February, 19...

Balance Sheet

	£	£		£	£
Capital	5 100		Goodwill		1 000
Add Net Profit	900		Freehold premises		4 000
		6 000	Sundry debtors	1 500	
Loan from S. Roberts		3 000	*Less* Provision for		
Sundry creditors		1 970	bad debts	100	
					1 400
			Stock		2 800
			Bank		1 700
			Cash		70
		£10 970			£10 970

(i) State the total of the Fixed Assets.
(ii) State the total of the Current Assets.
(iii) What is the figure of Working Capital?
(iv) If Goodwill were written off, what would be the effect on the Balance Sheet?
(v) If a Provision for Salaries due of £200 had to be made, what would be the effect on the Balance Sheet?
(vi) If goods bought on credit for £300 had been omitted, what would be the effect of the correction of this error on the Balance Sheet?
(vii) Was Williams solvent or insolvent? Give your reasons.

(viii) State the effect on the Balance Sheet of making the provision for bad debts 5% of the sundry debtors.

(ix) Re-write the Balance Sheet as it would appear after all necessary adjustments had been made and put the assets under appropriate headings.

9. From the following details draw up a Balance Sheet in such a way as to show within the Balance Sheet:

(i) The total of Fixed Assets.
(ii) The total of Current Assets.
(iii) The total of Current Liabilities.
(iv) The Working Capital.
(v) The net Book Value of the assets.
(vi) The Capital employed.

	Dr. £	*Cr.* £
Capital (1 Jan, 19..)		8 000
Net profit for year to 31st December, 19..		3 450
Drawings	3 000	
Machinery at cost	7 000	
Provision for depreciation on machinery		2 500
Furniture and fittings	250	
Stock	4 750	
Trade debtors	3 800	
Provision for bad debts		182
Sundry creditors: Trade		3 240
Expense		88
Loan (5 years) from X.L. Loan Co.		1 000
Bank overdraft		340
	£18 800	£18 800

10. J.K. started business on 1st January, 19.. with £2 000. He borrowed a further £1 000 from his uncle on a long-term basis. He paid both amounts into a business bank account.

During the ensuing six months J.K.:

(i) Purchases furniture and fittings £450 and a second-hand motor van £860 and paid both amounts by cheque.
(ii) Purchased stock-in-trade on credit for £6 150.
(iii) Sold goods (cost price £4 140) on credit for £5 240.
(iv) Paid business expenses by cheque £320.
(v) Received from trade debtors and paid into bank £3 310.
(vi) Paid trade creditors by cheques, £3 490.

On 30th June, 19.., J.K. depreciated the motor van by £70 and the furniture and fittings by £30. On that date £20 was still owing for business expenses.

(*a*) Calculate as at 30th June, 19. . :

(i) The bank balance.
(ii) The value, at cost price, of the stock-in-trade.
(iii) The total of trade debtors.
(iv) The total of trade creditors.

(*b*) Prepare a Trading and Profit and Loss Account for the half year ended 30th June, 19. . and a Balance Sheet as at that date.

Note: The Balance Sheet is to be prepared in such a way as to show *within the Balance Sheet* the totals of fixed assets, current assets and current liabilities; the amount of working capital, the net book value of the assets, and the capital employed.

24

Bills of Exchange: Bills Payable

The granting of a period of credit in business transactions implies that the seller of goods under such conditions must wait for payment, and that the purchaser takes possession of the goods but postpones payment. The advantage lies with the purchaser for he may sell the goods in the ordinary course of business and receive cash, including a profit, before the credit period expires. The seller knows that it is not always possible to expect cash against goods and that he will normally have to offer credit if he wishes to sell his goods. But it is to his own interest to shorten the credit period as much as possible.

One way open to the seller by which he may allow the purchaser to defer payment for a period and yet at the same time obtain cash for his own use, is to arrange for the transaction to be settled by a Bill of Exchange.

Consider the following transactions:

Jan. 1 M. Redman bought goods value £1 000 from A. Yesufu on three months' credit.

If this takes the ordinary course, Redman will pay the account at the end of March, meanwhile having the use of £1 000 worth of Yesufu's goods. Yesufu will have his own expenses to meet, but he cannot expect Redman to pay his account before the expiration of the agreed credit period.

It may be arranged, however, between buyer and seller that, for their mutual advantage, a *Bill of Exchange* shall be used to finance the transaction.

A Bill of Exchange is defined in the Bills of Exchange Act 1882, as:

> 'An unconditional order in writing, addressed by one person to another, signed by the person giving it, requiring the person to whom it is addressed to pay on demand, or at a fixed or determinable future time, a certain sum in money to, or to the order of, a specified person or to bearer.'

This is the legal definition. How it applies in practice will be gathered from the procedure followed for the above and subsequent examples. An inland Bill of Exchange is one that is both drawn and payable in Great Britain and Northern Ireland; all other bills are foreign bills. Formal Bills of Exchange are now very rarely used in domestic trade within the United Kingdom. It is generally found to be more convenient to use a mixture of normal trade credit, with bank overdraft financing where necessary. Payment is effected by cheque or bank giro credit. Technically these are forms of Bill of Exchange, addressed by the drawer of the cheque to his banker, instructing the banker to pay a stated sum in accordance with stated instructions, usually to a stated payee immediately. Most of the matters raised in this chapter and Chapter 25 arise from the delayed date of settlement of the Bill, which in the example below was three months after the date on which it was drawn up. However, Bills of Exchange are still used in international trade. They are particularly appropriate when the exporter wants prompt payment, but the importer wants to receive and inspect the goods before paying for them. If the goods are being sent by ship from, say, Hong Kong to Liverpool, the long period of the journey can be covered by a suitably drawn up Bill of Exchange. Chapter 25 explains how the exporter can use the Bill when it has been accepted. This Chapter concentrates on the position of the importer, together with some general points.

A Bill of Exchange in the form that would be used in the transaction between Redman and Yesufu is shown below:

£1 000 1st January, 19..

Three months after date pay to my order the sum of One thousand pounds value received.

A. Yesufu

To M. Redman,
Marlborough Street,
London, SW4 7AA

Reference to its wording will show that it is addressed by Yesufu to Redman, is signed by Yesufu, and orders Redman to pay him at a determinable future time – three months from 1st January – a fixed sum of money. This is expressed in pounds sterling. Many international trading transactions are priced in sterling, though other currencies are used where the parties to the transaction agree.

The person who draws up and signs the bill is known as the *drawer*.

The person on whom the bill is drawn is the *drawee*. The person to whom the drawee is ordered to pay is known as the *payee*.

In the example, Yesufu is both the drawer and payee, and Redman is the drawee.

On it being agreed to use a Bill of Exchange, Yesufu draws up the bill. He forwards it to Redman for his *acceptance*, which means that Redman accepts the liability under the terms of the bill, indicating his acceptance by signing his name across the face of it. His signature alone is sufficient to bind him, but the word 'accepted' is usually added. Redman may also obtain the signature of an Accepting House to support his own acceptance. An Accepting House is a reputable financial institution, often a bank or merchant bank, which specialises in this service. By accepting a Bill it accepts a liability to pay Redman's debt, should he fail to do so. Redman must, of course, pay the Accepting House for this service.

Redman may *domicile* the bill by adding to his signature the place of payment. This is usually the name and address of the drawee's bankers. In the event of the place of payment not being mentioned, the bill is payable at the acceptor's usual place of business.

Redman then returns the *acceptance*, as the accepted bill is called, to Yesufu. What Yesufu may do with the bill is discussed in the next chapter. To him, as he is to receive the money, the bill is a *Bill Receivable*. To Redman, who has to pay the money in due course, it is a *Bill Payable*.

Days of Grace

The acceptor, by accepting the bill, engages that he will pay it according to the terms of his acceptance. In this example, the date of maturity is three months from 1st January. Bills may be payable on demand or, as in this case, at some future date. Except for bills payable on demand, three extra *days of grace* beyond the date mentioned may be allowed for payment.

The day for payment may happen to fall on a Sunday, Christmas Day, or Good Friday. The bill is then payable on the preceding business day. Should it fall due for payment on a Bank Holiday, other than Christmas Day, or Good Friday, it is payable on the succeeding business day.

Days of grace have never been more than a custom, but their widespread and general application meant that they were considered to be part of the terms of a Bill of Exchange unless expressly excluded in some way. They have been abolished in many countries in recent years. In the United Kingdom this was done by section 3(2) of the Banking and Financial Dealings Act 1971. However, they continue to be used in some countries, and this can raise the possibility of a legal dispute about which country's law governs the situation in international transactions.

Bills Payable

The example given at the beginning of this chapter is now repeated.

> ***Example 31.*** On Jan. 1st M. Redman bought goods value £1 000 from A. Yesufu and gave his acceptance for three months for that amount.

The entry to be made in Redman's books for the purchase follows the normal course. It will first be entered in the Purchase Day Book, and posted from there to the credit of Yesufu's account in the Ledger.

The new point is that Redman accepts a Bill of Exchange, and forwards it to Yesufu. For Redman it is a Bill Payable. He is liable on the bill, and in three months' time it will be presented for payment either to him personally, or, if he has so arranged, through his bankers. Yesufu receives the bill in the first place but, as will be discussed. later, he may dispose of it without Redman's knowledge. Redman then has no means of knowing who will be presenting the bill for payment or, pending presentation, to whom he is liable.

In Redman's books, Yesufu's account will be debited with the amount of the bill. The Bills Payable Account will be credited to record the giving of the bill, as shown below:

A. Yesufu 81

19..			£	19..			£
Jan. 1	Bills Payable	40	1 000	Jan. 1	Purchases (Corresponding entry is in Purchases A/c.)	P.B.	1 000

Bills Payable

			£	19..			£
				Jan. 1	A. Yesufu	81	1 000

Yesufu's account is now closed. In place of the debt due to Yesufu which appeared on that account there is a debt due to an unknown holder of the bill, and this is shown in the Bills Payable Account.

Had no bill been given, and it had happened that a Balance Sheet was being prepared, the debt of £1 000 due to Yesufu would have been included under the item 'Sundry Creditors' on the claims side of the Balance Sheet. Now there is a change in the nature of the current liabilities, as Yesufu's Account is closed and cannot be included among the creditors. A new form of liability, 'Bills Payable', appears in the Balance Sheet.

Payment on Presentation

Redman will arrange with his bankers to pay the bill on presentation. He must, of course, see that his bank account is sufficiently in funds to meet it. The bill will be taken by the bank on presentation, and when payment is complete it will be returned to Redman in due course with his paid cheques, when he may cancel or destroy it.

The entries that are necessary in Redman's books to record the payment on April 1st are:

(i) A Credit to Bank Account in the Cash Book, as the money is paid away.
(ii) A Debit to Bills Payable Account, as the bill is received back.
The accounts will now appear as below:

A. Yesufu 18

19..			£	19..			£
Jan. 1	Bills Payable	40	1 000	Jan. 1	Purchases (Corresponding entry is in Purchases A/c.)	P.B.	1 000

Bills Payable 40

19..			£	19..			£
Apr. 1	Cash	C.B.	1 000	Jan. 1	A. Yesufu	81	1 000

Dr. **Cash Book** *Cr.*

			Bank				Bank £
				19..			
				Apr. 1	Bills Payable (A. Yesufu)	40	1 000

Ultimately, therefore, the Bills Payable Account is closed and a credit entry is made in the Bank Account. The financial position and the accounts are now as they would have been had a cheque been sent direct to Yesufu. The use of a bill has involved the opening of the Bills Payable Account, and the creation, temporarily, of a new liability called Bills Payable in place of the original creditor.

EXERCISES 24

1. Give the entries to record the following transactions in B. W. Payne's accounts:

Sept. 1.	Bought goods to the value of £500 on credit from J. Chanrai & Sons.
,, 2.	Accepted a Bill for three months for £500 drawn by J. Chanrai & Sons.
Dec. 5.	Bankers paid the Bill on presentation.

2. On 5th April T. Williams bought goods, £600, from R. B. Robledo and gave him his acceptance for two months for that amount. Williams arranged with his bankers to meet the Bill, and it was duly paid on presentation. Show how T. Williams should record these transactions in his books.

3. J. W. Firth bought gloves, £340, from the Delhi Garment Company on 12th June who drew on him at three months for the amount. Firth accepted the Bill and arranged with his bankers to meet the Bill on presentation. Record in Firth's books the purchase, the giving of the acceptance, and the payment of the Bill at maturity.

4. From the following particulars draw up a Bill of Exchange in the usual form:

Drawer: Yourself
Drawee: B. Worthington, 12 Mill Road, Ottawa, Canada.
Payee: W. Baxter
Date: 10th December, 19. .
Amount: £2 215
Term: Three months.

5. From the following balances, extracted from the books of G. Roberts as on June 30th, 19. ., you are required to prepare Trading and Profit and Loss Accounts for the month ended June 30th, and a Balance Sheet as on that date.

	£
Cash at bank: Current Account	198
,, ,, ,, Deposit Account	1 000
Warehouse salaries and expenses	1 462
Freehold property	14 876
Capital Account	18 000

	£
Office salaries	1 255
Discount received	76
Purchases	6 481
Sales	10 527
Stock at the beginning of the year	2 106
Office expenses	236
Bills payable	500
Sundry creditors	2 274
Sundry debtors	3 786
Bank deposit interest	23

The stock at the end of the month was valued at £1 968.

6. The following Balances were extracted from the books of Ernest Midgeley as on the 31st December, 19. . :

Dr.	£	*Cr.*	£
Cash in hand	200	Provision for doubtful debts	300
Cash at bank	6 270	Sundry creditors	6 410
Land and Buildings	10 800	Sales	69 420
Furniture and fittings	8 200	Returns outwards	760
Motor vehicle	3 650	Discount	1 490
Stock in hand, Jan. 1st	11 270	Bills payable	2 580
Sundry debtors	8 320	Capital Account	32 610
Purchases	49 640		
Returns inwards	400		
Discount	1 370		
Interest	800		
Wages	4 900		
Drawings A/c.	4 200		
Bad debts	300		
Rates	600		
Gas and electricity	530		
Sundry expenses	2 120		
	£113 570		£113 570

You are required to prepare the Trading and Profit and Loss Accounts and a Balance Sheet as on the 31st December. Before doing so the following information and adjustments must be taken into account:

Write 5% depreciation off fixtures and fittings, and depreciate the motor vehicle by 10%.

Make the provision for doubtful debts up to 5% on sundry debtors.

The value of the stock in hand on 31st December was £6 800.

N.C.T.E.C. (adapted).

25

Bills of Exchange: Bills Receivable

The person who is to receive the money on a Bill of Exchange regards it as a Bill Receivable. The transaction discussed in the preceding chapter may, therefore, be viewed from another standpoint, that of the holder of the bill. From his point of view the transaction would appear as follows:

Example 32. On Jan. 1st A. Yesufu sold to M. Redman goods valued £1 000 and received from him his acceptance for three months for that amount.

The problems of accounting for foreign currency transactions are considerable. It is therefore assumed that, even though the Bill in the example was probably international, Yesufu lives in a country which also uses the pound as its currency, that the exchange rate between the two currencies is parity, and that Yesufu incurs no currency conversion costs. These simplifying assumptions enable the Chapter to concentrate on the aspects of the transaction relating to the Bill of Exchange from Yesufu's point of view.

The sale of goods would be recorded in Yesufu's books in the usual manner. For the Bill of Exchange it is necessary to record the receipt of it and from whom it was received; credit the giver – in this example M. Redman—and debit Bills Receivable Account.

M. Redman 56

19..			£	19..			£
Jan. 1	Sales (Corresponding entry is in Sales Account)	S.B.	1 000	Jan. 1	Bills Receivable	74	1 000

Bills Receivable 74

19..			£	19..			
Jan. 1	M. Redman	56	1 000				

The effect of these entries is to close M. Redman's Account, and in the place of the debt due from him to show a new asset, a Bill Receivable for £1 000. In a Balance Sheet prepared at this point, the debit balance of the Bills Receivable Account would appear under that heading among the current assets.

Yesufu has a choice of methods of dealing with the bill in his possession. He may retain it until the *due date*, April 1st, and then present it through his bankers for payment. (Alternative methods are discussed later.) If he decides to do this, and the bill is met at maturity, his bankers will credit his account with the amount received. He will have given up the bill: Redman's recovery of possession of the bill is prima facie evidence that he has paid it. No other form of receipt is necessary. The entries to record the giving up of the bill and the receipt of the cash are:

(i) *Credit* Bills Receivable Account, and
(ii) *Debit* Bank Account in the Cash Book.

The whole transaction will appear in Yesufu's books as below:

M. Redman 56

19..			£	19..			£
Jan. 1	Sales (Corresponding entry in Sales A/c.)	S.B.	1 000	Jan. 1	Bills Receivable	74	1 000

Bills Receivable 74

19..			£	19..			£
Jan. 1	M. Redman	56	1 000	Apr. 1	Cash	CB	1 000

Cash Book

Dr. (Bank Columns only) *Cr.*

Apr. 1	Bills Receivable (Redman)	74	1 000				

In practice bills are deposited with the bank for collection soon after receipt, the bank holding them in safe custody and presenting them for payment at due date. The above entries in the Bills Account and the Cash Book are made on the bill being duly honoured at maturity. On being requested the bank will notify its customer immediately a bill is honoured.

Dishonoured Bills

If payment is refused or cannot be obtained for any reason, the bill is said to be *dishonoured* (i.e. not paid) on presentation. If the bill has been deposited with the bank for collection and it is dishonoured the bank will notify its customer. It will be necessary to revive the personal debt of the acceptor, as the bill is valueless as an asset, though it is valuable as legal evidence against the acceptor. The bank may have thought it necessary to have further evidence of dishonour, and may have taken steps for it to be re-presented by a *Notary Public* whose charges they will have paid. The Notary Public affixes to the bill a printed slip bearing his name, the reason for the dishonour, and a note of his charges. This expense being caused by the acceptor, it is recoverable from him and, until recovered, must be recorded as an additional debt due from him.

On dishonour:

(i) *Credit* Bills Receivable Account with the amount of the bill.
(ii) *Credit* Bank Account in the Cash Book with the amount of the bank charges.
(iii) *Debit* the personal account of the acceptor with the amount of the bill and the bank charges.

In the above example the dishonour would make Redman's Account appear as below:

M. Redman 56

19..			£	19..			£
Jan. 1	Sales	S.B.	1 000	Jan. 1	Bill Receivable	74	1 000
Apr. 2	Bill Receivable A/c. (Dishonoured Bill)	74	1 000				
„ 2	Bank Charges	C.B.	5				

Sometimes a trader may pay his bills into the bank for collection two or three days prior to the due date, and he may then credit Bills Receivable Account and debit his Bank Account on the assumption that the bill will be met. Should dishonour occur he would have to make a credit entry in his Bank Account to cancel the debit entry –

he corresponding debit entry being made in the acceptor's account for the amount of the bill and the charges.

Discounting Bills of Exchange

The holder of the bill may decide instead to *discount* it with his bankers, and not to retain it until maturity. This means that the bank will pay him the value of the bill immediately, and the bank will then recover the money from the acceptor when the bill reaches maturity. This will place the holder of the bill in funds at once and is one of the advantages afforded by the use of a Bill of Exchange to finance a business deal. Banks are prepared to discount bills for customers provided that the standing of the person liable on a bill offers reasonable prospect of payment at due date, or that the bank's customer is of good standing so that in the event of dishonour his account may be debited without risk or loss to the banker. The bank charges for the service, as it will not be re-imbursed until the bill is met. The amount of the charge depends upon the financial standing of the acceptor and upon the current rates for discounting and is calculated at a percentage on the face value for the period of the bill. If the discount rate is 8 per cent per annum, the charge on the above bill for £1 000 for three months would be £20, if discounted immediately after receipt from the acceptor.

The *discount charge* should not be confused with cash discount or trade discount. On discounting:

(i) *Credit* Bills Receivable Account, as the bill will be handed over to the bank.
(ii) *Debit* Bank Account in the Cash Book with the full value of the bill.

The bank credits its customer with the full amount of the bill discounted, but makes a *contra* (i.e. offsetting or opposite) entry of the discount charge. The holder, therefore, receives somewhat less than the face value of the bill but considers that the lesser sum is worth as much to him now as the full value would be in three month's time.

Later, examination of the Bank Statement will disclose the amount of the discount charges. For these charges:

(i) *Credit* Bank Account in the Cash Book.
(ii) *Debit* Discount on Bills Account, for eventual transfer to the debit of Profit and Loss Account.

Bills Receivable 74

19..			£	19..			£
Jan. 1	M. Redman		1 000	Jan. 3	Bank	C.B.	1 000

Dr. **Cash Book** *Cr.*

19..			BANK £	19..			BANK £
Jan. 3	Bill Receivable discounted (M. Redman)	74	1 000	Jan. 6	Discount charge on (Redman)	82	20

Discount on Bills 82

19..			£				£
Jan. 6	Bank (Redman's Bill)	C.B.	20				

In the event of the dishonour of a discounted bill the bank has the legal right to seek reimbursement from its customer. The trader will then *credit* his Bank Account in the Cash Book with the amount of the bill and the bank charges for presenting, and *debit* the acceptor's account with these sums to revive the debt and to record the additional debt for the charges. The bank's *original* charge for discounting *cannot* be placed to the acceptor's account, since that charge was for the personal convenience to the holder.

The following entries illustrate the example given above on the assumption that the bill was discounted and was dishonoured on presentation:

M. Redman 56

19..			£	19..			£
Jan. 1	Sales	S.B.	1 000	Jan. 1	Bill Receivable	74	1 000
Apr. 5	Dishonoured Bill	C.B.	1 000				
	Bank Charges	C.B.	5				

Bills Receivable 74

19..			£	19..			£
Jan. 1	M. Redman	56	1 000	Jan. 5	Bank	C.B.	1 000

Cash Book
(Bank Columns only)

Dr.							Cr.
19..			£	19..			£
Jan. 3	Bill Receivable discounted (Redman)	74	1 000	Jan. 6	Discount on B/R (Redman)	82	20
				Apr. 5	Redman Dishonoured Bill	56	1 000
				,, 5	Redman Bank Charges on dishonoured Bill	56	5

Discount on Bills Account

19..			£	19..			£
Jan. 6	Bank (Redman's Bill)	C.B.	20				

Contingent Liabilities

Bills under discount are not actual liabilities of the firm doing the discounting, (in this case Yesufu). They remain as *contingent liabilities* (liabilities which may occur) until payment at maturity precludes any possibility of dishonour. Discounted bills do not appear in the Balance Sheet, but it is important to draw attention to the fact that there are bills under discount at the date of the Balance Sheet, and that a contingent liability exists in respect of them by making a note at the foot for information only, e.g. 'Contingent Liabilities, Bills under Discount, £——'.

The Transfer of a Bill

A third method of dealing with a Bill of Exchange is to transfer it to another person who then acquires all the rights to it. A trader may arrange to do this to settle one of his own debts. To record the transfer a credit entry is made to Bills Receivable Account, and a debit entry to the account of the person to whom the bill is transferred.

Indorsement

A Bill of Exchange that is made payable to order requires the signature of the holder before being passed on, whether such transfer is to a bank for discounting or to another person. Such signature is an *indorsement*, and is usually made on the back of the bill. A bill may continue to be indorsed over, or transferred, until it is discharged by payment or otherwise, or until restrictively indorsed, such as 'Pay ——only.' Every indorser becomes liable as a party to the bill in the event of dishonour.

Renewing a Bill of Exchange

The acceptor of a bill may not be in a position to honour the bill on presentation, and it may be mutually arranged that he accepts a fresh bill in place of the existing one. This will extend the credit period by the duration of the new bill, but interest is usually added in the new bill as compensation for the delayed payment.

In the books of the holder the exchange of the old bill for the new bill will involve the cancellation of the old bill by crediting Bills Receivable Account and debiting the personal account of the acceptor. The new bill will be recorded in the usual manner, being credited to the acceptor's account and debited to Bills Receivable Account. If these entries include a sum for interest, further entries will be required, namely a debit entry to the acceptor's account for the interest, and a credit entry in the Interest Account for eventual transfer to Profit and Loss Account.

Assuming that Redman, in the above Example 32, renews his bill, the account would appear as below. Note the three transactions, the withdrawal of the bill, the charging of the interest, and the giving of the new bill.

M. Redman 56

19..			£	19..			£
Jan. 1	Sales	S.B.	1 000	Jan. 1	Bill Receivable	74	1 000
Apr. 1	Bill withdrawn	74	1 000	Apr. 1	Bill Receivable (new Bill)	74	1 020
„ 1	Interest	96	20				

Bills Receivable 74

19..			£	19..			£
Jan. 1	M. Redman	56	1 000	Apr. 1	M. Redman (Bill withdrawn)	56	1 000
Apr. 1	M. Redman (new Bill)	56	1 020				

Interest Account 96

			£	19..			£
				Apr. 1	M. Redman	56	20

Converse entries would be made in the books of the acceptor.

Retiring a Bill of Exchange

To take up a bill and to pay it before it is due is called retiring a bill. The holder may be willing to give up the bill and to allow a rebate on the full amount. In his books, he will credit Bills Receivable Account with the full value, and debit Cash for the cash received, and debit Interest Account or Discount on Bills Account for the rebate given. The acceptor, in his books, would credit the rebate to the Interest or Discount Account and the Cash payment to the Cash Book, debiting both items to the Bills Payable Account.

Bill Books

If bill transactions are not numerous, the original entries may be made in the Journal, to be posted from there to the appropriate Ledger Accounts. As the bills become numerous it will be advantageous to introduce special Bill Books for the original entries, and to discontinue the use of the Journal for this purpose. The Bill Books provide a means of keeping an adequate record of the particulars of the bills for reference, and at the same time permit periodical postings of the totals to be made to the Bill Accounts to avoid frequent use of the Ledger for the posting of individual entries. The Bill Books are subsidiary books, and, like the other subsidiary books discussed in earlier chapters, make for better organisation and efficiency in the work of the accounts department.

Specimen rulings of Bill Books for M. Redman are given on page 238. The first few columns gave the imformation for the bookkeeping record, the remainder are memoranda columns for particulars of the bills and the manner of their disposal.

Bills Payable Book

BILL NO.	DATE	DEBIT TO: –	LEDGER FOLIO	AMOUNT	DRAWER	PAYEE	WHERE PAYABLE	DATE OF BILL	TERM	DUE DATE	HOW DISPOSED OF
				£				19..		19..	
1	Jan. 1	A. Yesufu	81	1 000	A. Yesufu	A. Yesufu	London Bank, E.C.	Jan. 1	3 Mons.	Apr. 1	Paid Apr. 1

Bills Receivable Book

BILL NO.	DATE	CREDIT TO: –	LEDGER FOLIO	AMOUNT	DRAWER	ACCEPTOR	WHERE PAYABLE	DATE OF BILL	TERM	DUE DATE	HOW DISPOSE OF
				£				19..		19..	
1	Apr. 2	B. Banjul	96	2 000	SELF	B. Banjul	London and Counties Bank	Apr. 1	2 Mons.	June 1	Dis-counted Apr. 4

EXERCISES 25

1. On 1st September P. Beaumont sold goods to the amount of £350 to R. Sinclair who accepted that day a Bill of Exchange at two months for the sum due.

Beaumont paid the bill into his bank for collection, and the bill was met at the due date.

Record these transactions as in Beaumont's books.

2. Record the following transactions in R. Rosendale's books:

Feb.	10.	Sold goods to J. B. Whittaker, £250.
,,	10.	Drew on Whittaker at three months for £250.
		Received from Whittaker the bill duly accepted.
May	10.	Bank notified that Whittaker had paid the bill on presentation.

3. S. J. Hull sold goods to T. Yorke on 1st March to the amount of £500, and received from Yorke his acceptance for three months for the amount due. On 2nd March Hull discounted the bill with his bankers whose discounting charges were £10.

Make the entries to record these transactions in S. J. Hull's books.

4. Record the following transactions of R. J. Westrop in his books:

Feb.	1.	Sold goods, £400 to L. Newton.
,,	1.	Received from Newton his acceptance for two months for £400.
,,	4.	Discounted Newton's bill at bankers who charged £8 for discounting.

5. Record the following transactions in B. Johnson's books:

Mar.	1.	He sold to L. T. Smith, goods, £600.
,,	1.	Received from L. T. Smith his acceptance for £600 at three months.
,,	4.	Discounted Smith's bill with bankers.
		Discounting charges, £12.
June	1.	Bank returned Smith's bill as dishonoured on presentation.

6. On 1st May B. Leslie received from L. Herbert his acceptance for two months for £500 for goods supplied on that date. He at once discounted the bill with his bankers who charged £10. On due date his bankers notified him that Herbert had dishonoured his bill on presentation.

Record the sale, the receipt of the bill, the discounting, and the dishonour in B. Leslie's books.

7. On 1st January, 19.., the following balances appeared in the books of Oxford, Ltd.:

Debtors	£	*Creditors*	£
Hull Ltd.	250	Bristol & Sons Ltd.	300
Exeter & Co.	400	Cardiff Bros.	100

Open the accounts to record the above in the books of Oxford, Ltd., and record the following transactions in the Journal and Ledger and Cash Book:

19. .

Jan. 2. Accepted a bill drawn by Bristol & Sons Ltd., for the balance due at one month.
,, 9. Received bill for two months from Exeter & Co. for £400 duly accepted.
,, 16. Hull Ltd. forwarded draft duly accepted at two months for balance due.
,, 23. Accepted Cardiff & Co.'s bill for three months for £100.
Feb. 2. Bill due to Bristol & Sons Ltd., duly honoured.
,, 9. Discounted Exeter & Co.'s draft at 6% per annum.
Mar. 16. Proceeds of Hull Ltd's. bill collected by bankers and credited in account. *R.S.A.* (*adapted*)

8. R. Kingston had the following assets and liabilities on 1st June, 19. .: Cash in hand, £160; Cash at bank, £1 750; Plant and machinery, £850; Stock, £7 000; S. Jameson owed him £730; and £790 was owing to B. Luckworth.

Open the books of R. Kingston as on 1st June, 19. ., and record the following transactions:

June 2. Sold goods to R. Freeman, £740.
,, 3. Paid wages in cash, £190.
,, 3. Paid £50 into the bank.
,, 4. Cash sales, £2 060.
,, 5. Sold goods to S. Jameson, £790.
,, 7. R. Freeman proves insolvent and pays £0·50 in the £ in settlement of the amount owing.
,, 10. Drew cheque for private use, £300.
,, 12. Bought goods for cash, £210.
,, 14. S. Jameson sends his acceptance at 14 days for the amount due.
,, 15. Discounted S. Jameson's acceptance at bank, discounting charge being £5.
,, 16. Cash sales, £2270.
,, 17. Bought goods from B. Luckworth, £330.
,, 18. Paid into bank, £2 300.
,, 19. Bought by cheque, office furniture, £210.
,, 20. Paid B. Luckworth cheque £770 being allowed discount £20.
,, 21. Sold goods to S. Jameson, £760.
,, 22. Bought stationery for cash, £150.
,, 22. Paid rent in cash, £150.
,, 23. Bought on credit from R. Austin, plant and machinery, £580.
,, 24. Paid wages in cash, £830.
,, 25. Returned to B. Luckworth, goods, £70.
,, 30. Received a debit note from S. Jameson, £60.
,, 30. Bank returned S. Jameson's bill dishonoured.

You are required to extract a Trial Balance as at 30th June, and also a Trading Account, Profit and Loss Account, and Balance Sheet as at that date.

When preparing the Final Accounts, the following items are to be brought into account:

(1) Stock, 30th June, 19.., is £230.
(2) £150 is owing for wages.
(3) Plant and machinery is to be depreciated by £40.
(4) £30 is to be allowed for interest on capital.
(5) Value of unused stationery, £120.

U.E.I. (adapted)

9. (*a*) Enter the following transactions through their appropriate books.
(b) Post to Ledger.
(c) Take out Trial Balance.
(d) Prepare Profit and Loss Account and Balance Sheet.

A. ARMITAGE

Balance Sheet.

30 June, 19...

CLAIMS	£	£	ASSETS	£	£
Capital A/c.		11 100	Fixtures and fittings		1 800
Sundry Creditors:			*Sundry Debtors:*		
H. Hall	830		B. Bowen	650	
M. Marks	1 370	2 200	C. Charles	800	1 450
			Stock of goods		7 850
			Bill Receivable due 30th Sept.		1 500
			Cash at bank	580	
			Cash in hand	120	700
		£13 300			£13 300

During July 19.., Armitage's transactions were as follows:

Armitage paid into bank £3 900 as additional capital. Received cheque for £620 from B. Bowen in settlement of his account.
Paid to H. Hall a cheque for the amount of his account.
Sold goods, on credit, to B. Bowen, £1 160.
Purchased motor van by cheque, £5 400.
Paid by cheque, tax and insurance on motor van, £400.
Purchased goods, on credit, from H. Hall, £750.
Drew and cashed cheque, £380, for office cash.
Paid from cash salaries, £250, office expenses, £50, and private expenses, £150.
Discounted Bill Receivable, due 30th Sept., at bank, discount charged being £40.
Paid rent for month, £60 by cheque.
Write off 10% depreciation from fixtures and fittings.
Cash sales during month, £1 650, which was banked.
The stock on hand at 31st July, 19.., was valued at £8 100.

N.B. All cheques received were paid into bank same day.

10. On 1st June, 19. ., after trading for eleven months, B. Somers, a Wholesale Ironmonger, had the following balances on his books:

Capital Account	25 000
Drawings Account	2 750
Stock Account	33 450
Purchases Account	90 000
Sales Account	110 000
Furniture and fittings	6 000
Bank overdraft	500
J. Fish (Debtor)	1 400
R. Stagg (Debtor)	600
R. Blunt (Creditor)	3 420
Bills Receivable	2 300
Sundry expenses	2 420

At the end of each year 10% of the value of the furniture and fittings is to be written off foı depreciation.

After these deductions, £500 of the remaining net profit is to be set aside to meet possible future bad debts.

The remaining net profit, if any, is to be credited to the proprietor's Capital Account.

All the accounts are then to be closed, and the balances carried forward as on 1st July.

The transactions which took place during the month of June were as follows:

June 3. Bill Receivable £1 300 paid into bank for collection.
,, 6. Cheque for £360 received from B. Judge on May 31st and paid into bank on that day, returned dishonoured.
,, 8. Purchased from the Trustee in Bankruptcy, the whole of the stock of Williams & Co. for £12 000, payment to be made by two equal acceptances due 8th July and 8th August. The transaction was duly completed and the drafts accepted.
,, 15. Cash sales to date paid into bank, £4 000.
,, 17. Wrote off B. Judge's Account as a bad debt.
,, 19. Received cheque from R. Stagg in settlement of his account, less 5% discount.
,, 20. Paid R. Blunt cheque for £3 250 in settlement of his account.
,, 21. Received J. Fish's acceptance for £1 400.
,, 24. Discounted with bank all Bills Receivable in hand, the bank charging £30 for discounting.
,, 30. Drew cheque for sundry expenses, £120.

All payments were made by cheque and all amounts received were at once paid into the Bank.

Enter *direct into the Ledger* the opening balances and the transactions. Take out a Trial Balance. Make the adjustments required. Then prepare Trading and Profit and Loss Account for the twelve months ended June 30th, 19. ., and Balance Sheet at that date. *No subsidiary books whatever are to be used.*

The stock at June 30th was valued at £39 120.

Joint Matriculation Board (*adapted*)

26

Consignment Accounts

Much of the trade between different parts of the country and between different countries is carried on through *agents* who sell goods on behalf of their *principals*. In this way the manufacturer or merchant exporting the goods avoids the expenses of a local branch, and has the benefit of the agent's knowledge of local conditions and likely markets. The goods are forwarded for sale on commission. The agent deducts his expenses and commission from the gross proceeds, and remits the net proceeds to his principal. Goods so dispatched are called *consignments*. The principal, who forwards the goods, is known as the *consignor*, and the receiver (i.e. the agent) as the *consignee*. From the consignor's point of view a consignment is a *Consignment Outwards*; from the consignee's it is a *Consignment Inwards*.

A consignment outwards is not a sale to the agent. The goods are held by the agent for sale, and if he cannot sell them he may return them to the consignor. There is a change only in the location of the goods. It is necessary to bring the transaction into account when the sale takes place, but meanwhile the consignment must be treated separately from the ordinary trading transactions of the business.

The agent is usually remunerated by an agreed commission calculated as a percentage on the gross proceeds of sale. Should he guarantee the consignor against loss from bad debts he is paid an additional commission, called a *del credere* commission.

The consignor usually sends to the agent a *pro forma* invoice, giving a description of the goods consigned, the weight, quantity, shipping marks, and other relevant details, and sometimes including the price as an indication of the minimum selling price the consignor expects to be realised. The invoice does not charge the consignee with the value; it is sent to him for information and guidance only.

The agent informs his principal of his dealings with the consignment by rendering an *Account Sales*, which is a statement containing particulars of the consignment, the gross proceeds of sale, the agent's expenses and commission, and the net proceeds due to the consignor.

The transactions relative to the consignment are completed when the consignor receives the net proceeds from the consignee.

Example 33. Butcher & Co., of London, consigned ten cases of fancy goods to their agents, Patel & Vora, of Bombay, on 20th August, paying freight, insurance, etc., £400.

The goods were valued at cost, £10 000, and were shown on the *pro forma* invoice at £13 500. An Account Sales was received from the consignees on 10th October showing the gross proceeds of sale, £15 000; landing and dock charges and duty paid, £500; and commission at 5% + 1% *del credere*.

A banker's draft on London for the net proceeds was forwarded by the consignees with the Account Sales.

Show the entries for the consignment in the books of the consignors.

The Consignor's Accounts

The first step is to record the consignment of the goods to Patel & Vora. The entries cannot be made in the Sales Account as this is not a sale, and, until they are sold, the goods remain the legal property of the consignor. For the same reason Patel & Vora cannot be debited personally with the value of the goods consigned. They are not debtors until the goods are sold. Two special accounts are opened instead: one, the 'Goods Consigned Outwards Account' to record that the goods have left the warehouse on consignment, and the other, the 'Consignment to Patel & Vora Account', to record that Patel & Vora have received the goods, but on consignment only. The former account is credited, and the latter account is debited with the goods consigned at cost price, as until the sale takes place the entries are a record only of stock transferred from the warehouse to another place.

Journal

			Dr.	Cr.
19..			£	£
Aug. 20	Consignment to Patel & Vora Account		10 000	
	Goods Consigned Outwards Account			10 000
	being 10 cases of fancy goods consigned to Patel & Vora, Bombay.			

The purpose of the 'Consignment to Patel & Vora Account' is to show the dealings with the consignment, the expenses incurred, and the eventual profit or loss on the venture. The shipping and other charges paid by the consignor are debited to this account (and credited to Cash), and no other entries are made until the Account Sales is received from the consignee.

The Account Sales shows the gross proceeds of sale, the expenses paid, the commission deducted, and the net proceeds due to the consignor. When the goods are sold and the proceeds collected, the consignees become debtors for the net proceeds, but if they are acting *del credere* they are liable to the consignor as soon as the goods are sold.

ACCOUNT SALES of 10 cases of Fancy Goods *ex* SS. *Lamina* sold by Patel and Vora of Bombay for the account of Messrs. Butcher & Co., London.

B. Co. 1–10	10 Cases of Fancy Goods at £1 500		15 000
	Deduct charges and expenses:	£	
	Landing, dock charges, and duty	500	
	Commission, 5%	750	
	Del Credere, 1%	150	1 400
	Sight Draft herewith for		£13 600
	Bombay, 18 Sept., 19.. (Sgd.) *PATEL & VORA*		

The sum representing the net proceeds is credited to the Consignment to Patel & Vora Account, and is debited to the personal account of Patel & Vora as a debt due from them. An alternative method to the same effect is to credit the Consignment to Patel & Vora Account with the gross proceeds, and to debit the account with the expenses and commission shown in the Account Sales. The contra entries are made in Patel & Vora's personal account by debiting the gross proceeds and crediting the expenses and commission.

Patel & Vora's personal account is closed by a credit entry when they remit the proceeds, the debit entry being made to Cash.

The balance of the Goods Consigned Outwards Account is transferred to the Trading Account at the close of the year. It is preferable to show this balance, on taking it to the Trading Account, as a deduction from the total purchases and not as a credit entry, since the consignment figure is at cost. If shown as a credit entry it should be stated separately from the total sales, as the latter includes the gross profit. To include it with the sales figure would render that figure ineffective for purposes of comparison with previous sales figures and for the calculation of the percentage of gross profit on turnover.

The balance of the Consignment to Patel & Vora Account, which represents the profit on the venture, is transferred to Profit and Loss Account.

The following Ledger Accounts illustrate the record required:

Goods Consigned Outwards Account

19..			£	19..			£
Dec. 31	Transfer to Trading A/c.		10 000	Aug. 20	Consignment to Patel & Vora	J	10 000

Consignment to Patel & Vora, Bombay

19..			£	19..			£
Aug. 20	Goods Consigned A/c.	J	10 000	Oct. 10	Consignees' Account: Gross Proceeds		15 000
,, 20	Cash: Freight and Insurance		400				
Oct. 10	Consignees' Account: Landing and other expenses		500				
	Commission, 5%		750				
	Del credere, 1%		150				
	Profit and Loss A/c.		3 200				
			£15 000				£15 000

Patel & Vora's Account

19..			£	19..			£
Oct. 10	Consignment Account, Gross Proceeds		15 000	Oct. 10	Consignment Account: Landing and other expenses		500
					Commission, 5%		750
					Del credere, 1%		150
					Cash		13 600
			£15 000				£15 000

Remitting by Bill

The consignees may remit by Bill of Exchange, in which case the consignees' account is credited and Bills Receivable Account is debited with the amount of the bill. The Bills Receivable Account is credited, and Cash is debited when the bill is paid. The consignors are, of course, at liberty to discount the bill and should they so decide, the usual entries on discounting will be required.

Documentary Bill

The consignor may arrange to draw a bill on the consignee at the time of shipment. In that case the bill is drawn for about three-quarters of the value of the goods consigned, and for a period after sight (i.e. after the goods and the bill have been received) that will give the consignee time to sell the goods before the bill has to be met. The consignor attaches the shipping documents to the bill and sells the bill outright, subject to recourse (i.e. the right to recover the amount of the bill from him if it were dishonoured), to his bankers, who then proceed to obtain the consignee's acceptance against the handing over of the shipping documents. The *documentary bill*, as this is termed is credited to the consignee's personal account as part payment by him, and is debited to Bills Receivable Account. On selling the bill the consignor credits Bills Receivable Account with the cash and the discount charge, and debits the cash to the Cash Book and the discount charge to the Consignment Account. The balance due from the consignee will be treated as in the above example when the Account Sales is received and the amount is known.

Goods on Consignment and the Balance Sheet

Should the Final Accounts and the Balance Sheet have to be prepared before the goods are sold, it will be necessary to take the consignment into account. Reverting to the above example, the Consignment to Patel & Vora Account would be balanced and closed, and the balance carried down to the debit side for the next trading period. This balance would be shown in the Balance Sheet, among the assets, as *Stock on Consignment*.

If part only of the goods have been sold when the Balance Sheet has to be prepared, the value of the unsold portion must be ascertained in order that it may be shown in the Balance Sheet as *unsold stock on consignment*. As the consignors' expenses and some part of the consignees' expenses probably relate to the whole consignment, it will be necessary to apportion these between the sold and the unsold parts of the consignment, and to include the appropriate proportion of the expenses in the valuation figure of the unsold portion.

When this value has been ascertained it is credited to the *Consignment to Agent Account*, and is carried down as the opening debit balance of the Consignment to Agent Account for the new financial period.

The apportionment spreads the expenses over the whole of the stock on consignment and enables the correct profit on the sold

Consignment to Patel & Vora, Bombay

19..			£	19..			£
Aug. 20	Goods Consigned A/c.	J	10 000	Oct. 10	Consignees' A/c Gross proceeds of half consignment		7 500
	Cash: Freight and Insurance		400	,, 31	Unsold Stock on Consignment at cost (£5 000) and half consignors' expenses (£200 + £250) carried down		5 450
Oct. 10	Consignees' Account: Landing and other Expenses		500				
	Commission, 5%		375				
	Del credere, 1%		75				
,, 31	Profit and Loss A/c. (Profit on half consignment)		1 600				
			£12 950				£12 950
Nov. 1	Balance brought down (unsold stock on consignment proportion of expenses)		5 450				

portion to be ascertained. After the value of the unsold portion and its proportion of expenses have been credited, the balance of the Consignment to Agent Account represents the profit or loss on the sold portion, and is carried to the Profit and Loss Account in the ordinary way.

Assuming, as an example, that Patel & Vora sold only half the above consignment and forwarded an Account Sales conveying this information, and that the expenses should be related equally to the sold and unsold portions, the Consignment Account would appear at balancing time as shown on p. 248.

The sum of £5 450 would appear in the Consignors' Balance Sheet as an asset under the heading 'Stock on Consignment'.

If consignments form a considerable proportion of a firm's business it is the practice to keep special books comprising a *Consignment Ledger* and Cash Book. A special *Profits on Consignments Account* may also be used to summarise the profits, the balance of which is transferred to the Profit and Loss Account at the close of the financial year.

Consignments Inwards

The consignee, who receives the goods on consignment for sale on behalf of the consignor, is dealing with a Consignment Inwards. He is not a debtor for their value, so he makes no entry in his financial books on their arrival. He will find it necessary to keep an adequate record of the kind of goods and the quantities in an appropriate memorandum book – usually called a *Consignment Inwards Stock Book* – but apart from this his only concern is to record the expenses he has incurred, the sales, his commission, and his financial relationship with the consignor. A personal account for the consignor is the only additional account a Consignment Inwards involves.

The Consignee's Accounts

The above Example 33, taken from Patel & Vora's point of view, will also serve as an example of a Consignment Inwards. The same simplifying assumptions that were made in Chapter 25 about foreign currency must be made in this chapter also. Patel & Vora will open in their books a personal account for Butcher & Co., the consignors.

The entries must be summarised as follows:

EXPENSES: *Debit* Consignors' Account.
Credit Cash.

SALES: *Debit* the customers' personal accounts, or Cash, if sold for cash.
Credit Consignors' Account.

COMMISSION: *Debit* Consignors' Account.
Credit Commission Account for eventual transfer to Profit and Loss Account.

REMITTANCES: *Debit* Consignors' Account
Credit Cash or Bills Payable Account as the case may be.

After the expenses, sales, and commission have been entered in the Consignors' Account, the balance represents the sum due to the consignors. When the sum remitted is entered the account is closed.

The Consignors' Account for the above example would appear in the books of the consignees as below:

Butcher & Co.'s Account

19..			£	19..			£
Sept. 15	Cash, Landing and other expenses		500	Oct.	Sundry Debtors (Proceeds of Consignment)		15 000
	Commission A/c.		900				
	Cash (Banker's draft to settle)		13 600				
			£15 000				£15 000

Goods on Approval

Goods on approval should not be confused with consignments. In the latter case the goods are sent to an agent for sale on behalf of the consignor. In the former, the customer is given an option to purchase or return the goods, which he is expected to exercise within a reasonable or specified time.

The dispatch of goods on approval to a customer cannot be treated as an ordinary sale until the customer signifies his acceptance of them. Pending such acceptance the property in the goods remains vested in the sender. It is usual to keep a special *Goods on Sale or Return Journal* in which the goods sent out *on sale or return* are recorded, and from which the sales as they take place are posted to the Ledger Accounts. The ruling of such a Journal might be as below:

Goods on Sale or Return Journal

DATE	PARTICULARS	DISPATCHED		RETURNED		SALES		REMARKS
		DATE	AMOUNT	DATE	AMOUNT	SALES LEDGER FOLIO	AMOUNT	
			£		£		£	

When a sale takes place an entry is made in the appropriate sales column in the Journal, and is posted from there to the personal account of the customer. The periodical totals of the sales column are posted to the credit of the Sales Account. The goods still with customers on approval must be taken into account at the close of a trading period, being taken into stock at cost or market price, whichever is the lower.

EXERCISES 26

1. On 1st April, 19.., The Export Co. consigned 72 cases of cutlery to A. Dennis & Co. of Kingston, Jamaica, and forwarded a *pro forma* invoice at the cost price of £4 270. On the same day, the consignors paid freight charges £20, and insurance £10 per case.

On 1st August, 19.., the following was received by the consignor together with the bill as stated:

ACCOUNT SALES of part consignment of 72 cases, received from The Export Co. per S.S. *Calypso* by Dennis & Co., up to 30th June, 19..:

	£	£
72 cases at £90 per case		6 480
Less:		
Landing Charges, etc.	362	
Commission due to us	328	690
Sight draft herewith for		£5 790

Dennis & Co.

Record these transactions in the books of The Export Co., showing the profit on the consignment.

R.S.A. (adapted)

2. On Nov. 1st, 19.., Horrocks & Co. Ltd., of Manchester, shipped per the S.S. *Lancaster* 'on consignment' to Alva & Co., Buenos Aires, 5 bales of piece goods which were invoiced to them *pro forma* for £12 000. The following expenses were paid by the consignors:

Packing charges, £45; Shipping charges and freight, £125; Marine insurance, £100. Under date Jan. 26, Messrs. Alva submitted an Account Sales showing the consignment to have realised £18 600 gross, and showing the following deductions for expenses: Customs duty, £158; Landing charges, £40; Fire insurance, £80; Warehousing, £61; and their own commission of 5% on gross sales. A demand draft on the Anglo-South American Bank was enclosed. Show the whole of the entries which are necessary, and close off the accounts in the books of the consignors only.

N.C.T.E.C. (adapted)

3. Watson & Co., of London, consigned to New Way Co., of Mombasa, for sale, goods which cost £1 240, but were invoiced *pro forma* at £1 500. Watson & Co. paid freight, £83, and insurance, £21. In due course, New Way Co. sent an Account Sales showing that part of the goods had been sold for £1 210, and that their charges were £98 *plus* a commission of 4% on the gross proceeds. They also sent to Watson & Co. a sight draft for the amount due.

Show the Account Sales and the necessary accounts in Watson & Co'.s Ledger, noting that the unsold goods were valued at £573.

U.E.I. (adapted)

4. On 1st January, 19.., A.N. Exporter forwarded a consignment of 20 cases of goods to A. Trader, his agent in West Africa, together with a *pro forma* invoice for £360. On the following day, the consignor paid the freight charges amounting to £55 and insurance charges £9. On 15 March, 19.., an Account Sales was received from the agent showing that 15 cases had been sold for £380, and that landing and storage charges on the consignment amounting to £28 had been paid by the agent. The agent's commission of 5% of the gross sales was deducted and the balance due was remitted by sight draft.

Record these transactions in the books of the consignor showing the profit or loss on the consignment.

R.S.A. (adapted)

5. On 1st January, 19.., A. Exporter & Co. forwarded a consignment of 100 cabinets to J. Dyke, his agent in South Africa, and also sent a *pro forma* invoice showing the price at £75 each. On 7th January, 19.., the firm paid freight and insurance charges on the consignment amounting to £650.

On 30th June, 19.., an account sales was received from the agent showing that 50 cabinets had been sold at £100 each and that various landing and storage charges had been paid by him on the whole of the consignment amounting to £850. The agent also deducted his commission of 5% of the gross sales, forwarded a draft for the net proceeds of the sales, and intimated that the balance would be sold shortly at the same price. Record these transactions in the books of the consignor, showing the profit or loss at the 30th June, 19..

6. C. Cave received goods from A. Abdullahi, Karachi, invoiced at £4 000. Cave made the following payments on 1st April: Dock charges, £50; Carriage £100; Duty, £200. Cave sold the goods for cash, £5 500, on 14th April. His commission is agreed at 2½% on the gross proceeds. Cave remitted to Abdullahi the amount due to him on 16th April. Show the entries to record these transactions in Cave's books.

27

Incomplete Records

The term *incomplete records* is applied, in general, to any system of bookkeeping that does not adhere strictly to the principles of double entry.

A trader may deem it sufficient for his purposes if he has a Cash Book and a Customers' Ledger containing his customers' accounts. He records all his cash dealings in his Cash Book, and posts the sums received from customers to their respective accounts in the Ledger, but otherwise he makes no attempt to complete the two-fold aspect of his transactions. His Ledger, therefore, contains no record of his expenses, of his capital, or of the value of any business assets. He relies, probably, on the invoices which he receives as a record of his purchases, and the only entry in his books for these is the cash payment as and when he pays his creditors.

This is typical of the nature of incomplete records. As a variation from it, a trader may keep a Sales Book, and may post the entries to his Customers' Ledger Accounts, but refrains from posting the total sales in any form to the Ledger. Some traders may go further and keep a Purchases Day Book and also keep accounts for creditors in the Ledger but, even so, the record is still only one of the personal aspects of the business transactions with the exception of some of the Cash Book entries.

It is obvious that a record of this kind lacks the fullness and informative value of the double entry system, and that it has positive disadvantages. No Trial Balance, for example, can be extracted to test the arithmetical accuracy of the entries, and the gross and net profit cannot be ascertained without recourse to other sources of information. Further, in the absence of records of any assets and of any record of allowance for depreciation or other loss of value, it is difficult to present a Balance Sheet of reasonable accuracy.

Statement of Affairs under Incomplete Records

To ascertain the trading results when records are incomplete it is necessary to know the capital at the start of the trading period and also the capital at the close of the period under review. As a trader's capital on any given date is represented by the excess of the value of his assets over his liabilities, it follows that in order to ascertain his capital where proper books of account are not kept, it is necessary to prepare a statement of the trader's assets and liabilities. Such a statement is known as a *Statement of Affairs*. In appearance it is like an ordinary Balance Sheet. It follows, that, unless the capital at the commencement of the trading period is known, it is necessary to prepare two Statements of Affairs – one as at the beginning of the trading period, and the other as at the close of the period.

The steps to be taken to prepare a Statement of Affairs are:

(*a*) Value the stock on hand.
(*b*) Check the cash in hand and at bank.
(*c*) Ascertain the total of the debtors and creditors.
(*d*) Identify and value any other assets.
(*e*) Identify the liabilities, if any, which exist in addition to the trade creditors.
(*f*) Take into account all outstanding expenses and payments made in advance.
(*g*) Consider whether any provisions or reserves should be made.

This information having been obtained, the Statement of Affairs is formulated by placing the assets on the credit side and the liabilities on the debit side. The difference between the two sides represents the capital, and by inserting the amount of this difference on the appropriate side the two sides are made equal in total and the Statement is closed. It may be difficult to establish some of the facts with certainty. In that case, the best estimates possible must be made. If the estimated liabilities exceed the estimated assets, there is a *deficiency of capital*. The proprietor's Capital Account would then have a debit balance. This could indicate an imminent collapse of the business, or a mistake in the estimates, or very efficient operations whereby goods bought on credit are sold quickly for cash. In any case, it calls for further investigation.

By way of simple illustration of the principle involved in the foregoing paragraphs, let it be assumed that a trader's capital on a given date is calculated to be £10 000; that it is known that a year earlier it was calculated to be £9 000; and that during the year he drew from the business a weekly allowance, *totalling* £4 100 for the period. His profit for the year is arrived at as follows:

Statement of Profit

	£
Capital on 1st January, 19..	9 000
Capital on 31st December, 19..	10 000
Net *increase* of capital	1 000
add Drawings during the year	4 100
Profit for the year	£5 100

If his capital position had been the reverse, that is, his capital had been £10 000 at 1st January and £9 000 at 31st December, his profit would have been £3 100, arrived at as follows:

	£
Capital on 1st January, 19..	10 000
Capital on 31st December, 19..	9 000
Net *decrease* of capital	1 000
add Drawings during the year	4 100
Profit for the year	£3 100

In the above simplified illustration the only adjustment required is in respect of personal cash drawings. Various other adjustments may be necessary in practice, such as adjustment for additional capital brought into the business (whether it is in the form of cash or in the form of assets purchased for the business from private funds), or adjustment for withdrawals of capital. Thus, if, in the above example, new machinery had been bought during the trading period, it would be deducted, and the example would then appear as follows:

	£
Capital 1st January, 19..	9 000
Capital 31st December, 19..	10 000
Net increase of capital	1 000
Add Drawings	4 100
	5 100
Less Cost of machinery	800
Profit for year	£4 300

Provided the above particulars are grasped no difficulty should arise in following the examples given below.

Example 34. R. Benson prepared the following Statement of Affairs as at 1st January, 19..:

Statement of Affairs

1st January, 19...

CLAIMS	£	ASSETS	£
Sundry creditors	5 200	Freehold premises	12 800
Capital Account	12 800	Fittings	300
		Stock	1 800
		Sundry debtors	2 500
		Cash	600
	£18 000		£18 000

His liabilities and assets at 31st December of that year were valued as follows:

Sundry creditors, £4 900; premises, £12 800; fittings, £400; stock, £1 950; sundry debtors, £2 700; and cash, £320.
The fittings include £150 of new fittings purchased during the year and paid for by R. Benson from his private account.
Drawings during the year amounted to £400.
Find his profit or loss on the year.

The solution is as below:

Statement of Affairs

31st December, 19...

CLAIMS	£	ASSETS	£
Sundry creditors	4 900	Premises	12 800
Capital: excess of assets over liabilities at this date	13 270	Fittings	400
		Stock	1 950
		Sundry debtors	2 700
		Cash	320
	£18 170		£18 170

Statement of Profit

	£
Capital, 31st December, 19..	13 270
Add Drawings	400
	13 670
Deduct Capital introduced	150
	13 520
Deduct Capital as at 1st January	12 800
Net profit for the year	£720

Conversion to Double Entry

It has been shown that with due care in the compilation of the basic figures it is possible to prepare a survey of the trader's business for any given period from incomplete records. This can include the preparation of a Balance Sheet and the calculation of a figure of profit. While this may be so, the double entry system can provide a much greater amount of detail to show how the results were arrived at. The method for incomplete records cannot inform the trader of the ratio of his gross profit to turnover or of the relative proportions of the various expenses which represent the difference between his gross and net profit. This is the point where incomplete records fail in practice, and if the practical question of cost is not insurmountable the obvious remedy is to convert the records to double entry form. If Benson decides that his books are, in future, to be kept on double entry principles, the new set of books will be opened by recording all the items contained in the closing Statement of Affairs. The items should be journalised as opening entries and posted from the Journal to the respective Ledger Accounts, including the cash balance to the Cash Book. Proper subsidiary books will have to be brought into use and instructions should be issued that all transactions must be recorded strictly on double entry principles.

Unfortunately, however, it is not always possible in practice for a trader to bear the extra cost of a bookkeeper competent to keep a complete set of books on double entry principles. In such cases it is necessary to use such information as can be made available for the preparation of detailed accounts on double entry lines. If the trader already keeps, or agrees to keep in future, a Cash Book, together with a Sales Ledger and a Purchases Ledger (or Sales and Purchases Day Books), the work involved in preparing proper accounts is governed solely by the number and variety of the trader's transactions during the period under review. All the necessary information will have been recorded, and it will be necessary only to collate it in the desired manner. *It must be emphasised, however, that whilst the absence of personal Ledgers would only increase the amount of work necessary to prepare detailed accounts, the keeping of a Cash Book and the accurate recording in it of all receipts and payments (with sufficient narration to enable them to be identified) is vital.* Great care must be taken in cases where disbursements are made out of cash takings and only the net cash on hand is banked or otherwise disposed of. In such cases, the *gross* cash takings must be entered on the receipts side of the Cash Book, and the cash disbursements must be entered on the payments side of the Cash Book. To the extent to which this fundamental rule is broken, the Final Accounts are rendered inaccurate. The turnover or total sales, the gross profit ratio to turnover, and the expenses totals and their ratio to turnover will be correspondingly inaccurate.

If the trader is convinced of the importance of a correct record of the cash transactions, and agrees to keep such a record, he may be assured of a Profit and Loss Account comparable in accuracy to that prepared from a standard set of books kept on double entry principles.

As an example, let it be assumed that in Example 34, Benson had kept incomplete records, but that he had also kept a detailed Cash Book on the above lines. To prepare his Profit and Loss Account the first step is to classify all the entries in the Cash Book. The simplest method is to use multi-column analysis paper and to head the columns according to the information required for the Profit and Loss Account, with an additional column for items affecting the Balance Sheet. The following is an example of the summary of the cash transactions taken from the analysis paper and consisting of the totals under each of the appropriate headings in the columns:

		£
Debits:	Balance shown in Cash Book, 1st January	600
	Cash sales	3 000
	Cash from sundry debtors	21 300
		£24 900
Credits:	Cash paid to creditors	20 050
	Commission to assistants	2 750
	Rent and rates	810
	Fuel and light	250
	Insurance and telephone	120
	Carriage and packing	200
	Drawings	400
	Balance shown in Cash Book, 31st December	320
		£24 900

It is obvious that the foregoing summary contains most of the usual items appearing in the Trial Balance of a set of books kept by double entry. The following items, as at 31st December, are still required:

Sundry debtors.
Sundry creditors.
Stock.
Capital introduced by R. Benson, if any.
Drawings by R. Benson other than in cash, if any.
Sales on credit.
Purchases on credit.

Benson can supply the first five items, and the summary of the Cash Book provides the details from which the last two items may be obtained by the compilation of a *Sundry Debtors Summary Account* for the sales, and a *Sundry Creditors Summary Account* for the purchases.

When completed, these accounts would appear as below:

Sundry Debtors Summary Account

	£		£
Sundry debtors, 1st Jan.	2 500	Receipts from sundry debtors	21 300
Sales on credit	21 500	Sundry debtors, 31st Dec.	2 700
	£24 000		£24 000

Sundry Creditors Summary Account

	£		£
Cash payments to creditors	20 050	Sundry creditors, 1st Jan.	5 200
Sundry creditors, 31st Dec.	4 900	*Purchases on credit*	19 750
	£24 950		£24 950

All the items in these accounts are known from the two Statements of Affairs and the cash transactions analysis, with the exception of the sales and purchases figures respectively. In each case these are ascertained by simple arithmetic as the difference between the two sides of the respective accounts.

It is now possible to prepare a complete Trial Balance, Trading and Profit and Loss Account, and Balance Sheet. The Balance Sheet will be identical in content, though not layout, with the Statement of Affairs of the business shown on page 257. The Trial Balance and Trading and Profit and Loss Account will appear as below:

Trial Balance.

31st December, 19...

	£	£
Cash sales		3 000
Credit sales		21 500
Credit purchases	19 750	
Stock on hand, 1st January	1 800	
Fittings, 1st January	300	
Fittings purchased by R. Benson	150	
R. Benson for fittings		150
Provision for Depreciation		50
Profit and Loss Account (Depreciation)	50	
Freehold premises	12 800	
Capital Accounts, R. Benson, at 1st January		12 800
Commission to assistants	2 750	
Rent and rates	810	
Fuel and light	250	
Insurance and telephone	120	
Carriage and packing	200	
Drawings, R. Benson	400	
Cash in bank, 31st December	320	
Sundry creditors		4 900
Sundry debtors	2 700	
	£42 400	£42 400

Note: The Stock at 31st December is given at £1 950. The fittings were valued at £300 at 1st January, to which new purchases, £150, are added. At 31st December the fittings were revalued at £400 – hence the depreciation (£50) shown above.

Trading and
Profit and Loss Account
for year ended 31st December, 19..

	£		£
Stock on 1st Jan.	1 800	Cash sales	3 000
Purchases	19 750	Credit sales	21 500
Gross profit carried down (20% of turnover)	4 900	Stock, 31st December	1 950
	£26 450		£26 450
Commission to assistants	2 750	Gross profit brought down	4 900
Rent and rates	810		
Fuel and light	250		
Insurance and telephone	120		
Carriage and packing	200		
Depreciation on fittings	50		
Net profit transferred to Capital Account	720		
	£4 900		£4 900

Balance Sheet
as at 31st December, 19..

	£	£		£	£	£
CAPITAL			FIXED ASSETS	*Cost*	*Dep'n*	*Net*
Balance		12 800	Premises	12 800	—	12 800
Add: Capital introduced	150		Fittings	450	50	400
Net Profit	720					
				13 250	50	13 200
Less: Drawings	400	470				
			CURRENT ASSETS			
		13 270	Stock		1 950	
CURRENT LIABILITIES			Debtors		2 700	
Creditors		4 900	Bank		320	4 970
		£18 170				£18 170

It will be observed that the net profit, £720, is the same as the figure arrived at on page 258.

From the Trading Account figures it is now possible to inform the trader that his average gross profit on turnover is 20 per cent. This can also be calculated as follows:

	£	
Stock, 1st January	1 800	
add: Purchases	19 750	
	21 550	
Less: Stock, 31st Dec.	1 950	
Cost of sales	£19 600	
Actual sales	24 500	
Cost of sales	19 600	
Gross profit	£4 900	= 20% of £24 500 turnover

His return on capital employed is only 5·52%. It measures the net profit as a percentage of the average capital employed (or the average net assets). The average capital employed is:

$$(£12\,800 + £13\,270) \div 2 = £13\,035.$$

It is also possible to calculated the percentages of the various expenses to turnover. By comparison with the percentages of similar businesses, it is then possible to consider whether or not this particular business may be managed more efficiently, and whether efforts should be made to increase turnover or gross profit, in order to obtain a greater net profit for distribution.

In conclusion it may be remarked that the above example has referred to an extreme case in which only a Cash Book is kept. In practice the available information may be contained in books ranging from only a Cash Book to a case where all the books of original entry are kept, but no one in the business may possess the requisite knowledge to post the appropriate periodical totals to the proper impersonal accounts in the General or Private Ledger. In all cases, before commencing the preparation of a detailed Profit and Loss Account from incomplete records, full information should be obtained as to the extent and dependability of the existing records, as otherwise much unnecessary analysis work may be undertaken. Students should pay particular attention to this aspect of examination questions.

EXERCISES 27

1. The following 'Statements of Affairs' have been drawn up to give the financial position, as on 31st March, 19.., and 31st March, 19.1, respectively, of A. Brown, who keeps his books on a single entry basis:

Statement of Affairs

31st March, 19..

	£		£
Capital	61 920	Fixtures	2 500
Creditors	7 420	Stock	23 050
		Debtors	41 760
		Cash	2 030
	£69 340		£69 340

Statement of Affairs

31st March, 19..

	£		£
Capital	59 330	Fixtures	2 300
Creditors	8 170	Stock	25 620
		Debtors	37 770
		Cash	1 810
	£67 500		£67 600

Brown has transferred £1 000 a month regularly from his business banking account to his private bank account by way of drawings, and he has taken £250 worth of stock for his private use. The alteration in the value of the fixtures represents an amount written off by way of depreciation.

Calculate Brown's trading profit for the year.

R.S.A. (adapted)

2. A manufacturer, Philip Morgan, kept incomplete records. The position of the business at the 31st December, 19.. revealed the following:

	£
Freehold premises	10 000
Plant and machinery	6 000
Stock in trade	13 000
Sundry debtors	17 500
Cash at bank	3 000
Sundry creditors	18 750

At 1st January, 19.., his capital was £55 000.

During the year his drawings amounted to £5 000. The sale of his private motor car realised £2 000, which he paid into the business bank account.

You are required to prepare the Statement of Affairs showing the financial position of Philip Morgan as at the 31st December, 19.., compile his Capital Account at that date, and ascertain his profit or loss for the year.

R.S.A. (adapted)

3. **Balance Sheet**

	£		£
Creditors	7 210	Fixtures and Fittings	15 600
Capital	31 500	Machinery and plant	4 200
		Stock	8 760
		Debtors	9 820
		Cash	330
	£38 710		£38 710

The above is a copy of Samuel Wood's Balance Sheet as on the 31st December, a year ago. The only books kept are a Cash Book and a Ledger. The following is a summary of his receipts and payments for the year ended 31st December, 19..:

Receipts	£	**Payments**	£
Cash on account of credit sales	42 760	Creditors for goods purchased	39 540
		Wages	7 430
Cash sales	18 630	General expenses	6 270
Capital paid in	2 000	Additions to machinery	1 600
		Drawings	5 360
	£63 390		£60 200

On 31st December, 19.., the amount due to creditors was £8 160, and the debtors and stock amounted to £9 180 and £8 540 respectively. You are required to prepare Trading and Profit and Loss Accounts for the year ended 31st December, 19.., and a Balance Sheet as on that date, after making adjustments in respect of the following:

(*a*) Depreciation of 10% is to be written off the machinery and plant, including additions during the year.
(*b*) £1 500 is to be provided for doubtful debts.
(*c*) The sum of £380 for goods supplied to the proprietor was included in the debtor's balances at 31st December, 19...

R.S.A. (adapted)

4. A.N. Ironmonger's Statement of Affairs at 1st January, 19.., was as follows:

	£	£		£	£
Capital		15 776	Premises		11 000
Creditors:			Fixtures and fittings		285
Trade	1 372		Stock		2 740
Expense	100				
		1 472	Debtors		2 218
			Cash:		
			In hand	30	
			At bank	975	
					1 005
		£17 248			£17 248

Ironmonger's records are incomplete but you ascertain the following position at December 31st, 19..

Debtors	2 485	(including bad debts £115)
Creditors:		
Trade	1 588	
Expense	121	

and Ironmonger informs you that he estimates his stock at £2 800 and values his fixtures at £250.

An analysis of his Bank Pay-In Book and Bank Statement reveals the following:

	£
Bank lodgements:	
Cash sales	2 029
Received from credit customers	9 805
Interest from private investments	105
Bank drawn:	
For goods	6 490
Business expenses	2 515
Self	1 400
Income Tax	370

Ironmonger also informs you that approximately £250 of the cash takings have been retained and not banked, to cover petty items which included £120 for purchases. £20 of this sum was in hand at December 31st, 19...

You are required to prepare Trading and Profit and Loss Account for the year ended December 31st, 19.., and the Statement of Affairs at that date.

London Chamber of Commerce – Intermediate (adapted)

5. W. Fairfax does not keep proper books of account. The following information is available for the year ended 30th June, 19...

	1st July previous year	*30th June 19..*
	£	£
Stock-in-trade	18 410	17 620
Cash in hand and at bank	6 470	4 980
Trade debtors	4 700	3 500
Trade creditors	10 740	9 980
Fixtures and fittings	4 000	3 600
Motor van	3 700	7 650

Note: During the year Fairfax had sold the old motor van and purchased a new one for £8 500 which was valued at £7 650 at the end of the year of account.

(*a*) Find the profit or loss made by Fairfax for the year ended 30th June, 19.., taking into account the following:
(i) An account for light and heat, £110, is due.
(ii) Rates, £580, had been paid for the period 1st April, 19.., to 30th September, 19...
(iii) A provision of £350 is to be made for bad debts.
(iv) During the year Fairfax had withdrawn £1 000 from the business each month.
(*b*) Calculate the amount of Fairfax's working capital at 30th June, 19...

6. L. Akbar does not keep proper books of account. The following information is available for the year ended 31st December, 19...

	1st Jan. 19..	*31st Dec. 19..*
	£	£
Stock-in-trade	1 368	1 294
Trade debtors	428	386
Amounts prepaid	23	29
Bank overdraft	210	—
Cash in hand and balance at bank	—	147
Motor van	520	416
Furniture and fittings	340	323
Trade creditors	989	1 037
Expense creditors	17	14

(*a*) Prepare a statement to show the profit or loss made by Akbar for the year ended 31st December, 19.., taking account of the following:

(i) £38 of the trade debtors at 31st December, 19.., were considered to be bad debts and in addition it was decided to make a provision of £39 for doubtful debts.
(ii) During the year 19.. Akbar had withdrawn £90 each month from the business.
(iii) During the year Akbar had won a football pool and paid £200 of the proceeds into the business bank account.

(*b*) With the information given above and the following additional information calculate Akbar's gross profit for the year ended 31st December, 19...

	£
Receipts from trade debtors for the year	8 122
Payments to trade creditors for the year	6 262

28

Income and Expenditure Accounts of Non-Trading Institutions

The purpose of trading concerns is primarily to make a profit whereas the purpose of non-trading institutions is to render a service. It follows that the Trading and Profit and Loss Accounts required by the former would serve no purpose in the accounts of non-trading bodies; but as social and athletic clubs, benevolent and similar institutions are maintained by subscriptions from members or the public, an annual financial statement is desirable.

For small clubs or associations a *Receipts and Payments Account* may be suitable. Such an account is prepared by analysing the entries in the Club Cash Book and presenting the receipts and payments in summarised form as below. The use of a tabular Cash Book facilitates the preparation of the account.

DAFFODIL BADMINTON CLUB

Receipts and Payments Account

for the year ended 30th April, 19..

RECEIPTS	£	PAYMENTS	£
Balance brought forward	80	Wages	555
Subscriptions	930	Rent	255
Profit on refreshments	200	Hire of equipment	200
		Postage	20
		Printing	40
		Affiliation fees	20
		Balance in hand at year-end	120
	£1 210		£1 210

The Receipts and Payments Account is simply a cash account. If there are amounts owing or amounts prepaid it would not show these. It may also include items of capital expenditure and takes no account of depreciation of fixed assets.

To ascertain whether there is a surplus of income over expenditure or a deficiency for the period of account it is necessary to draw up an

Income and Expenditure Account. Like the Profit and Loss Account of a trading concern, this would show the actual revenue expenditure for the period taking account of expenses outstanding and prepaid and bringing into account such items as depreciation of fixed assets. The income for the period, appearing on the credit side of the account, would take into account items still due (e.g. subscriptions) and would exclude those paid in advance by adding the amounts due to and deducting those paid in advance from the amount actually received. Items of capital expenditure would not be included as these would be represented by fixed assets in the Balance Sheet.

An Income and Expenditure Account is similar in form to the Profit and Loss Account of a trading concern. The revenue appears on the credit side and the expenditure on the debit side, and when all outstanding income and expenditure is brought into account, the balance represents a surplus or deficiency for the period. This is added to, or deducted from, the opening capital or surplus, if any, shown in the Balance Sheet.

Example 35. The following Receipts and Payments Account for the Crocus Tennis Club for the year to 30th April, 19.1 was issued to the members by the secretary.

CROCUS TENNIS CLUB

Receipts and Payments Account
for the year ended 30th April, 19.1

RECEIPTS	£	PAYMENTS	£
Balance, 1st May, 19.0	120	Wages	1 000
Entrance fees	20	Stationery	200
Subscriptions	1 660	Printing, postage and misc. charges	150
Locker rents	40	New equipment	100
		Loss on refreshments	60
		Balance carried down	330
	£1 840		£1 840
Balance brought down	330		

A footnote showed that subscriptions, £100, were in arrear and unpaid, and that locker rents, £10, were due but not paid. No reference was made to the fact that the club owned its premises, valued at £5 000; that £20 was owing for printing charges, and that the club's equipment was worth £1 250.

In the above example, the first step is to eliminate the expenditure on new equipment (£100), and to bring in the locker rents and subscriptions outstanding and the unpaid printing bill. The next step is to ascertain the amount of the Capital Fund at the beginning of the period. This consisted of cash, £120; premises, £5 000; and equipment, £1 250 – a total of £6 370.

CROCUS TENNIS CLUB

Income and Expenditure Account

for the year ended 30th April, 19.1

	£		£
Wages	1 000	Subscriptions	1 760
Printing and postage	170	Locker rents	50
Stationery	200	Entrance fees	20
Loss on refreshments	60		
Balance carried to capital	400		
	£1 830		£1 830

Balance Sheet

as at 30th April, 19.1

	£	£		£	£
ACCUMULATED FUND *			Club premises		5 000
At 1st May 19.0	6 370		Equipment	1 250	
			Additions during year	100	
Add:					1 350
Surplus from Income and Expenditure A/c.	400		Debtors		110
		6 770	Cash in hand		330
Sundry creditors (Printing)		20			
		£6 790			£6 790

* The term 'Accumulated Fund' is often used to denote the capital of a non-trading institution.

Under Section 148 of the Companies Act, 1948, it is compulsory for a company registered under the Act as not trading for profit, to lay an Income and Expenditure Account before the company in general meeting.

EXERCISES 28

1. From the following Receipts and Payments Account and the given particulars, prepare an Income and Expenditure Account and, if necessary, a Balance Sheet.

LONGTOWN SPORTS CLUB

Receipts and Payments Account

to 31st December

RECEIPTS	£	PAYMENTS	£
Balance from last year	310	Wages	1 040
Entrance fees	60	Printing, postage and stationery	280
Subscriptions and donations	2 100	Purchase of new equipment	320
Competition fees	100	Prizes	160
Profit on refreshments	420	Sundry expenses	120
		Rent of grounds	600
		Balance carried down	470
	£2 990		£2 990
Balance brought down	470		

The Secretary stated that the club *now* possessed equipment of a total cost of £870, that subscriptions in arrear amounted to £170, and that a printing bill of £40 was unpaid.

2. The following Receipts and Payments Account is for the period ending 31st December, 19..:

THE WEST COAST CLUB

Receipts and Payments Account

RECEIPTS	£	PAYMENTS	£
Balance from last year	270	Payment for new lockers	320
Entrance fees	160	Wages	1 500
Subscriptions:		Printing and postage	360
Current year	2 200	Stationery	30
In advance	240	Sundries	80
Profit on refreshments	530	Lighting and fuel	190
Locker rents	120	Taxes and insurance	540
Interest on deposit	20	Balance carried down	520
	£3 540		£3 540
Balance brought down	520		

Of the subscriptions due for the current year, £210 are in arrear. Locker rents in arrear, £20. Printing bill unpaid, £20. Stationery account unpaid, £30. There is a sum of £2 000 on deposit at bank and the club house and equipment is valued at £11 250.

From the above particulars prepare an Income and Expenditure Account and a Balance Sheet as at 31st December.

3. The assets and liabilities of the Njala Social Club on 1st January, 19.. were: Cash in hand and balance at bank, £268; liquor stocks, £210; subscriptions outstanding for previous year, £20; insurance prepaid, £3; furniture and equipment, £430; creditors for liquor supplies, £150.

From the following summary of receipts and payments and the notes appended prepare the Income and Expenditure Account of the club for the year ended 31st December, 19.. and a Balance Sheet as on that date.

RECEIPTS	£	PAYMENTS	£
Subscriptions	845	Creditors for liquor	1 415
Sales of liquor	1 840	New furniture	60
Sale of old furniture	15	Dance and social expenses	269
Dances and socials	347	Rent and rates	645
		Wages	520
		Light and heat	106
		Insurance	8
		Postages and stationery	18

Notes:

(i) The subscriptions received included £15 relating to the previous year of account. The remainder of the subscriptions for that year were written off as a bad debt.

(ii) On 31st December, 19.., £45 subscriptions were outstanding for the current year of account.

(iii) The old furniture sold during the year of account had a book value of £9 at the date of sale.

(iv) The payment for insurance is a yearly premium paid on 1st July in each year.

(v) Depreciation £25 is to be written off furniture and equipment.

(vi) Liquor stocks on 31st December, 19.., were valued at £180.

(vii) On 31st December, 19.., there were outstanding amounts due to creditors for liquor £175 and for light and heat £27.

4. The following information is supplied to you by the treasurer of the O.K. Boys' Club. From these details you are required to prepare an Income and Expenditure Account for the year ended 30th September, 19.., and a Statement of the club's financial position on that date.

(*a*) The total membership of the club is 120, all of whom had paid their annual subscription of £2·50 except 10 members who are in arrears for one year's subscription.

(*b*) During the year ended 30th September 19. . the treasurer had paid the following expenses: Rent of club premises, £200; light and heat, £55; cleaning, £26; sundry expenses, £24. At the end of the year the treasurer had an outstanding account for electricity, £8.

(*c*) Socials held during the year brought gross proceeds, £500. Expenses in connection with the socials amounted to £200.

(*d*) Purchases of refreshments during the year amounted to £60 and sales of refreshments £80. There was a stock of refreshments in hand at 30th September, 19. ., valued at £10 compared with £15 at the beginning of the year of account.

(*e*) On the 30th September, 19. ., cash in hand and at bank was £343 and the value of furniture and fittings was estimated at £190.

(*f*) The capital of the club at the beginning of the year of account was £258.

5. The Social Club, which runs a snack bar for its members, has made up a summary of the Club's receipts and payments for the year ended 31st December, 1979:

Receipts and Payments Account

for Year ended 31st December 1979

		£		£
Balance at Bank			New Furniture	125
1st Jan.		460	General Expenses	350
Subscriptions:			Stationery	265
For 1978	21		Salaries	875
1979	1 257		Rent	200
1980	162	1 440	Snack Bar Purchases	1 000
Snack Bar receipts		610	Balance 31st Dec. c/d	585
Receipts from advertising on menus and snack bar posters		690		
Income from Investments		200		
		£3 400		£ 3400

Note the following adjustments:

(i) Amount due to Snack Bar creditors:
at 31st December, 1978, £266.
at 31st December, 1979, £354.

(ii) The amount owing to sundry creditors at 31st December 1979 included £113 for a quantity of stores intended specifically for a special function due to take place in January 1980.

(iii) The amount owing to the Club for advertising:
at 31st December, 1978, £128.
at 31st December, 1979, £107.

(iv) £172 was received in December, 1978, in advance for the annual subscriptions of 1979.

(v) £115 was due to salaried staff at 31st December 1979 but remained unpaid at that date.

(vi) £144 of the total cost of Stationery was in connection with the Snack Bar.

(vii) At 31st December, 1979, the assets of the Club comprised: Balance at Bank, £585; Debtors for advertisements, £107; Furniture and Equipment at Cost, £635; Investments at cost, £3 290.

You are required to prepare:

(*a*) A Profit and Loss Account for the Snack Bar for the year 1979.

(*b*) A general Income and Expenditure Account for the year 1979.

(*c*) A Balance Sheet as at 31st December, 1979.

Ignore the current market value of the investments, and Depreciation of Furniture and Equipment. Ignore also taxation.

29

Manufacturing Accounts

The explanation of bookkeeping in this book so far has been set in the context of wholesale or retail businesses. This chapter sets out briefly some of the additional considerations which must be taken into account by a manufacturer. It is concerned mainly with the manufacturer's Final Accounts, which include an additional section before the Trading Account, called the *Manufacturing Account*. In this account are analysed the separate and distinct costs of the manufacturing activities. These are of three main categories, which are *materials*, *labour*, and *overheads*.

The *materials* used may be raw materials, components, sub-assemblies, or partly-finished goods. There will normally be opening and closing stock valuations for each relevant category. These must be accounted for in the Manufacturing Account in exactly the same way that stocks of finished goods are accounted for in the Trading Account.

The normal basis of valuation of stocks of materials is *cost*, as it is also for finished goods. However, if the *net realisable value* of any particular type of stock falls below the cost price, then the net realisable value becomes the basis of valuation for those types of stock, cost continuing to be used for the others.

The *labour* employed is usually categorised as *direct* or *indirect*. Direct labour cost is the cost of employing people whose work can be related easily to output. Indirect labour cost is the cost of employing people such as managers, supervisors, and administrative staff, whose cost is less directly related to output.

Overheads include all of the other costs of running the manufacturing operations, including, for example, depreciation, rent, rates and insurance, and fuel costs. Those which vary approximately in relation to output are sometimes called variable overheads, the rest being known as fixed overhead. Overhead is sometimes called *burden*.

Normally some uncompleted work will be in hand at the close of any accounting period. This *work-in-progress* must be valued, and accounted for in the Manufacturing Account. The valuation is made on the basis of the cost of the materials used, to which is usually added a proportionate allocation of labour and overhead costs. This allocation can be difficult to assess. The same problem arises in valuing stocks of finished goods manufactured by the firm. Statement of Standard Accounting Practice (SSAP) no. 9 has a long discussion of how to make such allocations equitably. There are also arguments, similar to those noted in Chapter 10, against the principle of making any allocations of overheads. Furthermore, the new developments in current cost accounting introduce yet further variations into the valuation process.

However, at this stage of study, the student can normally expect to find that examination questions will give the amounts of the valuations to be placed on all types of stock, and also work-in-progress. The stocks and work-in-progress at the start of the accounting period are shown in the Trial Balance, or the list of account balances. All except the finished goods stock should be debited to the Manufacturing Account. The closing stocks and work-in-progress will normally be given as a further instruction. All except the finished goods should be credited to the Manufacturing Account, and all should be listed as Current Assets in the Balance Sheet. The opening and closing stocks of finished goods are, of course, respectively debited and credited in the Trading Account.

The Manufacturing Account should be set out so that it shows first the *prime cost of production* during the period. The prime cost includes those elements of cost which vary closely with output. It includes raw materials, components and partly finished goods, and possibly also wages, depending on the circumstances. Due allowance must be made for opening and closing stocks. If work-in-progress is valued without allocating indirect costs, then it must also be allowed for in the calculation of prime cost.

To the prime costs must be added the other manufacturing costs. If, as is usually the case, work-in-progress is valued to include an allocation of overheads, the opening valuation is debited, and the closing valuation is credited, to the Manufacturing Account at this stage. The figure thus calculated is the *cost of (completed) production* during the period. It is credited to the Manufacturing Account and debited to the Trading Account.

Alternatively, if the goods manufactured could have been bought from elsewhere instead of being manufactured, the transfer from the Manufacturing Account to the debit of the Trading Account may be done at the *market buying-in price* instead of at cost of production. If the market buying-in price is higher than the cost of production the Manufacturing Account will show a credit balance after the transfer to the Trading Account. This credit balance is the profit from manufacturing. It is debited to the Manufacturing Account and credited to the Profit and Loss Account. If the market buying-in price is the lower of the two, then it will be necessary to transfer the resultant loss on manufacturing to the debit of the Profit and Loss Account.

The Trading Account is debited with the cost of completed production, or with the buying-in price of the goods produced according to the system followed. In addition, it is also debited with the cost of any finished goods actually purchased for resale. In every other respect it is completed in exactly the way described in previous chapters, to show the gross profit on trading. The amount calculated as gross profit will, of course, vary according to whether the goods manufactured are debited to the Trading Account at manufacturing cost or market buying-in price.

Example 36. The Freetown Textile Company's books include the following balances at 31st December, 19. .

		£
Sales (less returns):	finished goods	82 000
Purchases (less returns):	raw materials	30 300
	finished goods	10 000
Stocks at 1st January 19. . :	raw materials	5 000
	work-in-progress	8 000
	finished goods	5 000
Factory wages and salaries:	direct	20 000
	indirect	2 000
Factory overhead costs:	fuel	1 500
	rent, rates, insurance	1 700
	depreciation	1 000

At 31st December stocks held were raw materials £4 000, work-in-progress £9 000, and finished goods £6 000. Prepare the Manufacturing Account and Trading Account for the Freetown Textile Company for 19. . .

FREETOWN TEXTILE COMPANY

Manufacturing and Trading Account

for year ended 31st December, 19...

		£		£
Materials consumed (or used):				
Stock of Raw Materials, 1st Jan. 19..		5 000	Cost of manufactured goods carried down to Trading Account	56 500
Purchases of Raw Materials		30 300		
		35 300		
Less Stock of Raw Materials 31st Dec. 19..		4 000		
Cost of Materials used		31 300		
Direct Wages and Salaries		20 000		
Prime cost		51 300		
Factory Overheads:				
Indirect wages and salaries	2 000			
Fuel	1 500			
Rent, Rates and Insurance	1 700			
Depreciation	1 000	6 200		
		57 500		
Add Work-in-Progress 1st Jan. 19..		8 000		
		65 500		
Less Work in Progress 31st Dec. 19..		9 000		
Cost of Manufactured goods (or cost of Production)		56 500		56 500

	£		£
Stock of Finished Goods 1st Jan. 19..	5 000	Sales (less returns)	82 000
Purchases of finished goods	10 000		
Cost of Manufactured Goods b/d	56 500		
	71 500		
Less Stock of Finished Goods 31st Dec. 19..	6 000		
	65 500		
Gross Profit carried to Profit and Loss Account	16 500		
	£82 000		£82 000

Example 37. The Freetown Textile Company's affairs are as described in Example 36. In addition it is known that the goods manufactured could have been purchased for £60 000. What was the profit or loss on manufacturing and on trading in 19.. ?

FREETOWN TEXTILE COMPANY

Manufacturing and Trading Accounts

for year ended 31st December 19...

	£		£
Cost of production (as in Example 36)	56 500	Market buying-in-price of production, transferred to Trading Account	60 000
Profit on manufacturing, transferred to Profit and Loss Account	3 500		
	£60 000		£60 000
Stock of finished goods at 1st January	5 000	Sales	82 000
Purchases of finished goods	10 000		
Manufactured goods	60 000		
	75 000		
Less: Stock at 31st December	6 000		
	69 000		
Gross Profit, transferred to Profit and Loss Account	13 000		
	£82 000		£82 000

Often the total expenditure on Rent, Rates, Insurance and similar expenses is given, and the student is asked to apportion the sum in certain proportions between the factory and the office. If instructions are given of outstanding or prepaid items relative to this total they should be taken into account before the apportionment is made. The part attributable to the factory is debited to the Trading Account, the remainder, attributable to the office, is debited to the Profit and Loss Account.

The preparation of a Manufacturing Account is only one small part of the additional accounting requirements of the manufacturing firm. Earlier chapters have indicated from time to time that extensive basic recording systems, such as invoicing and payroll, are necessary in any firm which aims to keep systematic and meaningful Ledger

Accounts. Firms must also keep careful records, analysed in such a way as to enable them to estimate the cost of carrying out each of their activities, and to assess the relative efficiency of alternative ways of carrying them out. This form of accounting is often called *Management Accounting*. It uses the basic principles of double entry book-keeping to prepare analyses of the firm's costs and revenues which may be useful to the managers in making decisions.

Even for the wholesale or retail business, the types of issue to be decided are many and varied. Which goods should be traded in? What prices should be charged? How many should be bought-in? How many warehouses, or shops should be operated, where should they be located, how many employees should each have? How much stock should be held of each product, and what kind of storage system should be used? What credit terms should be extended to customers? And so on.

The manufacturer is also concerned with each of these matters. However, he needs additional management accounting information. He has to estimate the costs of each manufacturing operation. He has to decide, for example, whether to make all his components for a particular product or to buy some of the components from another manufacturer, in the way that, for example, many motor vehicle assembly firms buy in the electrical equipment, tyres, and other parts that go into their vehicles. There are many other such decisions, which are within the province of management accounting.

One other important aspect of management accounting can be mentioned. Most firms find it useful to prepare *budgets* of their future activities. Subsequently, these can be compared with the results actually achieved. Such comparisons should help to lead to greater control being gained over the firm's operations. The system of budgeting normally extends to the completion of budgeted Manufacturing, Trading, and Profit and Loss Accounts and Balance Sheets.

EXERCISES 29

1. Prepare Manufacturing and Trading Accounts for year ending 31st Dec., 19. ., from the following balances:

	£
Stock of raw materials, 1st Jan., 19. .	22 370
Raw Material purchases	293 140
Carriage on purchases	2 760
Stock of raw materials, 31st Dec., 19. .	30 720
Manufacturing wages	219 840
Manufacturing power	94 310

	£
Work in progress, 1st Jan., 19..	5 860
Work in progress, 31st Dec., 19..	3 170
Stock of finished goods, 1st Jan., 19..	53 410
Sales	1 031 270
Purchases of finished goods	8 730
Stock of finished goods, 31st Dec., 19..	60 950
Manufacturing expenses	8 920

2. From the following Trading Account of a manufacturer calculate in relation to the period covered by the account:

(1) The cost of the materials used;
(2) The value at cost price of the goods manufactured;
(3) The percentage of gross profit on sales.
Do you think that the profit as stated below is adequate?

Trading Account
for the Year ended 31st December, 19..

	£	£		£	£
Stock:			Sales		50 000
Finished goods	3 500		Stock:		
Raw materials	1 700	5 200	Finished goods	3 000	
Purchases of raw materials		15 000	Raw materials	2 000	5 000
Wages		22 500			
Factory power		1 200			
Gross profit		11 100			
		£55 000			£55 000

London Chamber of Commerce – Intermediate

3. From the balances given below, prepare the Manufacturing and Profit and Loss Accounts of the Excelsis Manufacturing Company:

	£
Raw materials purchases	249 700
Travellers' salaries, expenses, and commission	34 610
Transport costs:	
On goods sold	5 960
On raw materials purchased	820
Stock of raw materials and work in progress:	
1st June, 19..	52 820
31st May in following year	49 420
Returns inwards	1 170

	£
Stock of finished goods:	
1st June, 19..	35 650
31st May in following year	41 160
Sales	519 660
Factory wages	118 610
Other factory expenses	37 470
Office and administration expenses	27 430

If it does not already appear in your answer as a separate figure, calculate the cost of goods manufactured.

4. The following particulars are extracted from the Final Accounts of R. Ransford for the year ended 31st December, 19..:

	£
Stock of raw materials (1st Jan., 19..)	27 840
Stock of raw materials (31st Dec., 19..)	23 210
Purchases	98 760
Sales of finished goods	247 000
Stock of finished goods (1st Jan., 19..) (valued at selling price)	32 870
Stock of finished goods (31st Dec., 19..) (valued at selling price)	29 450
Factory power	1 060
Factory heat and light	340
Factory rent and rates	8 400
Factory wages	78 500
Gross profit for the year	51 030
Net profit for the year	18 700
Capital	85 000

From the above figures calculate (where necessary) and state:

(*a*) The turnover for the year.

(*b*) Cost of raw materials *used* during the year.

(*c*) Cost of Production of goods manufactured during the year.

(*d*) The percentage of Net Profit on Capital, correct to two places of decimals.

(*e*) Value (at selling price) of goods manufactured during the year.

London Chamber of Commerce – Intermediate (adapted)

5. (*a*) Name, and explain briefly the purpose of the various sections of the Revenue Accounts of a manufacturing company. (*b*) From the following information prepare the necessary accounts to disclose the cost of goods manufactured and the gross profit for the six months ending 30th June, 19..

	1st Jan. 19..		30th June 19..
	£	£	£
Stock of raw materials	3 421		3 121
Stock of finished goods	5 932		6 360
Work in progress	1 180		1 420
Purchases of raw materials (net)		17 843	
Sales (net)		98 341	
Wages: Factory		33 248	
Warehouse		7 120	
Overhead expenses: Factory		4 360	
Warehouse		2 830	
Depreciation: Factory		2 050	
Machinery		6 241	
Warehouse		870	
Warehouse fittings		130	
Carriage inwards (raw materials)		261	

N.U.J.M.B

6. C.D. is in business as a manufacturer of packing cases and at 31st December, 19.., the following balances were extracted from his books.

	£
Stock at 1st January, 19..	
Raw materials	4 000
Partly finished cases	4 500
Finished cases	3 000
Wages	48 000
National Insurance	700
Purchases of materials	14 000
Workshop expenses	2 100
Workshop insurance	900
Workshop power and lighting	3 300
Carriage on raw materials	700
Carriage on sales	4 800
Office expenses, salaries, and insurance	11 200
Postage and telephone charges	850
Advertising	800
Sales of packing cases	113 000
Stocks at 31st December, 19..:	
Raw materials	3 400
Partly finished cases	2 800
Finished cases	4 200

(*a*) Prepare Manufacturing, Trading, and Profit and Loss Accounts for the year ended 31st December, 19... The following must be brought into account:

Depreciation at 12½% on the plant and workshop tools valued at £80 000.

Interest at 5% per annum on C.D.'s capital of £120 000.

C.D. is to be credited with a salary of £5 000.

(*b*) Express your reasoned opinion of the result of the year's trading.

30

Funds Flow Statements

A recent addition to the final accounts is a *funds flow statement*. It is sometimes called a *statement of the source and application of funds*. There is as yet no legal requirement to publish such a statement, but it is considered to be good professional practice. The publication of funds flow statements by companies whose annual turnover is at least £25 000 is therefore required by Statement of Standard Accounting Practice no. 10, issued in July 1975. The nature of a statement of standard accounting practice is described in Chapter 43.

A funds flow statement may be set out in many different ways. However, in essence its purpose is to show the sources of any increase in the firm's funds over a period of time, and the corresponding uses made of those funds. In doing this it provides a link between the balance sheets at the start and end of the period of time, in a way which is complementary to the profit and loss account. The information contained in a funds flow statement is useful in itself. The owners of the business would themselves find it useful, regardless of whether or not there is any requirement for their business to publish such a statement.

In its simplest form a funds flow statement can be prepared by comparing two successive balance sheets of the business. Any increases in claims *plus* any decreases in assets, which are found when the later balance sheet is compared with the earlier one, together constitute the sources of funds. Any increases in assets *plus* any decreases in claims together constitute uses of funds.

It will be noted that the sources of funds are all represented by increases in credit balances or decreases in debit balances over the period. Similarly, the uses of funds are represented by increased debit balances and decreased credit balances. Since the opening and closing totals of the balance sheets each balance, then so must a statement composed of differences between them in this way also balance. It is, in fact, simply another consequence of the equality of debit and credit entries in the basic bookkeeping records. This has been explained already in terms of the uses (debits) and sources (credits) of funds.

Example 38 illustrates the preparation of a funds flow statement by the process of comparing two successive balance sheets.

Example 38. The balance sheets of P and M, a business run by Patrick Michaels, were as set out below at 31st December 19.0 and 19.1. Prepare a funds flow statement for P & M for the year 19.1, assuming that the proprietor took out no drawings during 19.1.

	19.0	19.1
	£	£
Fixed assets	8 013	8 840
Current assets:		
Stocks	17 437	14 503
Debtors	19 902	21 075
Bank	9 504	15 808
	46 843	51 386
	£54 856	£60 226

	19.0	19.1
	£	£
Capital:		
Opening capital	6 000	6 000
Retained profits	30 819	37 553
	36 819	43 553
Current Liabilities:		
Creditors	16 429	9 924
Short-term borrowing	1 608	6 749
	18 037	16 673
	£54 856	£60 226

In order to prepare the required statement it is necessary to calculate the amount of the change between the two balance sheets, and to decide whether it represents a source of funds (i.e. an increase in a claim or a reduction in an asset) or a use of funds (i.e. an increase in an asset or a reduction in a claim).

	Nature of difference	Amount of difference Uses	Sources
		£	£
Fixed Assets	Increase in asset	827	—
Current Assets:			
Stocks	Decrease in asset	—	2 934
Debtors	Increase in asset	1 173	—
Bank	Increase in asset	6 304	—
Capital:			
Opening capital	No change	—	—
Retained profits	Increase in claim	—	6 734
Current Liabilities:			
Creditors	Decrease in claim	6 505	—
Short-term borrowing	Increase in claim	—	5 141
		£14 809	£14 809

It will be noticed that the calculations encompass the whole balance sheet, and do not distinguish between the Claims and Assets sections. Furthermore, both sources and uses may be derived from either section of the balance sheet. In some cases, such as the opening capital in the example, there may be no change, and therefore neither source nor use.

The funds flow statement could be set out by simply listing the sources and uses which have been calculated. Such a statement might appear as follows:

P & M: Funds Flow Statement for 19.1

	£
Source of Funds:	
Retained profits	6 734
Short-term borrowing	5 141
Reduction in stockholding	2 934
	£14 809
Uses of Funds:	
Increase in fixed assets	827
Increased credit extended to customers	1 173
Increase in bank balance	6 304
Reduced credit taken from suppliers	6 505
	£14 809

Such a statement should prompt several questions. Why has more borrowing been undertaken, despite a profit being made? Why was more borrowing undertaken when bank balances increased significantly? Would it be better to use some of the bank balance to pay off the borrowing? Why has more credit been extended to customers? Is it because there are more customers, or because they are taking longer to pay? Why has the credit taken from suppliers fallen? Does the reduction in stocks arise from increased sales? Furthermore, is it a temporary phenomenon, or the result of careful control? Is it likely to lead to loss of customers in the future?

Such questions could be asked following a study of the two balance sheets. The funds flow statement throws them into sharper perspective. The statement could be redrafted to suggest answers to any of them. For example, why was more borrowing undertaken, when a profit was made?

P & M: Funds Flow Statement for 19.1

	£	£
SOURCE OF FUNDS:		
Profit retained from operations in 19.1		£6 734
USES OF FUNDS:		
Fixed assets: additional capital expenditure		827
Working capital:		
Additional credit extended to customers	1 173	
Reduced credit taken from suppliers	6 505	
Increased bank balance	6 304	
	13 982	
Less: Reduced stockholding	2 934	
	11 048	
Less: Additional short-term borrowing	5 141	
Net increase in working capital		5 907
		£6 734

This statement has also been set out to show the working capital items grouped together. It shows only the same figures as the previous statement illustrated, but it suggest more clearly why additional short-term borrowing was undertaken when a profit was made.

Another variation which is widely adopted, and which is described in SSAP 10, is to group together all items constituting *net liquid funds*, i.e. cash and bank balances and short-term investments *less* bank overdrafts and other forms of short-term borrowing. 'Short-term' is usually defined for this purpose as meaning subject to realisation or settlement within one year.

Two important extensions of these ideas are common to most funds flow statements. The first is to include depreciation, and the second is to extend the treatment of fixed assets. They are obviously related issues. It will also normally be necessary to account for drawings (or dividends).

Example 39. The affairs of P & M were as described in Example 38. In addition, the following information is available:

(*a*) the profit of £6 734 in 19.1 is calculated after charging depreciation of £750;

(*b*) the profit includes the surplus on the disposal for £1 000 of a fixed asset which was included in the balance sheet at 31st December 19.0 at a net value of £800;

(*c*) the proprietor had taken out drawings for himself in respect of 19.1, amounting to £2 400, and which had not been recorded in the books.

The charge for depreciation has reduced the profit below the level which it would otherwise have been. However, it did not cause any outflow of funds during 19.1. The result of this is that the funds available from trading operations were not just the profitof £6 734, but the profit plus the depreciation charge, a total of £6 734 + £750, or £7 484. The second effect of introducing the depreciation charge is on the figure shown for capital expenditure. The depreciation of £750 has to be deducted from the fixed assets balance of £8 013 as at 31st December 19.0, giving a net figure of £7 263 at 31st December 19.1 had there been no capital expenditure. In fact, the balance at that date was £8 840. Therefore the capital expenditure on fixed assets in 19.1 was £8 840–£7 263, or £1 577. This is £750 greater than the figure shown in the various drafts of the funds flow statement set out above.

Thus, in order to incorporate depreciation, both the retained profits and the expenditure on fixed assets are increased by the amount of the year's depreciation.

The disposal of a fixed asset adds another complication. The surplus of £200 has been included in the retained profit. It is necessary to appreciate that the funds available for re-investment were in fact £1 000, the amount of the disposal, and not just the £200 profit. Therefore the retained profit shown in the funds flow statement is reduced by £200, and an additional source of funds is shown, i.e. Disposal of Fixed Assets £1 000. This is a net increase of £800 in the sources of funds. At the same time, it must be recognised that, as an asset valued at £800 in the balance sheet as at 31st December 19.0 was sold during 19.1, the balance sheet figure at 31st December 19.1 would be £8 013 – £750 (as above) – £800 in the absence of any capital expenditure during 19.1. This gives a figure of £6 463. Since the balance at 31st December 19.1 was in fact £8 840, total capital expenditure was £8 840 – £6 463, a total of £2 377. This can be checked as the total of £827 + £750 + £800.

The proprietor's drawings would have to be offset against the profit for 19.1, and would therefore constitute a reduction in the sources of funds available. At the same time, they would cause the closing bank balance to be £2 400 lower than stated in Example 38, and so reduce by £2 400 the use of funds represented by an increase in the bank balance.

Incorporating all these changes the following revised funds flow statement would be prepared:

P & M: Funds Flow Statement for 19.1

	£	£
SOURCES OF FUNDS		
Profit retained from operations in 19.1	6 534	
Add back: *depreciation*	750	
	7 284	
Deduct: *drawings*	2 400	
Funds available from operations		4 884
Disposal of fixed assets		1 000
		£5 884

	£	£
USE OF FUNDS		
Fixed assets: additional capital expenditure		2 377
Working capital:		
Additional credit extended to customers	1 173	
Reduced credit taken from suppliers	6 505	
Increased bank balance	3 904	
	11 582	
Less: reduced stockholding	2 934	
	8 648	
Less: additional short-term borrowing	5 141	
Net increase in working capital		3 507
		£5 884

The funds flow statement does not replace the profit and loss account or the balance sheet. It rearranges and summarises the information which they contain, to emphasise further complementary aspects of the firm's affairs. Its purpose is to show how changes in the firm's operations have been financed, and the ways in which those funds have been disbursed.

EXERCISES 30

Note: Question 5 should be completed before beginning question 4.

1. Explain how a firm's funds flow statement is related to the profit and loss account and the opening and closing balance sheets for the same period.

2. What is the purpose of preparing a funds flow statement?

3. Explain how to prepare a funds flow statement.

4. The balance sheets of the Georgia Company as at 31st December 19.0, 19.1 and 19.2 were as shown in question 5. In addition, you are advised that the following matters need to be taken into account:

		19.1	19.2
(*a*) Depreciation:	Plant	500	500
	Vehicles	1 500	3 000

(*b*) In 19.1 a vehicle was sold for £200. It was shown in the balance sheet at 31st December 19.0 at a value of £500. The difference arising on the disposal was included in the profits for 19.1.

(*c*) The proprietor, George McLennon, had taken out drawings of £5 000 in 19.1 and £6 000 in 19.2. These drawings have been allowed for in the balance sheets set out above.

(*d*) Bad debts of £1 000 are to be incorporated into the accounts for 19.2.

Prepare revised funds flow statements for 19.1 and 19.2.

5. The Georgia Company has the following balance sheets at 31st December 19.0, 19.1 and 19.2:

	19.0	19.1	19.2
Capital	17 000	24 000	24 000
Retained Profits	8 000	12 000	10 000
	25 000	36 000	34 000
Current Liabilities:			
Creditors	12 500	18 000	13 000
Bank overdraft	3 500	—	9 000
	16 000	18 000	22 000
	£41 000	£54 000	£56 000
Fixed Assets:			
Plant	5 000	4 500	4 000
Vehicles	2 500	10 000	12 000
	7 500	14 500	16 000
Current Assets:			
Stocks	15 000	24 000	20 500
Debtors	18 500	14 500	19 500
Bank	—	1 000	—
	33 500	39 500	40 000
	£41 000	£54 000	£56 000

Prepare funds flow statements for 19.1 and 19.2.

31

Mechanised Accounting

Students will appreciate that when there are many thousands of transactions, hand written methods of bookkeeping, as described in previous chapters, entail a great deal of labour and the services of large numbers of clerks and skilled bookkeepers. To this must be added the substantial task of operating the underlying accounting systems such as payroll etc., which were introduced in Chapter 16. Sales are usually the most numerous of all transactions and the writing up of Sales Books, Sales Ledgers, and customers' Statements of Account may involve many hours of work on the part of many clerks.

Hand written methods involve the ever-present possibility of error. Errors may be made in writing up the Sales Books, posting to the Sales Ledgers, and in making out Statements of Account at the end of each month. Moreover, there are peak periods of work, particularly at the end of each month when Statements are sent to customers and the books are 'proved' by means of a Trial Balance. If the Trial Balance does not agree, by reason of errors, then hours of search may be entailed before such errors are located.

Control Accounts, as described in Chapter 13, may help a great deal in locating such errors. Nevertheless, it would be a great advantage to have a system in which, at the time of making records, not only are the Sales Book, Ledger Account, and Statement of Account written up simultaneously, but also a system of control proves the postings correct after each run of work. This would save a great deal of labour in writing up the records, and by ensuring that all postings are correct from day to day.

This is possible by the adoption of a simple system of mechanised accounts which will give the advantages of accuracy, improved records, speed, economy, and up-to-date information.

The operation of a simple *accounting machine* now described is based on information kindly supplied by the British Olivetti Company Ltd. It is treated in its application to sales records.

The sources of information for compiling sales records will be copy invoices of goods sold to customers, copy receipts or bank paying-in slips for remittances received from debtors, copy credit notes sent to customers for returns and allowances, and Journal vouchers for miscellaneous items such as bad debts.

The Sales Ledger Accounts take the form of cards ruled in three money columns (debit, credit and balance) as shown on page 3. These cards may be kept in drawers in alphabetical order, or in numerical order if the customers' accounts are numbered. This facilitates the selection of cards for any particular run of postings. A run of postings may consist, for example, of posting copy invoices, copy credit notes or remittances from debtors.

Accounting machines are so constructed that they add or subtract automatically. They may supply narrative detail on documents.

Whichever the run may be, the material, e.g. copy invoices, is sorted into ledger card order, listed, and totalled on an adding machine. This is known as a *pre-list*. Its total should agree with the total of the postings made as shown by the accounting machine at the *end* of the run of postings.

The Ledger cards are then selected and placed in the same sequence as the material to be posted. For ease of operation when posting to Ledger cards, the cards and relevant documents (e.g. copy invoices) may be arranged in pairs in a tray from which card and relevant document are withdrawn together.

A Sales Day Book sheet with carbon jacket is inserted into the rear feed of the accounting machine and the machine is cleared ready for posting. The clearing operation (described below) is printed on to the Day Book so that in the event of non-agreement of totals after posting the error is known to be confined to the batch of postings just completed. A Ledger card and statement are then inserted with carbons.

A loose-leaf sheet in the form of a statement is also inserted, with a suitable form of carbon. This is normally the top copy, and all the remaining documents are prepared as carbon copies. The Statement Sheet is filed with the Ledger card.

The machines incorporate devices to ensure the accuracy of the postings. To do this it is necessary first to introduce the old balance into the machine. This is known as 'picking up' the old balance. It is necessary to prove the accuracy of this 'pick up'. In some machines when the posting has been made the 'pick up' balance is repeated and if the two 'pick ups' do not agree the machine locks. There is always the possibility of the operator making the same error in both 'pick ups'. To avoid this, more advanced types of machine are capable of giving an automatic proof of the entry of the correct 'pick up' of the old balance. This operates in the following manner. On completion of a line entry, and after recording the up-to-date balance, the machine automatically produces a non-accounting figure which is mathematically related to the account balance. It is printed in a special column on the card known as 'proof code'. When the next entry is to be made to an account *both* the account balance and the 'proof code' are picked up, i.e. *two different numbers*. The machine will then decide if the two numbers picked-up are correctly related. If they are, then it is virtually certain that the balance has been picked up correctly. If this proof has not been achieved the machine will not operate.

The postings are made from the copy invoices, copy credit notes, or whatever media are being posted. The new balance is calculated and printed by the machine. It is, of course, the insertion of the old balance and then the amount of the transaction that enables the machine to add (in the case of credit postings) or subtract (in the case of debit postings) and thus calculate and print the new balance on both Ledger card and statement. Where the system of proving the 'pick up' of the previous balance by printing it again is in use this is then done to prove the accuracy of the 'pick up'.

The only possibility of error now remaining is in the actual posting. This can be checked at the end of the posting run by comparing the automatic total of entries which is accumulated by the machine with the pre-list, i.e. the predetermined total of postings made by adding machine. This may be done visually, but some machines are made in such a way as to make this comparison by entering the pre-list total into the machine at the end of the run of postings. The machine will then automatically compare this total with the total of accumulated postings and if they agree make the total entry in the Sales Ledger Control Account. If they do not agree it is necessary to check the pre-list against the postings and to compare them entry by entry.

When the correct total of the postings is proved a Control Account card is inserted and the opening balance picked up and proved. The agreed total of postings is then entered on the Control Account card. The student will readily see that, unlike hand written methods, the accuracy of the posting is proved after each run of postings, and the Sales Ledger Control Account will show at a glance the total of trade debtors to date. This total can be proved against a pre-list, if this is desired as a final check.

Periodically, usually monthly, the statement sheets are reviewed. They are removed from the Ledger cards and are sent to the customer if he owes money, or has a credit balance (e.g. if he has returned goods for which he had previously paid, and has been given a credit note). Fresh Statement sheets are prepared recording the balance on the account and inserted with the Ledger cards, ready for the next month.

In the case of Purchases Ledgers the procedure of posting invoices received (credits), credit notes received (debits), and Cash Book summaries of accounts paid (debits) will be basically the same as for the Sales Ledgers, except that Statements are omitted. The Purchases Ledger Control Account will then show, at the end of each run of postings, the total of trade creditors.

Accounting machines may be used for Cash Book postings and analysis, the making up of Payrolls, Stock Sheets, and Stock Control Records.

Whilst many accounting machines of the type described above are still in use, there have been further major developments in forms of mechanisation.

The first of these, also now being superseded, was the *punched card accounting machine*. This is sometimes known as 'unit record equipment', because each transaction is recorded on its own unique punched card. All of the information about the transaction is contained within the code of holes punched into the card. It can be drawn from at will, and used in various ways, and then filed away again.

Like all mechanised systems, punched card systems depend for their success on the grouping of transactions so that each group contains a large number of entries requiring similar treatment. They have been surpassed in their technical capacity to handle large amounts of data quickly, by *electronic digital computers*. Until recently, and despite massive advances in technical capacity and speed of operation, most computers were too large and too expensive for most businesses. However, the situation is now rapidly arriving when computers and the ancillary equipment to go with them become relatively very cheap, physically very small, and yet remain capable of great versatility and speed of operation. These mini-computers will be very widely used in businesses.

A simple basic computer system can be represented in a flowchart form. The following example (see p. 299) is taken from *Accounting By Electronic Methods*, published by the Institute of Chartered Accountants in England and Wales.

Generally speaking, computers are used in bookkeeping and accounting work for the following main types of application:

(*a*) payroll and related records;
(*b*) invoicing, sales ledger bookkeeping, sales analyses;
(*c*) purchases ledger bookkeeping, purchases analyses;
(*d*) records of stocks, including raw materials, components, finished goods, and work-in-progress;
(*e*) labour cost analysis, and other cost analyses;
(*f*) preparing budgets and forecasts.

Like other forms of mechanised accounting equipment, electronic computers are desirable aids to bookkeeping and accountancy work to the extent that they give the following *advantages*:

(*a*) quicker, more accurate and cheaper processing of large quantities of uncomplicated data;
(*b*) greater control over the system;
(*c*) the elimination of much routine copying work;
(*d*) automatic preparation of books of original entry, or elimination of the need for written-out forms of these, by the maintenance of other forms of permanent record;
(*e*) more effective control of working capital through quicker and more accurate recording of debtors, stocks, and cash records;
(*f*) additional information, analysis, and statistics;
(*g*) fewer accounting and clerical staff.

The potential advantages under these headings must be offset against the possible *disadvantages* arising from:

(*a*) the inflexible arrangement of the programme, requiring that all transactions meet specified conditions;
(*b*) the absence of full written records at every stage;
(*c*) the possible manipulation of a highly-centralised system, with fraudulent intent;
(*d*) the difficulty of answering non-routine enquiries;
(*e*) the complications of introducing a new system;
(*f*) the tendency for the availability of a computer to cause new applications to be introduced which may be inefficient or even strictly unnecessary, but which may lead to pressure for more, or newer, equipment;

(*g*) the difficulty of designing a system of charging departments which use the machine for the time taken on a central facility by their work.

Some of these disadvantages are gradually being reduced by new developments in the equipment available.

EXERCISES 31

1. Give a brief explanation of the posting of Sales Ledger Accounts by means of a simple accounting machine.

2. What advantage does the use of an accounting machine have as compared with hand written methods of bookkeeping?

3. How would the use of an accounting machine economise in clerical labour?

4. How is the accuracy of posting ensured when using an accounting machine and what advantages ensue?

5. Why is the use of Control Accounts enhanced by the use of an accounting machine?

6. List the main applications of computer systems in bookkeeping and accounting work.

7. What advantages should be sought from operating computerised systems of bookkeeping and accounts?

8. Explain why a computerised system of bookkeeping may be less flexible than a clerical system.

9. Draw a flowchart of how a computer operates in accounting and bookkeeping work.

SIMPLIFIED FLOW CHART

To illustrate:
(i) the flow of data through an Electronic Data Processing installation, and
(ii) the action and output of the installation.

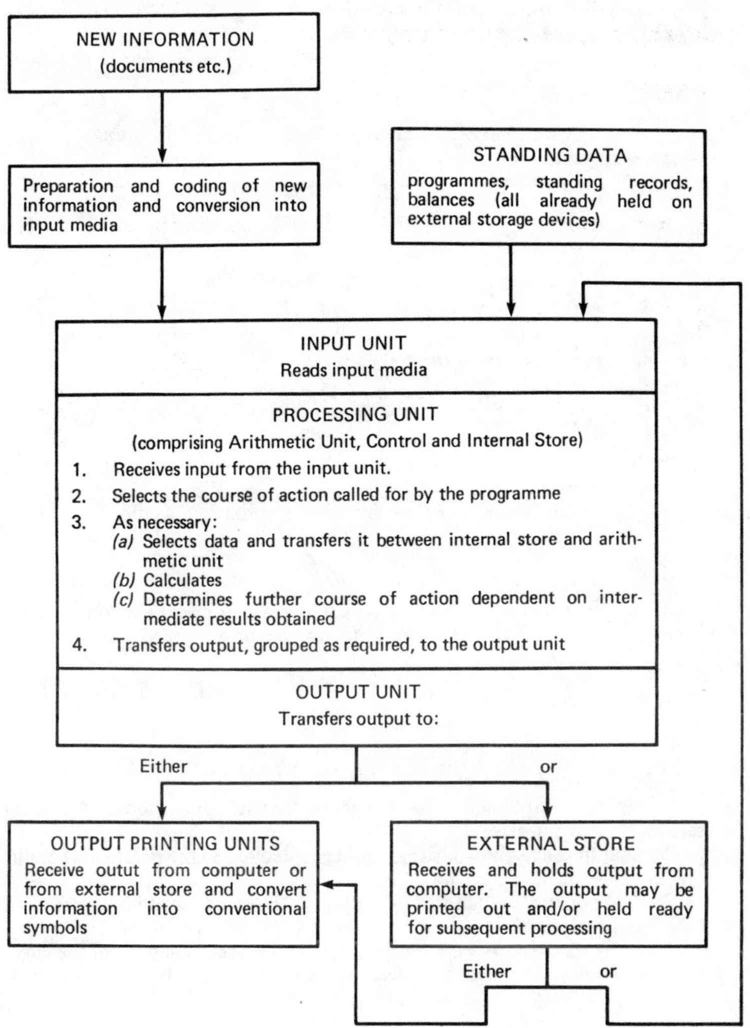

Courtesy of The Institute of Chartered Accountants (England and Wales)

Appendix I

Additional Exercises

1.

M. Butler's Ledger
B. Mitchell's Account

Dr.				*Cr.*			
19..			£	19..			£
(*a*) May	1.	Balance	600	(*b*) May	2.	Bank	570
(*d*) ,,	6.	Goods	280	(*c*) ,,	2.	Discount	30
				(*e*) ,,	9.	Returns	70

Examine the above account carefully and

(i) briefly interpret each of the items (*a*)–(*e*);
(ii) state in which of M. Butler's books each of the items (*b*)–(*e*) was entered before being posted to the Ledger;
(iii) state the account in M. Butler's Ledger where each of the items (*b*)–(*e*) has its double entry;
(iv) state the conclusions you draw from the account as a whole.

2. From what sources would you expect a wholesaler to obtain the information for writing up (*a*) the Sales Day Book, (*b*) the Returns Inwards Book, (*c*) the Purchases Day Book?

A.E.B., G.C.E. 'O' Level

3. Although the Trial Balance of A.B. agreed, the audit of his books of account revealed the following errors.

£150 paid for advertising charges had been debited to the personal account of the advertising contractor.

£300 paid for the purchase of an additional typewriter had been debited to the Purchases Account.

State (*a*) why these errors were not revealed by the Trial Balance, (*b*) the effect of their *correction* on the balance of the net profit at the end of the trading period.

4. During the audit of the books of a business the following errors were discovered:

(*a*) An amount of £200 for the sale of a typewriter used in the business had been credited to Sales Account.
(*b*) An amount of £160 paid for carriage on purchases had been debited to Carriage on Sales Account.
(*c*) A sale of goods £490 to J. Brown had been debited to the account of G. Brown.

You are required—
(i) to give the Journal entries necessary to correct the errors.
(ii) to state the effect of the corrections on the gross profit, the net profit, and on any items in the Balance Sheet.

College of Preceptors – Senior (adapted)

5. (*a*) Explain the Imprest Petty Cash system, clearly stating its main features.
(*b*) Prepare an analysed Imprest Petty Cash record from the following:

			£
January	1	Balance of cash in hand	40.00
	2	Postage stamps	8.00
	3	Stationery	2.40
	3	Taxi fares	2.50
	4	Window cleaning	1.50
	5	Notebook refills	1.00
	5	Parcel postage	1.10
	5	Typing paper	1.40
	5	Balance and reimbursement by Chief Cashier	

6. Trot, a retailer, finds himself in need of additional capital in order to pay for an expansion in his business, and arranges for a loan from the Downshire Bank to be drawn as required. You are asked to record the following in Trot's Ledger –

			£
Jan.	1.	Received loan from bank	5 000
,,	10.	,, ,, ,, ,,	7 500
,,	31.	,, ,, ,, ,,	2 500
Mar.	1.	Repaid on account of loan	3 250
,,	16.	,, ,, ,, ,, ,,	1 250
,,	31.	Paid interest	300

Balance the Loan Account on 31st March, 19...

Note. – Cash Book and Journal entries are *not* required.

R.S.A. – Elementary (adapted)

7. Included among the bookkeeping records of a firm of wholesalers is a 'Journal Proper'. What types of entry would you expect to find in this book?

At the close of the firm's financial year on 31st December, 19.., their stock in trade was valued at £12 900: give the journal entry to record this.

R.S.A. – Elementary (adapted)

8. From the following details find C.D.'s capital and show his Balance Sheet at 31st December, 19..:

Trade creditors, £1 977; expense creditors, £129; debtors, £2 845; stock, £3 848; amounts prepaid, £57; plant and machinery, £4 100; furniture and fittings, £680; freehold premises, £10 000; cash in hand, £40; bank overdraft, £2 600.

From the completed Balance Sheet answer the following questions:

(*a*) State the items which are current assets and give the total of such assets.
(*b*) State the items which are fixed assets and give the total of such assets.
(*c*) State the items which you consider to be current liabilities and give the total of such liabilities.
(*d*) How would you find the working capital and what is its amount?
(*e*) What is meant by 'Freehold' premises?

London Chamber of Commerce – Elementary

9. What is meant by saying a firm is insolvent and how would this fact be apparent from its Balance Sheet?

London Chamber of Commerce – Elementary (adapted)

10.

Ledger of E. Huish

T. Smith's Account

Dr.									*Cr.*
	19..			£		19..			£
(*c*)	May	5.	Returns	300	(*a*)	May	1.	Balance	1 800
(*d*)	„	5.	Bank	3 610	(*b*)	„	2.	Goods	2 300
(*e*)	„	5.	Discount	190	(*g*)	„	15.	Bank	1 520
(*f*)	„	12.	Goods	1 600	(*h*)	„	15.	Discount	80

Indicate in respect of each of the eight items (*a*)–(*h*):

(i) its meaning;
(ii) the subsidiary book in which it was first entered;
(iii) the Ledger Account in which the offsetting double entry is to be found.

What deductions do you make in respect of the account as a whole?

11. A. Gwynn's business is divided into two departments, A and B, and on 31st May, 19.., the following balances were extracted from the books.

	A	B
	£ thousands	
Stock at beginning of year	4·5	5·4
Sales	13·5	22·6
Purchases	11·5	15·6
Returns inwards	0·3	0·6
Returns outwards	1·4	2·2
Stock at 31st May, 19..	4·7	5·6

(*a*) Prepare, on the columnar system, Trading Account for the year ended 31st May, 19...

(*b*) Express the gross profit as a percentage of turnover in respect of each department and of the business as a whole.

W.J.E.C., G.C.E. 'O' Level

12. Indicate – *briefly* giving your reasons in each case – which of the following represents capital receipts, capital expenditure, revenue income, revenue expenditure:

(*a*) Bank overdraft interest;
(*b*) purchase of typewriters for re-sale by the Office Supplies Company;
(*c*) purchase of typewriter for office use by the H.T.C. Social Club;
(*d*) sale of a delivery van by the Office Supplies Company;
(*e*) receipt of commission by a firm of brokers.

W.J.E.C., G.C.E. 'O' Level (Commercial Subjects)

13. F. W. Pickles & Sons are manufacturers of sauces and pickles.

From the following information relating to the year ended 31st December, 19.., select the items which you consider should be charged to the Trading and Profit and Loss Accounts of the firm and draw up the accounts in proper form.

N.B. – A Balance Sheet is *not* required.

	£
Stocks of raw materials 1st January, 19..	310 000
Stocks of raw materials 31st December, 19..	287 000
Purchases of raw materials	6 910 000
Stocks of jars and bottles 1st January, 19..	98 000
Stocks of jars and bottles 31st December, 19..	106 000
Purchases of jars and bottles	925 000
Stock of packing cases and crates for despatch of finished goods 1st January, 19..	27 000
Cost of making new packing cases and crates during the year	184 000
Stock of packing cases and crates 31st December, 19..	21 000
Factory wages	7 510 000
Office wages and salaries	680 000
Delivery vanmen's wages	490 000
Salesmen's salaries, expenses, and commission	1 095 000
Advertising	650 000
Factory power	185 000
Light and heat (Factory $\frac{5}{6}$, Office $\frac{1}{6}$)	78 000
Rates (Factory $\frac{5}{6}$, Office $\frac{1}{6}$)	82 200
Delivery van expenses	210 000

	£
Insurance (Factory $\frac{5}{6}$, Office $\frac{1}{6}$)	42 000
Depreciation of machinery	161 500
Depreciation of office equipment	7 500
Drawings	1 800 000
Office and administrative expenses	95 000
Purchases of new machinery	350 000
Repairs to premises	34 000
Extension of premises	250 000
Sales	21 500 000
Stocks of finished goods 1st January, 19..	478 000
Stocks of finished goods 31st December, 19..	522 000
Notes –	
Factory wages due at 31st December, 19.., and not paid	120 000
Insurance prepaid at 31st December, 19..	10 200

College of Preceptors – Senior (*adapted*)

14. From the information given below prepare the account of T. Matthew as it would appear in the Ledger of O. Paul (Tableware dealer) for the month of April, 19...

April 1. Balance due to Matthew, £120.
,, 6. Purchased from Matthew 6 dozen table cloths at £2 each, *less* 25% trade discount.
,, 8. Returned to Matthew 6 damaged table cloths and received credit note therefor.
Paid carriage on returned goods (chargeable to Matthew) £2.
,, 15. Sold to Matthew an old board-room table for £15.
,, 20. Paid to Matthew the balance due on 1st April, *less* 5% cash discount.
,, 30. Purchased from Matthew a job lot of tableware for £20.

Balance the account on 30th April, 19...

(*a*) Has it a debit or credit balance?

(*b*) Is O. Paul due to receive or pay the amount?

R.S.A. – Elementary (*adapted*)

15. (*a*) What do you understand by Capital Expenditure and Revenue Expenditure? Why is this distinction important in bookkeeping?

(*b*) Steven and James, retailers, have spent £2 500 for complete redecoration of their premises. Steven says this is Capital Expenditure but James says it is Revenue Expenditure. State with your reasons which of them you consider to be right.

(*c*) What difference will it make to the profits for the year if Steven's rather than James's view is adopted, but one-fifth of the cost is written off?

R.S.A. Elementary – (*adapted*)

16. The following information is taken from the books of the X.Y.Z. Company.

	YEAR 1	YEAR 2 (following year 1)
	£	£
Turnover	110 000	120 000
Gross profit as a percentage of turnover	41	43
Net profit as a percentage of turnover	16	15

State, with reasons, the conclusions you draw from this information.

17. The following balances were extracted from the books of M.N., a retailer for two completed years of trading.

	YEAR 1	YEAR 2
	£	£
Stock at 1st January	40 000	50 000
,, 31st December	50 000	30 000
Purchases	200 000	210 000
Salaries	40 000	48 000
National Insurance	1 200	1 300
Rent and rates	12 000	15 000
Heating and lighting	4 000	6 250
Advertising	750	800
Sundry expenses	2 000	3 250
Depreciation of fittings	500	500
Cost of delivery of sales	2 200	3 500
Insurances	1 200	1 200
Sales	285 000	344 000

(*a*) Prepare accounts showing the gross and net profit in each year. Provide for interest at 5% per annum on M.N.'s capital, which for the year ended 31st December in Year 1, was £350 000, and for the year ended 31st December in Year 2, £360 000.

(*b*) State, with reasons for your opinion, which of the two years has yielded the better result.

18. (*a*) What is a Balance Sheet?

(*b*) How does it differ from –

(i) A Trial Balance?

(ii) A Trading and Profit and Loss Account?

(*c*) From the following list of balances prepare a Balance Sheet at 31st March 19.., in good style bringing out totals for the following –

Fixed Assets.
Current Assets.
Fixed Liabilities.
Current Liabilities.

The list is complete save for the balance on the Capital Account.

	£
Premises	2 500
Loan from A. Goodman	2 000
Bank overdraft	2 350
Plant	5 000
Fixtures	750
Accrued charges	150
Accounts payable	3 350
Accounts receivable	4 500
Sundry prepayments	120
Six months' interest accrued on Goodman's loan, payable 31st March, 19..	50
Petty cash imprest	30
Stock and work in progress	3 000

(*d*) Assuming that the proprietor had paid in additional capital during th year of £1 500, and had drawings as follows:

	£
Cash	450
Goods	150

and that the profit for the year ended 31st March, 19.., was £1 100, write up th proprietor's Capital Account for the year ended 31st March, 19.., bringing ou the balance at the beginning of the year.

London Chamber of Commerce – Elementar

19. On 31st December, 19.., A. Bass's Statement of Account (from the bank showed a balance in his favour of £650. On comparing the Statement with hi Cash Book he found that the following entries in the Cash Book had not yet bee entered on the statement:

Cheques paid in 31st December, £125.
Cheques drawn up to 31st December, £275.

and the following entries on the Statement had not yet been entered in his Cash Book:

Bank charges for the half year £26.
Payment direct to the bank by one of his debtors £116.

Draw up a bank Reconciliation Statement so as to show the bank balance according to his Cash Book on 31st December, 19...

W.J.E.C., G.C.E. 'O' Level (Commercial Subjects

20. The following Trial Balance was extracted from Peter Pliney's books *after* the Trading and Profit and Loss Account had been prepared –

Trial Balance, 31st December, 19..

	£	£
Profit and Loss Account (Net profit for year to date)		18 000
Cash in hand	100	
Cash at bank	5 000	
Bank Deposit Account	3 200	
Trade debtors and creditors	16 000	9 250
Bad debts provision		1 850
Plant and machinery (see note)	7 400	
Insurance unexpired	250	
Stock in trade	12 000	
Peter Pliney: Capital Account		15 000
,, ,, Drawings Account	5 000	
Rent accrued		1 600
Delivery van (see note)	4 500	
Loan Account: D. Garrick		4 000
Cibber Garages – balance due for van		3 750
	£53 450	£53 450

Notes. – (1) Plant and machinery has been depreciated by £1 200 during the year and stood in the books at £8 600 on 1st January, 19.., this being its cost less depreciation to date:

(2) The delivery van cost £5 000 during 19.. and £500 had been written off for depreciation.

From the above prepare Pliney's Balance Sheet as on 31st December, 19..

R.S.A. – Elementary (adapted)

21. Joan Peters is in business as a wholesale draper. It is her practice to maintain a bad and doubtful debts provision equal in amount to 5% of the debts outstanding at the end of each financial year.

From the following information prepare the Bad Debts Account for the year 19.. (including the provision for bad and doubtful debts) –

		£
Total Debtors on 31st December in previous year		3 220
,, ,, ,, ,, 19..		4 340
Debts written off as irrecoverable –		
On 30th June, 19..	– A. Luke	15
	N. Abel	120
30th November	– B. John	97
	K. Simon	49

On 1st November, 19.., a first and final dividend of 10p in the £ was received in respect of the debt due from Abel (previously written off on 30th June, 19..) and on 18th December, £20 in respect of a debt due from O. Adam (written off in a previous year).

Balance the account as on 31st December, 19.., and show the amount chargeable against the Profit and Loss Account for the year.

R.S.A. – Elementary (adapted)

22. (i) Distinguish between (*a*) a Receipts and Payments Account, (*b*) an Income and Expenditure Account, and (*c*) a Profit and Loss Account.

(ii) Prepare the Income and Expenditure Account for the Western Vale Hockey Club for 19.. from the following information:

	£
Subscriptions for the year	2 500
Receipts for hire of pitch	250
Club dances (net income)	180
Rent paid	600
Secretarial expenses	300
Wages (groundsman)	1 040
Paid for repairs to club house	400
Lighting and other club house expenses	560

On 31st December, 19.., £150 was due to the club for the hire of the pitch and £260 was unpaid for repairs to the club house.

R.S.A. – Elementary (adapted)

23. Jack Store owns a group of shops to which goods are charged at selling prices (*i.e.* the prices at which they are expected to be sold) so as to secure a check on the shop stocks held at any time, the theory being that to the extent that the goods sent to the shops have not been sold, goods of that invoice value ought to be on hand.

(*a*) From the following details relative to his Argyle Street shop you are required to bring out – in statement or account form – what the actual physical stock at 30th April, 19.., ought to be.

	£
Shop stock, 1st April, 19.., at invoice values	3 500
Shop stock, 30th April, 19.., at invoice values	?
Goods charged to shop during April	10 000
Goods returned by shop to suppliers at invoice value	200
Goods returned to shop by credit customers	60
Shop cash sales	9 000
Shop credit sales (gross)	1 160

(*b*) On the basis that the actual stock at 30th April, 19.., was also the theoretical stock and that the invoice value of the goods is such that a profit of 25% on cost price is earned and that the shop expenses for April were £1 000, calculate –

(i) the shop gross profit;
(ii) the shop net profit for the month.

London Chamber of Commerce – Elementary

24. Distinguish between:

(*a*) Capital and Revenue Expenditure. Give *two* examples of each;

(*b*) Capital and Working Capital.

W.J.E.C., G.C.E. 'O' Level (Commercial Subjects)

25. George Makin is in business as an engineer. His business, which is expanding, owns its factory and distributes its products by its own motor lorries.

(*a*) Give one example each of capital expenditure, revenue income and revenue expenditure that you might expect to find in the above firm.

(*b*) How would you deal with the examples chosen in the final Accounts of the business?

26. S. J. started business on 1st January, 19.., with a balance at the bank of £20 000, of which he had borrowed £5 000 from R. T. At the end of the year some of the records kept by S. J. were lost but at 31st December, 19.., a valuation showed the following assets and liabilities.

	£
Fittings	6 000
Van	4 500
Stock in trade	8 500
Sundry debtors	2 700
Cash at bank	6 000
Sundry creditors	6 200

The loan from R. T. was outstanding and interest at 5% per annum was to be charged on this loan. During the year S. J. had drawn £80 per week in anticipation of profits.

From the above information draw up a statement showing the profit or loss for the year ended 31st December, 19.., and a Balance Sheet at that date.

27. R. C. Workman has a small business and does not keep proper accounts. At the end of the year 19.. he submits the following statement to show his profit or loss for the year.

You are required to draw up the accounts in proper form to show his true profit or loss for the year.

Statement of Trading

	£	£		£	£
Stock on 1st January	12 150		Sales	213 000	
Less Stock on 31st December	11 400		*Less* Purchases	103 000	110 000
		750	Goods returned to suppliers		2 100
Carriage on goods bought		1 250	Discount allowed		4 650
Carriage on goods sold		2 150			
Light and heat		950			
Rent and rates		5 250			
Office expenses		1 500			
Office salaries		16 000			
Workmen's wages		61 400			
Depreciation		2 100			
Sales returns		6 500			
Drawings		9 500			
New office furniture		2 200			
Profit		7 200			
		£116 750			£116 750

Note. – There is an outstanding electricity bill for the September–December quarter, £170.

College of Preceptors – Senior (adapted)

28. The Furzdown School has a Social Fund for school journeys and visits and for social functions.

From the following details prepare the Receipts and Payments Account of this fund for the year 19...

Use a total column and columns for (*a*) school journeys, (*b*) social functions.

	£
Balance at bank at 1st January, 19..	1 600
Amounts paid in for journey to Paris	5 000
Amounts paid in for summer camp	1 300
Fares and passport expenses to Paris	1 800
Amount paid in France for coach trips	450
Amount paid in France for food and accommodation	2 750
Rail fares to summer camp	570
Expenses of Parents' Open Day	180
Sales of refreshments on Open Day	130
Sales of tickets for school play	250
Printing of tickets for school play	40
Hire of costumes for school play	150
Cost of food and accommodation at summer camp	1 270
Earnings from harvest work at summer camp	650
Hire of equipment for summer camp	100
Decorations for Christmas party	30
Refreshments for Christmas party	120

	£
Prizes for Christmas party	50
Sale of tickets for Christmas party	170
Contribution by pupils to Social Fund	350

College of Preceptors – Senior (adapted)

29. The following is the Trial Balance of the Carefree Social Club on 31st December, 19. .

	Dr.	*Cr.*
	£	£
Capital at 1st January, 19. .		568
Office and club room equipment	210	
Sports equipment	135	
Subscriptions received for year of account		490
Subscriptions outstanding for previous year	7	
Receipts from club room games		157
Maintenance of club room games, and sports equipment	21	
Rent and rates	132	
Postages	67	
Insurance	12	
Wages	196	
Sundry expenses	64	
Printing and stationery	67	
Cash in hand and at bank	304	
	£1 215	£1 215

You are requested to prepare an Income and Expenditure Account for the year ended 31st December, 19. ., and a Balance Sheet at that date, taking into consideration the following:

(*a*) Sports equipment to be depreciated at 20% per annum and office and club room equipment at 10% per annum.

(*b*) The outstanding subscriptions for previous year to be written off as a bad debt.

(*c*) Subscriptions due for year of account and not yet paid, £6.

London Chamber of Commerce – Elementary

30. The following details relate to the manufacturing and selling activities of a business for the year ended 31st March, 19. .:

	£	£
Stocks, 1st April, in year of account –		
Raw materials		2 000
Finished goods		5 000
Purchases (raw materials)		50 200

		£
Carriage inwards (raw materials)		1 495
Returns outwards (raw materials)		3 100
Sales (finished goods)		76 000
Returns inwards		1 000
Wages (productive)		10 970
Work in progress, 1st April, in year of account, made up of –		
Raw materials	650	
Wages	150	
Carriage	20	
	—	820
Stocks, 31st March, 19. .:		
Raw materials		2 200
Finished goods		7 000
Work in progress, 31st March, 19. ., made up of:		
Raw materials	550	
Wages	120	
Carriage	15	
	—	685

You are required to set out the foregoing in such a form as to bring out:

(*a*) the material cost
(*b*) the labour cost
(*c*) the prime cost *i.e.* material plus labour cost)
} of the production for the year.
(*d*) the cost of the goods sold
(*e*) the gross profit.

London Chamber of Commerce – Intermediate

31. R. L. is a small builder and contractor who does not keep proper books of account.

From the following particulars you are required to prepare Trading and Profit and Loss Accounts for the year ended 31st December, 19. ., and a Balance Sheet at that date.

The Balance Sheet at the end of the previous year was as follows:

	£		£
Trade creditors	3 250	Cash in hand	400
Capital	38 500	Cash at bank	5 600
		Rates and insurance prepaid	150
		Debtors	4 900
		Stock	2 700
		Tools and equipment	3 000
		Premises	25 000
	£41 750		£41 750

		£
Bank Statements for the year showed –		
Credits:	Customers' remittances paid in	36 100
Debits:	Paid to creditors	13 350
	Withdrawn for office cash	6 800
	Withdrawn for private use	8 000
	Rates and insurances	760
	Telephone	520
Cash payments were –		
	Wages	4 160
	Lighting and heating	180
	Van expenses	2 050
	Sundry expenses	420
At 31st December, 19. ., the following valuations were made –		
	Stock	2 100
	Debtors	3 800
	Unexpired rates and insurance	160
	Tools and equipment	2 700
	Premises	25 000
and there were the following liabilities:		
	Trade creditors	2 900

Notes. – Candidates must show below their accounts how they arrive at the amount of sales and purchases.

London Chamber of Commerce – Intermediate (adapted)

32. (*a*) State how each of the following errors would affect the net profit of a firm for the year ended 31st December, 19. . :

(i) Stock at 1st January, 19. ., overvalued by £100.
(ii) Stock at 31st December, 19. ., undervalued by £150.
(iii) Discounts received £210, debited to Profit and Loss Account.
(iv) Proprietor's drawings £1 000 charged to Profit and Loss Account.
(v) Interest on loan from bank £113, omitted from the accounts.
(vi) Omission from Purchases Book of a purchase of £65.

(*b*) What information is conveyed to you by each of the following in the books of a sole trader after balancing for Final Accounts.

(i) A debit balance on Packing Materials Account.
(ii) A debit balance on Rates Account.
(iii) A debit balance on Capital Account.
(iv) A credit balance on Bank Account as it appears in the Cash Book.
(v) A credit balance on Wages Account.

London Chamber of Commerce – Intermediate

33. On 31st December, 19.., the Trial Balance of J. Smith included the following balances:

		£	£
Stock (1st January, 19..)	Dept. A	76 860	
,, ,,	,, B	44 850	
Purchases and sales	Dept. A	63 120	157 360
,, ,,	,, B	76 880	117 020
Inter-departmental transfers of goods.	Dept. A	2 000	
,, ,, ,,	,, B		2 000
Returns inwards	Dept. A	4 000	
,, ,,	,, B	2 000	
Rent, rates, and taxes		8 400	
General expenses		15 040	
Salaries		12 000	
Carriage inwards		7 280	
Wages (productive)	Dept. A	16 600	
,, ,,	,, B	9 000	

Stocks on 31st December, 19.., were: Dept. A, £2 734; Dept. B, £3 063.

From such of the above items as you think should be included prepare, in columnar form, a Departmental Trading Account for the year ended 31st December, 19...

You should also enter any charges not already shown separately, in such proportions to the nearest £ as you consider proper, stating below your accounts the basis on which you have made the apportionment.

London Chamber of Commerce – Intermediate (adapted)

34. The following balances appeared in the books of a business at 1st January, 19...

	£
Cash balance	2 620
Bank balance (credit)	11 170
Debtors' Ledger Control Account	20 370
Creditors' Ledger Control Account	18 120

During the month of January, 19.., the following transactions took place:

			£
Jan.	2.	Received cheque from A. Debtor (discount allowed £10)	100
,,	3.	Paid petty cash by cheque	170
,,	7.	Received cheque from C. Debtor (discount allowed £60)	1 140
,,	7.	Paid cheques to bank	1 240
,,	9.	Received cheque from C. Debtor	2 920
,,	9.	Paid L. Creditor by cheque	4 500
,,	17.	Received cheque from D. Debtor	2 130
,,	20.	Paid M. Creditor by cheque (discount received £110)	2 220
,,	30.	Paid wages for month by cheque	4 120
,,	30.	Paid petty cash expenses	270

The Credit Sales for the month were £6 120 (less Returns and Allowances £120) and the Purchases £4 970.

Write up the Cash Book for the month and compute the amounts of trade debtors and creditors at 31st January.

35. From the following details you are required to write up the Sales Ledger and Purchase Ledger Control Accounts for the month of January.

	£
Debtors at January 1st, 19..	9 753
Creditors at January 1st, 19..	3 456
Credit sales for month	19 506
Credit purchases for month	6 912
Returns outward for month	115
Returns inward for month	97
Cash got from customers	18 912
Customers cheques dishonoured	100
Cash paid to suppliers	5 814
Discount allowed	178
Discount received	117
Interest charged to customers on overdue accounts	5
Bad debts written off	76
Accounts settled by 'contra'	345
Dr. Balances in Purchases Ledger at January 31st, 19..	28
Cr. Balances in Sales Ledger at January 31st, 19..	49

London Chamber of Commerce – Intermediate

36. The following balances were extracted from the books of A. Trader, a wholesale merchant, on March 31st, 1978. You are required to draw up a Trial Balance – ascertaining his capital as you do so – and from it prepare the Trading and Profit and Loss Account for the year.

	£
Drawings	9 500
Returns Outwards	900
Carriage Outwards	1 050
Debtors	21 750
Creditors	6 450
Motor Car	6 000
Cash in Hand	550
Sales	239 000
Furniture, Fixtures and Fittings	16 000
Bank Overdraft	9 000
Wages and Salaries	43 000
Returns Inwards	1 040
Commission Paid	9 100

	£
Commission Received	1 030
Motor Car Expenses	1 200
Stock at April 1st, 1977	22 500
Purchases	170 500
Bank Interest and Charges	570
Rent, Rates and Insurance	5 700
General Expenses	7 140
Bad Debts	910
Discount Allowed	700
Discount Received	3 300

In preparing the Trading and Profit and Loss Account note the following:

(i) The stock was valued at £31 535 on 31st March, 1978.

(ii) Wages and salaries should be apportioned as to one-quarter to Trading Account and three-quarters to Profit and Loss Account.

(iii) Rent, rates and insurance should be apportioned as to two-thirds to the Trading Account and one-third to the Profit and Loss Account.

(iv) The Furniture, Fixtures and Fittings are to be depreciated by 20 per cent.

(*Note:* You are not required to produce a balance sheet.)

The following questions have been selected from ***West African Examinations Council, School Certificate*** *papers.*

Questions are set in the currencies of The Gambia, Ghana, Liberia, Nigeria and Sierra Leone, but there are no mathematical or accounting differences as all the currencies are now decimal.

Table of Currencies

The Gambia	100 bututs	= 1 Dalasi (D)
Ghana	100 pesewas	= 1 Cedi (₵)
Liberia	100 cents	= 1 Dollar ($)
Nigeria	100 kobo	= 1 Naira (₦)
Sierra Leone	100 cents	= 1 Leone (Le)

37. On 1 January 1978, Kojo commenced business as a sole trader selling provisions. He provided, out of his savings, ₵5 000 with which to start the business.

The following transactions took place during the month of January, 1978.

		₵
Jan. 1	Opened a Bank Account for the business and paid in cash	5 000
,, 6	Rented premises and paid for 1 month by cheque	100
,, 10	Bought furniture and fittings by cheque	200
,, 12	Purchased goods for resale by cheque	600
,, 17	Cash sales to date	800

			₵
,,	18	Paid cash into bank	600
,,	20	Purchased goods for resale from Asani & Sons	1 000
,,	25	Cash sales	750
,,	26	Paid cash into bank	750
,,	27	Sold goods to Smiths	180
,,	28	Paid Asani & Sons on account by cheque	500
,,	31	Paid salaries by cheque	77
		Paid electricity bill for Kojo's house by cheque	90
		Paid sundry expenses by cheque	40

From the above transactions you are required to prepare the following:

(*a*) Cash Account,

(*b*) Bank Account,

(*c*) Trial Balance,

(*d*) Trading and Profit & Loss Account for the month of January, 1978,

(*e*) The Balance Sheet as at 31 January, 1978.

Note: Closing Stock was valued at ₵600.

W.A.E.C.

38. The following is a summary of the cash book of Ola-Olu Company Ltd. at 31st December, 1978.

Cash Book

	₦		₦
Opening Balance b/d	1 407	Sundry Payments	15 520
Sundry Receipts	15 073	Closing Balance c/d	960
	₦16 480		₦16 480
Balance b/d	960		

On investigation, the following errors were discovered:

(i) Bank charges of ₦35 shown on the bank statement had not been entered in the cash book;

(ii) A cheque drawn for ₦47 had been entered in error in the cash book as a receipt;

(iii) A cheque for ₦18, had been returned by the bank marked 'R/D', but this had not been recorded in the cash book;

(iv) The opening balance in the cash book was wrongly brought down as ₦1 470;

(v) Three cheques paid to suppliers, for ₦214, ₦370 and ₦30, had not been presented to the bank;

(vi) The last page of the paying-in book showed a deposit of ₦1 542 which had not yet been credited to the Account by the bank;

(vii) The bank had debited a cheque for ₦72 in error to the company's account;

(viii) The bank statement showed an overdrawn balance of ₦124.

You are required:

(*a*) To write up the cash book;

(*b*) To prepare a bank reconciliation statement.

W.A.E.C.

39. (*a*) Distinguish between *capital* and *revenue* expenditure.

(*b*) State whether each of the items of expenditure in (i) – (vii) below is a capital or a revenue expenditure, stating the reason in each case:

(i) Purchased a delivery van for Le2 500;
(ii) Paid in advance an amount of Le240, representing the rent of premises for three months January to March;
(iii) Bought various types of goods for resale, all amounting to Le3 000;
(iv) Acquired some fixtures and fittings for the office costing Le180;
(v) Paid for the company sign post Le50;
(vi) Paid Le60 to the men who unloaded the goods purchased in (iii) above;
(vii) Advertised the shop in a local newspaper for Le100.

W.A.E.C.

40. The following balance sheet was extracted from the books of A. Lyon on 30 November, 1978.

	D		D
Capital	12 155	Premises	11 000
Loan from D. Silver	1 000	Furniture & Fittings	1 340
Creditors	215	Stock	795
		Cash at Bank	225
		Cash in Hand	10
	D13 370		D13 370

You are required to show the balance sheet after the following transactions have taken place during the first week of December, 1978:

(*a*) Goods which had cost D250 were sold for D325 in cash;

(*b*) Interest on Loan D70 paid by cheque;

(*c*) Drawings by A. Lyon in cash D20;

(*d*) Goods at cost taken by A. Lyon for private use D7;

(*e*) Cheques totalling D170, sent to creditors; Discount received D8;

(*f*) All cash except D10 float had been paid to the bank at the end of the week

All working notes should be clearly shown.

W.A.E.C.

41. On 1st April, 1977, the assets of the Eko Youth Centre were:

	₦
Cash in hand and balance at bank	460
Furniture and fittings	1 500
Games equipment	640
Tools and hobbies equipment	410
Subscriptions in arrear	30
Insurance prepaid	20

There were no liabilities at this date. For the year ended 31st March, 1978 the treasurer produced the following summary of receipts and payments:

	₦		₦
Subscriptions	520	Electricity	270
Donations	500	Expenses of Annual Fete	310
Sale of Tickets for Annual Fete	590	New Tools	90
Sale of Dance Tickets	670	New Games equipment	60
		Expenses of Dance	270
		Cleaners' Wages	520
		Printing & Stationery	50
		Repairs	140
		Insurance	120

Notes:

(i) Subscriptions received included the amount in arrears for the previous year: ₦20 was in arrears for the current year.

(ii) Repairs outstanding amounted to ₦30.

(iii) Annual Insurance premiums ₦120 were paid to 30th June, 1978.

(iv) 10% depreciation is to be written off the balance at 31st March, 1978, of furniture and fittings, games equipment and tools and hobbies equipment.

You are required to prepare:

(*a*) The Income and Expenditure Account for the year ended 31st March, 1978 and

(*b*) a Balance Sheet as at that date. *W.A.E.C.*

42. From the following information prepare Manufacturing and Trading Accounts for the year ended 31st March, 1977.

	Le
Stocks at 1st April, 1976:	
Finished Goods	6 724
Raw materials	2 400
Work-in-Progress	955
Carriage on Purchases	321
Sales	69 830
Purchases of Raw Materials	21 340
Manufacturing Wages	13 280
Factory Power	6 220
Other Manufacturing expenses	1 430
Factory Rent & Rates	2 300

Stocks at 31st March, 1977:	
Raw Materials	2 620
Work-in-Progress	870
Finished Goods	7 230

W.A.E.C.

43. On 1st January, 1976, B. Adegun started business as a wholesale confectioner. The following were among the balances extracted from his books at 31st December, 1976.

From the following information you are required to prepare:

Trading and Profit and Loss Accounts for the Year ended 31st December, 1976.

	₦
Purchases	11 377
Sales	13 475
Returns Inwards	242
Returns Outwards	268
Carriage on Purchases	47
Advertising	110
Motor Van Expenses	155
Wages of Driver	652
Office Expenses	104
Bad Debts	79
Insurances	26
Electricity	30
Interest on Loan	21
Discounts Allowed	337
Discounts Received	210
Rent and Rates	365
Rent of Premises Sublet	104

You are given the following additional information:

(i) Stock in hand at 31st December, 1976, was valued at ₦898.
(ii) A motor van which costs ₦660 is to be depreciated by 15% on cost.
(iii) Provide ₦105 for Bad and Doubtful Debts.
(iv) A half year's interest ₦21 was due on the loan.
(v) A demand notice for rates for the half year ending 31st March, 1977, ₦56 had been received but no payment made.
(vi) Insurance ₦6 was prepaid.
(vii) ₦12 was owing in respect of repairs to the motor van.

W.A.E.C.

44. The Trial Balance of Jinja & Co. – Traders, drawn up at 31st December: 1977, failed to agree, its credit side exceeding the debit side by $125. A Suspense Account was opened and the Trading and Profit and Loss Account prepared which revealed a net profit of $17 172. The following errors were later discovered:

(i) The owner had taken goods worth $70 *each month* for his personal use but no entry was made to record this fact.
(ii) A credit sale of goods for $940 to Juma was recorded correctly in the Sales Book but as $490 in his personal account.
(iii) The Returns Outward Book was under-cast by $100.
(iv) Goods worth $225 were returned by P. Okot. This was correctly recorded in Returns Inwards Book but not posted to the ledger.
(v) Motor expenses $1 475, were debited to Motor Car Account.

You are required to:

(*a*) Prepare the necessary journal entries to correct the mistakes;
(*b*) Draft a Suspense Account;
(*c*) Show the effect of each error on the net profit and calculate the correct net profit.

W.A.E.C.

Appendix 2

Examination Questions

THE ROYAL SOCIETY OF ARTS EXAMINATION BOARD

SINGLE-SUBJECT EXAMINATIONS

BOOK-KEEPING

STAGE I (Elementary) – THURSDAY, 8th MARCH, 1979

[TWO HOURS ALLOWED]

You have TEN *minutes to read through this question paper before the start of the examination.*

ALL *questions in Section A and* TWO *questions in Section B are to be attempted.*
Marks may be lost for untidy work.
Answers must be written in pen or biro.

SECTION A

ALL *questions are to be attempted.*

1. J. Goode sub-divides his Purchases Ledger into three alphabetical sections: A–G, H–M and N–Z, the creditors' accounts being entered according to their surnames.

Draw up a Purchases Day Book (or Journal) with appropriate analysis columns and enter the following invoices. Rule and total for the period 1st to 6th February, 1979.

Date	*Supplier*	*Invoice No.*	*Invoice Total* £
Feb. 1	F. Archer	21	960
2	J. Potter	22	360
3	J. Harris	23	575
4	C. Clay	24	106
5	B. Sidwell	25	91
6	F. Lake	26	450

Ignore V.A.T. *(15 marks)*

2. George Anson commenced business as a wholesaler and importer on 1st January, 1978. The following Trial Balance was extracted from his books on 31st December, 1978:

	£	£
Capital 1st January, 1978		21 700
Drawings	4 800	
Leasehold Premises (Lease has 10 years to run from 1st Jan., 1978)	10 000	
Fittings and Equipment at cost	4 000	
Purchases and Sales	48 250	61 440
Warehouse wages	3 654	
Customs duties on imported goods	872	
Carriage on purchases	464	
Carriage on sales	708	
Rates and Insurance	350	
Light and Heat	260	
Office Expenses	194	
Hire of security system	490	
Debtors and Creditors	5 200	4 818
Commission paid and received	616	502
Office wages	4 540	
Bad debts	132	
Cash at bank	3 930	
	£88 460	£88 460

Prepare the Trading and Profit and Loss Account for the year ended 31st December, 1978 taking into consideration the following matters. A Balance Sheet is not required.

(*a*) Stock at 31st December, 1978 was valued at £8 106.

(*b*) Light and Heat and Rates and Insurance are to be allocated four-fifths to warehouse and one-fifth to office.

(*c*) Depreciation should be written off Fittings and Equipment at 10 per cent of cost.

(*d*) An appropriate amount of depreciation should be written off the Leasehold Premises.

(*e*) Commission receivable of £38 was outstanding at 31st December, 1978.

Note that a Balance Sheet is not required. (*25 marks*)

3. (i) What is meant by depreciation and why is it important that a businessman should provide for depreciation in his accounts?

(ii) On 1st January, 1976. A. Swain, a haulage contractor, purchased three tipper lorries for £4 800 each. Mr. Swain estimated that his lorries would have an effective working life of five years with a disposal value of £300 each. The straight-line method of depreciation is to be used. The financial year ends on 31st December. One of the lorries kept breaking down and was sold on 1st January, 1978 for £2 500.

You are required to show the relevant entries for the years 1976, 1977 and 1978 in the following ledger accounts:

(*a*) Lorries.

(*b*) Lorries Disposal.

(*c*) Provision for Depreciation on Lorries.

All workings are to be shown.

(*21 marks*)

4. The following is a Trial Balance which has been incorrectly drawn up:

Trial Balance 31 January 1979

	£	£
Capital 1st February, 1978	5 500	
Drawings	2 800	
Stock 1st February, 1978		2 597
Trade Debtors		2 130
Furniture and Fittings	1 750	
Cash in hand	1 020	
Trade Creditors		2 735
Sales		7 430
Returns Inwards		85
Discount Received	46	
Business expenses	950	
Purchases	4 380	
	£16 446	£14 977

As well as the mistakes evident above, the following errors were also discovered:

(i) A payment of £75 made to a creditor had not been posted from the cash book into the purchases ledger.

(ii) A cheque for £56 received from a customer had been correctly entered in the cash book but posted to the customer's account as £50.

(iii) A purchase of fittings £120 had been included in the purchases account.

(iv) The total of Discounts Allowed column in the cash book of £38 had not been posted into the general ledger.

(v) A page of the sales day book was correctly totalled as £564 but had been carried forward as £456.

Show the Trial Balance as it would appear after all the errors had been corrected. You are required to show all workings.

(*15 marks*)

SECTION B

Answer TWO *questions from this Section.*

5. The following account appeared in the Purchases ledger of D. Ledbury on 1st February, 1979:

J. Grubb

			£				£
Jan. 14	Bank		342	Jan. 1	Balance	b/d	360
	Discount		18	7	Purchases		564
18	Returns		25	15	Purchases		480
25	Bank		1 019	28	Purchases		618
31	Balance	c/d	618				
			2 022				2 022
				Feb. 1	Balance	b/d	618

D. Ledbury received the following statement of account from J. Grubb,

Statement 31st January, 1979

D. Ledbury Dr.		Debits	Credits	*Balance*
1979		£	£	£
Jan. 1	Balance			360
7	Goods	564		924
14	Cash		342	582
15	Goods	480		1 062
28	Goods	746		
	Goods	618		2 426

Prepare a statement reconciling the balance shown in the ledger of D. Ledbury with that shown by the statement of account.

(*12 marks*)

6. (i) State which commercial documents you should use in writing up the following:

(*a*) Petty Cash book

(*b*) Sales Returns book

(*c*) Bank Cash book (credit side)

(*d*) Sales Day book

(*e*) Wages book

(*f*) Purchases Returns book

(*ii*) Draft an example of one of the documents you have mentioned in your answer to (*d*), (*e*) or (*f*) above.

(*12 marks*)

7. D. Brown owns a petrol filling station. Petrol is sold at cost plus 25 per cent. The petrol pumps automatically record by meter the number of gallons sold. Stock of 4-star petrol on 1st January, 1979 was 8 000 gallons valued at 60 pence per gallon.

During the month of January, 1979 Brown took delivery of 4-star petrol as follows:

Jan. 6 000 gallons costing 60 pence per gallon
16 Jan. 8 000 gallons costing 62 pence per gallon
24 Jan. 12 000 gallons costing 64 pence per gallon

Meter readings taken from the 4-star petrol pump were:

1 January, 1979	35 609
31 January	56 609

You are required to calculate:

(*a*) The number of gallons of 4-star petrol in stock on 31st January, 1979.

(*b*) The value of that stock of petrol on 31st January, 1979.

(*c*) The number of gallons of 4-star petrol sold during January, 1979.

(*d*) The revenue from sales of 4-star petrol during January, 1979.

(*e*) The gross profit on sales of 4-star petrol for January, 1979.

Show your workings.
Ignore V.A.T. (*12 marks*)

THE ROYAL SOCIETY OF ARTS EXAMINATIONS BOARD

SINGLE-SUBJECT EXAMINATIONS

BOOK-KEEPING

STAGE I (Elementary)–TUESDAY, 8th MAY, 1979

[TWO HOURS ALLOWED]

You have ten minutes to read through this question paper before the start of the examination.

All questions in Section A and TWO *questions in Section B are to be attempted.*

SECTION A

ALL *Questions are to be attempted*

1. From the following information prepare a Profit and Loss Account for G. Jones, Accountant:

Trial Balance as at 31st December, 1978

	Dr. £	*Cr.* £
Capital—G. Jones		9 000
Drawings	3 600	
Telephone	200	
Salaries	4 000	
Office Premises—at cost	30 000	
Stationery	1 100	
Postage	806	
Fees Received from Clients		48 500
Creditors		610
Debtors	5 410	
Office Equipment—at cost	3 400	
Cash at Bank	2 410	
Cash in Hand	504	
Rates	180	
Motor Vehicle—at cost	4 500	
Petrol and Oil	800	
Vehicle Road Tax and Licence	230	
Rental—Automatic Phone Answering Equipment	70	
Office Cleaner's Wages	750	
Annual Fees – Professional Society	50	
Petty Cash Balance	100	
	58 110	58 110

Take into consideration the following:

1. Debts amounting to £20 are to be written off as irrecoverable.
2. Depreciate the Motor Vehicle at 20% on cost.
3. Depreciate the Office Equipment at 10% on cost.
4. Telephone Account Accrued Due is £53.
5. Salaries Accrued Due are £120.
6. Rates Paid in Advance are £45.

(*30 marks*)

NOTE – A Balance Sheet is not required.

2. The following draft Balance Sheet was prepared for Hotel Splendid, a small private hotel, on 31st December, 1978.

Produce the final Balance Sheet in Narrative (Vertical) form, correctly set out.

Balance Sheet

Liabilities	£	*Assets*	£
Bank Loan (long term)	6 000	Stock	6 000
Creditors	4 000	Premises – cost	48 000
Capital	50 000	Cash at Bank	3 000
Profit	10 000	Furniture – cost	10 000
		Debtors	3 000
	£70 000		£70 000

Adjust the Balance Sheet for:

(*a*) Depreciation on furniture £1 000;

(*b*) Stock was valued at £5 600.

(*14 marks*)

3. On 31st March 1979 the Bank column in the Cash Book of Catering Services showed a debit balance of £137 510.

At preparation of a reconciliation statement the following differences appeared:

(i) Cheques debited in the Cash Book but not yet received by the bank – £1 731.

(ii) Cheques credited in the Cash Book but not yet presented for payment – £1 235.

(iii) The bank has charged the account with £115 bank charges and credited the account with £220 dividend received direct. Neither item has been entered in the Cash Book.

You are required to produce:

(*a*) a statement showing the revised Cash Book balance;

(*b*) a statement reconciling the revised Cash Book balance, showing the balance which appears on the Bank Statement.

(*14 marks*)

4. Air Frames are manufacturers, commencing business on 1st January 1978. They purchased plant as follows:

1978	£
1st January	400 000
1st July	200 000

1979

On 30th April 1979, the machine purchased on 1st May 1978 was sold for £120 000.

Depreciation is provided by the 'Straight Line Method' at 10 per cent per annum, from date of purchase.

(i) Write up the accounts which you think are necessary to record the above transactions.

(ii) Show clearly your treatment of the resulting Profit or Loss.

(*14 marks*)

SECTION B

Answer TWO *questions from this section*

5. Record the following in a columnar Purchases Day Book

January 1 Invoice 1362, Purchase from J. A. Smith, Ltd.

	£
Goods Costing	300
Freight Costs	30
Total Invoice	330

January 30 Invoice 1720, Purchase from J. Brown, Ltd.

Goods Costing £800
Subject to 20% Trade Discount and Freight Charges £50.

Post the Day Book to Ledger Accounts.

(*14 marks*)

6. Record the following in a three column Cash Book.

Opening balances are £125 cash in hand and £1 300 at the bank.

January 2nd, 1979
Received cheque from James Ltd., £120;
Cash Discount £10.
Received cash from S. Smith, £140;
Cash Discount, £20.
Dividend on investment paid direct to Bank, £10.

January 1st, Payments
Paid A. Robbs Ltd. by cheque £33;
Cash Discount £4.
Drew £20 from bank for cash.
Paid cleaner's wages £18 in cash.
Private drawings in cash £10.
Paid £65 cash into bank.

(*14 marks*)

7. The following are items of information often stated on a Pay Advice (Pay Slip.)

(*a*) Tax code;

(*b*) Gross pay to date;

(*c*) Superannuation deducted;

(*d*) Tax paid to date;

(*e*) Net pay;

(*f*) National Insurance deducted to date;

(*g*) Works or Pay Reference Number.

Write a brief explanation of the meaning of each of the above items.

(*14 marks*)

32

The Purchase of a Business, Amalgamation of Existing Businesses

The purchase of a business as a going concern is of fairly frequent occurrence. There is the attraction of existing Goodwill, and the trend of future trade may be estimated more easily for an established concern than for a newly started business that has to make its entry into the market. Such businesses may, of course, be owned by sole traders or partnerships or companies, and the purchase may be made by one of these forms of business ownership. For the most part the method of recording the purchase of the business in the books of the purchaser is the same whether the purchaser is a sole trader, a partnership firm, or a company. Any difference will be in the Capital Accounts and, probably, in the case of a company as a purchaser, in the form the purchase consideration may take, as it may be wholly or partly in shares. Matters relating to shares are explained in Chapters 37, 38 and 39.

The purchase price is usually based partly on the particulars disclosed in the final Balance Sheet of the vendor, and partly on the profits expected in the future. The assets may be subject to independent valuation. The agreement will include some reference to the settling of the liabilities, if any, as they may not all be taken over. Each sale stands by itself, as the terms vary considerably. One purchaser may take over only the assets; another may take over all the assets and liabilities. Sometimes the cash balance is taken over and in other cases it is retained by the vendor. A further provision in the agreement may refer to the Goodwill of the business and the price to be paid for it. There may also be a clause restraining the vendor from starting a similar business within a certain radius of the present concern, although great care must be taken in drafting such clauses to ensure that they are not in restraint of trade. On the sale of Goodwill the vendor is prevented from canvassing former customers, but unless he binds himself to the contrary, he is not prevented from starting a similar business and dealing with former customers if they come to him unsolicited.

Purchase of Business Account

The following example will illustrate the entries that are necessary to record the purchase of a business in the purchaser's books and to open the accounts. The illustration is of a purchase by a sole trader. The differences in the record when a limited liability company makes a similar purchase and pays partly in shares are discussed in a later chapter. In the case of a partnership making the purchase, the only difference would be that the entries relating to the sole trader's Capital Account would have to be split between the partners' Capital Accounts. Partnerships and partnership accounts are discussed in Chapters 33–36.

Example 40. B. Rose arranges to take over the business carried on by R. Briar, as a going concern from 1st January, 19.1. The final Balance Sheet of R. Briar was as follows:

Balance Sheet

as at 31st December 19.0

	£		£
Capital – R. Briar	20 000	Freehold premises	9 000
Sundry creditors	4 500	Plant and machinery	6 000
		Furniture and fittings	800
		Stock	5 000
		Debtors	3 300
		Cash	400
	£24 500		£24 500

The purchase price was £24 000, and was paid by cheque by Rose direct to Briar. R. Briar retained the cash balance. All other assets and the liabilities were taken over by Rose, who contributed a further sum of £2 000 in cash to the firm's capital.

Make the necessary Journal entries in Rose's books, and show the new firm's Cash Book and opening Balance Sheet.

Temporary accounts called the *Business Purchase Account* and the *Vendor's Account* are opened, and the following is the sequence of entries to record the purchase:

1. *Debit* the Business Purchase Account } with the agreed pur-
   Credit the Vendor's Account } chase price.

2. *Debit* the assets, including Goodwill, if any, to their respective accounts.
   Credit the total value of assets taken over in one amount to the Business Purchase Account.
3. *Debit* the total value of liabilities taken over in one amount to the Business Purchase Account.
   Credit the liabilities to their particular accounts.
4. *Debit* Vendor's Account } with the purchase price when
   Credit Rose's Capital Account } paid.

Usually the vendor is paid by the purchasing firm itself, in which case Cash Book is credited with the purchase price. By paying directly himself Rose is introducing new capital into his business.

The cash balance taken over, if any, should be debited to Cash.

The posting of these entries will bring all the assets and liabilities into the firm's books, and will close the Business Purchase Account and the Vendor's Account.

These steps are evident in the working of the above example:

Journal

			£	£
19.1 Jan. 1	Business Purchase Account R. Briar (Vendor) being purchase price as agreed.		24 000	24 000
„ 1	Freehold premises Plant and machinery Furniture and fittings Stock Debtors Business Purchase Account being assets acquired from R. Briar.		9 000 6 000 800 5 000 3 300	24 100
„ 1	Business Purchase Account Sundry creditors being liabilities taken over from R. Briar		4 500	4 500
„ 1	R. Briar (Vendor) B. Rose – Capital Account being purchase price paid direct to vendor.		24 000	24 000
„ 1	Goodwill Business Purchase Account being value of Goodwill acquired.		4 400	4 400

Balance Sheet
as at 1st January, 19.1

	£	£		£	£
CAPITAL:			FIXED ASSETS:		
B. Rose		26 000	Freehold premises	9 000	
CURRENT LIABILITIES			Plant and machinery	6 000	
Sundry creditors	4 500		Furniture and fittings	800	
	——	4 500		——	15 800
			GOODWILL		4 400
			CURRENT ASSETS:		
			Stock	5 000	
			Sundry debtors	3 300	
			Cash	2 000	
				——	10 300
		£30 500			£30 500

Cash Book

			£				£
19.1				19.1			
Jan. 1	B. Rose: Capital		2 000				

Alternative method of Example 40

An even simpler approach is to show in the buyer's Journal all of the Opening Entries, consisting of the items shown in the Vendor's balance sheet, and such other items as are necessary, as illustrated below:

Journal—B. Rose

			Dr. £	*Cr.* £
19.1				
Jan. 1	Freehold Premises		9 000	
	Plant and Machinery		6 000	
	Furniture and Fittings		8 000	
	Stock		5 000	
	Debtors		3 300	
	Goodwill (Being excess of liabilities over assets)		4 400	
	Creditors			4 500
	Vendor – R. Briar (Purchase price of business)			24 000
	Being assets, liabilities and goodwill acquired on purchase of business.		£28 500	£28 500
Jan. 1	Vendor		24 000	
	Capital – B. Rose			24 000
	Being purchase price of business transferred		£24 000	£24 000

If the assets are purchased at prices different from those shown on the vendor's balance sheet, then the *new prices*, at which the assets have been purchased should be shown in the opening entries. Rose is not concerned with the values shown in Briar's books for their own sakes, but only so far as they are relevant in determining the price to be paid.

The Ledger Accounts are not shown in the example. Their preparation from the Journal entries above would show clearly the use of the Business Purchase Account as a means of transferring the assets and liabilities.

The balance of the Business Purchase Account after the entry of purchase price, and the liabilities and assets taken over, is the value of the Goodwill acquired. Should the purchase price be less than the nominal value of the net assets bought (i.e. the assets minus any liabilities) then the credit balance of the Business Purchase Account should be treated as a Capital Reserve against which the value of the assets might be written down, should the need arise.

The Amalgamation of Existing Businesses

Independent traders engaged in the same kind of business, or persons practising the same profession, may agree to amalgamate and merge their assets and liabilities in a partnership concern with a view, possibly, to the reduction of overhead charges or the elimination of competition. The special legal nature of a partnership is described in Chapter 33.

The decision to amalgamate will involve the fixing of the date on which the amalgamation is to take place, and agreement on the terms under which it shall be carried out. Each trader must be prepared to make full disclosure of the financial position of his business, and there must be some assessment of the relative values of the businesses as going concerns. A satisfactory plan is the preparation of a Balance Sheet by each trader as at the amalgamation date, and mutual agreement upon the adjustments that may be necessary in the value of the assets or the extent of the liabilities. If the Goodwill of the businesses are unequal, then it may be more equitable to make allowance for this in the amalgamation by compensating the owner of the more valuable business. The Balance Sheet of each business is re-drafted, taking into consideration the adjustments agreed upon, and these re-drafted Balance Sheets are then combined to form the initial Balance Sheet of the partnership.

Example 41. Butcher and Baker decide to amalgamate their businesses as from 1st January, 19.1. Their respective Balance Sheets as 31st December, 19.0, preceding, being as follows:

Butcher's Balance Sheet

31st December, 19.0

	£		£
Capital:	20 000	*Fixed Assets:*	
Current liabilities:		Freehold property	4 000
Sundry creditors	2 900	Fixtures and fittings	900
		Current assets:	
		Stock	10 000
		Sundry debtors	7 000
		Cash at bank	1 000
	£22 900		£22 900

Baker's Balance Sheet

31st December 19.0

	£		£
Capital:	5 000	*Fixed Assets:*	
Current Liabilities:		Fixtures and fittings	500
Bills Payable	1 500	*Current Assets:*	
Sundry creditors	3 000	Stock	4 200
		Sundry debtors	4 000
		Cash	800
	£9 500		£9 500

The agreement provides that the stocks of each business are to be reduced in value by 10%; that a provision for doubtful debts of 5% is to be made on the sundry debtors: that Baker's fixtures and fittings are to be kept by him and disposed of as he thinks best; that Butcher's fixtures and fittings are to be re-valued at £800, and that Butcher is to be credited with £3 000 for Goodwill.

Show the initial Balance Sheet of the partnership as at 1st January, 19.1, after taking into account the above adjustments.

Butcher and Baker will each make the necessary adjustments in their own books so that these show the financial position immediately before amalgamation. In Baker's case the Journal entries required will be as follows.

Journal

		£	£
19.1			
Jan. 1	Capital Account	1 120	
	Stock		420
	Provision for double debts		200
	Fixtures and fittings		500
	being reductions on revaluation and by amalgamation agreement.		

His adjusted Balance Sheet will be:

Baker's Balance Sheet

1st January, 19.1

	£	£		£	£
Capital:	5 000		*Current Assets:*		
less reduction on revaluation	1 120		Stock		3 780
		3 880	Sundry debtors	4 000	
Current Liabilities:			*less* Provision for doubtful debts	200	
Bills payable		1 500			3 800
Sundry creditors		3 000	Cash at bank		800
		£8 380			£8 380

Butcher will make the following entries in his books:

Journal

		£	£
19.1			
Jan. 1	Capital Account	1 450	
	Stock		1 000
	Provision for doubtful debts		350
	Fixtures and fittings		100
	being reduction on revaluation of assets.		
Jan. 1	Goodwill Account	3 000	
	Capital Account		3 000
	being agreed value of Goodwill on amalgamation		

His adjusted Balance Sheet will be:

Butcher's Balance Sheet
1st January, 19.1

	£	£		£	£
Capital:	20 000		*Goodwill*		3 000
add Goodwill	3 000		*Fixed Assets:*		
	23 000		Freehold property		4 000
less reduction on revaluation	1 450		Fixtures and fittings		800
		21 550			
Current liabilities:			*Current Assets:*		
Sundry creditors		2 900	Stock		9 000
			Sundry debtors	7 000	
			less Provision for doubtful debts	350	
					6 650
			Cash at bank		1 000
		£24 450			£24 450

It remains to combine the adjusted Balance Sheets to provide the initial Balance Sheet of the new firm:

BUTCHER & BAKER
Balance Sheet
1st January, 19.1

	£	£		£	£
Capital:			*Goodwill*		3 000
Butcher	21 550				
Baker	3 880		*Fixed Assets:*		
		25 430	Freehold property	4 000	
			Fixtures and fittings	800	
					4 800
Current liabilities:			*Current assets*		
Bills Payable	1 500		Stock		12 780
Sundry creditors	5 900		Sundry Debtors	11 000	
		7 400	*less* Provision for doubtful debts	550	
					10 450
			Cash at bank		1 800
		£32 830			£32 830

EXERCISES 32

1. R. B. Graham agrees to purchase R. Foreman's business as at 1st January, 19.1 on the basis of the Balance Sheet shown below. Graham agrees to take over all the assets and liabilities with the exception of the cash balances, and to pay Foreman the sum of £4 500 as the purchase price.

R. Foreman's Balance Sheet

31st December, 19.0

	£		£
Capital	4 450	Machinery	1 500
Creditors	1 412	Fittings and fixtures	160
		Stock	2 180
		Debtors	1 550
		Cash at Bank	452
		Cash in hand	20
	£5 862		£5 862

Graham paid the purchase price by cheque on 1st January, 19.1. Record the purchase in Graham's books, and show his Balance Sheet as at 1st January, 19.1.

2. R. Jacobs and B. Mosley enter into partnership to purchase and take over as from 1st January, 19.1 the business carried on by B. Macintosh. They are to share profits and losses equally, and the purchase is to be on the basis of the last Balance Sheet as shown below.

B. Macintosh's Balance Sheet

31st December 19.0

	£		£
Capital	10 000	Premises	4 800
Sundry creditors	2 640	Machinery	2 750
		Furniture and fittings	100
		Sundry debtors	1 920
		Stock	2 800
		Cash at bank	270
	£12 640		£12 640

Jacobs and Mosley each contributed £6 000 in cash as capital, and the sums were paid into a banking account opened in the firm's name. The purchase price was agreed at £11 000, and a cheque for that amount was paid over to Macintosh. All the assets and liabilities were taken over with the exception of the cash balance. The purchase price includes a sum for Goodwill, and a Goodwill Account is to be raised in the firm's books. Record the purchase in the partnership books, and show the firm's opening Balance Sheet.

3. T. B. Jones and A. M. Wilmot entered into partnership as equal partners to acquire the business carried on by J. B. Duncan as from 1st January, 19.1. The purchase is to be made on the basis of the following Balance Sheet:

J. B. Duncan's Balance Sheet

31st December, 19.0

	£		£
Capital	9 500	Freehold premises	4 000
Sundry creditors	2 165	Machinery and plant	2 200
		Furniture and fittings	350
		Sundry debtors	1 840
		Stock	2 900
		Cash at bank	375
	£11 665		£11 665

The purchase price is agreed at £10 500, and Jones and Wilmot pay this sum in equal shares by cheques direct to Duncan. A firm's banking account is opened, into which Jones and Wilmot pay £750 each. All the assets and liabilities are taken over with the exception of the cash balance.

The partners decide to re-value the assets for the purposes of the partnership, and the following reductions were made:

The stock was reduced to £2 750; furniture and fittings to £200; and the machinery to £1 800.

These reductions are to be considered as an appreciation of the value of the Goodwill included in the purchase price.

Record the purchase and the adjustments in the partnership books, and give the firm's opening Balance Sheet.

4. George Wright and Henry Dobson enter into partnership, as equal partners, to acquire the business carried on by Andrew Atkinson. The business was taken over as at 1st January, 19.1, on the basis of the Balance Sheet at 31st December, 19.0 which was as follows:

Andrew Atkinson's Balance Sheet

31st December, 19.0

	£		£
Capital Account:		Freehold premises	14 200
Andrew Atkinson	26 000	Plant and machinery	8 100
Sundry creditors	3 400	Furniture and fittings	600
Reserve for bad debts	300	Stock in trade	4 100
		Sundry debtors	2 700
	£29 700		£29 700

The purchase price was agreed at £28 000, and was paid in equal shares by Wright and Dobson direct to Atkinson. A Bank Account was opened in the name of the firm, into which each partner paid the sum of £1 000. For the purpose of the partnership the assets were revalued, and the following reductions in value were made:

Plant and machinery, £500; Stock, £450; and Furniture and fittings, £200.

A Goodwill Account is to be raised in the partnership books for the difference between the total purchase price paid and the amended valuation.

You are required to make the Journal entries necessary to record the above transactions in the Books of Messrs. Wright and Dobson, and prepare a Balance Sheet as at the commencement of the new partnership.

R.S.A. (adapted)

5. The Balance Sheets shown below are those of two independent traders who have agreed to amalgamate their businesses as from 1st January, 19.1, on the basis of these Balance Sheets, subject to the adjustments mentioned.

Barnett's Balance Sheet

31st December, 19.0

	£		£
Capital	9 000	Premises	2 000
Creditors	840	Fittings	300
Bills Payable	500	Stock	5 250
		Debtors	1 750
		Bills Receivable	200
		Cash at bank	840
	£10 340		£10 340

Marsden's Balance Sheet

31st December, 19.0

	£		£
Capital	3 000	Furniture and fittings	180
Creditors	1 200	Stock	3 100
		Debtors	800
		Cash at bank	120
	£4 200		£4 200

The adjustments are: Marsden to retain the furniture and fittings and to dispose of them privately; Marsden to write off £150 of the sundry debtors as a bad debt, and to reduce his stock valuation to £2 500. Barnett's stock valuation is to be reduced to £5 000, and he is to be credited with £1 000 for the Goodwill of his business. Subject to these adjustments the new firm is to take over all the assets and liabilities.

Show the opening Balance Sheet of the partnership as at 1st January, 19.1.

6. Lucas and Cave agree to amalgamate their businesses from 1st January, 19.1 on the basis of the following Balance Sheets, subject to the adjustments mentioned below:

Lucas's Balance Sheet

31st December, 19.0

	£		£
Capital	65 000	Plant and machinery	30 000
Sundry creditors	8 500	Stock	20 000
		Fittings	4 000
		Sundry debtors	10 500
		Cash at bank	9 000
	£73 500		£73 500

Cave's Balance Sheet

31st December, 19.0

	£		£
Capital	2 200	Plant and machinery	1 200
Creditors	700	Stock	1 510
Overdraft	450	Fittings	140
		Sundry debtors	500
	£3 350		£3 350

Prepare the opening Balance Sheet of the partnership as at 1st January, taking the following adjustments into consideration: Lucas is to be credited with £10 000 for Goodwill. Cave's machinery and plant is to be reduced in value to £1 000. Both stocks are to be reduced in value by 10%. Cave is to pay off his overdraft from his private funds. Each trader is to create a provision for bad and doubtful debts at 5% of the sundry debtors.

7. X and Y are independent traders in the same line of business, their respective Sheets on 31st December, 19.0, being as follows:

X. Balance Sheet

31st December, 19.0

	£		£
Capital	22 400	Goodwill	2 000
Sundry creditors	2 047	Machinery	2 400
		Fixtures and fittings	530
		Stock	10 854
		Debtors	7 591
		Cash at bank	1 072
	£24 447		£24 447

Y. Balance Sheet

31st December, 19.0

	£		£
Capital	46 600	Fixtures and fittings	1 800
Bills payable	12 000	Stocks	51 710
Sundry creditors	23 180	Debtors	31 460
Bank overdraft	3 190		
	£84 970		£84 970

X and Y decided to amalgamate their businesses as from 1st January, the firm taking over all the assets and liabilities at the figures stated except for Y's fixtures and fittings, which he was to retain and dispose of, and Y's stock which is to be written down by £2 800. The Goodwill of Y's business was agreed to be valued at £6 000.

Draw up the opening Balance Sheet of the partnership.

R.S.A. (adapted)

33

Partnerships; Joint Ventures

The ownership of a business may take one of several forms. Hitherto consideration has been given chiefly to one form of proprietorship – that of the sole trader, who is entitled to all the profits of his business, and who is personally liable for the debts incurred. When two or more persons carry on a business in common with a view to profit, the relationship subsisting between them is termed a *partnership*. The legal position of the partners to each other, and to those with whom they have business dealings, is governed by the *Partnership Act, 1890*. Under the Companies Act, 1948, no partnership or association consisting of more than ten persons may be formed for the purpose of carrying on a banking business, or of more than twenty to carry on any other kind of business, unless it is registered as a company. These rules were relaxed, although not completely repealed by sections 119–122 of the Companies Act, 1967.

The fact that the business is owned by two or more persons does not affect the trading records. Whether under the proprietorship of a sole trader or of partners, the records of sale and purchases and the accounts of customers will be similar in all respects. *The part of the bookkeeping record that is affected is the part showing the financial relationship of the business to the proprietors, namely the Capital Account*. With two or more partners there are two or more ownership claims, and the single Capital Account of the sole trader will not suffice. If this point is borne in mind the new matters to be discussed should present little difficulty.

Articles of Partnership

As there are two or more members of a partnership, the legal position of the partners to each other should be defined so that dispute may be prevented. Usually a *Deed of Partnership* or *Partnership Agreement* is drawn up containing the terms under which the partnership shall be carried on. The points usually covered by such agreements are as follows:

1. The duration of the partnership.
2. The sum to be contributed by each partner to the capital of the firm.
3. When, and in what ratio, the profits or losses are to be shared and profits may be drawn out.
4. The rate of interest, if any, to be allowed on capital.
5. Whether partnership salaries shall be paid and to whom.
6. The keeping of proper accounts.
7. How any dispute which may arise shall be settled.
8. The firm name under which the business shall be carried on.

The partners may determine for themselves all such matters affecting their relationship to each other, but *in the absence of any agreement to the contrary* certain rules laid down by Section 24 of the Partnership Act, 1890, apply. The chief of these are as follows:

1. All the partners are entitled to share equally in the capital and profits of the business, and must share equally in its losses.
2. No partner is entitled to interest on his capital before the profits are ascertained.
3. No partner may receive a salary or remuneration for acting in the partnership business.
4. Advances by a partner beyond his capital are to bear interest at 5 per cent per annum.
5. A new partner may be brought into the firm only with the consent of all the existing partners.
6. Every partner may take part in the management of the business.
7. In the event of any differences arising between the partners on matters of ordinary business the will of the majority shall prevail, but the consent of all the partners is necessary to any change in the nature of the business.
8. The books of the firm shall be at the principal place of business, and all partners have the right of free access to inspect or copy them.

The above rules are for guidance, in the absence of any agreement otherwise, in the relationship of partners with each other. As to their relationship with the outside public, Section 5 of the Partnership Act, 1890, expresses the chief points:

> Every partner is an agent of the firm and his other partners for the purpose of the business of the partnership. The acts of every partner, who does any act for carrying on in the usual way business of the kind carried on by the firm of which he is a member, bind the firm and his partners, *unless* the partner so acting has in fact no authority to act for the firm in the particular matter, and the person with whom he is dealing either knows he has no authority or does not know or believe him to be a partner.

The name under which a partnership is carried on is the 'firm name' and the partners are collectively known as the 'firm'. Where the firm name does not consist of the true surnames or full names of all the partners the firm name must be registered under the Registration of Business Names Act, 1916, and the full names of all the proprietors disclosed to the Registrar. These full names must also appear in all trade catalogues, circulars, and business letters of the firm. The Registration of Business Names Act also applies to a sole trader carrying on business in a name not his own.

Liability of Partners

Every partner in a firm is liable for the debts of the firm incurred while he is a partner. In England a partner is liable jointly with all the other partners. If judgement is obtained against the firm as a joint liability of all the partners, each partner is liable for the full amount of the judgement. If, however, judgement is obtained only against some members of the firm without satisfaction, action cannot be taken against the remaining partners. In Scotland the partners are jointly and severally (i.e. jointly but also independently) liable, and the firm is a separate legal entity and can sue and be sued.

Limited Partnerships Act, 1907

This Act provides that a *Limited Partnership* may be formed in which one member at least is a general partner, and one at least a limited partner. The limited partner invests capital in the partnership, but may not take any part in the management of the firm. He may, however, offer advice on the management to the other partners. He shares in the profits, but his liability for the debts and obligations of the firm is limited to the amount of capital he has put into the partnership. The management of the business is in the hands of the general partners whose liability is that of ordinary members of a partnership firm. Should a limited partner withdraw any part of his capital he is liable for the debts of the firm to the extent of the capital so withdrawn.

Limited Partnerships must be registered with the Registrar of Joint Stock Companies. They are rare.

Sleeping or Dormant Partners

A 'Sleeping (or Dormant) Partner' is one who takes no active part in the management of the business, although he continues to share in the profits, and his capital remains in the firm. He is as fully liable for the debts and obligations of the firm as any active partner.

Partnership Accounts

The Capital Account in the books of a sole trader contains the record of the financial position between the business and the owner. It shows the capital invested in the business at the beginning of a trading period and, at the close of that trading period, the net profit or loss and any drawings made by the proprietor. Where there are two or more owners of the business, as in the case of a partnership, there must be two or more Capital Accounts; a separate one for each partner in which is recorded his contribution to the firm's capital.

Partners' Current Accounts

In the case of the sole trader the net profit is credited and his drawings debited to his Capital Account, so that his capital at the start of a new period varies from his capital at the opening of the previous period of trading by the excess of net profit over drawings. As, however, the capital contribution of each partner in a partnership business is usually fixed by agreement, the Capital Accounts are reserved for a record of the capital contributions only. An account for each partner, separate from his Capital Account, is opened to record his share in the net profit or loss, and any drawings he may make on account of profit. The separate account is called the partner's *Current* (*or Drawings*) *Account*. The Current Account and the capital Account together would correspond with the Capital Account of the sole trader.

Example 42. M. Redman and J. Butcher are in partnership under the firm name of Redman and Butcher. Each has contributed £15 000 as capital and is entitled to half share of profits. The partnership agreement provides that Redman may draw £2 000 and Butcher £2 500 half-yearly on account of profits. The profits for the year to 31st December amounted to £11 000.

Show the Capital Accounts and Current Accounts of the partners.

The trading record in the partnership books will differ in no way from the record required had the business been under the proprietorship of a sole trader.

The net profit will appear as usual as the balance of the Profit and Loss Account. The profit, however, is shared between the partners in the agreed proportions, and is placed to the credit of their Current Accounts, the Capital Accounts remaining unaffected.

The Cash Book contra entries for the drawings are not shown below as they are simple credit entries.

M. Redman's Capital Account

19..				19..			£
				Jan. 1	Cash	C.B.	15 000

J. Butcher's Capital Account

19..			£	19..			£
				Jan. 1	Cash	C.B.	15 000

M. Redman's Current Account

19..			£	19..			£
June 30	Cash	C.B.	2 000	Dec. 31	½ share of profit	T	5 500
Dec. 31	Cash	C.B.	2 000				

J. Butcher's Current Account

19..			£	19..			£
June 30	Cash	C.B.	2 500	Dec. 31	½ share of profit	T	5 500
Dec. 31	Cash	C.B.	2 500				

The credit balances of the Current Accounts represent undrawn profit, and as such are a claim against the firm by the respective partners.

An alternative way of preparing the Ledger Accounts giving the ownership claims is to set them out in columnar form, as illustrated on the next page.

Capital Accounts

			M. REDMAN	J. BUTCHER				M. REDMAN	J. BUTCHER
					19.. Jan. 1	Cash	C.B.	15 000	15 000

Current Accounts

			M. REDMAN	J. BUTCHER				M. REDMAN	J. BUTCHER
19.. June 30	Cash Drawings	C.B.	2 000	2 500	19.. Dec. 31	½ share of Profit	T	5 500	5 500
Dec. 31	Cash Drawings		2 000	2 500					
,, 31	Balances	c/d	1 500	500					
			£5 500	£5 500				£5 500	£5 500
					19.. Jan. 1	Balances	b/d	1 500	500

Profit and Loss Account

Partnership Profit and Loss Accounts vary slightly in form from those of sole traders. They are prepared in two sections. The first part shows the ordinary gross profit brought down from the Trading Account and the expenses to be charged against it, giving as the balance, in the usual way, the net trading profit or loss for the period. The net profit or loss is then carried down to a second section – sometimes called the *Appropriation Section* – in which the division of the balance between the partners is shown.

The second section of the Profit and Loss Account for the above example would appear as below:

Profit and Loss Account

(Appropriation Section only)

19..		£	19..		£
Dec. 31	M. Redman, ½ share of profit	5 500	Dec. 31	Balance (net trading profit) brought down	11 000
	J. Butcher, ½ share of profit	5 500			
		£11 000			£11 000

The corresponding credit entries for the half-shares of the profit are made in the partners' respective Current Accounts as shown above.

Interest on parters' capital, partners' salaries, and interest on drawings are also entered in the Appropriation section of the Profit and Loss Account.

The Balance Sheet

A further slight variation *in form* is the setting out of the partners' accounts in the firm's Balance Sheet. This makes the Balance Sheet more informative, as it discloses the financial position of each partner in relation to the firm.

The Balance Sheet for the above example would contain the following details in addition to the ordinary assets and liabilities.

Balance Sheet

as at 31st December, 19 . .
(ownership claims only shown)

	£	£	£
CAPITAL:			
M. Redman	15 000		
J. Butcher	15 000		
		30 000	
CURRENT ACCOUNTS:			
M. Redman			
Share of Profits	5 500		
less Drawings	4 000		
		1 500	
J. Butcher			
Share of profits	5 500		
less Drawings	5 000		
		500	

In columnar form the Balance Sheet would appear as follows:

Balance Sheet

as at 31st December, 19..
(Ownership claims only)

	£	£	£
CAPITAL ACCOUNTS:			
M. Redman		15 000	
J. Butcher		15 000	
			30 000
CURRENT ACCOUNTS	*M. Redman*	*J. Butcher*	
Share of Profits	5 500	5 500	
Less Drawings	4 000	5 000	
	1 500	500	
			2 000

The balance on a Current Account, whether debit or credit, is carried forward to the next accounting period. Occasionally it may be found that a debit balance is shown on a Current Account, indicating that the partner is in debt to the firm to that extent. Such debts are carried forward in partnership accounts and are not placed against the partner's capital in the Ledger Accounts, but, in the Balance Sheet, the debit balance of a partner's Current Account is best shown as a deduction from his capital.

Joint Ventures

A *joint venture* is a partnership of a restricted kind, formed to carry out a particular trading operation, undertaking, or speculation, and is confined to that particular purpose. The trading operation may be on a scale to warrant the opening of a separate set of books to record the transaction. In such a case the record will follow the lines of the ordinary partnership accounts. In other cases each of the *adventurers* takes a part in the conduct of the business and records in his own books the transactions he carries out on behalf of the joint enterprise.

Each adventurer opens in his own books a *Joint Venture Account*. This is treated as a personal account; all payments and charges in respect of the venture are debited to the account, and all receipts and other credit items are credited to it. On completion of the venture, each adventurer sends a copy of his own account to his co-adventurer.

The separate accounts are combined into a single Joint Venture Account, which is of the nature of a Profit and Loss Account for the venture. It will show the profit to be divided between the adventurers or the loss to be borne by them. Each adventurer debits his own venture account in his own books with his share of the profit, or credits his account with his proportion of the loss, as the case may be. The contra entry is made in his Profit and Loss Account in his own books.

The balance of each adventurer's account after the entry of the profit or loss is the amount due from him to the other adventurer or due to him from the other adventurer. With the entry of the adjusting payments the separate accounts are closed.

Example 43. Jackson and Dawson enter into a joint transaction to purchase and sell a quantity of salvaged goods, and agree to share expenses and profits equally. Jackson acquires the goods, paying £5 000 by cheque. Dawson gives a cheque for £2 500 to Jackson as his proportion of the outlay. Dawson pays for advertising, £250. Jackson pays warehousing charges, £100; carriage expenses, £20; and sundry minor expenses, £6. Jackson is allowed £50 for office expenses. Dawson sells three-quarters of the goods for £5 200 in cash. Jackson sells the remainder for £1 600, taking a Bill at three months which he discounts at once. The discount charge, £16, is an expense of the venture. Prepare the Joint Venture Account and the appropriate Ledger Accounts as in Jackson's and Dawson's books.

Combined Account—a memorandum account only:

Joint Venture in Salvaged Goods

	£		£
Purchase of goods	5 000	Proceeds of sales	6 800
Warehouse charges	100		
Carriage expenses	20		
Sundry expenses	6		
Discount charges	16		
Office allowance	50		
Advertising	250		
Profit, Jackson	679		
Dawson	679		
	£6 800		£6 800

In Jackson's Books:

Joint Venture with Dawson

	£		£
Cash purchase of goods	5 000	Cash received from Dawson	2 500
Cash, warehouse charges	100	Bill received for proceeds of sale	1 600
Cash, carriage expenses	20	*Cash from Dawson*	1 771
Cash, sundry expenses	6		
Discount charges on bill	16		
Office allowance	50		
Share of Profit to Profit and Loss Account	679		
	£5 871		£5 871

In Dawson's Books:

Joint Venture with Jackson

	£		£
Cash to Jackson	2 500	Cash – proceeds of sale	5 200
Cash, advertising	250		
Share of Profit to Profit and Loss Account	679		
Cash to Jackson	1 771		
	£5 200		£5 200

EXERCISES 33

1. D. P. Graves and E. Coffin enter into partnership, profit and losses to be shared in proportion to their capitals which are respectively £5 000 and £3 000. Graves drew £6 000 and Coffin £5 000 during the year on account of profits. The net trading profit for the year amounted to £20 000.
Show the partners' Capital Accounts and Current Accounts as at 31st December.

2. J. Groom and T. B. Bride entered into partnership with capitals respectively of £2 000 and £1 000. Profits and losses are to be shared in proportion to their capitals. The net trading profit for the year ending 31st December amounted to £7 800. During the year Groom drew £4 000 and Bride £3 000 on account of profits.

Show the partners' Capital Accounts and Current Accounts as at 31st December and, also, how these particulars should appear in the firm's Balance Sheet.

3. M. J. Childs and T. Carr are in partnership, sharing profits and losses equally. Their respective capitals are £2 000 and £1 200. Childs drew £400 a month and Carr £300 a month on account of profits. At 31st December the net trading profit for the year amounted to £12 200. Show the Capital Account and Current Account for each partner as at 31st December.

4. G. Reader and A. Storey are in partnership sharing profits and losses as to two-thirds and one-third respectively. On 1st January, 19. ., the total capital of the firm was £5 000, held by the partners in equal shares, and on 1st July each partner paid into the business Bank Account £500 as additional capital. During the year each partner drew from the business £800 at the end of each quarter. On 31st December the credit balance of the Profit and Loss Account was £8 400. Show the Ledger Accounts of the partners as they would appear after the books had been balanced on 31st December, 19. . .

R.S.A. (adapted)

5. Palmer and Pye are partners in a garage business. They share profits and losses: Palmer $\frac{3}{5}$ths; $\frac{2}{5}$ths.

Prepare their Trading and Profit and Loss Accounts for the year ended 31st December, 19. ., with a Balance Sheet as at that date, from the following Trial Balance.

The stock at 31st December, 19. ., was valued at £2 621.

Trial Balance

31st December, 19...

	Dr. £	*Cr.* £
Fixed Capital Accounts:		
Palmer		11 400
Pye		7 600
Current Accounts, 1st January, 19..:		
Palmer		182
Pye	230	
Drawings during year:		
Palmer	1 582	
Pye	912	
Freehold property	15 000	
Stock, 1st January, 19..	1 939	
Sundry debtors	1 413	
Sundry creditors		1 324
Sale of motor cars		6 430
Sale of petrol, oils, etc.		2 948
Charges for repairs to cars		989
Plant and machinery	750	
Breakdown lorry	925	
Advertising	75	
Wages: Works	2 100	
Office	412	
Electric power (Works)	427	
Electricity (Office)	48	
Purchases	4 307	
Office expenses	156	
Insurances	89	
Cash at bank	508	
	£30 873	£30 873

R.S.A. (*adapted*)

6. D. Sinclair and B. Clark are partners sharing profits and losses, three-fifths and two-fifths respectively.

On 31st March, 19.., the balances in their books were as follows:

	£
Sinclair, Capital Account	68 830
,, Drawings Account	18 000
Clark, Capital Account (Dr. Balance)	2 300
,, Drawings Account	12 000
Plant and machinery	26 000
Furniture and fixtures	1 800
Stock, 1st April	37 420

	£
Creditors	38 140
Debtors	51 900
Cash in hand	1 220
Cash at bank	9 770
Provision for doubtful debts	850
Rent and rates	2 300
Purchases, less returns	50 430
Insurance	340
Manufacturing wages	39 000
Carriage inwards	1 680
Discounts allowed	3 870
,, received	820
Salaries	7 200
Sundry manufacturing expenses	8 700
Sundry expenses (other than manufacturing)	1 160
Sales, less returns	166 450

Draw up a Trial Balance as at 31st March, 19..; then prepare Trading and Profit and Loss Accounts and Balance Sheet, noting that:

(*a*) Stock at balancing date was valued at £30 821.

(*b*) On 30th March, 19.., goods valued at £1 250 were returned by a customer and were taken into stock, but no record of this return was made in the books until 1st April.

(*c*) Depreciation should be written off as follows: Furniture and fixtures, 5%; Plant and machinery, 7½%.

(*d*) £720 of book debts should be written off as bad and the Provision for Doubtful Debts raised to £1 000.

(Journal entries are not required).

U.E.I. (adapted)

7. C. Nelson and S. Bennett join in the purchase of a cargo of flour and agree to share the expenses and profits in equal proportions.

Nelson agrees to arrange the purchase and Bennett undertakes the sale of the flour. The cost of the cargo was £9 600 and Bennett at once paid £4 800 to Nelson for his share.

Nelson incurred the following expenses: Unloading, £185; Carriage, £103; Warehousing, £211.

Bennett sold the flour for cash for £12 500, his expenses amounting to £56, and he remitted to Nelson cheque for the amount due to him.

Show the necessary accounts in Bennett's Ledger.

U.E.I. (adapted)

8. A. Blake entered into a joint venture with M. Day. A. Blake agreed to manage the joint venture and on 1st March, M. Day remitted a cheque value

£700 to A. Blake to assist in financing the venture. Profits and losses are to be divided two-thirds to A. Blake and one-third to M. Day.

On 4th June, A. Blake bought goods to the value £1 130 and incurred the following expenses: carriage, £21 and insurance, £9. By agreement, he is allowed to charge a commission of £10. The goods were sold for £1 590 on 11th June.

You are required to show the joint venture account.

U.E.I.

9. Adams and Bell were art dealers who agreed to purchase certain pictures on joint account, the arrangement being that the party effecting the sale was to be allowed a commission of 5% on the amount realised, the remaining profit being divided equally.

On 25th June, 19.., Adams bought three pictures for £1 600 and Bell purchased two others for £1 350. Expenses of £35 were incurred, of which Adams paid £25 and Bell £10.

On 17th July, Adams sold one of the pictures for £600 and on 25th July forwarded another picture to Bell, the cost of carriage and insurance (paid by Adams) being £7. Bell sold this picture on 5th August for £720 and on the same day sent Adams a cheque for the amount realised, less 5%. The pictures purchased by Bell were sold by him on 10th and 29th July for £850 and £780 respectively.

At 30th September the remaining picture was still unsold and it was arranged that Adams should take this over for £400. On 5th October the amount due from one party to the other was settled by cheque.

Prepare a general statement showing the result of the venture and write up the joint account as it would appeaı in the books of Adams.

R.S.A.

10. A and B enter into a venture to purchase a cargo of timber from Kotka. The expenses, profits or losses, are to be shared equally. It is arranged that A should make the purchase and B undertake the selling. A purchased timber valued at £4 800 and B at once paid half this amount to A. The following expenses were incurred by A: – freight, £160; unloading, £70; carriage, £93. Sundry expenses incurred by B: £30. The timber was sold by B for £6 500, payable by bill at three months, which he immediately discounted at the rate of 5% p.a.

You are required to prepare accounts as they would appear in A and B's Ledgers when the venture was completed.

N.C.T.E.C. (adapted)

34

Partnership Accounts

The terms of a Partnership Agreement may be such that further accounts than those already discussed are required to record the financial relationship of the partners.

Partners' Salaries

It may happen that there are certain inequalities between the partners. One may give more time to the firm's business, another may have exceptional skill or experience. A junior partner may have brought little capital and be entitled to a small share only of the profits, yet he may devote considerable skill and attention to the business. In such cases the reward for this work may take the form of a fixed salary.

A partnership salary is a charge against profits before they are divided between the partners. It may be dealt with in one of two ways, namely:

(*a*) Paid direct to the partner in cash at stated intervals.

(*b*) Placed to the partner's credit at the close of the financial year, or at another agreed time.

In either case a new account, *Partnership Salaries Account*, is required. It is debited with the amount of the salary. The balance of this is transferred to the second section of the Profit and Loss Account at the close of the trading period.

If the salary is paid in cash, *credit* Cash book; *debit* Partnership Salaries Account at the time of payment.

If the salary is to be credited to the partner, *credit* the partner's Current Account; *debit* Partnership Salaries Account.

Interest on Capital

The capital introduced by the partners is an important factor in the success of an undertaking, especially if the nature of the business requires considerable quantities of fixed assets, such as plant and machinery, or considerable capital resources to finance business deals.

Where there are equal contributions of capital in such cases, equal sharing of profits is a satisfactory proposal for equally hard-working partners. But some agreements bind the partners to a *ratio of profit distribution* different from the *ratio of capital contribution*. A and B may, for example, contribute £10 000 and £5 000 respectively as capital, but agree to share profits equally. Any benefit to the firm from A's larger capital comes equally to A and B in the sharing of profits.

A method of rewarding A for the larger capital he has introduced, is is to give A and B a first share (or *prior allocation*) of the profits in the form of interest on the capital they have invested. The remainder of the profit is then shared on the agreed basis (in this case equally).

Below is an example of how the sharing of profits would work out (*a*) without allowing interest on capital (*b*) allowing interest on capital.

A and B are in partnership, sharing profits equally.

A's capital = £10 000
B's capital = £5 000
Profits = £7 500

(*a*) Without allowing interest on capital, each partner would be credited with £3 750 as half share of the profits.

(*b*) If interest on capital is allowed at 10% per annum, the first allocation to the partners is £1 500 (£1 000 to A, £500 to B). This leaves £6 000 to be divided equally by A and B.

	A	B	Total
	£	£	£
Interest on capital	1 000	500	1 500
Share of remainder	3 000	3 000	6 000
Total	£4 000	£3 500	£7 500

Under this method A receives £500 more than B as reward for the use of his greater capital. Note that interest on capital is credited only if the terms of the Partnership provide for it (see Chapter 32).

No immediate payment of cash is involved – interest on capital is a book entry only. The method of recording it in the accounts at the end of the trading period is to debit the interest to a separate account, the *Interest on Capital Account*, the corresponding entry being made in the partners' respective Current Accounts at the close of the trading period. The Interest on Capital Account is closed by transferring the balance to the debit of the Appropriation section of the Profit and Loss Account. The balance remaining in the appropriation section is then the profit available for division in the usual way.

The credit for interest on capital is intended to give roughly the same return which might be expected if the capital were invested outside the business. This is sometimes called its 'opportunity cost'. The remainder of the profit may therefore be regarded as the reward for the labour and skill exercised in the business by the partners. If this remainder is a very small amount, it should be considered whether or not to dissolve the partnership. The labour and skill also have an 'opportunity cost', which is the income that could be earned by employing them in other work.

New accounts, namely, the Partnership Salaries Account and the Interest on Capital Account, have been suggested, but in the case of small partnerships the entries may be made direct from the credit of the Current Accounts to the debit of the Profit and Loss Account, thus avoiding the opening of new accounts for one or two entries only which are immediately transferred to the Profit and Loss Account.

Interest on Drawings

Reasons somewhat similar to those for allowing interest on capital are advanced for charging interest on drawings. If A draws £500 each quarter on account of profits, and B draws nothing until the end of the financial year, A has had the use of money which, had it not been drawn, would probably have been of use to the business and to the profit of both A and B. An advantage is given to A which B does not enjoy. If, however, the Partnership Agreement provides that interest shall be charged on drawings, the partners pay for the use of money drawn in anticipation of profits. They pay the firm, and the firm's profits are increased to that extent. The partners who do not draw, or who draw smaller sums, are compensated by the proportion of the interest that is included in their share of profits. The interest is charged by adjustments in the partnership accounts, not by direct payment of cash by the partner to the firm. The amount to the credit of a partner shown in his Current Account is diminished by debiting the interest to that account. A credit entry is made in a new account called *Interest on Drawings Account*. At the close of the trading period the balance of the Interest on Drawings Account is transferred to the credit of the second section of the Profit and Loss Account. It is included in the balance of profit to be shared between the partners, including the partner who has been charged the interest.

The interest, usually charged at the 'opportunity cost' rate, is calculated for the period from the date of the drawing to the date of the closing of the books for the financial year.

To facilitate the calculations and the entries it is usual to have two additional columns on the debit side of the partners' Current Accounts, one for the number of days and the other for the amount of interest. The total of the interest column is carried to the ordinary debit column of the Current Account at the close of the financial year, and the credit entry is made in the Interest on Drawings Account.

The following example illustrates the entries required for partners' salaries, interest on capital, and interest on drawings, and for the distribution of the balance of profit.

Example 44. J. Moore and B. Burgess began to trade in partnership on 1st January, 19.., under the firm name of Moore & Co., Moore contributing £6 000 and Burgess £2 000 in cash. They agree as follows:

To share profits equally. To allow interest on capital at 6% per annum. To charge interest on drawings at 6% per annum. That prior to division of profits Burgess shall be credited with £1 000 as partnership salary. That Moore may draw £1 000 on 1st July and Burgess £600 on 1st April, 1st July, and 1st October in each year on account of profits.

The net trading profit for the year to 31st December, 19.., amounted to £10 000. Show the accounts rendered necessary by these provisions.

J. Moore. Capital Account

19..			£	19..			£
				Jan. 1	Cash	CB	6 000

B. Burgess. Capital Account

19..			£	19..			£
				Jan. 1	Cash	CB	2 000

Interest on Capital

19..			£	19..			£
Dec. 31	J. Moore		360	Dec. 31	Transfer to Profit and Loss A/c		480
	B. Burgess		120				
			£480				£480

Interest on Drawings

19..			£	19..			£
Dec. 31	Transfer to Profit and Loss A/c		84	Dec. 31	J. Moore		30
				,, 31	B. Burgess		54
			£84				£84

Partner's Salary Account

19..			£	19..			£
Dec. 31	B. Burgess		1 000	Dec. 31	Transfer to to Profit and Loss A/c		1 000

Profit and Loss Appropriation Account

For the Year ended 31st December, 19...

		£			£
Interest on capital		480	Trading profit	b/d	10 000
Partner's salary		1 000	Interest on drawings		84
Share of profits:					
J. Moore		4 302			
B. Burgess		4 302			
		£10 084			£10 084

Cash Book

(Showing only appropriate items, Bank Columns)

Dr. *Cr.*

			BANK				BANK
19..			£	19..			£
Jan. 1	Capital:			Apr. 1	B. Burgess		600
	J. Moore		6 000	July 1	B. Burgess		600
	B. Burgess		2 000	July 1	J. Moore		1 000
				Oct. 1	B. Burgess		600

J. Moore. Current Account

			MONTHS	INTEREST	DRAWINGS ETC.				
19..				£	£	19..			£
July 1	Cash			30	1 000	Dec. 31	Interest on capital		360
						,, 31	½ share of profits		4 302
Dec. 31	Interest		6		30				
,, 31	Balance	c/d			3 632				
					£4 662				£4 662
						Jan. 1	Balance	b/d	3 632

B. Burgess. Current Account

			MONTHS	INTEREST	DRAWINGS, ETC.				
19..				£	£	19..			£
Apr. 1	Cash		9	27	600	Dec. 31	Interest on capital		120
July 1	Cash		6	18	600	,, 31	Salary		1 000
Oct. 1	Cash		3	9	600	,, 31	½ share of profits		4 302
Dec. 31	Interest			54	54				
,, 31	Balance	c/d			3 568				
					£5 422				£5 422
						Jan. 1	Balance	b/d	3 568

Balance Sheet
as at 31st December, 19...
(Claims side and required items only are shown)

	£	£	£
CAPITAL:			
J. Moore		6 000	
B. Burgess		2 000	
			8 000
CURRENT ACCOUNTS:			
J. Moore			
Share of profits	4 302		
Interest on capital	360	4 662	
less Drawings	1 000		
Interest on drawings	30	1 030	
			3 632
B. Burgess			
Share of profits	4 302		
Interest on capital	120		
Salary	1 000		
		5 422	
less Drawings	1 800		
Interest on drawings	54	1 854	3 568

Had Burgess been permitted also to withdraw the salary of £1 000 during the year, the debit entry for it would have been made in the Partners' Salary Account as shown above, but the credit entry would have been made in the Cash Book. No credit entry would have appeared in the Partner's Current Account.

Note that the crediting of salary, interest or profit to a partner's account is not necessarily the same as the amount that the partner takes out as drawings. Note also that interest on capital is credited (and interest on drawings is charged) only for that part of the accounting period after the capital was introduced (or the drawings were taken out).

Partners' Advances and Sundry Adjustments

If the partnership firm is in need of more working capital or requires money temporarily to help over a difficult financial period, a partner may give assistance by making a loan to the firm. There is an advantage to the partner is assisting by way of a loan rather than by an addition to his capital, as partners' loans have priority of repayment over capital in the event of dissolution. On the other hand, if things go well the interest on a loan is likely to be less than an increased share of profits. A separate Partner's Loan Account is kept in respect of each loan. The interest on the loan is debited periodically to the Interest on Loan Account for eventual transfer to the Profit and Loss Appropriation Account. The credit entry for the interest is made to the Partner's Current Account unless it is paid to him in cash – in which case the Cash Book is credited.

In the preparation of the Trading and Profit and Loss Accounts and Balance Sheet of a partnership, the usual adjustments have to be made to take into account outstanding liabilities, payments in advance, allowances for depreciation and for bad and doubtful debts. These are necessary for sound accounting whatever form the business takes. Some adjustments may be required, in addition, arising from the type of ownership. These include the taking into account of the interest on partner's capital, interest on drawings, and any partnership salary outstanding. The treatment of these items in the accounts has already been discussed. In examination questions the items are often given as instructions with a Trial Balance from which Final Accounts are to be prepared. If the Ledger Accounts are not required in answering a question, only the effect on the Final Accounts has to be shown. Such adjustments are, of course, normally entered in the appropriate Ledger Accounts but, if the question is concerned only with the Final Accounts, it is necessary to show in them the two-fold effect of each adjustment.

For interest on capital the appropriate sum should be debited to the second section of the Profit and Loss Account, and added to the balance of the Partner's Current Account in the Balance Sheet (reflecting the credit to his Account in the Ledger).

The interest on drawings is credited to the appropriation or second section of the Profit and Loss Account, and shown in the Balance Sheet as a deduction from the balance of the Partner's Current Account (reflecting the debit to his Account in the Ledger).

The partnership salary for which credit is to be given to the partner is entered to the debit of the second section of the Profit and Loss Account, and the sum is added to the Partner's Current Account balance in the Balance Sheet (reflecting the credit to his Account in the ledger).

In each of these cases one entry of the two-fold aspect is entered in the Balance Sheet. It does not follow that the Balance Sheet is treated as a Ledger Account. The Balance Sheet item has been adjusted to show the figure at which it would stand if the item had been extracted from the Ledger after the proper Ledger entries for the adjustments had been made. As, however, in this kind of question the Ledger Accounts are neither given nor required, it is necessary to arrive at the Balance Sheet figure without presenting them, although they may, of course, be prepared as working papers.

Partnership Profits from Incomplete Records

The preparation of a Statement of Profit as shown on pp. 256–258 must not be assumed to be a process restricted to a sole trader. It may also be necessary in the case of a partnership. The only addition needed to adapt the system to partnership records is to elaborate the Statement of Profit to give effect to the relationship existing between the partners. Let it be assumed by way of further illustration that, in Example 34 above, R. Benson had brought his son, S. Benson, into the business on 1st January, 19.., on the following terms:

(*a*) R. Benson to credit £2 800 of his capital to his son, leaving a sum of £10 000 to his own credit as at 1st January.

(*b*) Each partner to be credited with 5 per cent per annum interest on opening capital.

(*c*) R. Benson to draw £20 and S. Benson to draw £5 a calendar month on account of profits, S. Benson also drawing £50 on 31st December.

(*d*) S. Benson to draw a further sum of £25 each half-year as salary.

(*e*) The profits remaining, after provision for interest on capital and for S. Benson's salary, to be divided between father and son in the proportion of two thirds to R. Benson and one third to S. Benson.

The Statement of Profit would then have been as follows:

Statement of Profit

	£	£
Surplus of assets over liabilities at 31st December, 19.. (Details in Example 34.)		13 270
add Drawings: R. Benson	240	
S. Benson	60	
Salary: S. Benson	100	
	400	
less Capital introduced by R. Benson (see Example 34)	150	250
		13 520
Capital on 1st January, 19..		
R. Benson	10 000	
S. Benson	2 800	12 800
Profit for the year		£720

Division of Profit:

	R. Benson	S. Benson	Total
	£	£	£
Interest at 5% p.a.	500	140	640
Salary	—	50	50
Balance of profit in ratio 2:1	20	10	30
	£520	£200	£720

Statement of Affairs at 31st December, 19..

CLAIMS	£	£	ASSETS	£
Sundry creditors		4 900	Premises	12 800
Capital Accounts:			Fittings	400
R. Benson			Stock	1 950
As at 1st Jan.	10 000		Sundry debtors	2 700
add Capital addition	150		Cash	320
Interest	500			
Profit	20			
	£10 670			
less drawings	240	10 430		
S. Benson				
As at 1st Jan.	2 800			
add Salary	50			
Interest	140			
Profit	10			
	£3 000			
less drawings and salary	160	2 840		
		£18 170		£18 170

Comparison of the above Statements with Example 34 will reveal that the total profit at £720 is the same in both cases, and that in the former case the capital in the business was shown as R. Benson's at £13 270, whereas, in the latter case, the capital has been apportioned between the two partners but remains in total the same. Thus, R. Benson's capital is £10 430, S. Benson's capital £2 840 – total partnership capital, £13 270.

EXERCISES 34

1. Laxton and Bexley were in partnership sharing profits equally. The following information was extracted from their books at 31st December, 1971:

Total Bank Account for 1971

	£		£
Opening balance	768	Cash paid to suppliers	24 171
Cash received from credit customers	39 847	Salaries	6 319
		Insurances	129
		Rent and rates	980
		General expenses	1 197
		Lighting and heating	218
		Drawings:	
		Laxton	1 762
		Bexley	1 696
		Closing balance	4 143
	£40 615		£40 615

	31st Dec. 1970	31st Dec. 1971
	£	£
Stock	2 529	2 876
Debtors	3 171	3 349
Creditors for:		
Purchases	1 622	2 048
Rates	44	56
Insurance paid in advance	28	24

Delivery vans which cost £3 500 on 1st January 1970 are still in use and are to be written down by an annual depreciation charge of 20 per cent on cost.

Laxton and Bexley entered into partnership on 1st January 1970 and each partner contributed £3 250 as his capital. The net profit for 1970 was £3 808 and the partners' drawings during 1970 were: Laxton £1 382 and Bexley £1 296.

Required:

Laxton and Bexley's trading and profit and loss account for 1971 and balance sheet as at 31st December 1971.

R.S.A. II

2. Robinson and Jones are in partnership, sharing profits and losses equally. Their fixed capitals are: Robinson £11 500, Jones £9 400. Jones is entitled to a salary of £4 000 per annum which is to be credited to him at the close of the year. During the year Robinson drew £3 000 on account of profits. The net profit at 31st December, prior to these adjustments, amounted to £12 100.

Show the final section of the Profit and Loss Account, the partners' Capital Account and Current Accounts, and the appropriate entries in the Balance Sheet.

3. Brown and Tomlinson are in partnership, sharing profits and losses in equal proportion. Brown's capital is £10 000, and Tomlinson's capital is £4 000.

The partners are entitled to 10% interest on capital and are to be charged interest on drawings at 10% per annum.

Brown drew £200 on 1st March and 1st August.

Tomlinson drew £200 on 1st April, 1st July, and 1st October.

Prior to any of the above adjustments the profits for the year to 31st December were £6 000.

Give the accounts to record the above information, and the partners' accounts as they would appear in the Balance Sheet.

4. Toogood and Waring are equal partners whose capitals are £12 000 and £8 000 respectively. They are entitled to interest on capital at 10% and are to be charged interest on drawings at 10% per annum.

Waring drew £100 on 1st March, 1st June, 1st September, and 1st December.

The profits prior to these adjustments amounted at 31st December to £12 130.

Show the accounts required to record this information, including the partners' Capital and Current Accounts, and show the details that should be given in the firm's Balance Sheet.

5. Record the following facts in the personal accounts of A. and B. Ajayi, two partners, who share profits and losses in the ratio of 5 to 3; and allow interest on capital at the rate of 4 per cent per annum. No interest is to be allowed on Current Accounts or charged on drawings. B. Ajayi is to be credited with a salary of £300 for the year.

	A. Ajayi	B. Ajayi
	£	£
Jan. 1. Capital Accounts	4 000	3 000
June 30. Additional capital brought in and banked	1 000	—
Jan. 1. Current Accounts	72 (*Dr.*)	100 (*Cr.*)
Jan. 1–Dec. 31. Drawings	3 650	3 650

The partnership's total divisible profit for the year, after charging the salary, was £7 188.

R.S.A. (adapted)

6. Dickson is a partner in a business and is entitled to an eighth of the net profits of the firm. From the following particulars write up the Capital and Current Accounts of Dickson for the year to 31st December, 19.., as they would appear in the Ledger of the partnership.

19..			£
Jan.	1.	Balance on Dickson's Capital Account (*Cr.*)	1 000
,,	1.	,, ,, ,, Current ,, ,,	300
July	1.	Additional cash capital brought in by Dickson	600
Dec.	31.	Dickson's drawings for year	520
,,	31.	Interest charged on Dickson's drawings	13
,,	31.	Interest allowed on Dickson's capital	65
,,	31.	Interest allowed on Dickson's Current Account	15
,,	31.	Net profits for year (after adjustment of partners' interest) divisible between the partners	16 400
,,	31.	Amount transferred from Dickson's Current Account to his Capital Account	400

R.S.A. (adapted)

7. The Partnership Agreement between A, B and C contains the following provision:

(*a*) The partners' *fixed* capitals shall be: A, £10 000; B, £8 000; C, £6 000.

(*b*) A and B are each to receive a salary of £600 a year.

(*c*) Interest on capital is to be calculated at 5% per annum.

(*d*) A, B, and C are to share profits and losses in the ratio 3:2.1.

(*e*) No interest to be charged on Drawings or Current Accounts:

On January 1st, 19.., the balances on Current Accounts were: A, credit, £500; B, credit, £200; C, credit, £350.

During the year the drawings were: A, £4 200; B, £3 000; and C, £5 000. The Profit and Loss Account for the year showed a profit of £14 500 before charging interest on capital and partners' salaries.

Show the Capital and Current Accounts of A, B, and C, as at 31st December, after the division of the profit.

U.E.I. (adapted)

8. X, Y, Z are in partnership. They share profits: X two-fifths, Y two-fifths, and Z one-fifth. The partnership provides that interest at 8% per annum shall be paid on the credit balance of each partner's Capital Account as it was at the beginning of each financial year, that no interest is to be charged on drawings, and that Z is to receive a salary of £750 per annum and 2% commission on the balance of trading profit after charging his salary but before charging interest on capital.

The balances of the Capital Accounts at 1st January, 19.., are: X, credit £4 000; Y, credit £3 000; Z, credit £1 000.

The balances of the Current Accounts at 1st January, 19.., are: X, credit £250, Y, debit £50; Z, debit £100.

Drawings during the year amount to: X, £1 300; Y, £925; Z, £1 200. The trading profit for the year ended 31st December, 19.., was £3 650.

Prepare:

(*a*) An account showing the division of the trading profit in accordance with the terms of the partnership agreement.

(*b*) The Capital and Current Accounts of each of the partners for the year.

College of Preceptors – Senior (adapted)

9. Copping and Watts were equal partners in a business, and a Trial Balance is taken from their books on 31st December, 19..:

Trial Balance.

31st December, 19...

	Dr.	*Cr.*
	£	£
Copping, Capital		10 000
Watts, Capital		5 000
Sales, net		86 730
Purchases, net	73 280	
Freehold premises	25 000	
Copping, Drawings Account	2 500	
Watts, Drawings Account	4 000	
General expenses	4 620	
Bad debts	500	
Discount	1 360	290
Creditors		28 740
Debtors	31 180	
Cash	860	
Bank		40 710
Stock, 1st January	23 170	
Repairs to premises	1 500	
Fixtures and fittings	3 500	
	£171 470	£171 470

Prepare a Trading Account and Profit and Loss Account for the year ending 31st December, and a Balance Sheet as at that date, making the necessary allowances for the following:

Watts is entitled to a salary of £2 500 per annum, which has not been paid.

Fixtures and fittings to be depreciated at the rate of 10%. Allow interest on capital at the rate of 5% per annum. Insurance premium prepaid, £360, included in general expenses. Stock on hand, 31st December, valued at £28 850.

U.L.C.I.

10. A. Carrick and G. Furgus are trading in partnership, and the following list of balances appeared in the books of the firm on 31st March, 19..:

	£
Fixtures and fittings	400
Machinery	5 000
A. Carrick – Capital Account	20 000
G. Furgus – Capital Account	2 250
A. Carrick – Drawings Account	1 200
G. Furgus – Drawings Account	600
Rent received	150
Telephone charges	177
Bank balance (in hand)	1 645
Discount allowed	461
Factory wages	13 397
Freehold premises	9 000
Sales	53 944
Factory power	1 592
Salaries	2 479
Sundry creditors	4 392
Sundry expenses	849
Purchases	34 118
Stock at 31st March (previous year)	3 763
Sundry debtors	5 649
Bad debts	158
Discount received	121
Cash in hand	369

You are required to prepare:

(*a*) The Trial Balance at 31st March, 19...

(*b*) The Trading and Profit and Loss Account for the year ending 31st March, 19.., and Balance Sheet as on that date, taking into consideration the following:

1. The Stock at 31st March, 19.., was valued at £6 545.
2. Provide for further bad debts, £102.
3. Depreciate machinery by 10% of cost (£10 000).
4. Depreciate fixtures and fittings by $12\frac{1}{2}$% of cost (£800).
5. A. Carrick is entitled to three-quarters and G. Furgus one-quarter of the profits or losses.

R.S.A.

11. The following is the Trial Balance extracted from the books of William and James on the 31st March, 1980.

The partners share profits and losses equally.

	£	£
Capital – William		3 500
,, – James		3 500
Drawings – William	1 175	
,, – James	1 151	
Sales		32 010
Purchases	23 015	
Discounts allowed	850	
Discounts received		1 021
Rent	1 180	
Rates	200	
Lighting and heating	193	
Insurance	168	
Wages and salaries	2 154	
Printing and stationery	155	
General expenses	170	
Motor lorry and van expenses	1 110	
Stock (1st March, 1980)	3 209	
Bad debts	80	
Trade debtors	3 500	
Trade Creditors		3 309
Motor Lorry and Van at Cost	2 000	
Furniture and fittings at Cost	700	
Balance at Bank	2 430	
Provision for bad debts, 1st March, 1980		100
	£43 440	£43 440

You are requested to prepare the partners' Trading and Profit and Loss Account for the month ended 31st March, 1980 and a Balance Sheet as at that date, taking the following matters into consideration:

(i) The Stock in trade at 31st March 1980, amounted to £3 004.
(ii) Rent in arrears at 31st March 1980, £160.
(iii) An amount of £38 was owing at 31st March 1980, for repairs to the Motor Van.
(iv) Rates paid in advance at 31st March 1980, £40.
(v) Provide for depreciation of Motor Lorry and Van, £400.
(vi) Furniture and Fittings are to be depreciated by £100.
(vii) Included in the sum of £193 for Lighting and Heating is an amount of £32 paid for a new convector heater, purchased on 21st March 1980.
(viii) The provision for Bad Debts is to be increased to 5% of the Trade Debtors.

12. L. and M. are in partnership sharing profits and losses equally. Before profits or losses are shared each partner is entitled to 5% per annum interest of capital, after which M. is entitled so far as profits are available to a bonus of £500 per annum. Final Accounts are made up half-yearly.

From the following details extracted from the books at 30th June, 19. ., you are required to prepare the Profit and Loss Appropriation Account for the half year ended 30th June 19. . and a Balance Sheet as on that date.

	£
Capital Accounts (1st January, 19. .):	
L. £4 000; M. £6 000	10 000
Current Accounts (Credit balances at 1st January, 19. .)	
L. £250; M. £300	550
Cash in hand and at bank	2 335
Stock	2 705
Sundry debtors	2 475
Provision for bad debts	100
Sundry creditors: Trade	2 510
Expense	104
Advertising brought forward (debit balance)	800
Furniture and equipment	475
Freehold premises	8 000
Mortgage on freehold premises	3 500
Credit balance of Profit and Loss Account (before providing for interest on capital and M's bonus)	3 126
Partners' drawings for the half year:	
L. £1 250; M. £1 850	3 100

13. F. Winter and G. Frost are in partnership trading as 'Utensils Supply Company'. The partners have fixed capital contributions: Winter, £6 500, and Frost, £5 500. Each partner is allowed interest on capital at 6% per annum and profits and losses are shared equally. Winter has made a loan to the firm of £2 500 at 7% per annum interest which is credited to his Current Account at the end of each year. At the 30th September, 19. ., one year's interest was still due on this loan.

The Net Trading Profit (before allowing for any sums due to partners) for the year ended 30th September, 19. ., was £4 369.

In addition the following balances were extracted from the books at 30th September, 19. .:

	£
Current Accounts:	
Credit balances at start of year: Winter	40
Frost	30
Drawings for year of account: Winter	2 300
Frost	2 000
Sundry creditors	2 570
Sundry debtors	5 490
Provision for bad debts	170
Goodwill	2 000
Stock-in-trade	5 980
Furniture and equipment	740
Cash in hand and balance at bank	3 169

(*a*) Prepare the Appropriation Account of the partnership for the year ended 30th September, 19. ., and a Balance Sheet at that date.

(*b*) If there had been no agreement between the partners with regard to interest on capital and loans and the division of profits:

(i) Would partners be entitled to interest on capital and, if so, at what rate?
(ii) Would Winter be entitled to any interest on loan and, if so, at what rate?
(iii) How would profits and losses be shared?

A.E.B., G.C.E. 'O' Level

35

Partnership Accounts: The Admission of a New Partner

When a business grows it may need additional supervision or additional capital, and the decision may be to take in a new partner to supply the need. Whether the existing business is owned by a sole trader or a partnership firm, the admission of a partner brings a new firm into being. It is essential to agree upon the terms of his admission and the conditions of a new partnership.

Take the example in Chapter 33 in which Redman and Butcher are shown as trading in partnership, each with a capital of £15 000, and sharing profits equally. They may decide to admit Robinson to partnership, who is to contribute £10 000 as capital, and is to have $\frac{1}{5}$ share of the profits of the new firm; Redman and Butcher to share the remaining profits equally.

If that is all, the entries in the firm's books are simple, requiring only a credit entry for £10 000 in Robinson's Capital Account, and a corresponding debit entry for the sum in the firm's Cash Book. But the matter is seldom so simple as that. The new partner is being admitted to an existing business, and he will benefit from the connections and reputation already established. The old partners, on their part, forgo these advantages to the extent that the new partner shares in them. In short, *Goodwill* attaches to the business created by the old firm, and will continue for the new firm of which Robinson is a member. Not only will Robinson derive present benefit in the form of profits, but should any event happen, such as the dissolution of the partnership, and the Goodwill be realised by sale, he has the right to share in its value. It is therefore customary for the new partner to pay for the privilege of admission to an existing business. Such payment, called a *Premium*, is made to the old members by the new member and may be regarded as compensation to them for the share in the Goodwill that will accrue to the new partner at their expense.

The premium must not be confused with the capital the new partner may introduce. His capital is credited to his own account, whilst the premium is for the benefit of the partners of the old firm.

It is normally anticipated that the cash or other assets brought in by the new partner and credited to his Capital Account will produce additional profits. If cash is brought in, the corresponding entry to the credit of the new partner's Capital Account is a debit to the Bank Account through the Cash Book. If the new capital is in kind, such as book debts, stock, and other assets, an appropriate Journal entry is made from which the agreed values are posted to the debit of the respective asset accounts, and the total value to the credit of the new partner's Capital Account.

The premium, however, may be treated in one of several ways, and in none of these is the new partner's Capital Account affected.

Example 45. On 1st January, Redman and Butcher, trading in partnership, each with a capital of £15 000 and sharing profits equally, decide to admit Robinson as a partner on the condition that he brings in £10 000 as capital and pays them a premium of £10 000. The profits in future are to be shared as follows: Redman, $\frac{2}{5}$; Butcher, $\frac{2}{5}$; Robinson $\frac{1}{5}$.

Method 1. The premium is to be paid by Robinson direct to Redman and Butcher.

In this case no entries are made in the firm's books. The premium is shared between Redman and Butcher in the proportion in which they shared profits before admission of the new partner, so that Robinson hands direct to each of them a cheque for £5 000 as a private transaction between him and the old partners.

Method 2. The £10 000 premium is to be paid by Robinson into the firm, but it is to be paid out to Redman and Butcher in the proportions in which they are entitled to share it (i.e. in the proportions in which they shared profits before Robinson was admitted). This method differs from Method 1 only in that an entry is made of the premium in the firm's books (see below and on pp. 378–9). It may be the wish of the partners to have the transaction on record.

Dr. **Cash Book** *Cr.*

19..			£	19..			£
Jan. 1	Robinson:			Jan. 2	Redman:		
	Capital	10	10 000		$\frac{1}{2}$ Robinson's		
	Premium	9	10 000		Premium		5 000
					Butcher:		
					$\frac{1}{2}$ Robinson's		
					Premium		5 000

Current Accounts 11

			Redman	Butcher				Redman	Butcher
19..			£	£	19..			£	£
Jan. 2	Cash:	C.B.			Jan. 1	½ Premium from			
	Premium					Robinson	J	5 000	5 000
	Withdrawn		5 000	5 000					

Robinson. Premium Account

			£				£
19..				19..			
Jan. 1	Current Accounts:			Jan. 1	Cash	CB 20	10 000
	Redman	J	5 000				
	Butcher	J	5 000				
			£10 000				£10 000

Robinson. Capital Account 10

			£				£
19..				19..			
				Jan. 1	Cash	CB 20	10 000

Method 3. The premium is to be paid by Robinson into the firm and is to remain in the business. The premium is the property of Redman and Butcher. As they agree that it shall be left in the business and not withdrawn by them, the effect is to increase their capital contributions by the amount of the premium. This is recorded in their respective Capital Accounts. (See below and on p. 380). If interest is allowed on capital they will receive interest on these sums in addition to the interest on their original capital.

20

Dr. **Cash Book** *Cr.*

			£				£
19..				19..			
Jan. 1	Robinson:						
	Capital	10	10 000				
	Premium:						
	Redman, £5 000	13					
	Butcher, £5 000	14	10 000				

Whichever of these methods is decided upon for the treatment of the premium, the old partners have been compensated in cash for the share in the Goodwill and for the proportion of future profits they surrender to the new partner. It has not been necessary to raise a Goodwill Account in the firm's books.

Cases may arise, however, where the new partner may be unable, or may find it inconvenient, to pay the premium in cash, and some other method must be devised to compensate the old partners for

Capital Accounts

		Robinson £	Redman £	Butcher £	19..			Robinson £	Redman £	Butcher £
					Jan. 1	Balances	b/d	—	15 000	15 000
					,, 1	Cash	C.B.	10 000	5 000	5 000

what they forego on admitting the new partner. As no value in either cash or other form passes between the old partners and the new partner, the method of compensation becomes a series of bookkeeping entries to increase the old partners' claims on the new firm.

As a set-off against the bookkeeping entries of these additional claims an increase is made in the total value of the assets. A value is placed upon the Goodwill of the business, and is included among the assets of the new firm – a *Goodwill Account* is opened to record it.

Example 46. On January 1st Redman and Butcher, trading in partnership, each with a capital of £15 000 and sharing profits equally, decide to admit Robinson as a partner on condition that he brings in £10 000 as capital and pays them a premium of £10 000. Profits to be shared in the new firm: Redman, $\frac{2}{5}$; Butcher $\frac{2}{5}$; Robinson $\frac{1}{5}$.

Robinson is unable to pay the premium in cash. It is agreed that in place of the cash premium a Goodwill Account of £50 000 shall be created, and that a similar sum shall be credited to Redman and Butcher in the same proportion in which they shared profits.

The £10 000 capital will be debited on receipt to the firm's Cash Book, and credited to Robinson's Capital Account. A Goodwill Account will be opened, and the following entries made in the Journal and posted from there to the Goodwill Account and to the old partners' Capital Accounts (see below and on p. 382):

Journal

			Dr.	*Cr.*
19..			£	£
Jan. 1	Goodwill Account	17	50 000	
	Redman's Capital Account	13		25 000
	Butcher's ,, ,,	14		25 000
	being the apportionment of the Goodwill valuation as agreed on admission of Robinson to partnership.			

Goodwill Account 17

19..			£	19..			£
Jan. 1	Sundries	J	50 000				

By this method the old partners have an additional capital claim against the new firm, and will be further compensated by the larger sum which will accrue to them annually as interest on their increased capitals.

The debit balance of the Goodwill Account is usually written off

Capital Account

		Redman	Butcher	19..			Redman	Butcher
		£	£				£	£
				Jan. 1	Balance	b/d	15 000	15 000
				,, 1	Goodwill A/c.	J	25 000	25 000

over a number of years, the Profit and Loss Appropriation Account being debited and the Goodwill Account credited. In this way the new partner contributes out of his share of the profits to writing off the amount of Goodwill which was credited to the Capital Accounts of the existing partners when he entered the partnership.

EXERCISES 35

1. Budd and Benson, each with a capital of £2 000 and sharing profits and losses in equal proportion, decide to admit Bentley as partner on condition that he brings in £1 000 in cash as capital and pays £1 000 as premium for admission. The premium is paid directly by Bentley to Budd and Benson. The profits in future are to be shared: Budd and Benson, each $\frac{2}{5}$, Bentley $\frac{1}{5}$.

Show the effect of the admission of the new partner on the partnership accounts.

2. Thomas and James are in partnership with capitals respectively of £2 500 and £1 500, sharing profits and losses in equal proportions. They decide to admit Jackson as partner on condition that he brings into the business £2 000 of which £1 000 is Jackson's capital contribution and £1 000 is the premium for his admission to the partnership. The sum of £2 000 is paid into the firm's Banking Account, and the premium of £1 000 is paid out to Thomas and James in the proportions in which they are entitled to share it. The profits in future are to be shared: Thomas $\frac{2}{5}$, James $\frac{2}{5}$, Jackson $\frac{1}{5}$.

Record the new partner's admission and the payment out of the premium in the firm's accounts.

3. Wise and Wisdom are in partnership, sharing profits and losses in proportion to their capitals which are £30 000 and £20 000 respectively. They agree to admit Woolley as partner on condition that he pays into the firm £25 000 of which £15 000 is to be Woolley's capital contribution, and £10 000 the premium he is to pay for his admission.

The cash is paid into the firm's Banking Account, and the premium is paid out to Wise and Wisdom.

The profits are to be shared in future, Wise and Wisdom, $\frac{3}{8}$ each; Woolley $\frac{1}{4}$.

Record Woolley's admission to the firm and the payment out of the premium.

4. West and Wilson are equal partners, each with a capital of £3 000. They agree to admit Williams as partner provided he pays in £4 000 of which £3 000 is to be his capital contribution and £1 000 the premium he pays for his admission. Williams paid in the cash which was paid into the firm's Banking Account. The premium is to remain in the business. The profits are to be shared in future equally between the three partners, but 5% interest is to be allowed on capital.

Record the admission of the new partner.

5. Acton and Ascott, trading in partnership, share profits and losses in proportion to their capitals, which are £20 000 and £15 000 respectively. They admit Bennett as partner on his contributing in cash £10 000 as capital and £7 000 as premium. The premium is to remain in the business, and profits in future are to be shared, Acton $\frac{4}{9}$, Ascott ^{1}, and Bennet $\frac{2}{9}$.

Record Bennett's admission to the partnership.

6. Caton and Coutler are in partnership, sharing profits and losses equally. Each has a capital of £4 000 in the firm. They agree to admit Denton as partner, who, however, can provide only £2 000 as his cash contribution. It is arranged that this sum shall be his capital, that a Goodwill Account shall be raised for £2 000, and that Caton's and Coulter's Capital Accounts shall be credited with £1 000 each.

Give the entries to carry these decisions into effect. The partners are to share profits in future in proportion to their capitals. State the ratio in which the future profits will be shared.

7. Dunn and Dugald, trading in partnership each with a capital of £2 000 and sharing profits and losses equally, decide to admit Everton as a partner on condition that he brings in £1 000 in cash as capital and pays them £1 000 as premium for his admission. Everton cannot find sufficient cash to carry out these terms. It is agreed, therefore, that in place of the cash premium a Goodwill Account for £3 000 shall be raised, and that this sum shall be credited to Dunn and Dugald in the proportion in which they formerly shared profits and losses.

Record Everton's admission under these terms.

8. A and B are partners sharing profits in the same proportion as their capital, which is £6 000 and £3 000 respectively. They agree to admit their Manager C into partnership. Under the original agreement C was to pay £3 000 to A and B by way of premium for admission to the firm, and was to pay in a further £3 000 as his capital in the business.

C, however, is only able to raise £4 000; it is therefore, agreed that a Goodwill Account of £8 000 is to be created, and £1 000 only paid to A and B by way of cash premium.

Prepare the necessary entries to record these transactions.

R.S.A.

9. A, a sole trader owning an established business, took B into partnership on 1st January, 19. ., at which date the Goodwill of the business was agreed to be worth £6 000. A's capital (exclusive of Goodwill) was £10 000 and B brought in £3 000 as his capital. Interest on Capital Accounts was to be allowed at 5% and A and B were to divide the remaining profit in the ratio of 2 to 1.

The profit for the year, before charging interest, was £2 600. Calculate the division of this sum between A and B on the alternative assumptions that (1) Goodwill was ignored on B's entering the business. (2) Goodwill was taken into account at its correct value.

36

Dissolution of Partnerships

A partnership is a voluntary association of persons, and just as its inception is by mutual agreement, so it may be dissolved at any time by the mutual consent of the partners.

The Partnership Act, 1890, enacts that, subject to any agreement between the partners, a partnership is dissolved:

(*a*) If entered into for a fixed term, on the expiration of that term.

(*b*) If entered into for a single adventure or undertaking, on the termination of that adventure or undertaking.

(*c*) If entered into for an undefined time, on any partner giving notice to the other member or members of his intention to dissolve the partnership.

(*d*) On the death or bankruptcy of a partner.

(*e*) At the option of the other partners, if a partner suffers his share of the partnership property to be charged under the Act for his separate debt.

Also, on application of a partner, the Court may decree a dissolution when a partner is found lunatic or permanently incapable of performing his part of the partnership agreement or is guilty of such conduct as may be prejudicial to the carrying on of the partnership business. The Court may also decree dissolution, on application of a partner, when the business can only be carried on at a loss.

On dissolution the assets of the partnership are realised, and Section 44 of the Partnership Act, 1890, decrees that, in settling the accounts between partners on dissolution, the following rules shall be observed:

(*a*) Losses, including capital losses, shall be paid first out of profits, next out of capital and, if necessary, by the partners individually in the proportion in which they shared profits.

(*b*) The assets of the firm, including any contribution by the partners as above to make up losses, are to be applied in the following order:

1. Firstly, to the payment of outside debts and liabilities; then

2. To the repayment, *pro rata*, of loans from partners (i.e. if the funds were insufficient to repay all loans by partners, then each partner is to be repaid the same proportion of his outstanding loan).

3. To repayment of the partners' capital.

4. The surplus, if any, after the satisfaction of these claims, to be divided among the partners in the proportion in which they shared profits.

It follows from this that any losses are first to be charged against any undrawn profits shown in the partners' Current Accounts. If this is insufficient or if no such undrawn profits exist, then the losses are to be charged against the partners' Capital Accounts. Should undrawn profits and capital be together insufficient to meet the losses then the partners must contribute in actual cash sufficient to make good the remaining deficiency. After such adjustments the distribution of the assets must proceed according to the above rules subject to any agreement otherwise between the partners. Such agreement, however, cannot affect the first rule which grants to outside creditors the first claim upon the assets.

Closing the Partnership Books on Dissolution

Where there are no complicating circumstances the procedure adopted to close the partnership books is as follows:

1. Open a *Realisation of Assets Account* in the Ledger in order to ascertain the financial result of the realisation of the partnership assets. This is often called simply the *Realisation Account*.

2. Close all the asset accounts, except the cash, by transfer to the debit of the Realisation Account.

3. When the assets are realised, debit the Cash Book with the proceeds and credit the Realisation Account.

If a partner takes over an asset at an agreed value, debit the value to the partner's Capital Account and credit Realisation Account.

4. Credit the Cash Book and debit the Realisation Account with the expenses of the dissolution.

The balance of the Realisation Account now shows a profit or a loss on realisation of the assets. The profit or loss is divisible among the partners in the proportion in which they shared profits. In the event of a loss, credit Realisation Account and debit the partners' respective Capital Accounts with the appropriate shares of the loss. In the event of a profit – debit Realisation Account and credit the partners' respective Capital Accounts with the appropriate shares of the profit.

5. Discharge the liabilities, crediting cash and debiting the various liability accounts.

The balance of cash in hand, after payment of the outside liabilities, should now exactly equal the aggregate of the balances of the partners' Capital Accounts if they are in credit. The entries consequent on the payment to the partners of the capital sums will close the Cash Book and the partners' Capital Accounts.

Example 47. F. Lynch and B. Finch decide to dissolve partnership as on 30th June, 19... Profits and losses are shared equally. The firm's Balance Sheet as at date of dissolution was as follows:

Balance Sheet. 30th June, 19..

	£		£
Capital:		Machinery	1 200
F. Lynch	2 500	Fittings	250
B. Finch	2 000	Stock	2 500
Sundry creditors	1 500	Sundry debtors	1 750
		Cash	300
	£6 000		£6 000

The results of the realisation were: Machinery, £1 400; Stock, £2 700; Debtors, £1 700; B. Finch took over the fittings at an agreed price of £200. The expenses of dissolution amounted to £100. Prepare the necessary accounts.

The solution is given below:

F. Lynch. Capital Account 1

19..			£	19..			£
June 30	Balance	c/d	2 600	June 30	Balance	b/d	2 500
				,, 30	Realisation A/c	J	100
			£2 600				£2 600
June 30	Cash	CB	2 600	June 30	Balance	b/d	2 600

Journal

			Dr.	Cr.
19..			£	£
June 30	Realisation Account	8	5 700	
	Sundry assets:			
	Machinery	4		1 200
	Fittings	5		250
	Stock	6		2 500
	Sundry debtors	7		1 750
	being transfer of assets on dissolution.			
„ 30	B. Finch. Capital Account	2	200	
	Realisation Account	8		200
	being agreed value of fittings taken over.			
„ 30	Realisation Account	8	200	
	F. Lynch. Capital Account.	1		100
	B. Finch. Capital Account.	2		100
	being profit on realisation transferred.			

B. Finch. Capital Account 2

19..			£	19..			£
June 30	Fittings	J	200	June 30	Balance	b/d	2 000
„ 30	Balance	c/d	1 900	„ 30	Realisation A/c	J	100
			£2 100				£2 100
June 30	Cash	CB	1 900	June 30	Balance	b/d	1 900

3

Sundry Creditors

19..			£	19..			£
June 30	Cash	CB	1 500	June 30	Balance	b/d	1 500

4

Machinery

19..			£	19..			£
June 30	Balance	b/d	1 200	June 30	Realisation A/c	J	1 200

5

Fittings

19..			£	19..			£
June 30	Balance	b/d	250	June 30	Realisation A/c	J	250

6

Stock

19..			£	19..			£
June 30	Balance	b/d	2 500	June 30	Realisation A/c	J	2 500

7

Sundry Debtors

19..			£	19..			£
June 30	Balance	b/d	1 750	June 30	Realisation A/c	J	1 750

8

Realisation Account

19..			£	19..			£
June 30	Sundry assets	J	5 700	June 20	Cash – (Proceeds of sale of assets)	CB	5 800
	Cash – (Dissolution expenses)	CB	100	,, 30	B. Finch (Fittings)	J	200
	Balance	c/d	200				
			£6 000				£6 000
June 30	F. Lynch	J	100	June 30	Balance	b/d	200
	B. Finch	J	100				
			200				200

9

Dr. **Cash Book** **Cr.**

19..			£	19..			£
June 30	Balance	b/d	300	June 30	Dissolution expenses	8	100
,, 30	Proceeds of sale of assets	8	5 800		Sundry creditors	3	1 500
					F. Lynch	1	2 600
					B. Finch	2	1 900
			£6 100				£6 100

Loss on Realisation

In the above example a profit was made on realisation of the assets. If the assets realise less than their book values and a loss results, such loss will appear as a debit balance in the Realisation Account. The contra entry is made to the debit of the partners' Capital Accounts. The loss is shared by the partners in the proportions in which they agreed to share the profits or losses of the partnership. If each partner's Capital Account is still in credit the final settlement in cash will follow the lines shown in the above worked example. The cash balance will exactly equal the aggregate of the credit balances of the Capital Accounts.

Partner's Capital Account in Debit

If realisation of the assets results in a loss and a partner's Capital Account is already or is thereby placed in debit, the partner must pay in enough cash to clear the balance. Otherwise the remaining partners cannot be paid the sums shown to their credit. This point is illustrated in the following example:

Example 48. T. More and W. Morris are trading in partnership, sharing profits two-thirds and one-third respectively.

They decide to dissolve partnership and realise the assets. The firm's Balance Sheet at the date of dissolution was as follows:

Balance Sheet
31st December, 19...

	£		£
Capital:		Sundry assets	1 800
T. More	3 000	Stock	2 450
W. Morris	500	Cash at bank	450
Sundry Creditors	1 200		
	£4 700		£4 700

The sundry assets realised £1 400 and the stock £1 450.
The expenses of realisation amounted to £190.
Prepare the necessary accounts to show the results of the realisation as they should appear in the books of the firm, and the position of the two partners after satisfying the firm's liabilities.

The solution to the example is given below, where it will be observed that there is a loss on realisation. The share of the loss to be borne by W. Morris places him in debt to the firm, and he has to pay in cash to enable More to be paid the sum due to him.

1

Realisation Account

			£				£
Dec. 31	Sundry Assets		1 800	Dec. 31	Cash:		
	Stock		2 450		Proceeds of sale of assets	C.B.	2 850
	Cash: (Dissolution expenses)	CB	190		Balance carried down		1 590
			£4 440				£4 440
Dec. 31	Balance brought down		1 590	Dec. 31	T. More $\frac{2}{3}$ share of loss		1 060
					W. Morris $\frac{1}{3}$ share of loss		530
			£1 590				£1 590

Cash Book

Dr.							*Cr.*
19..			£	19..			£
Dec. 31	Balance	b/d	450	Dec. 31	Sundry creditors		1 200
	Proceeds of sale of assets	1	2 850		Expenses of dissolution	1	190
	W. Morris, Cash paid in	3	30		T. More	2	1 940
			£3 330				£3 330

2

T. More. Capital Account

19..			£	19..			£
Dec. 31	Realisation Account, share of loss	1	1 060	Dec. 31	Balance	b/d	3 000
,, 31	Balance	c/d	1 940				
			£3 000				£3 000
Dec. 31	Cash	CB	1 940	Dec. 31	Balance	b/d	1 940

W. Morris. Capital Account

19..			£	19..			£
Dec. 31	Realisation Account share of loss	1	530	Dec. 31	Balance	b/d	500
				,, 31	Balance	c/d	30
			£530				£530
Dec. 31	Balance	b/d	30	Dec. 31	Cash	CB	30

The Ledger Accounts for the assets and liabilities (i.e. claims other than owner's capital) are not shown in this worked example. One of the partners has a credit balance on Capital Account, and the payment in of cash by the partner in debit makes it possible to extinguish the credit balance and to close the books. It may happen that the loss on realisation is so great that all the partners are placed in debit, which would mean that the cash balance would be insufficient to discharge the Sundry Creditors. Each partner would, in that case, have to pay in sufficient cash to extinguish his debit balance and so to provide enough cash to pay the outside creditors.

EXERCISES 36

1. McArthur and Dickson are partners sharing profits as to $\frac{3}{5}$ and $\frac{2}{3}$ respectively. They agree to dissolve partnership and realise the business assets. Upon the conclusion of the realisation the position was as follows:

McArthur, Capital Account, £5 000; Loan Account, £1 000.
Dickson, Capital Account, £3 000; Sundry creditors, £1 456.
Net amount realised by the assets, £11 441.

Submit a statement showing how you would deal with the amount realised.

R.S.A.

2. A. Adams and B. Bates were in partnership, sharing profits and losses two-thirds and one-third respectively. On 31st January, 19.., their Balance Sheet showed as follows:

	£		£
Sundry creditors	18 000	Cash in hand	700
Capital Accounts		Sundry debtors	36 000
A. Adams	23 000	Stock in hand	15 800
B. Bates	11 500		
	£52 500		£52 500

On this date they decided to dissolve the partnership and realise the assets. The stock realised £12 000; and the sundry debtors, £31 500. The sundry creditors were paid, and discount to the amount of £400 was received. The expenses of realisation amounted to £180. Make the entries necessary to complete the above, and show the Ledger Accounts of the partners in their final form.

N.C.T.E.C. (adapted)

3. Brown and Green are in partnership, sharing profits and losses two-thirds and one-third respectively, and on the 31st January, 19.., their Balance Sheet shows as follows:

	£		£
Sundry creditors	2 800	Cash in hand	700
Capital Accounts:		Sundry debtors	2 100
A. Brown	3 800	Stock in hand	4 200
W. Green	1 900	Furniture, etc.	1 500
	£8 500		£8 500

On this date they decided to dissolve partnership, and the assets realised were as follows: The furniture was taken over by Brown at an agreed price of £1 450; sundry debtors realised £2 025; and the stock, £4 500. The expenses of realisation amounted to £91. Make the entries necessary to close the books of the firm, and show the Ledger Accounts in their final form.

N.C.T.E.C.

4. A and B, trading in partnership, decide, as on March 31st, 19.., to dissolve partnership and to liquidate their business.

Their Balance Sheet as on that date was as follows:

Balance Sheet

31st March, 19..

	£		£
Capital Account: A	20 000	Cash	18 000
Capital Account: B	15 000	Sundry debtors	28 000
Sundry creditors	27 500	Other assets	8 500
		Goodwill	8 000
	£62 500		£62 500

Profits and losses are shared equally.

The debtors realised £27 000, other assets £9 500, and the Goodwill of the business was sold for £4 000. The expenses of liquidation amounted to £1 000.

Prepare the necessary accounts to show the result of the realisation as it would appear in the books of the firm, and the position of the two partners as regards the disposal of the balance of cash remaining after satisfying the firm's liabilities.

R.S.A. (adapted)

37

Limited Liability Companies

Companies have been the subject of legislation in the UK since the first Companies Act of 1855. They are now governed by the provisions of the Companies Act, 1948, as amended and extended by the Companies Act, 1967, the European Communities Act, 1972, and the Companies Act, 1976. There is likely to be further legislation in the 1980s. There is also a substantial body of case law on companies. Except where specifically stated, sections of the Companies Acts referred to in this chapter are in the Companies Act 1948.

As a form of business ownership, a company differs from the sole trader or partnership in that it is a corporate body sanctioned by Act of Parliament, and has a legal personality distinct from the persons comprising it. The company may sue and be sued in its own name in an action at law, and neither the death or bankruptcy of any of its members nor any change in the personnel of the membership affects its independent existence. Over 600 000 companies are in existence in the UK, and they are a popular form of business ownership because, with certain rare exceptions, the members are limited in their liability for the debts contracted by the company. The most that a member can lose if the company fails is the amount he has contributed or has agreed to contribute towards the capital of the company. This principle of *limited liability* has attracted investors who are willing to become part owners of a business under such conditions, and has made possible the formation of companies with very large capitals to carry on large-scale businesses. At the other extreme, many sole trading and partnership concerns have been converted into companies to take advantage of the limitation of liability.

A few companies have been incorporated by special Act of Parliament, as were British Railways, or by Royal Charter, like the Hudson Bay Company. Most were incorporated under the Companies Acts.

The reader must not assume that the word 'Company' as part of a firm name indicates that the concern is an incorporated company. A sole trader or partnership may adopt a title such as 'John Brown & Company' for trading purposes.

Three types of company may be formed under the Companies Act, 1948, namely:

(*a*) Companies limited by shares.

(*b*) Companies limited by guarantee.

(*c*) Companies with or without share capital, the liability of whose members is unlimited.

The first type is the most appropriate for business undertakings, and is the subject-matter of this chapter.

Memorandum of Association

Under the Companies Acts any seven or more persons may apply to be registered as a private company. The application is made in writing to the Registrar of Companies, and is in the form of a *Memorandum of Association* signed by the applicants, who are known as the *signatories*, and is accompanied by certain other documents required by the Act.

The Memorandum must state:

(*a*) *The name of the company with 'Limited' as the last word of its name.* The purpose of this is to inform all persons having dealings with the company of the fact that it is a limited liability company.

(*b*) *Whether the registered office of the company is to be situated in England or Scotland.* Later the company must register its address with the Registrar, and its registered office is the address for all notices and communications. The company's name must be affixed or painted in a conspicuous position on the outside of every place where the company carries on its business, and must be on all notices, advertisements, bills of exchange, cheques, orders, invoices and receipts. There is a penalty for default.

(*c*) *The Objects of the company.* These are normally fully stated. However, the former rule, which was derived from case law, that a company cannot legally undertake any business other than that set out in this clause of its Memorandum, has been over-ruled by one of the provisions of the European Communities Act, 1972.

(*d*) *That the liability of its members is limited.*

(*e*) *The amount of share capital with which the company proposes to be registered and the division thereof into shares of a fixed amount.* The capital as stated is known as the *authorised* (or *nominal*, or *registered*) *capital* of the company. The capital may be, say £10 000. The shares of fixed *nominal value* into which this is divided may be £1 shares or £0·25 shares or whatever value is agreed upon. If they are to be £1 shares then the capital, if £10 000, is made up of 10 000 shares of £1 each. The signatories to the memorandum must state opposite their names how many shares they propose to take up. It is seldom that more than one share each is taken up initially, and it is also only very infrequently that the number of signatories exceeds the minimum of seven, or two for a private company, required by the Act.

Articles of Association

Usually another document, called the *Articles of Association*, is also filed with the Registrar of Companies. This contains the regulations for the internal management and organisation of the company. If no such Articles are filed then the company is bound by the model set of regulations contained in the first schedule to the Companies Act, 1948, and known as Table A, except that a private company, as defined below, cannot adopt Table A without the amendment that is necessary to comply with the statutory definition of a private company.

These documents, properly stamped, are lodged with the Registrar of Companies, who on accepting the registration, issues a *Certificate of Incorporation*. A private company may then commence business, but a public company has only power to issue a prospectus, i.e. an invitation to the public to subscribe for shares. Certain other formalities are necessary before a public company may commence to trade.

Private Companies

A 'private company' is a company which by its articles:

1. Restricts the right to transfer its shares.
2. Limits the number of its members to a maximum of fifty, excluding employees who may be members and ex-employees who became members whilst so employed and continue to be members.
3. Prohibits any invitation to the public to subscribe for any shares or debentures of the company.

As mentioned above, two or more persons as against seven or more in the case of a public company, may apply to form a private company. Private companies are a popular form of ownership, especially for small businesses and family concerns, and many sole trading and partnership firms have been converted into private companies in order to take advantage of the limitation of liability. However, other factors, such as taxation, have to be considered also. Furthermore, the advantage of limited liability may be restricted for the owner of a small business if banks, or others considering whether to lend to him, insist that he *personally* guarantees any loan or other credit extended to his company.

Except for the restrictions above mentioned the remarks hereafter apply equally to public and private companies.

Directors

The members of a company have no right to share in the management of the company and cannot bind the company or fellow members in any way. The business is conducted by *Directors* whose activities are governed by the provisions of the company's Articles of Association. The first directors are appointed by the signatories to the Memorandum of Association or by being declared as such in the Articles of Association. The Articles of Association usually fix a minimum share qualification (i.e. a minimum number of shares that must be held) for each director; but unless the Articles make such a provision a director need not necessarily hold any share qualification. The directors are known, collectively, as the *Board of Directors* and usually have power to fill any casual vacancies in their number. One of their number is elected to be the Chairman. There are also special responsibilities attaching to the post of Managing Director. These posts differ in that the office of Managing Director has executive responsibilities, but the office of Chairman does not. The Articles usually contain a clause to the effect that one or more of the Board shall retire annually but shall be eligible for re-election for a further period. Many Boards are composed of four or five directors, but large companies may have many more. The Articles state the maximum number and also set out the arrangements which govern their remuneration.

Annual Meeting and Directors' Report

Under Section 131 of the 1948 Act every company must hold a general meeting of its members once at least in every calendar year, and not more than fifteen months after the holding of the last preceding general meeting. At the general meeting the directors, by Section 148 of the 1948 Act, must lay before the company a Profit and Loss Account made up to date not more than nine months earlier than the date of the meeting, and also a Balance Sheet as at the date to which the Profit and Loss Account is made up. To every Balance Sheet must be attached a report by the directors on the state of the company's affairs, and the amount, if any, which they recommend should be paid as dividend, and the amount, if any, which they propose to carry to reserve, together with the auditors' report. The *dividend* is the distribution of the profits of the company which is made to the members in proportion to their holdings in the share capital, and in accordance with the provisions of the Articles of Association.

It is at this annual general meeting that the election or re-election of directors takes place.

The Prospectus and the Kinds of Capital

Immediately after the formation of the company the directors have to consider the question of obtaining capital. A public company may invite subscriptions from the public. The invitation takes the form of a *prospectus*, in which general particulars regarding the company are set out and a formal invitation is made to the public to subscribe for the shares on the terms stated. Private companies and small public companies may obtain capital from relatives, friends, or business acquaintances of the owners, or the capital may be contributed by the signatories only, but private companies may not offer shares for public subscription.

As the prospectus is the basis of the contract between the company and the shareholder, the Act contains very strict provisions regarding prospectuses to safeguard the public as far as possible from fraud. A copy of the prospectus, dated and signed by the directors, must be filed with the Registrar of Companies on or before the date of publication.

The prospectuses are distributed to possible subscribers, and among banks and stockbrokers for their clients. As a further means of publicity, press advertising of abridged copies of the prospectus may be undertaken. The full prospectus must contain a copy of the company's Memorandum of Association.

For the use of subscribers an application form for the shares accompanies each prospectus. The required particulars are to be filled in, and the form, together with the first instalment on each share, known as the *application money*, is to be handed in to the company's bankers.

The capital of the company mentioned in the Memorandum of Association is the maximum amount which it has authority to issue. The directors may decide that not all of the *authorised capital* is needed immediately, and may offer part only for immediate subscription. The shares applied for may exceed, or may be less than, the number offered. In the former case an issue is said to be 'over-subscribed', and the directors have to find some way of reducing the applications. If fewer are subscribed for than offered, the issue is said to be 'under-subscribed'. (It is obvious that unless at least a certain minimum, varying according to circumstances, is subscribed, the company may be handicapped for want of funds and may find it impossible to commence trading or, having commenced, to continue to trade. However, public issues of shares by companies in this way are now unusual. A very small number of private companies goes public in any one year by making a public issue. Existing public companies making an issue normally do so by way of a *rights issue* to their existing members on advantageous terms.) The prospectus of any offer of shares must state the minimum subscription on which the directors will proceed to allotment and each subscriber makes his application for shares on the assumption that such minimum will be obtained before allotment. The Companies Acts impose penalties on directors for allotments made where the minimum subscription has not been received, and such allotments may be repudiated by the subscribers within one month after a special meeting known as the *Statutory meeting* of the company. Section 47 of the 1948 Act provides that where the minimum subscription has not been received within forty days after the first issue of the prospectus the directors must refund the application money without interest, and after forty-eight days the directors are personally liable for the repayment with interest at five per cent per annum.

It follows that the uncertainty which this possibility creates constitutes a severe handicap to genuine business propositions. Consequently a third party, known as an *underwriter*, is usually approached to guarantee that the minimum subscription shall be made. The underwriter is a financier who undertakes to subscribe for all shares in the offer not otherwise subscribed in consideration of a commission based on the number of shares underwritten. If 100 000 shares of £1 each are underwritten, and only 90 000 are subscribed, the underwriter must personally subscribe for 10 000 shares. Against the cost of these shares he will receive his commission on the whole 100 000 shares underwritten by him.

In most instances the shares applied for are payable by instalments. The first instalment, which must not be less than five per cent of the nominal value of the share, is paid on *application*. The second instalment is paid on *allotment* of the shares to the applicant, and the remainder, if any, at times decided by the directors, which may or may not be specifically mentioned in the prospectus. Such remaining instalments are known as *Calls*. It is usual to give shareholders fourteen days' notice by a Call Letter that a call is due.

The total amount paid up on the shares at any given date is referred to as the *paid-up capital* of the company, and the shares are *fully-paid* shares when the instalments have been paid.

The directors may decide not to call up the final instalment until such time that further working capital is required. Meanwhile the paid-up capital will be less than the subscribed capital by the amount of *uncalled capital*. The paid up capital may not, however, agree with the actual amount of *called-up* capital. Not all the calls may be met at due date by shareholders, and such outstanding instalments are referred to as *Calls in arrear*. Other instances arise where the shareholder pays the instalments before the due date, and these are known as *Calls in advance*.

The following example illustrates the various terms referred to above as applied to the capital of a company.

Example 49. Brown & Fox Limited is registered with a nominal capital of £1 200 000 divided into 120 000 shares of £10 each. 80 000 shares were offered to the public, and were fully subscribed. By 30th June, 19. ., £5 per share on application and allotment, and the first call of £2·50 per share had been paid up except for the call of £2·50 on 2 000 shares, held by L.T. Green, which remained unpaid.

In this example:

	£
The Authorised or Nominal Registered Capital is	1 200 000
The Issued Capital	800 000
The Subscribed Capital	800 000
The Called-up Capital	600 000
The Paid-up Capital	595 000
The Uncalled Capital	200 000
The Calls in Arrear	5 000

Various Classes of Shares

Though the capital of a company is divided into shares of fixed amount, the capital may comprise groups or classes of shares distinguished according to the rights and privileges attaching to each class. The three principal classes are Preference Shares, Ordinary Shares, and Deferred Shares.

Preference Shares usually carry the right to a fixed dividend from the profits each year before any other class is paid a dividend. In some cases preference shares have not only the prior right to dividend but also first claim to return of capital in the event of liquidation.

Ordinary Shares usually have no special dividend rights. The holders are entitled to the surplus profits remaining after the fixed dividend has been paid on the Preference Shares, subject to the right of the Deferred Shares, if any, to participate in any distribution above a given amount or percentage.

Deferred Shares rank for dividend only after the other classes have received payment of dividend. Where deferred shares exist the dividend payable on the ordinary shares may be fixed or the ordinary shares may be given prior right up to a certain amount and thereafter be entitled to share in any balance with the deferred shareholders.

Preference shares may be *cumulative* or *non-cumulative*. With Cumulative Preference Shares the arrears of dividend, if any, consequent on insufficient profits to pay the dividend in any year, are carried forward. The current dividend and all arrears must be paid before any distribution may be made to the subordinate classes of shares. Non-cumulative Preference Shares carry no right to payment of arrears of dividend. Unless the Articles of Association state otherwise, Preference Shares are assumed to be cumulative.

Participating Preference Shares carry an additional right to a fixed share in the profits over and above the fixed dividend, after the payment of a fixed dividend on the subordinate classes of shares.

There are also many instances of gradations of Preference Shares, such as First Preference and Second Preference Shares. In all cases, the basis is the order in which dividend is payable. An example is the Preferred Ordinary Shares which rank for dividend after the Preference Shares but before the Ordinary Shares. The classification is made to encourage investors of all temperaments since some wish for safety and a fixed rate of dividend from year to year, and others are less anxious and are attracted by the larger dividend that is usual on the Ordinary Shares.

Redeemable Preference Shares are a class permitted to be issued under the Companies Act. By Section 58 a company may issue redeemable Preference Shares, if so authorised by its Articles, but the shares may be redeemed only if fully paid and only out of profits which would otherwise be available for dividend or out of the proceeds of a fresh issue of shares made for the purpose of the redemption. If redemption is to be made from the profits of the company, a sum equal to the amount to be applied in redeeming the shares must be set aside out of profits to a reserve fund called the 'Capital Redemption Reserve Fund.' Any premium on redemption must also be provided for out of the profits before redemption.

The relative proportions of the different types of capital give an indication of what is known as the company's *gearing* (or *leverage*). The higher the proportion of preference shares to the total capital, the higher the gearing. High gearing is suitable only for secure companies, since the varying levels of profit in a risky business might lead to inability to meet the company's dividend commitments. In other words, gearing must reflect the risk facing the company. This is discussed further in Chapter 40.

Distinguishing Numbers and Share Certificates

Each share in a company having a share capital is usually distinguished by its appropriate number. Where shares are numbered consecutively, the numbers must be stated on the Share Certificates to which each shareholder is entitled. The share certificate is usually signed by two directors and the secretary, and bears the seal of the company. It certifies that the person named therein is the registered proprietor of the stated number of shares, and mentions the distinguishing numbers of such shares. The company must have such certificates ready for delivery within two months after the shares have been allotted, unless the conditions of issue otherwise provide.

The shareholder may transfer his shares to another person who then takes over all the rights and obligations, including the liability for outstanding calls, of the previous holder. Such transfer must be in writing and in proper form. Printed forms of transfer are obtainable from law stationers. The company must have the new certificate made out in the new member's name ready for delivery within two months from the date on which the transfer was lodged with the company.

The shares of most public companies are marketable, and those of many companies may be bought and sold on the Stock Exchange. In other cases the shares can be disposed of only by private treaty, and if the prospects of the company are not bright it may be difficult to find a purchaser. A shareholder can realise his investment only by sale. He cannot demand the return of his invested capital from the company, and only under rigid and special conditions set out in the Companies Acts may a company make any return of capital to shareholders.

The price which a shareholder may obtain for his shares depends upon the prospects of future dividends, the financial standing of the company, and the value the intending purchaser places upon these. The holder may have subscribed £1 for each £1 share, but that does not determine the selling value at a later time. The shares may be worth more or less in the market than their nominal value. The selling price concerns only the buyer and seller. The company is not affected other than to record the change in the ownership of shares bearing certain distinguishing numbers.

It will be seen that a person may become a member of a company by signing the Memorandum on its formation, or by applying for and being allotted shares, or by the transfer of shares to him by an existing shareholder.

The Statutory Books of a Company

Every company must keep certain books of record in addition to proper books of account relating to its trading activities. Also, many periodical returns to the Registrar of Companies have to be made.

The Register of Members. Under Section 110 of the Act every company must keep in one or more books a register of its members, and enter therein the following particulars:

The names and addresses of the members.

A statement of the shares held by each member, distinguishing each share by its number (as long as the shares are numbered), and of the amount paid or agreed to be considered as paid on the shares of each member.

The date at which each person was entered as a member in the register.

The date at which any person ceased to be a member.

Every company having more than fifty members must keep an index of the names of the members unless the register of members is in a form as to constitute in itself an index. It may be a card index, and any necessary alteration in the index consequent on an alteration in the register must be made within fourteen days.

The register of members and the index must be kept at the company's registered office or office where the work is done, and must be available for inspection for not less than two hours each day during business hours.

There is no special form of register. It is sufficient if the ruling permits of the entry of the above information. In practice it is usual to find the Register of Members combined with the Share Ledger to which reference is made in a later chapter.

The register may be closed for a period not exceeding thirty days in the year on giving notice by advertisement. The purpose is to allow time for the preparation of the dividend lists. Most companies close their register for fourteen days prior to the date of the Annual General Meeting. Where there are different classes of shares, it is usually more convenient to have separate registers of each class of shareholders.

Annual Return. Under Section 124 of the 1948 Act, every company having a share capital must once at least in every year make a return containing a list of all persons who, on the fourteenth day after the first or only ordinary general meeting in the year, are members of the company, and of all persons who have ceased to be members since the date of the last return. The list must state the names and addresses of all these persons, the shares held by them, the shares transferred since the last return, and the date of transfer. The company's registered address must be stated, and a complete summary of the company's capital must be given. The particulars required are given in Section 124 of the 1948 Act as extended/amended by the 1967 Act, and in Schedules to these Acts. Forms suitably printed containing all the particulars required may be purchased from company or law stationers, and are used for the purpose of making the copy required to be forwarded annually to the Registrar of Companies. The actual return itself must be contained in a separate part of the Register of Members. The return must include a Profit and Loss Account and Balance Sheet, and Directors' Report, all conforming to the requirements of the Companies Acts.

Minute Book. Under Section 145 of the Act every company shall cause minutes of all proceedings of general meetings and all proceedings of directors' meetings to be entered in books kept for that purpose.

Members have the right to inspect the minutes of the general meetings of the shareholders and to receive copies of the minutes at a specified charge.

Register of Directors or Managers. Under Section 200 every company shall keep at its registered office a register of its directors or managers containing full names, residential address, nationality, and occupation of each director or manager, and shall notify the Registrar of any change within fourteen days.

Register of Mortgages and Charges. Under Sections 95 to 106 every limited company shall keep at its registered office a register of charges and enter therein all charges specifically affecting the company's property and all floating charges and the names of the persons entitled thereto. Every such mortgage or charge and all releases therefrom must be registered with the Registrar of Companies.

EXERCISES 37

1. State briefly the difference between (*a*) The Authorised Capital and the Issued Capital of a Limited Liability Company; (*b*) Preference Shares and Ordinary Shares in a Limited Liability Company.

2. What is meant by:

(*a*) The Memorandum of Association;

(*b*) The Articles of Association;
of a Joint Stock Company?

3. In what ways does a *Private* Limited Liability Company differ from a *Public* Limited Liability Company?

4. What is gearing?

5. What must be shown in:

(*a*) The Register of Members,

(*b*) The Annual Return
of a Joint Stock Company?

38

Company Accounts. Share Capital and the Issue of Shares

The prospectus makes an offer of shares for subscription, and contains particulars regarding the number and kind of shares offered, and the way in which the shares may be paid for. The usual method is to accept payment by instalments through the company's bankers with whom it may be arranged that a special temporary account shall be opened to keep the payments separate from the ordinary banking account. The special Bank Statement is a help in checking the receipts, and the work of the share department does not affect the routine of the accounting department. Similar arrangements apply in the case of a rights issue to existing members.

The period during which applications may be received is limited, and for a first issue is fixed by Section 47 of the 1948 Act to forty days, so that the response to the offer may be known and the applications dealt with as a whole. The application forms are first checked against the Bank Statement and the total number of shares applied for is ascertained. If the offer is over-subscribed the directors must decide the method to adopt to reduce the applications to the limits of the offer. A proportionate reduction of all applications may answer the purpose, or individual applications for only a small number of shares may be declined.

The next step is to allot the shares to the applicants. *Allotment* is the formal act of the directors expressed in a resolution that the shares be allotted to the applicants in accordance with the allotment list which is prepared and submitted to the meeting. The allotment list shows the names, addresses, and occupations of the applicants, the number of shares alloted to each of them, and the balance due on the shares. The applicants are notified by an Allotment Letter that the shares have been allotted to them, and the posting of these letters signifies the acceptance by the company of the offer of the applicants to take the shares. The contract between the applicant and the company is then complete, and the applicants, once allotment is made, become shareholders in the company and are liable for the balance due on the shares.

The allotment letter states the number of shares allotted, the sum already paid, the sum due upon allotment, and concludes with a request that the latter sum be paid immediately.

The applicants for shares to whom no allotment is made have their application money returned in full. Applicants who are allotted a smaller number of shares than they applied for do not have part of their money returned to them. The amount they have overpaid on application is carried forwards towards the amount due from them on allotment.

Within one month the company must make a return of allotments to the Registrar of Companies, a document stating full particulars of the *allottees*, the number and nominal value of the shares allotted, and the amount paid or due and payable on each share.

If no allotment can be made to an applicant he is notified to this effect by a *Letter of Regret*, and his application money is returned.

Entries in the Accounts

The financial aspect of the issue of shares must be recorded, and the entries required are illustrated in Example 50.

The issue of Ordinary Shares only is illustrated. If the capital of a company is divided into several classes of shares, for example, Ordinary, Preference, and Deferred Shares, and a public issue were made of each, then separate accounts in the following form would be required for each class of shares. The company would have separate Registers of Members and Share Ledgers for each class of share.

Example 50. Wilkes and Boon Limited was registered with a nominal capital of £10 000 000 divided into 10 000 000 ordinary shares of £1 each. 8 000 000 shares are offered for public subscription on June 1st, 19. ., payable by instalments as follows:

£0·25 a share on application;
£0·25 a share on allotment;
£0·25 a share one month after allotment;
£0·25 a share two months after allotment.

All the shares offered were subscribed and allotted, and the application and allotment money received.

Show the entries required in the company's books to record the issue and allotment.

The first financial effect of the offer and subscription is the receipt of the application money. This is debited to the Cash Book. Often it is more convenient to use a temporary Shareholders' Cash Book. The credit entry is made to an *Application and Allotment Account* in the Ledger as shown below.

The allotment is made and the allotment letters are posted. The instalments due on allotment are received and the entries required are similar to those for the application money. These also are shown below.

Cash Book

19..			£	19..			£
June 1	Application and Allotment Account being instalments of £0·25 a share on application.	1	2 000 000				
,, 8	Application and Allotment Account being instalments of £0·25 a share on allotment.	1	2 000 000				

1

Application and Allotment Account

19..			£	19..			£
				June 1	Cash: Application instalments	CB	2 000 000
				,, 8	Cash: Allotment instalments	CB	2 000 000

Had too many applications been received, the excess would have been returned. In the accounts above the cash on application would have been a larger sum. On the return of the excess cash the Cash

Book is credited and the Application and Allotment Account debited with the amount returned.

As the contract to take shares is completed by the posting of the allotment letters, the allottees are then actual shareholders, and the instalments paid by them are contributions towards the company's capital. At this point it is necessary to record that fact, which is done by transferring the balance of the Application and Allotment Account to a *Share Capital Account* in the Ledger. The effect is to close the Application and Allotment Account, which has served the purpose of a temporary resting place for the items, and to open, for the first time, a Capital Account in the Ledger. The transfer is recorded in a Journal entry.

Journal

			Dr.	*Cr.*
19..			£	£
June 5	Application and Allotment Account	1	4 000 000	
	Ordinary Share Capital Account	2		4 000 000
	being £0·25 a share on application, and and £0·25 a share on allotment on 8 000 000 ordinary £1 shares by resolution of directors on 5th June, 19...			

2

Ordinary Share Capital Account

19..			£	19..			£
				June 5	Application and Allotment A/c	J	4 000 000

1

Application and Allotment Account

19..			£	19..			£
June 5	Ordinary Share Capital Account	J	4 000 000	June 1	Cash: Application instalments	CB	2 000 000
				,, 8	Cash: Allotment instalments	CB	2 000 000
			£4 000 000				£4 000 000

It is, of course, essential to keep a record of the liability of the company to its members for the contributions each has made towards the capital of the company. The Ordinary Share Capital Account, as above, represents the total of the individual contributions; details are entered in the *Share Ledger*, a subsidiary book in which an account is kept for each contributor.

The Register of Members, mentioned in the preceding chapter, is usually ruled to contain Ledger Accounts as well as the particulars required as a register proper. Actually the Register is a combined Share Ledger and Register of Members, and it is in these Shareholders' Ledger Accounts that the individual contributions towards the company's capital are recorded. The Share Capital Account in the Ledger is a totals account, the details of which are to be found in the Share Ledger. It would be inconvenient to have a large number of individual Capital Accounts in the general Ledger, as the changes may be frequent and the Ledger would then be in constant demand for this purpose alone, to the exclusion of its use for general purposes.

Calls

The third and fourth instalments in the above example are due on certain dates. If no date is given in the prospectus for the payment of the remaining instalments, they are payable at the discretion of the directors who are said to 'make a call' on the shareholders. It is usual for the Articles to provide that any one call should not exceed 25 per cent of the nominal value of the share, and for calls to be made at an interval of not less than one month.

The procedure in making a call is that the directors pass a resolution to the effect that a call be made, and send a *Call Letter* to the shareholders, giving, usually, fourteen days notice to pay the instalment due on their shares.

First Call

The passing of this resolution creates a liability on the part of the shareholders for the amount. An entry is made to the credit of the Share Capital Account and to the debit of a new account, the *First Call Account*. It is recorded in the Journal.

As the cash is received from the shareholders the Cash Book is debited and the First Call Account is credited. The Call Account will show at any time whether all the calls have been received.

The total entered in the Share Capital Account must be entered in detail in the shareholders' accounts in the Share Ledger so that the position of each shareholder is on record.

The entries for the first call are shown below:

Journal

19..			£	£
July 5	First Call Account	3	2 000 000	
	Ordinary Share Capital Account	2		2 000 000
	being first call of £0·25 a share on 8 000 000 Ordinary £1 shares by the terms of the issue.			

2

Ordinary Share Capital Account

19..			£	19..			£
				June 5	Application and Allotment A/c	J	4 000 000
				July 5	First Call Account	J	2 000 000

3

First Call Account

19..			£	19..			£
July 5	Ordinary Share Capital A/c	J	2 000 000	July 10	Cash	CB	2 000 000

Dr. **Cash Book** *Cr.*

19..			£	19..			£
June 1	Application and Allotment A/c, being instalments of £0·25 a share on application	1	2 000 000				
„ 8	Application and Allotment A/c, being instalments of £0·25 a share on allotment	1	2 000 000				

July 10	First Call A/c. being first call of £0·25 a share	3	2 000 000				

Final Call and Calls in Arrear

At due date of subsequent instalments, or on the directors resolving that a second or final call be made, the full amount is debited to a *Second* or *Final Call Account*, and is credited to the Share Capital Account.

Suppose that a holder of 50 000 shares fails to pay the final call of £0·25 per share. The cash receipts will be £12 500 less in consequence, and the amount outstanding will appear as a balance on the Call Account, remaining as such until payment is made or the directors decide to forfeit the shares, i.e. to advise the debtor that he is no longer considered to be the owner of the shares. The procedure and entries for forfeiture are beyond the scope of this book.

For the final call of the above example the entries would be:

Journal

			Dr.	*Cr.*
19..			£	£
Aug. 5	Second and Final Call Account	4	2 000 000	
	Ordinary Share Capital Account	2		2 000 000
	being second and final call of £0·25 a share on 8 000 000 shares by the terms of the issue			

Ordinary Share Capital Account

19..			£	19..			£
				June 5	Application and Allotment A/c	J	4 000 000
				July 5	First Call A/c	J	2 000 000
				Aug. 5	Second and Final Call A/c	J	2 000 000

Second and Final Call Account

19..				19..			£
Aug. 5	Ordinary Share Capital A/c	J	2 000 000	Aug. 15	Cash	CB	1 987 500
				,, 15	Balance	c/d	12 500
			£2 000 000				£2 000 000
Aug. 16	Balance	b/d	12 500				

Dr. **Cash Book** *Cr.*

19..			£	19..			£
June 1	Application and Allotment A/c, being instalments of £0·25 a share on application	1	2 000 000				
,, 8	Application and Allotment A/c, being being instalments of £0·25 a share on allotment	1	2 000 000				
July 10	First Call A/c, being first call of £0·25 a share	3	2 000 000				
Aug. 15	Second and Final Call Account, being final call of £0·25 a share	4	1 987 500				

If the calls are still in arrear at the date of the preparation of the Balance Sheet and the shares have not yet been forfeited, it will be necessary to take them into account as debts due to the company. The practice is to show them in the Balance Sheet as the deduction from the liability to which they relate, and not as an asset.

The capital in the above example will therefore appear in the Balance Sheet as below. It should be observed that the Balance Sheet presents to the shareholders full information regarding the capital of the company. The issued capital is the only actual capital claim against the company. The authorised or nominal capital is given as background information only.

Balance Sheet. Wilkes & Boon Limited
(Showing claims side only)

	£	£
AUTHORISED CAPITAL		
10 000 000 Ordinary Shares of £1 each	10 000 000	
ISSUED CAPITAL		
8 000 000 Ordinary Shares of £1 each fully called	8 000 000	
less Calls in arrear	12 500	
		7 987 500

The Balance Sheet of a company having different classes of shares should show each class of share separately.

Uncalled Capital

The directors may decide not to make calls until such times as the extra capital is needed, but as shares with a liability for calls are not popular as investments, the practice is infrequent. Section 60 of the 1948 Act provides that a company may, by special resolution, determine that the uncalled portion of its share capital shall not be capable of being called up except in the event and for the purposes of the company being wound up.

Calls in Advance

A company may be empowered by its Articles to accept calls in advance, and to pay a fixed rate of interest on them. Such calls paid in advance of the general call being made are loans to the company at interest, and the interest is payable even though the company may have no profits.

Example 51. A shareholder, Thomas Haynes, when making payment on 1st July of the first call, paid in advance the remaining instalment of £0·25 a share on 20 000 £1 shares.

The payment in advance of £5 000 is debited to the Cash Book and credited to a *Calls in Advance Account.*

Calls in Advance Account

19..			£	19..			£
				July 1	Cash:		
					T. Haynes	CB	5 000

When the directors make the call, the payment ceases to be in advance and becomes the shareholder's current instalment. A debit entry is then made to the Calls in Advance Account, which is thus closed, and a corresponding credit entry is made in the Share Capital Account.

Should a Balance Sheet be prepared before the call is made, the call paid in advance will appear under that heading on the claims side.

Such interest is usually paid half-yearly and should be recorded as follows:

Journal

			Dr.	*Cr.*
19..			£	£
Jan. 1	Interest Account		125	
	Thomas Haynes			125
	being interest at 5% per annum on calls paid in advance for half-year to 31st December.			
	(Income Tax ignored)			

These entries will be posted to the respective Ledger Accounts. The payment by cheque will be credited to Cash and debited to Thomas Haynes's Account. The payment closes the shareholder's account and the balance of the Interest Account is transferred to the Profit and Loss Account on closing the books for the financial year.

EXERCISES 38

1. The Manchester Goods Company Limited, whose registered capital is 8 000 000 Ordinary Shares of £1 each, offered on 1st July, 5 000 000 shares for public subscription, payable £0·15 a share on application and £0·85 on allotment.

All the shares were applied for and allotment was made on 16th July, and all the money was received by the company.

Make the entries to record the issue of the shares in the company's books, and show the statement of the company's capital in its Balance Sheet.

2. Godfrey & Co. Limited, registered with a capital of £1 200 000, comprising 120 000 Ordinary Shares of £10 each, offered 100 000 shares on 1st April for public subscription, payable £2·50 a share on application and £7·50 on allotment. All the shares were applied for and were allotted on 15th April. The cash was duly received.

Show the entries required to record the issue in the books of the company, and show how the capital would appear in the company's Balance Sheet.

3. Godfrey & Co. Limited, whose registered capital consists of £1 200 000 divided into 120 000 Ordinary Shares of £10 each, of which 100 000 shares have been issued, decide to issue the balance of its shares for public subscription on 1st October. The shares were payable, as to £1·25 a share on application, £3·75 a share on allotment, and £5·00 a share one month after allotment.

Record the issue in the company's books, all the shares being subscribed and allotted, and all instalments being paid at their due dates.

Show also the capital of the company as it would appear in its Balance Sheet.

4. Gilbert's Stores Limited was registered with a nominal capital of £750 000 divided into 750 000 Ordinary Shares of £1 each. Of these shares, 600 000 were offered for public subscription on 1st November, payable as to £0·15 a share on application, £0·25 a share on allotment, and the balance one month after allotment. Show the entries required to record the issue in the books of the company on the basis that the whole of the issue was subscribed and allotted and all the cash received. Show also the capital as it would appear in the company's Balance Sheet.

5. Richard's Stores Limited, registered with a nominal capital of £5 000 000 consisting of 5 000 000 Ordinary Shares of £1 each, make a public issue on 15th March of 4 000 000 shares, payable as below:

On application, £0·15 a share.
On allotment, £0·35 a share.
On 30th April, £0·25 a share.
On 30th June, £0·25 a share.

All the shares were applied for and allotted on 30th March, and all cash was received on allotment and for the two calls. Make the entries required to record the issue in the company's books, and show the capital as it should appear in the company's Balance Sheet.

6. Richmond & Co. Limited, registered with a capital of £6 000 000 in 6 000 000 Ordinary Shares of £1 each, offer for public subscription on 1st June, 5 000 000 shares payable as follows:

£0·15 a share on application.
£0·35 a share on allotment.
£0·25 a share one month after allotment.
£0·25 a share two months later.

All the shares were subscribed for and allotted on 15th June, and all the cash received on allotment and for the two calls. Give the entries that are necessary to record the issue in the company's books, and show the company's capital as it should appear in its Balance Sheet.

7. Richmond & Kew Limited, registered with a capital of £150 000 divided into 150 000 Ordinary Shares of £1 each, offer, on 1st January, 120 000 shares for public subscription, the terms of payment being:

£0·15 a share on application.
£0·35 a share on allotment.
£0·25 a share on 15th February.
£0·25 on 15th March.

All the shares on offer were subscribed for and allotted, and all the money on application, allotment and for both calls were received, with the exception of the final call of £0·25 a share on 2 000 shares allotted to Henry Watson.

Give the entries required to record the issue in the books of the company and show the capital as it would appear in the company's Balance Sheet.

8. Gillingham & Sons Limited was registered with a capital of £400 000, consisting of 400 000 shares of £1 each. An offer of 300 000 shares was made for public subscription on 1st May, payable as to £0·15 a share on application, £0·35 a share on allotment, and £0·50 a share one month after allotment.

All the shares were subscribed for and allotted on 15th May, and all the cash due on allotment and for the final instalment was received, with the exception of the call of £0·50 a share on 15 000 shares allotted to James Chatham.

Record the issue in the company's books, and show the capital as it should appear in the company's Balance Sheet.

9. Bedford & Luton Limited was registered with a capital of £100 000, comprising 40 000 6% Preference Shares of £1 each, and 60 000 Ordinary Shares of £1 each. All the Preference Shares and 50 000 Ordinary Shares were offered for public subscription on 1st October, payable in each case as follows:

£0·15 a share on application.
£0·35 a share on allotment.
£0·50 a share on 1st December.

All the shares were subscribed for and allotted on 15th October, and the allotment money and the first call paid on due date.

Make the required entries in the books of the company, and show the company's capital as it would appear in the Balance Sheet.

10. Kent & Essex Limited, registered with a capital of £5 000 000 in 40 000 Ordinary Shares of £10 each and 4 600 000 6% Preference Shares of £1 each, offer for public subscription all the Preference Shares and 30 000 Ordinary Shares on 1st March, payable in each case as to 12½% on application, 37½% on allotment and 50% on 1st May.

All the shares offered were subscribed for and allotted on 15th March, and the allotment money received. In addition, B. Bryson and W. Tanner who subscribed for 400 Ordinary Shares and 600 Ordinary Shares respectively, paid the final instalment of £5 a share with their allotment instalment. Make the entries in the company's books as at allotment, and show how the capital of the company would then appear in its Balance Sheet.

11. Explain the difference in treatment in the books of account between (*a*) a Partner's Capital Account, and (*b*) a Share Capital Account of a company limited by shares.

R.S.A.

39

The Issue of Shares at a Premium or a Discount

The Issue of Shares at a Premium

When the market price of a company's shares is *above par* (i.e. above their nominal value) the amount by which the market price exceeds the nominal value of the share is termed the *premium*.

When new shares of the same class are issued, they are very often issued at a premium approximately equal to the premium at which the already issued shares stand. This would bring to the company a sum over and above the nominal value of the issue, which would increase its financial resources but is not part of its issued share capital. The premiums are in the nature of a capital gain, and under the Companies Acts must be transferred to an account called the *Share Premium Account*.

This account is considered to be part of the company's long-term ownership capital and may only be reduced under the following circumstances:

(*a*) In writing off the *preliminary expenses* of the company. The nature of these expenses is explained on page 442.

(*b*) In writing off any expenses or commission paid, or discount allowed, on the issue of any shares or *debentures* of the company. The nature of debentures is explained in Chapter 40.

(*c*) In providing for the premium payable on redeeming any of the company's redeemable preference shares or debentures.

(*d*) If not used in any of these ways the Share Premium Account may be used for issuing *bonus shares*. An issue of bonus shares is a 'capitalisation of reserves'. A company which has traded successfully may show substantial reserves in its balance sheet as a result of retaining profits in the business as was described in Chapter 20. The ploughing back of these profits into the business is likely to increase future profits. This is likely to cause the market price of the shares to rise. If additional shares are *given* to all existing members in exact proportion to their existing shareholdings (e.g. one new share for every three old ones) then the shareholders each have more shares, but the price of each of them is lower than the price of each old share before the bonus issue.

A bonus issue has the appearance of a gift, but it is a gift with no real substance.

In the books of the company the entries are to debit the Reserve Accounts (including, where appropriate, the Share Premium Account) and to credit the Share Capital Account. There is no entry in the Cash Book as no payment is made for the shares.

So long as there is any balance left to the credit of the Share Premium Account it must be shown as a separate item in the Balance Sheet.

Should the premium be used for writing down any of the items allowed in the Act, the writing down is effected by a credit entry to the Expense Account and a corresponding debit entry to the Share Premium Account. The entry is first passed through the Journal.

Example 52. Wilkes and Boon Limited, whose nominal capital is 10 000 000 Ordinary Shares of £1 each, of which 8 000 000 shares have been issued and fully paid up, decide to offer the unissued capital for the subscription at £1·50 a share, payable as to £0·25 a share on application, £1·00 a share (including the premium of £0·50 a share) on allotment, and £0·25 a share two months after allotment.

All the shares were subscribed and were allotted on 5th July. The allotment money was paid by 8th July and the calls by 8th September.

In the example, as is usual in practice, the premium is payable with the instalment due on allotment. A combined Journal entry is made for the allotment instalment and the premium.

The entries for the application and allotment instalments and the final call follow the procedure already illustrated. The new point is the treatment of the premium on the shares.

The following are the entries required:

Journal

			Dr.	*Cr.*
19..			£	£
July 5	Application and Allotment Account	2	2 500 000	
	Ordinary Share Capital Account	1		1 500 000
	Premium on Ordinary Shares Account	3		1 000 000
	being £0·25 a share on application and £1·00 per share, including £0·50 premium a share, on allotment on 2 000 000 Ordinary £1 shares allotted by resolution of Directors dated 5th July, 19. . .			
Sept. 8	First and Final Call Account	4	500 000	
	Ordinary Share Capital Account	1		500 000
	being first and final call of £0·25 a share on 2 000 000 shares by terms of issue.			

Below are the Ledger Accounts for the new issue, the new account being the Premium on Ordinary Shares Account in which the premium is recorded. (See below and on pages 423–4).

1

Ordinary Share Capital Account

19..			£	19..			£
Sept. 8	Balance	c/d	10 000 000	Jan. 1	Balance (original issue)	b/d	8 000 000
				July 5	Application and Allotment A/c (New issue)	J	1 500 000
				Sept. 8	First and Final Call A/c (new issue)	J	500 000
			£10 000 000				£10 000 000
				Sept. 8	Balance	b/d	10 000 000

2

Application and Allotment Account

19..			£	19..			£
July 5	Ordinary Share Capital Account	J	1 500 000	July 6	Cash: Application instalment	CB	500 000
	Premium on Shares A/c	J	1 000 000	,, 8	Cash: Allotment instalment and premium	CB	2 000 000
			£2 500 000				£2 500 000

3

Premium on Ordinary Shares Account

19..			£	19..			£
				July 8	Application and Allotment A/c	J	1 000 000

4

Dr. **Cash Book** *Cr.*

19..			£	19..			£
July 6	Application and Allotment A/c	2	500 000				
July 8	Application and Allotment A/c being £0·50 a share on allotment and £0·50 a share premium	2	2 000 000				
Sept. 8	First and Final Call Account	4	500 000				

4

First and Final Call Account

19..			£	19..			£
Sept. 8	Ordinary Share Capital Account	J	500 000	Sept. 8	Cash	CB	500 000

The capital of the company and the premium will appear in the Balance Sheet as below:

Balance Sheet, Wilkes & Boon Limited
(Showing claims side only)

	£	£
AUTHORISED CAPITAL		
10 000 000 Ordinary Shares of £1 each	10 000 000	
ISSUED CAPITAL		
10 000 000 Ordinary Shares of £1 each, fully paid		10 000 000
Premium on Ordinary Shares		1 000 000

The Issue of Shares at a Discount

Section 57 of the Companies Act, 1948, provides for companies to issue shares at a discount. This provision is of value to a company whose issued shares stand at a discount as in such circumstances it is normally impossible to obtain subscriptions to a further issue of shares at par value. The section, however, imposes the following restrictions:

The proposed issue must be of a class of share already issued, and must be authorised by resolution passed in general meeting of the company, and must be sanctioned by the High Court.

The resolution must specify the maximum rate of discount.

The issue may not be made until at least one year after the date on which the company was entitled to commence business.

The shares must be issued within one month of the date of sanction by the Court, or within such extended time that the Court may allow.

Every *subsequent* prospectus and balance sheet must state the discount allowed, or that part of it which has not been written off by then.

Example 53. Wilkes & Boon Limited, whose nominal capital is 10 000 000 Ordinary Shares of £1 each, of which 8 000 000 shares are issued and fully paid up, decide to offer the unissued capital for subscription at a discount of 10%, payable as to £0·25 a share on application, £0·25 a share on allotment, and £0·40 a share two months after allotment.

All the shares were subscribed and were allotted on 5th July. The allotment money was paid on 8th July and the final instalment on 8th September.

Show the entries for the issue in the company's books and how the capital would appear in the company's Balance Sheet. The company has a credit balance of £1 006 606 in the Profit and Loss Account.

The entries for the applications and allotment follow the procedure already illustrated. The final instalment is affected by the discount, and the following entries are required on the call being made:

Journal

			Dr.	*Cr.*
19..			£	£
Sept. 8	First and Final Call Account	2	800 000	
	Discount on Ordinary Shares Account	3	200 000	
	Ordinary Share Capital Account	1		1 000 000
	being first and final call of £0·40 a share on 2 000 000 Ordinary £1 shares and the discount of 10% thereon.			

1

Ordinary Share Capital Account

19..			£	19..			£
				Jan. 1	Balance (original issue)	b/d	8 000 000
				July 5	Application and Allotment (new issue)		1 000 000
				Sept. 8	First and Final Call Account (new issue)	J	800 000
				,, 8	Discount on Shares A/c	J	200 000

2

First and Final Call Account

19..			£	19..			£
Sept. 8	Ordinary Share Capital Account	J	800 000	Sept. 8	Cash	CB	800 000

3

Discount on Ordinary Shares Account

19..			£	19..			£
Sept. 8	Ordinary Share Capital Account: 10% discount on on 2 000 000 £1 shares	J	200 000				

Dr. **Cash Book** *Cr.*

19..			£	19..			£
Sept. 8	First and Final Call of £0·40 per share on 2 000 000 £1 shares	2	800 000				

The discount appears in the Balance Sheet as below, but steps should be taken to write off the amount as soon as possible by transferring it to the debit of the Profit and Loss Account.

Balance Sheet 8th September, 19..

	£	£
AUTHORISED CAPITAL		
10 000 000 Ordinary shares of £1 each		10 000 000
ISSUED CAPITAL		
10 000 000 Ordinary Shares of £1 each, fully paid		10 000 000
RESERVES		
Profit and Loss Account	1 006 606	
Less: Discount on Issued Shares	200 000	806 606

Stock

Under Sections 61–63 of the 1948 Act a company may, if so authorised by its Articles, decide in general meeting (*a*) to increase its share capital by new shares; (*b*) to consolidate and then divide its capital into shares of larger amount than its existing shares; (*c*) to subdivide its shares into shares of smaller amount; (*d*) to convert all or any of its paid up shares into stock and to reconvert the stock again into shares; and (*e*) to cancel that part of its authorised capital represented by unissued shares.

To convert shares into *stock* is to convert an aggregate of shares into one mass or block of capital. The holder of 100 shares of £1 then holds, not 100 separate shares each bearing a distinguishing number, but a £100 portion of the total block of stock forming the company's capital.

Stock is usually transferable in units, of, for instance, £5 or multiples thereof. In some cases smaller units are permitted and even fractions of a pound as with Government stocks. The same procedure for transfer applies to stock as for shares.

EXERCISES 39

1. York & Lancaster Limited, whose authorised capital is £1 000 000 in 1 000 000 Ordinary Shares of £1 each, of which 600 000 have been issued, offer the remaining 400 000 shares for public subscription on 1st June at a premium of £0·25 a share payable as follows:

£0·15 a share on application.
£0·60 a share, including the premium, on allotment.
£0·50 a share one month after allotment.

All the shares offered were subscribed for and were allotted on 15th June, and all the cash due on allotment and for the final instalment was received at due date.

Make the necessary entries in the company's books, and show the capital and the premium as it would stand in the company's Balance Sheet.

2. A private company issued 40 000 Ordinary shares of £1 each at a premium of £0·05 per share. The amounts due upon the shares were payable as follows: £0·55 per share on application (including the premium); £0·25 per share on allotment; and £0·25 per share three months after allotment. All the shares were duly applied for and the cash paid with the exception of the final call on 1 000 shares. Show the entries necessary to record the above transactions in the books of the company, and draw up a Balance Sheet.

(*N.C.T.E.C. adapted*)

3. A limited company was registered with a nominal capital of £150 000, divided into 50 000 6% Preference Shares of £1 each, and 100 000 Ordinary Shares of £1 each. The Preference Shares were offered for subscriptions at par, and the Ordinary Shares at a premium of £0·12½ per share. On February 1st, 19. ., subscriptions were received for 45 000 Preference shares and 80 000 Ordinary Shares, payable as follows:

On application, £0·12½ per share in both cases; on allotment (February 10th) £0·25 per share on the Preference Shares, and £0·37½ per share (including the premium) on the Ordinary Shares. On March 15th, £0·62½ per share in both cases.

On March 20th, all money due on the shares had been received except the final call on 100 Preference Shares which remained outstanding.

Submit the entries necessary to record the above issue in the books of the company.

R.S.A. (adapted)

4. On January 1st, 19. ., Blanks Limited offered for public subsciiption 1 000 000 Ordinary Shares of £1 each at £1·50 per share, payable as to £0·50 per share on application, and £1 per share (including premium) on January 15th. The public applied for 1 115 000 shares, and duly paid the application moneys. 1 000 000 shares were allotted on January 17th, and application moneys were returned to the unsuccessful applicants. The final call was duly paid on or before the due date.

Give the entries necessary to record the above share issue in the company's books.

R.S.A. (adapted

5. Townley & Sons Limited, whose registered capital is £120 000, consisting of 120 000 Ordinary Shares of £1 each, of which 80 000 have been issued and are fully paid, have received the sanction of the Court to issue the remainder of its capital at a discount of 5%, payable £0·25 a share on application, £0·25 a share on allotment, and £0·45 a share two months after allotment. All the shares offered were subscribed for and were allotted on 15th June. All the cash due on allotment and for the final instalment was received. Show the entries for the issue in the books of the company, and show the capital of the company as it should appear in its next Balance Sheet.

6. Beauval & Woodwarde Limited obtained the sanction of its shareholders in general meeting and of the Court to offer its unissued capital of 50 000 £1 Ordinary Shares for subscription by the existing members at a discount of 10%. The shares were payable to £0·12½ on application, £0·37½ on allotment, and £0·40 two months after allotment.

All the shares were subscribed for and were allotted on 15th May, and all the cash due on allotment and on 15th July was received.

Show the entries for the issue in the company's books, and how the capital would appear in the company's Balance Sheet.

40

Loan Capital; Debentures

The legal process of increasing the share capital of a company is not difficult, and many companies take this step to increase the working capital. Other companies may require the use of additional cash resources for developments but, owing to the state of the market for their shares, they may be able to obtain further cash only by offering greater security to the investor. Moreover, an increase in the share capital involves a wider spread of the profits by way of dividend, and, unless profits increase in proportion, this may lead to a diminution in the dividend percentage. In such cases a company may raise money by means of loans. These are referred to as the *loan capital* of the company.

As security for the money lent, the company may give *security* to the lender of certain of the company's specific assets, or may give a *floating charge* (or security) over the whole of the company's assets including its stock and book debts. Only companies may give floating charges.

The document issued to the lender acknowledging the debt and creating a charge in his favour on the company's property, is called a *Debenture*.

A debenture issue may be made for public subscription. In such circumstances, the terms of payment of interest and of repayment of the capital will be included in the debentures. Property specifically charged to the debenture holders cannot be disposed of, or otherwise dealt in, by the company to the detriment of the debenture holders. In the event of default in regard to any covenant entered into, the debenture holders may take possession of, and deal with, the property charged to them. A floating charge covers all the property of the company, including its stock, cash, and book debts. It does not prevent the company dealing with these in the ordinary course of business. However, it gives the debenture holders priority over all unsecured creditors, should it be necessary to intervene owing to the company's default in payment of interest or in repayment of the loan.

Debentures giving a specific charge are often referred to as

Mortgage Debentures. They must be registered, like all charges on the company's property, with the Registrar of Companies.

The issue of debentures involves entries in the books of account similar to those for an issue of shares. A sum is payable on application and the remainder by periodical instalments, but usually the the balance is payable in full on allotment.

Debenture interest is usually paid half-yearly. As the interest is a debt due from the company secured by the terms of the debenture, it is payable whether profits have been made or not. Outstanding debenture interest must be brought into account as an accrued liability at the close of an accounting period. This point should not be overlooked by students, as the fact that interest is outstanding is sometimes purposely omitted from the information in an examination question, although the fact can be deduced by the observant student.

Debentures are transferable and the common form of transfer is used. Debentures may be transferred only as units. Debentures also may be converted into debenture stock. Debenture stock may be transferred in multiples or fractions of a pound. Debentures may be issued at par, at a discount, or at a premium, and there are no restrictive conditions on the issue of debentures at a discount as there are for shares.

Debenture holders are loan creditors of the company. They are *not* members of the company, though Section 158 of the 1948 Act states that a copy of the last Balance Sheet and a copy of the last Profit and Loss Account, together with the auditor's report, must be sent to all holders of debentures of a public company. The rights of the debenture-holders are safeguarded by specially-appointed *Trustees for the Debenture Holders.*

The Issue of Debentures

The following example illustrates the record required for an issue of debentures.

Example 54. Wilkes & Boon Limited offered for public subscription on 1st July, 19. ., 5 000 5% Debentures of £100 each, payable as to £20 a debenture on application, £30 a debenture on allotment, and £50 a debenture two months after allotment. The whole of the debenture issue was subscribed and allotment was made on 6th July. The final instalment was paid on 6th September.

Show the entries for the issue in the company's books and how the debentures should appear in the company's Balance Sheet.

It will be observed from the working of the example shown below that the entries in the books of account for a debenture issue are similar to those for an issue of shares as discussed in an earlier chapter.

Journal

			Dr.	*Cr.*
19..			£	£
July 6	5% Debenture Application and Allotment Account	2	250 000	
	5% Debentures Account	1		250 000
	being £20 a debenture on application and £30 a debenture on allotment on 5 000 5% debentures allotted on resolution of directors, dated 6th July, 19..			
Sept. 6	Call Account (5% Debentures)	3	250 000	
	5% Debentures Account	1		250 000
	being final instalment of £50 each on 5 000 5% Debentures by the conditions of issue.			

5% Debentures Account

19..			£	19..			£
				Dec. 31	Application and Allotment A/c	J	250 000
				Sept. 6	First and Final Call Account	J	250 000

5% Debentures Application and Allotment Account

19..			£	19..			£
July 6	5% Debentures A/c.	J.	250 000	July 3	Cash	CB	100 000
				,, 10	Cash	CB	150 000
			£250 000				£250 000

First and Final Call (Debentures) Account

19..			£	19..			£
Sept. 6	5% Debentures A/c	J	250 000	Sept. 6	Cash	CB	250 000

Dr. **Cash Book** *Cr*

19..			£	19..			£
July 3	Application A/c		100 000				
,, 10	Allotment A/c	2	150 000				
Sept. 6	First and Final Call	3	250 000				

The 5% Debentures Account is a total account comprising the sundry amounts subscribed by the debenture holders. The details appear in a Register of Debenture Holders which contains a Ledger Account for each debenture holder.

The debenture issue is shown in the Balance Sheet as a liability. The issue is usually placed immediately below the share capital, as in the following illustration. It is assumed, for the purpose of illustration, that the share capital is as shown in the Balance Sheet on page 415.

Balance Sheet, Wilkes & Boon Limited
(Showing claims side only)

	£	£
AUTHORISED CAPITAL		
10 000 000 Ordinary Shares of £1 each	10 000 000	
ISSUED CAPITAL		
8 000 000 Ordinary Shares of £1 each, fully called	8 000 000	
Less Calls in arrear	12 500	
		7 987 500
LOAN CAPITAL		
5% Debentures		
5 000 Debentures of £100 each, fully paid		5 000 000

Issue of Debentures at a Discount

A company may be authorised by its Articles of Association to issue debentures at a discount. Had the company in the above example doubted the success of an issue at par, they may have sought to make the issue more attractive by offering £100 debentures at say £95 each.

The nominal rate of interest is payable on the par value so that the investor obtains a higher rate of return on the money he actually invests. Further, the debenture for which £95 is subscribed may contain an undertaking to repay at par value (or even higher) at a later date.

Example 55. Wilkes & Boon Limited offer for public subscription on 1st July, 19.., 5 000 10% Debentures of £100 each at a price of £95 each, payable as to £20 a debenture on application, £30 a debenture on allotment, and £45 a debenture two months after allotment. The whole issue was subscribed and allotted on 6th July. The final instalment was paid on 6th September.

The full face value of the issue is £500 000 which is the extent of the company's liability to the debenture holders. Only £475 000 is received in actual cash as there is a discount of £25 000 on the issue. The full liability of £500 000 must be recorded in the books and shown in the claims section of the Balance Sheet. The discount is posted to a separate *Discount on Debentures Account* and appears on the assets side of the Balance Sheet. In effect it is part of the cost of the debenture issue. The amount is written off against profits during the life of the debentures.

The Journal and Ledger entries for the example are as shown below:

	Journal		*Dr.*	*Cr.*
19..			£	£
July 6	10% Debentures Application and Allotment Account	2	250 000	
	10% Debentures Account	1		250 000
	being £20 a debenture on application and £30 a debenture on allotment on 5 000 10% Debentures allotted on resolution of Directors, dated 6th July, 19..			
Sept. 6	Call Account (10% Debentures)	3	225 000	
	10% Debentures Account	1		225 000
	being final instalment of £45 a debenture on 5 000 10% Debentures issued at £95 by the conditions of issue.			
Sept. 6	Debenture Discount Account	4	25 000	
	10% Debentures Account	1		25 000
	being discount of £5 a debenture on 5 000 10% Debentures issued at £95.			

1

10% Debenture Account

19..			£	19..			£
				July 6	Application and Allotment A/c	J	250 000
				Sept. 6	First and Final Call A/c	J	225 000
				,, 6	Debenture Discount A/c	J	25 000

2

10% Debentures Application and Allotment Account

19..			£	19..			£
July 6	10% Debentures A/c	J.	250 000	July 3	Cash	C B	100 000
				,, 10	,,	C B	150 000
			£250 000				£250 000

3

First and Final Call (Debentures) Account

19..			£	19..			£
Sept. 6	10% Debentures A/c	J	225 000	Sept. 6	Cash	C B	225 000

Dr.			**Cash Book**				*Cr.*
19..			£	19..			£
July 3	Application A/c (Debentures)	2	100 000				
,, 10	Allotment Account (Debentures)	2	150 000				
Sept. 6	First and Final Call (Debentures)	3	225 000				

4

Debenture Discount Account

			£				£
19..				19..			
Sept. 6	10% Debentures A/c	J	25 000				

Balance Sheet

	£		£
LOAN CAPITAL: 10% DEBENTURES 5 000 Debentures of £100 each, fully paid	500 000	DISCOUNT ON DEBENTURES	25 000

Issue of Debentures at a Premium

Debentures, like shares, may be issued at a premium to take full advantage of the popularity of the company's securities and the demand for them in the investment market. They may also be issued at a premium if the interest rate offered on the par value is higher than long-term interest rates generally at the time of the issue.

Example 56. Wilkes & Boon Limited offer for public subscription on 1st July, 19.., 5 000 10% Debentures of £100 each at a price of £105 each, payable as to £20 a debenture on application, £35 a debenture on allotment, including the premium, and £50 two months after allotment. The whole issue was subscribed and allotted on 6th July. The final instalment was paid on 6th September.

Show the entries required in the company's books and how the debenture issue and the premium should appear in the Balance Sheet.

The entries for the applications and allotment will follow the usual procedure. The premium is treated similarly to the premium on shares, requiring the opening of a *Premium on Debentures Account*.

The entries for the example are shown below:

	Journal	Dr.	Cr.
19..		£	£
July 6	10% Debentures Application and Allotment Account	275 000	
	10% Debentures Account		250 000
	Debentures Premium Account		25 000
	being £20 a debenture on application and £35 (including premium of £5) a debenture on allotment on 5 000 10% Debentures allotted on resolution of Directors, dated 6th July.		
Sept. 6	Call Account (10% Debentures)	250 000	
	10% Debentures Account		250 000
	being final instalment of £50 a debenture on 5 000 10% Debentures by the terms of issue.		

1

10% Debentures Account

19..			£	19..			£
				July 6	Application and Allotment A/c	J.	250 000
				Sept. 6	First and Final Call Account	J.	250 000

2

10% Debentures Application and Allotment Account

19..				19..			
July 6	10% Debentures Account	J	250 000	July 3	Cash	CB	100 000
	Debentures Premium Account	J	25 000	,, 10	Cash	CB	175 000
			£275 000				£275 000

3

First and Final Call (Debentures) Account

19..			£	19..			£
Sept. 6	10% Debentures A/c.	J	250 000	Sept. 6	Cash	CB	250 000

4

Premium on Debentures Account

19..			£	19..			£
				July 6	Application and Allotment A/c	J	25 000

Dr. **Cash Book** *Cr.*

19..			£	19..			£
July 3	Application A/c. (Debentures)		100 000				
,, 10	Allotment Account (Debentures)		175 000				
Sept. 6	First and Final Call Account (Debentures)		250 000				

The premium on debentures is not part of the loan capital but is a gain to the company. Though the premium may be treated as ordinary revenue, the usual policy is to regard it as a capital reserve. As such it must be shown separately as a claim in the Balance Sheet.

Balance Sheet
(Showing claims side only)

	£
LOAN CAPITAL:	
10% DEBENTURES	
5 000 Debentures of £100 each, fully paid	500 000
Premium on Debentures Account	25 000

Expenses of Debenture Issues

The expenses involved by a debenture issue have been ignored in the above examples. With every issue, printing, advertising, and law costs as well as stamp duty, filing fees, and, possibly, underwriting commission have to be paid. These will be debited to a *Debenture Issue Expenses Account* in the Ledger, the balance of which represents the total expense of the debenture issue. The balance of the account must be shown as a temporary asset in the Balance Sheet in so far as it is not written off. The amount may be written off by instalments during the life of the debenture issue. By this method the cost of the issue is spread over the period of the debentures instead of being charged in one sum against the profits of the year of issue. The same remarks apply also to the issue of shares.

EXERCISES 40

1. The authorised capital of Newton & Co. Limited is £150 000, consisting of 50 000 6% Preference Shares of £1 each and 100 000 Ordinary Shares of £1 each, all of which have been issued and are fully paid. It is decided to offer for public subscription on 1st June, 1 000 12% Debentures of £100 each, payable £20 on application and £80 on allotment. The issue was fully subscribed and allotment made and the cash received by 9th June.

Show the entries for the debenture issue in the company's books and set down the company's share capital and the debenture issue as it should appear in the Balance Sheet.

2. Give the entries to record in the books of the Essex Ironworks Ltd., the issue of 1 000 11% Debentures of £100 each. The issue was made on 1st January, and the debentures were payable:

£20 for each debenture on application.
£30 for each debenture on allotment.
£50 for each debenture one month after allotment.

The issue was fully subscribed and the Directors went to allotment on 5th January. The cash was received for the remaining instalments on the due date.

3. Riverhead Mills Limited offered for public subscription on 1st February 1 000 10% Debentures of £100 each at the price of £105, payable £20 on application, and £85, including the premium, on allotment. The whole issue was subscribed and allotted and the cash was paid by 8th February.

Show the entries for the issue as in the company's books.

4. Kemsing Cotton Mills Limited offered for public subscription on 1st May 5 000 15% Debentures of £100 each at a price of £102, payable £25 on application and £77 on allotment, including the premium.

The whole issue was subscribed and allotted and the cash due was received by 9th May.

Record the issue as in the books of the company.

5. Record in the books of Remington & Sons Limited the issue of 500 7% Debentures of £100 each at a price of £98 a debenture, the costs of the issue being £500. Show the particulars of the issue as it would appear in the company's Balance Sheet.

6. Give the entries in the books of Jennings Stores Limited necessitated by the issue of 5 000 13½% Debentures of £100 each at a price of £102 a debenture. The costs of the issue amounted to £16 000. Show also how the issue would be recorded in the company's Balance Sheet.

7. The Woodside Manufacturing Company Limited offered for public subscription on 1st March, 1 000 12% Debentures of £100 each at a price of £98 a debenture, payable £20 on application, £40 on allotment and £38 one month after allotment. The issue was fully subscribed and allotted on 9th March, and final instalment was paid by 9th April.

Show the entries for the issue as in the company's books.

8. Lawson's Limited offered for subscription on 1st January, 50 000 10% Debentures of £100 at a price of £95, payable £20 on application and £75 on allotment. The issue was fully subscribed and allotted and the cash received.

Give the entries to record the issue in the books of the company and show how the issue would appear in the Balance Sheet of the company.

9. Draw up the Journal entries in proper form to record the following in the books of A. B. Company, Ltd., when preparing the accounts for the year ending 31st March, 19. . :

(*a*) It was decided that £30 000 of the Bad Debts Provision of £67 500 was no longer required.

(*b*) The interest on an issue of £1 000 000 6% Debentures had been paid to 30th September, 19. ., in the year of account to 31st March, 19. . .

(*c*) Included in purchases is £75 000 and in wages £65 000 relating to expenditure which was incurred in building an extension to the company's factory.

R.S.A. (*adapted*)

41

The Purchase of a Business by a Company

An existing company may buy an additional business or a company may be formed for the express purpose of taking over a going concern. The purchase price may be paid wholly in cash, or partly in cash and partly in shares in the company, or as in some cases, wholly in shares. Whole or part payment may also be made in debentures. The method of payment is arranged between the company and the vendor of the business. If the company makes a public issue of shares to obtain capital to make the purchase, a statement in the prospectus that the vendor is to be paid either wholly or in part in shares encourages investors, as it may be taken as a sign that the vendor himself has faith in the future prospects of the business under the new ownership. The shares allotted as consideration for the purchase become part of the issued capital of the company.

It is essential to know the terms of the contract under which the business is to be acquired. It is probable that the purchase price will include payment for Goodwill and for the assets, which may or may not include the cash balance. If the liabilities are taken over it is usual for the vendor to guarantee that they shall not exceed the figures in the Balance Sheet agreed before the purchase is made.

The entries in the company's books to record the purchase of a business will be similar to those discussed in Chapter 32, with the possible addition of the allotment of shares or debentures as part of the purchase price. In some instances a special issue of shares, part of the company's unissued capital, is made for cash to finance the purchase. The procedure for the issue and allotment will follow the usual course already described.

The following example illustrates the purchase price being paid partly in cash and partly in shares.

Example 57. Weston & Sons Limited was registered with a capital of £150 000 divided into 100 000 Ordinary Shares of £1 each and 50 000 6% Preference

Shares of £1 each. The company was formed to acquire an existing business as from 1st January, taking over the following assets and liabilities:

	£
Freehold Premises	25 000
Plant and Machinery	22 000
Stock	19 000
Sundry Debtors	11 000
Sundry Creditors	7 000

The purchase price, including Goodwill, was £80 000, payable as to £30 000 in cash and as to £50 000 in fully paid Ordinary Shares.

The directors subscribed for 10 000 Ordinary Shares and paid in full on allotment, thus a total number of 60 000 Ordinary Shares were issued. The whole of the Preference Share capital was subscribed for by the directors and was fully paid up. Preliminary expenses amounted to £2 000.

Give the Journal entries and the Cash Book entries to record these transactions, and show the opening Balance Sheet of the company.

	Journal		*Dr.*	*Cr.*
19..			£	£
Jan. 1	Business Purchase Account		80 000	
	Vendor's Account			80 000
	being purchase price by contract dated			
	Freehold Premises		25 000	
	Plant and Machinery		22 000	
	Stock		19 000	
	Sundry Debtors		11 000	
	Goodwill		10 000	
	Business Purchase Account			87 000
	being assets taken over by contract dated			
	Business Purchase Account		7 000	
	Sundry Creditors			7 000
	being liabilities as by contract dated			
	Vendor's Account		50 000	
	Ordinary Share Capital Account			50 000
	being 50 000 £1 Ordinary Shares allotted fully paid as part purchase price.			
	Ordinary Shares Application and Allotment Account		10 000	
	Ordinary Share Capital Account			10 000
	being 10 000 £1 Ordinary Shares allotted by Directors' resolution dated			

Preference Shares Application and Allotment Account	50 000	
Preference Share Capital Account being application and allotment money on 50 000 £1 Preference Shares allotted by resolution of Directors dated		50 000

The *preliminary expenses* incurred cover such items as the legal charges, stamp duty, and printing costs on the formation of the company. For present purposes it is sufficient to remark that they are considered to be capital expenditure. It is usual for this item to be written off out of profits over a short period of years. In the meantime it is best deducted from reserves when setting out the Balance Sheet.

In some instances debentures may be issued and allotted by a company in payment of the purchase price. Entries similar to those for shares would be required.

Dr. **Cash Book** *Cr.*

19..			£	19..			£
Jan. 1	Preference Shares Application and Allotment Account		50 000	Jan. 1	Vendor		30 000
,, 1	Ordinary Shares Application and Allotment Account		10 000	,, 1	Preliminary Expenses		2 000
				,, 1	Balance	c/d	28 000
			£60 000				£60 000
Jan. 2	Balance	b/d	28 000				

Balance Sheet, Weston & Sons, Limited

	£	£		£	£
AUTHORISED CAPITAL:			PRELIMINARY EXPENSES		2 000
50 000 6% Preference Shares of £1 each	50 000		FIXED ASSETS:		
100 000 Ordinary Shares of £1 each	100 000		Freehold Premises	25 000	
		150 000	Plant and Machinery	22 000	
					47 000
			GOODWILL		10 000
ISSUED CAPITAL:					
50 000 6% Preference Shares of £1 each	50 000		CURRENT ASSETS:		
			Stock	19 000	
			Debtors	11 000	
60 000 Ordinary Shares of £1 each	60 000		Cash	28 000	
				58 000	
		110 000	LESS: CURRENT LIABILITIES:		
			Creditors	7 000	
			WORKING CAPITAL		51 000
		£110 000			£110 000

EXERCISES 41

1. The Balance Sheet of Grace and Robins at 31st December 19.. is as follows:

Balance Sheet, Grace and Robins, 31st December, 19..

	£			£
Grace, Capital Account	4 750	Goodwill		250
Robins, ,,	7 236	Land and buildings		3 100
Bank Overdraft	464	Machinery and plant		2 720
Bills Payable	300	Fixtures and fittings		416
Sundry creditors	1 250	Stock		4 891
		Debtors	2 340	
		Less Reserve for bad debts	117	
				2 223
		Bills Receivable		400
	£14 000			£14 000

On 31st December, 19.., the business was acquired by Grace Bros. Ltd., specially formed for that purpose, with a nominal capital of 15 000 Ordinary Shares of £1 each, and 15 000 6% Preference Shares of £1 each.

The company took over all the assets except the Bills Receivable, and undertook to pay off the sundry creditors, but not the Bank Overdraft nor the Bills Payable. The purchase consideration was £15 000 consisting of 10 000 £1 Ordinary Shares and 4 000 £1 Preference Shares and the balance in cash.

The company revalued the land and buildings at £3 800 and the machinery and plant at £2 500.

On the 31st January the balance of the Ordinary Shares was issued to the public, and by the 28th February all moneys due had been received. On the 28th February, the purchase consideration was discharged. The preliminary expenses paid were £436.

You are required to give:

(1) The Journal entries in the books of Grace Bros. Ltd.

(2) All the Ledger Accounts affected in the books of Grace Bros. Ltd.

(3) The Balance Sheet of Grace Bros. Ltd. as on the 28th February, 19..

U.E.I. (adapted)

2. Enterprise Limited was registered in 19.. with a nominal capital of £500 000, divided into 250 000 7% Preference Shares of £1 each, and 500 000 Ordinary Shares of £0·50 each.

The company was formed to acquire an established business, the purchase price, £300 000, including Goodwill, being payable as follows: £50 000 in Preference Shares, £50 000 in Ordinary Shares (both fully paid), £100 000 in 9% Debenture Stock, and the balance in cash.

The balance of the Preference Shares were subscribed by the public and fully paid up, and 200 000 Ordinary Shares were subscribed by the Directors and fully paid up.

The assets and liabilities taken over (at agreed values) were:

	£		£
Freehold works	75 000	Plant and machinery	31 000
Stock	66 000	Sundry debtors	112 000
Patents and trade marks	8 000	Sundry creditors	12 000

Give the Journal entries necessary to record the above transactions in the books of the Company, and show its initial Balance Sheet.

R.S.A. (adapted)

3. Chatenays Limited was registered with a nominal capital of £200 000 (100 000 Ordinary Shares of £1 each and 100 000 6% Preference Shares of £1 each), to purchase the old established business of Abel Chatenay. The purchase price was agreed at £120 000, payable as to £30 000 in cash, £40 000 in Ordinary Shares of £1 each, and £50 000 in 6% Preference Shares of £1 each.

The company was to discharge the liabilities of the old firm.

The Balance Sheet of Abel Chatenay as on the date of purchase was as follows:

Balance Sheet

	£		£
Capital	100 000	Freehold works	36 000
Creditors	14 040	Machinery and plant	37 860
Bank loan	2 000	Sundry debtors	18 764
		Stock	22 440
		Cash in hand	976
	£116 040		£116 040

The balance of the Ordinary and Preference Shares was issued to the public and fully subscribed and paid up.

Prepare the accounts necessary to record the above purchase in the company's books, and give the initial Balance Sheet of the new company.

R.S.A.

4. A. Alpha carried on business as a manufacturer and his position at 31st December, 19.., was as follows: Freehold property, £5 000; loan from J. Alpha, £1 200; machinery, £3 250; debtors, £3 786; creditors, £1 100; balance at bank, £254; and cash in hand, £10.

It had been arranged that a limited company should be formed to take over all the assets and liabilities of the business as shown for the purchase price of £15 000, and the price was to be satisfied by the issue of 15 000 shares of £1 each.

A. Alpha Limited was duly formed with an authorised capital of £20 000 divided into shares of £1 each, and the transfer took place on 1st January, 19.., when the remaining 5 000 shares were allotted to J. Alpha, as to £3 800 in consideration of cash and as to the balance in consideration of the cancellation of his loan.

Draft the Balance Sheet of the company on the completion of these transactions.

R.S.A.

5. Woodcraft, Ltd., was registered to take over the business of Joseph Andrews at 31st December 19.., whose Balance Sheet at that date was as follows:

	£		£
Capital	149 170	Goodwill, Patents, etc.	33 300
Creditors	32 760	Plant	33 110
		Furniture, etc.	18 090
		Stock	54 910
		Debtors	41 070
		Cash at bank	1 450
	£181 930		£181 930

The purchase price was fixed at £135 000, payable as to £50 000 in cash, and £50 000 in fully paid Ordinary Shares, and the balance in 10% debentures of £100 each.

The company took over all the assets with the exception of the cash and debtors. It agreed to collect the debtors for the vendor and remit him the proceeds less 2½% collecting commission. The company did not take over the creditors.

The shares and debentures were allotted on 1st January, 19.., on which date 200 000 Ordinary Shares of £0·50 each were offered to the public, payable as to £0·25 per share on application and £0·25 per share on allotment.

Applications were received for 196 000 shares by 16th January, and these were duly allotted and the allotment money received by 30th January on which date the balance of the purchase money was paid over to the vendor. On 31st January the vendor's debts had all been collected, and the amount due to the vendor paid over. The formation expenses of the company, £6 420, were also paid on that date.

Open the books of Woodcraft, Ltd., record the above transactions in Cash Book and Ledger Accounts, and prepare a Balance Sheet as at 31st January 19...

Journal entries are not required, but all accounts should be presented.

U.E.I. (adapted)

42

The Final Accounts of a Company: Legal Provisions

The ordinary trading records do not differ whether the business is owned by a company, an individual, or a partnership firm. The form of ownership affects the proprietorship accounts, and the preceding chapters make clear the material differences in form of the Capital Accounts of a company from those of the sole trader and partners. Another point of difference in company accounts is in the treatment of the profit. A company may not increase its capital except under the conditions laid down in the Companies Act, 1948. Any profit, therefore, that remains after payments of dividends and transfers to Reserve Accounts cannot be transferred to the Capital Accounts but must remain on the books as the balance of the Profit and Loss Account. Further, the Companies Act makes certain provisions regarding the contents of the company Balance Sheet and Profit and Loss Account, and usually, certain adjustments, peculiar to company accounts, may be necessary in the final accounts at balancing time.

The Companies Acts and the Final Accounts of a Company

Companies are required by Section 148 of the Companies Act, 1948 to publish a Profit and Loss Account and Balance Sheet at least once a year. This is so that all shareholders and debenture holders may have necessary information about the company. Copies of such published accounts are sent annually to all shareholders and debenture holders, on the registers of the company at the date of publication. Other interested parties may inspect a copy of these accounts at the office of the Registrar of Companies.

These published accounts may differ *in form* from the accounts as made up for the purpose of ascertaining the profit or loss of the company. The 1948 and 1967 Companies Acts lay down detailed requirements as to the items which must be shown in the published accounts of a company and matters which must be dealt with in the Directors' Report. These requirements were greatly extended by the 1967 Act and it is not proposed to go fully into them at this stage. A detailed study of these requirements must be left to a more advanced stage of study. Students who are interested will find full details in the Companies Acts and, in particular, in Sections 3–12 and Schedule 2 of the Companies Act, 1967. These set out the legal requirements for the published Profit and Loss Accounts and Balance Sheets of Joint Stock Companies.

The Published Profit and Loss Account

The published profit and loss account is required to show only certain items. It must show the sales turnover and investment income on the credit side. Only some debit items are required. They include depreciation and renewals of fixed assets, interest on loans and overdrafts, directors' emoluments, auditor's remuneration, plant hire costs, taxation, dividends and transfers to and from reserves. Comparative figures for the previous year must be given. It is customary to show much of the detail in notes attached to the accounts. Some other expenses are normally shown in the Directors' Report. These include the number of UK employees and their total remuneration, the expenditure on political and other donations, the amount of exports, and an outline summary analysis of the company's results in each of its main business activities.

The Balance Sheet

Schedule 2 of the 1967 Companies Act lays down many requirements relating to the published Balance Sheets of Companies. While it would be unwise to enter into a full discussion of these requirements at this stage, students should observe the following rules when preparing the Balance Sheet of a Limited Liability Company, as a preliminary stage to more advanced study.

On the *claims* side:

1. The Authorised Share Capital, the Issued Share Capital, Reserves, Provisions (other than provisions for depreciation which are normally shown by way of deduction from the asset to which they relate) Loans and Current Liabilities should be shown under separate headings.

2. Share premiums must be shown separately under the heading 'Share Premium Account'.
3. The aggregate amount of bank loans and overdrafts must be shown.
4. The aggregate amount (before deduction of tax) recommended for distribution as dividends.

On the *assets* side:

1. Fixed assets, current assets and assets that are neither fixed nor current must be separately identified.
2. Fixed assets and current assets should be grouped and the total of each group should be shown.
3. The basis of valuation of fixed assets must be shown. These will generally be shown 'at cost' less the aggregate amount of depreciation written off to date.
4. Investments should be shown separately. Trade, quoted and unquoted investments should be separately identified. The market value of quoted investments must be shown if different from the Balance Sheet valuation.
5. The following should be shown under separate headings:
   (*a*) Goodwill and Trade Marks in so far as the amount is ascertainable and has not been written off.
   (*b*) Preliminary expenses not written off.
   (*c*) Expenses, commission and discount on any issue of shares or debentures in so far as it has not been written off.

At this stage of study students will not usually be called upon to prepare the *published* Profit and Loss Account of a limited liability company. In doing exercises and in examination work the Profit and Loss Account and its Appropriation Section will be prepared as explained below. In preparing a company Balance Sheet students should observe the rules set out above.

Auditor's Report

A company must appoint an auditor or auditors at its annual general meeting to hold office until the next annual general meeting.

The auditors have right of access at all times to the company's books, accounts and vouchers and shall be entitled to require from the officers of the company such information and explanations as they think necessary for the performance of their duties as auditors. They must report to the members on the accounts examined by them.

This report is usually confined to statements as to whether, in the opinion of the auditors:

(*a*) the Balance Sheet and Profit and Loss Account have been properly prepared in accordance with the provisions of the Companies Acts;

(*b*) the Balance Sheet and Profit and Loss Account give a true and fair view respectively of the state of affairs and the profit and loss of the company.

The Companies Acts provide that every Balance Sheet of a company must be signed on behalf of the board by two directors or by the sole director, and that the auditor's report must be attached and read before the company in general meeting.

The Appropriation Account

The net trading profit of a company is carried down to a second section of the Profit and Loss Account. This second section is called the *Appropriation Account* and contains all the appropriations of the net profit. It shows the disposal of the profit. It follows that the first section should contain all charges against profits such as directors' fees, debenture interest, depreciation, interest, rent, rates, and similar expenses. The Appropriation Account should contain only the appropriations of the profit that the first section shows available for distribution.

Examples of such appropriations are the payment of preference share dividends, allocations to pension funds and any sums written off Goodwill or preliminary expenses.

The balance remaining after the other appropriations have been made is available for distribution as dividend to the ordinary shareholders, or for retention and ploughing back into the business. In this latter case the retained profits may be transferred to the credit of a reserve account.

The directors set out the net trading profit in their report to the shareholders at the Annual General Meeting and include a statement of their recommendations for its disposal by way of dividend, transfers to reserve, etc. A resolution is proposed that the dividend specified shall be paid on a certain date, and, if the resolution is carried, the dividend becomes a debt due from the company to the shareholders. Only when the dividend has been declared is the entry for it made in the Appropriation Account. The shareholders cannot authorise the distribution of a larger dividend than that recommended by the directors, but they may recommend less.

The Appropriation Account is closed after the entry of the various allocations of profit and the final dividend. Any balance, whether a profit or a loss, is carried forward to the next period. The Appropriation Account is treated as a continuous account. It follows that after the first year's working the Account will show the balance brought forward from the preceding financial year and the balance to be carried forward to the next. In a company Balance Sheet the profit or loss is shown as a separate item – a profit is shown on the claims side; a loss as a deduction from reserves on the same side.

The balance brought down to the Appropriation Account for the new trading period appears in the Trial Balance extracted at the close of that period. In a Trial Balance given in an examination question it usually appears under the heading of 'Profit and Loss Account Balance'. In the preparation of the final accounts, the item should be entered in the Appropriation Account (which should directly follow the Profit and Loss Account) first ensuring whether the Trial Balance item represents a profit or a loss brought forward.

Example 58. A typical example of the appropriation section of a Profit and Loss Account is given on page 452.

The contra entries in the Ledger for the debit entries in this Appropriation Account would be as follows:

The interim dividend would be credited to the Ordinary Shares Dividend Account.

The transfer to reserve would be credited to the Reserve Account.

The sums written off Goodwill and preliminary expenses would be credited respectively to the Goodwill Account and the Preliminary Expenses Account.

The balance on the Appropriation Account (£8 000) is sufficient to allow the directors to declare a final dividend on the Ordinary Shares of 5% per annum. This would absorb £5 000, leaving £3 000 to be carried forward to next year.

The *final dividend* would be credited to the Ordinary Shares

Profit and Loss Account

for the year ended 31st December, 19. .

Date			£	Date			£
19. .				19. .			
Dec. 31	Total Expenses		20 000	Dec. 31	Gross Profit		38 000
	Balance carried down		18 000				
			£38 000				£38 000

Appropriation Account

Date			£	Date			£
19. .				19. .			
Dec. 31	Interim dividend on 100 000 Ordinary Shares		5 000	Dec. 31	Trading Profit brought down		18 000
„ 31	Transfer to Reserve Account		3 000	„ 31	Balance brought forward from last year		1 500
„ 31	Goodwill written off		1 500				
„ 31	Preliminary expenses written off		2 000				
„ 31	Balance	c/d	8 000				
			£19 500				£19 500
				Dec. 31	Balance	c/d	8 000

Dividend Account. The payment out of the dividend would be credited in the Cash Book and debited to the Ordinary Shares Dividend Account. The payment is made by special forms of cheque known as dividend warrants. If all the warrants are cashed the Dividend Account is closed, but a balance would remain should any dividends not be claimed. Such balance must be shown on the claims side of the Balance Sheet under the heading of Unclaimed Dividends.

The Articles usually give the directors power to pay *interim dividends*. These are dividends paid during the financial year before the annual accounts are made up. They are usually paid at the end of the first half-year, but the directors must take care that the profits justify the payment.

The transfer fees paid by transferees on the lodging of transfers of shares are credited to the Profit and Loss Account as a gain.

Preliminary expenses are usually written off against profits by instalments over a period of three to five years.

EXERCISES 42

1. If you were the accountant to a limited company and had drawn up a Trial Balance as at 31st December, 19.., prior to preparing the accounts, state how you would deal with the following items appearing therein, giving reasons for your replies:

(*a*) Premium on an issue of Shares, £5 000.
(*b*) Cash at bank, £6 800 (including proceeds of £2 500 Bills receivable, discounted with the Company's Bankers and falling due during January and February).

(*c*) Discount on an issue of Debentures, £4 000.

(*d*) Reserve for Bad and Doubtful Debts (previously made) £2 000.

(*e*) Preliminary (or Formation) Expenses, £950.

U.L.C.I.

2. The Crystal Glass Works Ltd., having made a profit of £29 448 during the year decided to appropriate it, together with a balance of profit of £3 329 brought forward, as follows:

(*a*) In payment of a dividend of $6\frac{1}{4}\%$, on 56 400 Preference Shares of £1 each, fully paid.
(*b*) In payment of a dividend of 17%, on 94 600 Ordinary Shares of £1 each, £0·50 paid.
(*c*) In transfer of £3 000 to a Reserve Fund Account with a corresponding investment of cash in securities.
(*d*) In writing off the figure of Goodwill, £1 600.

The balance of profit remaining was to be carried forward. The cash balance at the date prior to the payment of the dividends and the investment stood at £18 628.

Show the Profit and Loss Appropriation Account and the entries in all the other accounts necessary to give effect to the above resolution, allowing for unclaimed dividends £219 on the ordinary shares. Ignore taxation.

U.E.I. (adapted)

3. The A.B. Engineering Co. Ltd. has an authorised capital of £50 000 divided into 100 000 shares of £0·50 each.

On 31st December, 19. ., the following balances appear in the books of the company.

	£
Share capital (fully paid)	30 000
General reserve	5 000
Profit and Loss Account (credit balance)	10 480
Machinery and plant (at cost)	34 000
Furniture and fittings (at cost)	3 000
Provisions for depreciation:	
Machinery and plant	9 700
Furniture and fittings	800
Sundry debtors	4 780
Sundry creditors	2 340
Cash in hand and balance at bank	9 140
Stocks	7 400

For the year ended 31st December, 19. ., the directors decided to transfer £2 000 to reserve and to recommend a dividend of 20% on the ordinary shares.

Prepare the Appropriation Account of the company for the year ended 31st December, 19. . and a Balance Sheet as at that date.

The Balance Sheet is to be prepared in such a way as to show clearly *within the Balance Sheet:*

(i) The total of fixed assets;
(ii) the total of current assets;
(iii) the total of current liabilities;
(iv) the total of revenue reserves;
(v) the working capital;
(vi) the net book value of the assets.

Note: Ignore Taxation *A.E.B., G.C.E. 'O' Level.*

4. You are required to prepare the Balance Sheet of a limited company as on the 31st December, 19. ., from the following information: The Alma Manufacturing Company Limited was formed in the previous December, with a nominal capital of £80 000 in ordinary shares of £1 each. Up to and including December 31st, 50 000 shares had been issued and fully paid with the exception of 2 000 shares on which £0·12½ per share was still unpaid. Cash in Hand, £100; Cash at Bank, £3 400; Investments, £4 000; Sundry Debtors, £16 071; Leasehold Property, £6 700; Stock in Hand, £36 297; Plant and Machinery, £7 800; Goodwill, £10 000; Provision for Bad and Doubtful Debts, £800; Sundry Creditors, £29 000; Interim Dividend paid, £4 975; Profit for the year ending December 31st, 19. ., £9 793.

N.C.T.E.C.

5. A. B. Ltd., was formed and commenced trading on 1st January, 19. . . The authorised capital was £20 000 divided into 20 000 Ordinary Shares of £1 each, all of which were issued at £1·50 each and fully paid.

The following balances remained on the books after the revenue accounts had been closed at 31st December, 19. . :

Share Capital Account, £20 000; preliminary expenses, £500; sundry creditors, £4 820; freehold premises, £9 800 (cost £10 000, *less* depreciation £200); cash in hand, £120; Profit and Loss Account (*Cr.*), £2 000; Share Premium Account, £10 000; Goodwill at cost, £10 000; machinery, £6 800 (cost £8 500, *less* depreciation £1 700); general reserve, £1 000; sundry debtors, £7 975; stocks as valued by officials of the company, £2 270; provision for dividend, £1 000; provision for bad debts, £50; and balance with bank, £1 405.

Draft the Balance Sheet as at 31st December, 19. ., for presentation to the members of the company.

R.S.A.

6. C.D. Ltd., manufacturers, had an Authorised Capital of £150 000 of which £100 000 was in Ordinary Shares of £1 each and the balance in 5% Preference Shares of £1 each.

From the following list of balances at 30th June, 19. ., prepare the Balance Sheet of the company at that date for presentation to the members:

Formation expenses, £2 050; Ordinary Share Capital Account, £100 000; cash in hand, £255; sundry creditors, £14 326; General Reserve Account, £30 000; leasehold premises at cost, £42 000, less depreciation, £8 000; stocks on hand as valued by officials of the company, £15 826; Profit and Loss Account – undistributed profits, £23 739; machinery at cost, £126 056, *less* depreciation £16 056; equipment and tools at cost, £10 763, *less* depreciation £5 382; Preference Share Call Account (*Dr.*) £150; Preference Share Capital Account, £50 000; office furniture at cost, £2 978, *less* depreciation £952; sundry debtors, £37 377; balance at bank £11 000.

R.S.A.

7. Beta Gamma Limited was formed to take over as from 31st March 19. ., the business of a private trader whose Balance Sheet on that date was as follows:

	£		£
Capital	46 000	Plant and machinery	17 300
Sundry Creditors	5 471	Vans and lorries	3 940
		Fixtures and fittings	600
		Stock	19 731
		Debtors	7 978
		Cash	1 922
	£51 471		£51 471

The company took over all the assets, including cash, at the book values and assumed responsibility for the liabilities. The Goodwill was valued at £9 000.

The authorised capital of Beta Gamma Limited consisted of 40 000 6% Preference Shares of £1 each, 236 000 Ordinary Shares of £0·25 each, and 20 000 Deferred Shares of £·05 each. The vendor took the whole of the Deferred Shares and the balance of the purchase consideration in Ordinary Shares, all at par, and on 30th April, 19.., 20 000 of the Preference Shares were subscribed privately at a premium of £0·05 per share and fully paid. £15 000 was spent on new machinery, the balance being retained as working capital.

Six months' dividend on the Preference Shares was paid on 31st October, 19...

On closing the books on 30th December, 19.., £3 000 was provided for depreciation of plant and machinery, £440 for depreciation of vans and lorries, and £30 for depreciation of fixtures and fittings, and £620 was provided as a reserve for bad and doubtful debts. The remaining balances, after closing the Profit and Loss Account, in addition to those already indicated, were:

	£
Sundry Creditors	4 597
Stock, 31st December	29 388
Sundry Debtors	11 396
Cash	5 605
Net Profit for the period	8 142

You are required to draw up the Company's Balance Sheet as on 31st December, 19... Ignore Taxation.

R.S.A.

8. The Chromium Steel Company, Ltd., having a nominal capital of £500 000 divided into 300 000 Ordinary Shares of £1 each and 200 000 6% Preference Shares of £1 each, was formed to acquire the business of C. Barnby & Sons as from January 1st, 19...

The purchase consideration was fixed at £200 000 for which tangible assets to the value of £150 000 were acquired.

On the following 31st December the purchase price had been discharged by the issue of £100 000 in fully paid Ordinary Shares, £50 000 in 7% Debentures of £100 each and the balance in cash. 75 000 Ordinary Shares had been taken up by the directors and fully subscribed, with the exception of £620 calls in arrear, and 100 000 Preference Shares had been issued and fully subscribed.

The following balances stood in the books of the company on 31st December, 19.., in addition to those indicated by the above transactions:

	£
Plant and machinery	61 500
Salaries	19 380
Directors' fees	10 000
Investments	30 100
Fixtures and fittings	2 500
Carriage inwards	3 970
Fuel, light and heating (factory)	3 820
Freehold factory	39 460
Wages	154 730
Manufacturing expenses	9 650
Stock at 1st January	214 210
Rates and insurance	9 680
Purchases	549 300
Sales	782 260
Returns inwards	4 710
Returns outwards	5 210
Discount Account (*Cr.*)	2 140
Bank loan	24 120
Cash in hand	42 940
Creditors	203 530
Debtors	144 800
Office expenses	6 470
Repairs to buildings	6 860
Transfer fees	60
Apprentices' premiums (P. and L. Account)	2 500
Bad debts	2 310
Provision for bad and doubtful debts	4 000
Interest and bank charges (*Dr.*)	980
Solicitors' fees	1 250
Bills Payable	51 420
Motor lorries	22 000
Loose tools	9 000

Prepare Trading and Profit and Loss Accounts for the year ended 31st December, 19.., and a Balance Sheet at that date.

Make provision for the following:

(i) Motor lorries were re-valued at £17 600 and loose tools at £9 600.
(ii) Depreciation: plant and machinery, $7\frac{1}{2}$%, fixtures and fittings, 5%.
(iii) Unexpired rates and insurance, £1 190.
(iv) Provision for bad debts to be made up to 5% on the debtors.

(v) Debentures interest due (12 months).
(vi) Closing stock, £144 190.

U.E.I. (adapted)

9. Derry Ltd., a company with an authorised share capital of £25 000 in shares of £1 each, had the following balances at 31st December, 19..:

Trial Balance

	£	£
Share Capital Account (15 000 shares of £1 each, £0·75 called)		11 250
Debtors	5 500	
Rent received		400
Rent paid	600	
Bank balance	4 250	
Purchases and returns	28 500	150
Sales and returns	650	35 000
Stock at 1st January	3 000	
Bad debts written off	400	
Bad debts provision		450
Cash in hand	260	
Rates	240	
Salaries	3 520	
Profit and Loss Account at 1st January		5 150
Fixtures and fittings	1 530	
Creditors		2 150
Discount (net)		200
Advertising	300	
Interim dividend paid (ignore income tax)	750	
General expenses	250	
Goodwill	5 000	
	£54 750	£54 750

You are required to prepare the Trading and Profit and Loss Accounts for the year ending 31st December 19.., and Balance Sheet at that date, taking into consideration the adjustments required by the following:

(*a*) The stock at 31st December, 19.., was valued at £4 500.
(*b*) Depreciate fixtures and fittings at the rate of 10% of cost (£1 700).
(*c*) Set aside £1 000 for General Reserve.
(*d*) Included in the rate account is £40 paid in respect of the following year.
(*e*) The sum of £50 is due to the company for the rent owing at 31st December, 19...
(*f*) Included in the Advertising Account is the sum of £100 paid in December for advertising abroad, but the advertisements did not appear until the following year.

10. The Loamshire Garage, Ltd., is a company with an authorised share capital of £50 000 in shares of £1 each.

The following Trial Balance is extracted from the books of the company at 31st December, 19. . :

	£	£
Share Capital Account		50 000
Calls in arrear	250	
Plant and machinery	22 500	
Petrol pumps	8 500	
Purchases of spares	13 260	
Purchases of petrol	52 680	
Stock at 1st January: Spares	5 910	
Petrol	1 270	
Sales: Repairs Department		80 110
Petrol Department		59 700
Wages: Repairs Department	29 480	
Petrol Department	3 160	
Premises	42 000	
Creditors		2 660
Debtors	5 720	
Rates	630	
Salaries	9 240	
Insurance	720	
Light, heat and power	970	
Office expenses	480	
Bank balance	8 500	
Cash in hand	910	
Profit and Loss Account at 1st January		14 200
General expenses	490	
	£206 670	£206 670

You are required to prepare separate Trading Accounts for each department and a general Profit and Loss Account for the year ending 31st December, 19. ., together with the Balance Sheet at that date, after making such adjustments as are necessary in respect of the following:

(*a*) The plant and machinery to be depreciated at the rate of 10% on cost £25 000.
(*b*) The petrol pumps to be depreciated at the rate of 15% on cost £10 000.
(*c*) Provide £200 in respect of doubtful debts.
(*d*) Included in the Insurance Account is £120 in respect of the following year.
(*e*) The stock on hand at 31st December, 19. ., was valued at spares £4 670; and petrol £2 200.
(*f*) Provide for a dividened of 5% on the called up capital (ignore taxation)

R.S.A. (adapted.)

11. The following are the final accounts of M. Barton Co. Ltd., for the year 1978:

Trading and Profit and Loss Account – Year ended 31 December, 1978

Materials & Wages		314 660	Sales		441 200
Depreciation		38 300			
Gross Profit	c/d	88 240			
		441 200			441 200
Expenses		44 120	Gross Profit	b/d	88 240
Net Profit Trading	c/d	44 120			
		88 240			88 240
Balance	c/d	84 200	Net Trading Profit	b/d	44 120
			Balance 31st December, 1977		40 080
		84 200			84 200
			Balance	b/d	84 200

Balance Sheet as at 31st December, 1978

Authorised & Issued Capital		*Fixed Assets*		
360 000 Ordinary Shares of £1 each fully paid	360 000	Freehold Premises at cost		200 000
		Plant at Cost Purchased 1.1.76)	306 400	
		Less Depreciation	114 900	191 500
				391 500
Revenue Reserves		*Current Assets*		
Profit & Loss Account	84 200	Stock	48 120	
		Debtors	32 480	
		Cash at bank	24 800	
Current Liabilities				105 400
Creditors	52 700			
	496 900			496 900

The directors of the Company decided upon a programme of expansion, and by the end of 1979, they had succeeded in doubling the Company's turnover. But to achieve that, the following expenditure had become necessary:

1. A new building, costing £1 000 000 was purchased and paid for.

2. New plant costing £200 000 with an eight year life was purchased and paid for.
3. The cost of materials, wages and expenses were doubled.
4. At 31st December, 1979 the value of stock was £82 200. Total debtors amounted to £62 480 and total current liabilities was £102 560.
5. To meet this additional expenditure, the company's bankers agreed to allow a suitable overdraft.

Required

(*a*) The cash Account for the year 1979.
(*b*) The Trading and Profit and Loss Account for 1979 and a Balance Sheet as at 31st December, 1979.

Calculate the amount that will be available for overdraft repayment at the end of 1980, assuming that there was no additional Capital expenditure in 1980 and that trading receipts and expenses were as in 1979.

Note: No dividends are proposed. Ignore Taxation.

43

The Final Accounts of a Company: Standard Accounting Practices

It will be apparent from the discussion in some of the previous chapters that, although the principles of double entry bookkeeping can be applied to any transaction, in some cases there may be more than one way of doing this. For example, the chapter on depreciation describes several methods of calculating an appropriate provision.

It is clearly desirable that if possible, there should be some general understanding about the relative merits of these alternative approaches. In the United Kingdom the accountancy profession has contributed to such an understanding in respect of some important issues by issuing a series of Statements of Standard Accounting Practice. These are generally known as SSAPs.

SSAPs do not have the force of law. They are not referred to in the Companies Acts, which have, indeed, generally avoided saying *how* various matters should be accounted for, whilst nevertheless specifying clearly that certain matters must be shown, as outlined in Chapter 42. SSAPs have significance only when they are generally accepted by the accountancy profession, and by companies publishing accounts. If a company ignores one of them when preparing its accounts, then the company's auditor should draw attention to this fact in his report on the accounts, so that it can be seen clearly that in some respect, the company has followed unorthodox, although perfectly legal, procedures.

The SSAPs are published by a body known as the Accounting Standards Committee, which is a joint committee on which the six main bodies of accountants are represented. The subjects considered for publication are decided by the Accounting Standards Committee, after consultation within the accountancy profession, and also on the advice of a Consultative Group of non-accountants. The Consultative Group has representation from over twenty bodies, including the Stock Exchange, the Confederation of British Industry, the Trades Union Congress, the Inland Revenue, and the Department of Trade.

When a subject has been decided upon, some research is undertaken, and eventually a document known as an Exposure Draft (usually abbreviated to ED) is published. Any interested person can submit comments on an ED to the Accounting Standards Committee. When these have been collated and considered the Committee has to decide whether to publish an SSAP, and if so whether and how to amend the ED.

At the time of writing fifteen SSAPs have been issued, although two have been withdrawn subsequently for reconsideration. Six further EDs have been issued, and most of them are likely to lead to the publication of SSAPs.

The subjects on which SSAPs and EDs have been issued, other than those subsequently withdrawn, are as follows:

SSAPs

SSAP 1 Accounting for the results of associated companies
SSAP 2 Disclosure of accounting policies
SSAP 3 Earnings per share
SSAP 4 The accounting treatment of Government grants
SSAP 5 Accounting for VAT
SSAP 6 Extraordinary items and prior-year adjustments
SSAP 7 (Withdrawn)
SSAP 8 Treatment of taxation under the imputation system in the accounts of companies
SSAP 9 Stocks and work-in-progress
SSAP 10 Statements of source and application of funds
SSAP 11 (Withdrawn)
SSAP 12 Accounting for depreciation
SSAP 13 Accounting for research and development
SSAP 14 Group accounts
SSAP 15 Accounting for deferred taxation
SSAP 16 Current Cost Accounting

EDs

ED 3 Accounting for acquisitions and mergers
ED 16 Supplement to SSAP 6
ED 21 Accounting for foreign currency transactions
ED 22 Accounting for post-balance sheet events
ED 23 Accounting for contingencies

Those of greatest relevance to readers of this book are likely to be SSAPs 2, 5, 9, 10 and 12.

Reference is made to some of the contents of SSAPs 5, 9, 10 and 12 in other chapters. It is relevant to outline the content of SSAP 2 in this chapter. Mention is also made of the subject matter of ED 24.

SSAP 2 requires that companies disclose their accounting policies. These are the particular bases of accounting which are adopted by the company. The significance of disclosure is that it assists the reader of the accounts to understand them better if he knows which policies have been followed.

The policies are developed to implement in a practical way certain broad basic assumptions, or accounting concepts. SSAP 2, paragraph 14, identifies four of these as follows:

(*a*) *the 'going concern' concept*: the enterprise will continue in operational existence for the foreseeable future. This means in particular that the profit and loss account and balance sheet assume no intention or necessity to liquidate or curtail significantly the scale of operation;

(*b*) *the 'accruals' concept*: revenue and costs are accrued (that is, recognised as they are earned or incurred, not as money is received or paid), matched with one another so far as their relationship can be established or justifiably assumed, and dealt with in the profit and loss account of the period to which they relate; provided that where the accruals concept is inconsistent with the 'prudence' concept (paragraph (*d*) below), the latter prevails. The accruals concept implies that the profit and loss account reflects changes in the amount of net assets that arise out of the transactions of the relevant period (other than distributions or subscriptions of capital and unrealised surpluses arising on revaluation of fixed assets). Revenue and profits dealt with in the profit and loss account are matched with associated costs and expenses by including in the same account the costs incurred in earning them (so far as these are material and identifiable);

(*c*) *the 'consistency' concept*: there is consistency of accounting treatment of like items within each accounting period and from one period to the next;

(*d*) *the concept of 'prudence'*: revenue and profits are not anticipated, but are recognised by inclusion in the profit and loss account only when realised in the form either of cash or of other assets the ultimate cash realisation of which can be assessed with reasonable certainty; provision is made for all known liabilities (expenses and losses) whether the amount of these is known with certainty or is a best estimate in the light of the information.

Other accounting concepts are also generally accepted as being of wide application. One in particular may be noted here.

The *entity concept* is the name given to the idea developed in several chapters in this book, that the business is to be treated for accounting purposes as an independent body, an entity distinct from its owners. The accounts must show how the transactions which are accounted for affect the *business*. The entity concept is applied even when there is no legal distinction between the owner and the business, as in the case of a sole trader. In the case of a company, where there is a clear legal distinction between the owners and the business, the directors and managers are responsible to use wisely the funds which are in their care. In this context the final accounts may be seen as a report on their stewardship of those funds.

SSAPs are not comprehensive rigid rulings. The inevitability of variety and innovation must be recognised. In such cases the accounts need not follow the rules set out in SSAPs if they are seen as inappropriate. However, any significant departure from the standards should be disclosed and explained, and its financial effect calculated and disclosed.

The first SSAP was published in 1971. Before this the Institute of Chartered Accountants in England and Wales had published a long series of Recommendations on Accounting Principles, starting in 1942. These were guidance statements and indicators of good contemporary practice at the date of issue. They continue in effect in this way insofar as they are not replaced by SSAPs.

In some other countries documents similar to SSAPs are also published. In particular, there is a long history of such publication in the USA. There is also a body known as the International Accounting Standards Committee, with very wide membership, which had published over ten standards by the end of 1979. There is a wide measure of agreement between these various sets of standards, but also some important differences. Two topics on which standards vary are accounting for foreign currency transactions, and accounting for price inflation.

Current Cost Accounting

The continuing, and accelerating, increases in prices experienced world-wide for over thirty years led to the early consideration of systems of accounting which would specifically recognise the effects of price inflation. For a long time it was not felt necessary to make any change, and the system of 'historic cost accounting' remained in almost universal use.

However, in several countries there was extensive consideration of the problem throughout the 1970s. After considering various other alternatives the accounting Standards Committee published a relevant Exposure Draft in April 1979. This recommended that a system known as *Current Cost Accounting* (or CCA) be implemented by companies of at least a certain size.

What is Current Cost Accounting? Current cost accounting sets out a complete basis for preparing accounting reports of business activity. It incorporates the obvious fact that prices change over time, but it is not just a system of 'inflation accounting' – it is more fundamental and far-reaching than that.

CCA differs from traditional accounting in some very important respects. These centre round the way of valuing tangible assets and the way of charging expenses.

Traditional accounting shows tangible assets at a valuation based on the purchase price originally paid for them. In other words, it is a historic cost system. Similarly, it charges expenses against revenues first, on the basis of expenditures actually outlaid at some time in the recent or distant past, and second, by allocating these expenditures across time periods so that all revenue earned bears an appropriate proportion of them.

CCA show tangible assets at their 'value to the business', which will often (though not always) be based on their replacement cost. Similarly, it charges expenses against revenues on the basis of their current value to the business (i.e. their 'current cost'), whilst attempting to allocate this across time periods in the same way as in historic accounting. The principal items in each case are fixed assets (and their depreciation) and inventory (and the cost of sales).

CCA therefore produces different accounting results to historic cost accounting. In present-day conditions it tends to show a higher figure for capital employed and a lower figure for profit.

The CCA profit is in 'real' terms, in the sense that it is struck only after charging depreciation and cost of sales on the basis of maintaining intact the firm's productive capacity. In a historic cost system, profit is found after charging depreciation and cost of sales on the basis of maintaining intact the sum of money originally invested in the fixed assets and inventory. This may be too little to maintain the firm's capacity if prices are rising. Conversely, it may be too much if prices are falling.

Of course, if all prices remain stable both systems give the same result. But it is the very essence of the price system that they don't remain stable, because they mirror constantly-shifting relative preferences for different goods and services.

What Are The Ideas On Which CCA Is Based? CCA aims to show (a) the 'value to the business' of its capital employed, and (b) the division of any change in that 'value to the business' over time into a 'current cost operating profit' (which is a 'real gain') and a 'holding gain' (which arises only from holding assets whose money price is increasing).

Value to the business is central to the system. It is defined as the 'deprival value', i.e. the loss which the business would suffer if hypothetically deprived of the asset concerned. This is the lower of *either* the replacement cost of the asset *or* the income benefit which could be derived from it. If the income benefit were the lower of the two, then the firm would be fully compensated for any deprival of the asset by the restitution of a sum equal to that benefit. If the replacement cost were the lower then the firm would be fully compensated for any deprival of the asset by the restitution of a sum equal to that replacement cost, because the asset could be replaced and the higher benefit could then be gained from the replacement asset.

What, then, is the 'income benefit'? The asset could be *either* kept and used *or* disposed of, according to which produces the better return. The benefit in use is the discounted net present value of the expected future income streams. The disposal value is the net realisable selling price. Whichever of these two is the higher would obviously determine whether the firm would keep or sell the asset. In the event of a hypothetical deprival the 'keep or sell' policy would determine the 'income benefit'.

It is important to realise that CCA is *not* exclusively a system of replacement cost accounting and does *not* depend on the firm being willing to replace an asset of which it is deprived for whatever reason.

'Current cost operating profit' measures 'real' profit, defined as profit after making due allowance for changes in price levels. This might therefore be viewed as the figure of profit most suitable to use for purposes of dividend distribution and income taxation. Similarly, current costs rather than historic costs are seen as relevant for considerations such as determining prices, negotiating wages, etc.

EXERCISES 43

1. Explain how an exposure draft differs from a statement of standard accounting practice.

2. Given that they are not legal requirements, what is the significance of SSAPs?

3. List five topics on which SSAPs have been published.

4. Define the entity concept, and state its significance for bookkeeping and accounting work.

5. What do you understand by the following terms:

(*a*) the accruals concept.

(*b*) the consistency concept.

(*c*) the prudence concept.

6. Define the going concern concept, and explain what differences you consider would be made to final accounts if they were not prepared on a going concern basis.

7. If a company's accounts do not comply with an SSAP, what should happen?

Appendix 3

Additional Exercises

1. A and B enter into partnership on 1st March, 19. . . A contributes £2 000 cash and B £1,200 cash and a motor van valued at £650. The cash is paid into a bank account, which is also credited with an additional £2 000 borrowed from the bank.

Premises are rented and £500 paid as rent in advance.

The following items were purchased and paid by cheque. Furniture and fittings, £400; machinery, £1 500; stock in trade, £2 000.
Items purchased on credit were: Machinery, £500; stock in trade, £900.

Cash £50 is withdrawn from the bank to be used as petty cash. Draw up A and B's Balance Sheet on the opening of business.

College of Preceptors – Senior.

2. B. Graham and P. Thorton enter into partnership to take over from 1st January, 19. ., the business carried on by O. Jessop. They are to share profits and losses equally. The following is the final Balance Sheet of O. Jessop: –

Balance Sheet

	£		£
Capital – O. Jessop	20 000	Leasehold premises	9 000
Sundry creditors	4 500	Plant and machinery	6 000
		Furniture and fittings	800
		Stock	5 000
		Debtors	3 300
		Cash	400
	£24 500		£24 500

The purchase price was £24 000, and was paid by cheques by Graham and Thorton direct to Jessop in equal shares. O. Jessop retained the cash balance. All other assets and the liabilities were taken over by the partners. Each partner contributed a further sum of £1 000 in cash to the firm's capital.

Make the necessary Journal entries, and show the firm's Cash Book and opening Balance Sheet.

3. R and T are in partnership, sharing profit and losses equally. On 1st January, 19.., the following balances appeared in the partners' personal accounts:

Capital Accounts; R, £40 000; T, £30 000.
Current Accounts – credit balances; R, £170; T, £100.

From the above and the details which follow, show the Balance Sheet of the partnership at 31st December, 19...

Net profit for the year was £37 500 after providing for interest on capital R, £2 000; T, £1 500 and interest on drawings R, £330; T, £390.

	£
Partners' drawings for the year:	
R	20 000
T	20 000
Sundry creditors	19 800
Sundry debtors	29 800
Provision for bad and doubtful debts	1 500
Stock	27 600
Amounts pre-paid	400
Furniture and fixtures	4 700
Machinery and equipment, at cost	26 000
Depreciation fund for machinery and equipment	12 500
Cash at bank	15 350
Petty cash	500

Set out the Balance Sheet to show clearly the amount of current assets and the amount of fixed assets.

College of Preceptors – Senior (*adapted*)

4. The following balances were extracted from the books of M and N respectively at 31st December, 19...

	M	N
	£	£
Freehold premises	20 000	17 500
Machinery and tools	15 000	14 000
Delivery vans		3 500
Stock of materials	5 000	4 000
Stock of finished goods	8 000	6 000
Cash at bank	6 000	
Cash in hand	400	250
Bank overdraft		5 750
Sundry creditors	13 800	9 650
Rates and insurance prepaid	400	
Provision for bad debts		400
Sundry debtors	9 000	4 800

M and N agreed to combine and trade as partners from 1st January, 19.., on the following terms:

(*a*) N was to pay off the amount of his bank overdraft out of his private funds.

(*b*) Profits and losses were to be shared in proportion to the amount of capital brought in by each partner.

Draft the opening Balance Sheet of the new firm at 1st January, 19.., and state the ratio in which the profits and losses are to be shared.

5. A and B are in partnership as wholesalers, sharing profits and losses equally, and at the 31st December, 19.., the following balances were open in their books after the compilation of the Trading and Profit and Loss Account for the year which ended on that date.

		£
Capital Accounts	A (Cr.)	20 000
	B (Cr.)	20 000
Current Accounts	A (Cr.)	600
	B (Cr.)	400
Sundry creditors		7 000
Sundry debtors		8 000
Bank overdraft		2 650
Loan from C.D. (secured by mortgage of warehouse)		5 000
Freehold warehouse (at cost)		30 000
Fixtures and fittings at cost less depreciation		2 000
Delivery vans at cost less depreciation		4 000
Office furniture at cost less depreciation		250
Stock on hand		11 000
Cash in hand		80
Item prepaid (rates)		70
Provision for items outstanding:	Salaries	300
	Interest on loan	50
Profit and Loss A/c. Dr. Balance at 31st December, 19..		600

You are required:

(*a*) to transfer the Balance of the Profit and Loss Account to the partners' Current Accounts in equal shares;
(*b*) to prepare the Balance Sheet of the firm at the 31st December, 19..;
(*c*) to state what you consider to be the net value of the current assets of the firm at that date.

6. A. Anson and B. Benson are in partnership, sharing profits and losses equally. On 31st March, 19.., their Trial Balance is:

	Dr.	*Cr.*
	£	£
Capital: A. Anson		7 000
B. Benson		4 000
Drawings: A. Anson	340	
Cash	56	
Bank Current Account	134	
Bank Deposit Account	600	
Interest on bank deposit		10
Debtors and creditors	2 500	1 755
Stock, 1st October, in year of account	2 400	
Purchases and sales	14 080	19 437
Returns	177	352
Carriage inwards	182	
Carriage outwards	432	
Commission		152
Leasehold premises (cost £10,000)	8 000	
Furniture and fittings	860	
Salaries and wages	2 260	
Discounts	334	276
General expenses	727	
Provision for doubtful debts		100
	£33 082	£33 082

Prepare Trading and Profit and Loss Accounts for the half-year ended 31st March, 19.., and a Balance Sheet as at that date, taking the following into consideration:

(*a*) Value of stock, 31st March, 19.., £3 240;

(*b*) Leasehold premises are to be written down at the rate of 10% per annum on the orignal cost;

(*c*) Bank Deposit interest on £600 accrued for 3 months at 4% per annum not yet entered in books;

(*d*) Provision for doubtful debts: 5% of debtors;

(*e*) For managing the business B. Benson is to be credited with £800 salary for the half-year before distribution of profit or loss;

(*f*) Interest at the rate of 5% per annum on the partners' capitals is to be allowed.

7. The following balances appear in the books of J. & R. Brown on 31st May, 19.., after the Trading and Profit and Loss Accounts for the half-year ending that day have been prepared.

	Dr.	*Cr.*
	£	£
Cash in hand	450	
Bank Current Account		2 660
Debtors and creditors	28 940	35 430
Stock	46 840	
Freehold premises at cost	60 000	
Furniture and fittings	13 500	
Loan from W. Brown		15 400
Rent owing by tenant	650	
Commission owing to traveller		400
Investment in War Loan valued at cost	8 500	
Profit and Loss Account balance		18 000
Capital: J. Brown		60 000
R. Brown		30 000
Current Accounts: J. Brown	3 920	
R. Brown		910
	£162 800	£162 800

The partners share profits and losses in proportion to the balances shown in the Capital Accounts, these shares being transferred to the Current Accounts.

Before the Balance Sheet as at 31st May, 19. ., is drawn up, it is decided to give effect to the following:

(*a*) sell War Loan for £9 100; cheque for that amount is received and banked that day;

(*b*) accepting expert advice, to write up the value of the freehold premises from £60 000 to £90 000;

(*c*) loan from W. Brown is reduced to £10 000 by giving him cheque for £5 400;

(*d*) transfer shares of balance of Profit and Loss Account for the half-year to partners' accounts.

Draw up the Balance Sheet, assuming the necessary entries in the books to give effect to the above adjustments have been made.

8. **Balance Sheet of B. Barclay & C. Courage** 1st June, 19. .

	£		£
Capital: B. Barclay	8 500	Premises	5 600
C. Courage	8 500	Plant	4 200
Creditors	2 045	Furniture, etc.	1 200
		Stock	6 050
		Debtors	1 260
		Cash	735
	£19 045		£19 045

The partners share profits and losses equally.
On 1st June, 19.., they –

(*a*) re-valued premises at £7 000;

(*b*) received payment £360 from debtors;

(*c*) pay creditors £245;

(*d*) sell one-fifth of the stock for £1 350 cash;

(*e*) write off £160 debts as bad.

Re-write the Balance Sheet at the end of the day.

9. A. Flower started up business as a provision merchant on 1st April, 19.., taking over the business of B. Rice, whose Statement of Affairs at 31st March, 19.., was as follows:

	£	£		£
Capital – B. Rice		22 800	Fixtures	7 500
Creditors –			Stock	20 000
Trade Accounts	7 200		Prepayments (Insurance)	200
Expense	500		Bank	2 800
	—	7 700		
		£30 500		£30 500

All the assets were taken over save the bank balance and Flower also assumed responsibility for the creditors. The purchase price was £25 000 which was the first withdrawal from a Bank Account which Flower opened up in the sum of £40 000.

The only records which Flower kept were of cash sales which amounted to £165 000 at the end of the first year of trading. There were no credit sales.
The following facts are ascertained:

(*a*) All the expenses of the business have been met by cheque and an analysis of the Bank Statements for the year showed the following payments:

	£
Purchases	127 500
Wages	22 000
Rent and rates	5 200
Advertising	2 800
Other expenses	5 760

(*b*) At the end of the first year of trading.

(i) The sum standing to his credit with the bank was £13 000.

(ii) The value of the stock was £30 000.

(iii) Liabilities outstanding were as follows:

Trade creditors for goods supplied	15 000
Advertising	500
Other expenses	350

(iv) Amounts paid in advance were:

	£
Rates	200
Other expenses (Insurance)	150

(*c*) Goods had been taken for private consumption of an estimated cost value of £1 500 during the year.

(*d*) Private drawings were met out of cash receipts, the balance being banked.

(*e*) Private income of £2 000 had been paid into the Bank Account during the year.

On the basis of the foregoing information you are required to prepare –

(1) Trading and Profit and Loss Accounts for the first year of trading.

(2) Balance Sheet as at the end of the year.

London Chamber of Commerce – Intermediate (adapted)

10. X, Y, and Z entered into partnership on 1st July, 19.., without any agreement as to profit sharing save that X guaranteed that Z's share of profit, after bringing interest into account, would not be less than £8 500 per annum.

The initial capital provided was as follows:

X £50 000.
Y £30 000.
Z £10 000 increased on the following 1st January, to £15 000.

In addition to the above capital X and Y made temporary loans to the partnership as follows:

X £20 000 advanced 1st October, 19.., and repaid 1st April, following.
Y £40 000 advanced 1st September, 19.., and repaid 1st December, 19...

The profit for the following year ended 30th June, before providing for any interest, was £22 000.

You are required to show the Profit and Loss Appropriation Account for the year.

London Chamber of Commerce – Intermediate (adapted)

11. E. Flint and S. Stone are manufacturers, sharing profits and losses: Flint two-thirds and Stone one-third. The following is the Trial Balance of the firm as on 31st December, 19...

	Dr.	*Cr.*
	£	£
Stock (1st January, 19..)	5 002	
Purchases and sales	8 236	14 300
Returns inwards and outwards	306	160
Wages	2 575	
Discount allowed and received	85	120
Insurance	175	
Heating and lighting	384	
Salaries	724	
Carriage outwards	271	
Trade expenses	72	
Loan interest	100	
Cash in hand	55	
Bank	370	
Debtors and creditors	2 248	1 900
Loan		2 000
Machinery (1st January, 19..)	3 000	
Machinery additions	500	
Land and buildings	3 200	
Goodwill	300	
Capital Accounts: E. Flint		5 700
S. Stone		4 300
Current Accounts: E. Flint		400
S. Stone	100	
Drawings: E. Flint	832	
S. Stone	400	
Provision for doubtful debts		55
	£28 935	£28 935

(*a*) The stock at 31st December, 19.., was valued at £4 700.

(*b*) £125 was owing in respect of wages.

(*c*) The balance of machinery at 1st January, 19.., is to be depreciated by 10% and the additions by 5%.

(*d*) Interest on capital at 5%.

(*e*) Provide 5% for bad debts.

You are required to prepare the firm's Trading and Profit and Loss Accounts for the year ending 31st December, 19.., and a Balance Sheet as on that date.

12. A. Back and B. Bite started up in partnership on 1st April, 19.., contributing capitals of £8 000 and £15 000 respectively but without any formal agreement as to profit sharing. On 1st October, 19.., Bite made available an additional £9 000 as a loan but without any agreement as to interest.

The accounts for the year ended 31st March, in the following year, disclose a profit of £9 150, but the partners are unable to agree as to its allocation. Bite contends that interest at 6% ought to be brought into account and Back for his part that the technical knowledge which he made available ought to be remunerated by way of a salary allowance of £5 000 per annum which he reckons he could have earned in outside employment.

You are asked to show the distribution of the profit between the partners: the partners' accounts are not, however, required.

London Chamber of Commerce – Intermediate (adapted)

13. **Balance Sheet of A. Bishop, Grocer.**
31st March, 19...

	£		£
Capital	88 000	Premises	52 000
Creditors	2 300	Furniture and equipment	12 400
Expenses accrued	300	Stock	18 000
		Debtors	880
		Cash at bank	7 320
	£90 600		£90 600

(*a*) On 31st March, 19.., Bishop sells the business to Canon and Dean for £95 000 it being agreed that Bishop retains cash at bank and pays outstanding liabilities – which he does the same day. The purchase price is paid into Bishop's banking account.

Prepare Bishop's Realisation Account and show his Capital Account at the end of the day, when he closes his business accounts.

(*b*) On 31st March, 19.., Canon and Dean enter into partnership on equal terms to purchase Bishop's business. Canon pays £60 000 into the new firm's banking account, Dean £40 000, and Dean also brings into the firm stock valued at £20 000. They draw cheque for £95 000 payable to Bishop and take over his assets (other than his cash at bank).

As agreed between them, the partners write up the value of the premises to £65 000, revalue Bishop's stock at £15 000 and write down the furniture and equipment to £10 000.

Prepare Canon and Dean's opening Balance Sheet on 31st March, 19.., after effect has been given to the foregoing.

14. Pheasant and Partridge are in partnership sharing profits and losses equally. Pheasant's capital is £8 000 and Patridge's £7 000. On January 1st, 19.., they admit Grouse to partnership. The Goodwill of the existing partnership is to be capitalised at £4 000 and Grouse is to bring in cash £4 000 as his capital. Pheasant is to be allowed to withdraw £5 000 of his capital.

The terms of the new partnership provide that before division of the profits each partner is entitled to 5% per annum interest on his capital and that the remaining profits be divided: Partridge, one-half, Pheasant and Grouse, one-quarter each.

(*a*) Show, *by means of Journal Entries*, the records necessary to give effect to the above.

(*b*) At the end of the first year of trading the following details are available *in addition* to those arising from the above.

You are required to prepare a Balance Sheet as at the end of the first year of the new partnership.

	£
Net trading profit *before* charging interest on capital and *before* writing £500 off Goodwill	6 400
Cash in hand and at bank	1 772
Freehold premises	10 000
Mortgage on freehold premises	6 000
Stock	4 950
Sundry debtors	5 800
Provision for bad debts	290
Sundry creditors:	
Trade	4 450
Express	350
Machinery and equipment at cost	9 790
Furniture and fittings	670
Depreciation Fund for machinery and equipment	6 980
Current Accounts at January 1st, 19. .:	
Partridge: Balance at January 1st. Cr.	29
Drawings duiing year	2 800
Pheasant: Balance at January 1st. Dr.	17
Drawings during year	1 350
Grouse: Drawings during year	1 350

College of Preceptors – Senior

15. The following are the Balance Sheets of John Smith as at December 31st, in two successive years.

	YEAR 1	YEAR 2		YEAR 1	YEAR 2
	£	£		£	£
Capital, January 1st	50 000	47 000	Premises	15 000	15 000
Profit for year	12 000	20 000	Fixtures	4 000	3 500
Proceeds from sale private investment		6 000	Motor vehicles		7 000
	62 000	73 000	Stock	11 000	15 000
Deduct: Drawings	15 000	18 000	Debtors	26 000	29 000
	47 000	55 000	Bank	9 000	
Mortgage on premises	5 000				
Bank		6 500			
Sundry creditors	13 000	8 000			
	£65 000	£69 500		£65 000	£69 500

Smith looks at his overdraft of £6 500 and says that he cannot understand how he can have made a profit of £20 000 in year 2.

You are asked to prepare a statement showing Smith where his profit has 'gone'.

London Chamber of Commerce – Intermediate (adapted)

16. Explain the following in relation to the accounts of a Limited Liaaility Co., and state exactly where you would look in the Ledger for information on the amount of the item:

(*a*) Preference Share Capital:

(*b*) Reserve:

(*c*) Preliminary expenses:

(*d*) Depreciation Fund.

College of Preceptors – Senior

17. Record the following by way of Journal entries:

(*a*) The purchase of a new motor vehicle for £5 800 after bringing into account an allowance of £4 000 for the one which it replaced and which cost £4 600. The depreciation element has been passed through a separate Depreciation Provision Account and £1 000 of the balance on this account at the date of the purchase of the new vehicle related to the vehicle sold.

(*b*) The sale of goods on behalf of I. Trust for £1 500 cash. No entries with regard to the goods had previously been passed through the books. The sellers' remuneration is on a commission basis: 3% of the gross sale proceeds.

(*c*) The adjustment, at the financial year end, of the existing balance on a Doubtful Debts Provision Account of £750 to 5% of the total of the debtor's balances which amounted to £18 000.

(*d*) The directors' allocation of their company's available profit, viz.,

(1) Transfer to Reserve, £5 000.

(2) Proposed final dividend of £0·10 per share on an issued capital of 100 000 shares of £1 each fully paid.

London Chamber of Commerce – Intermediate (adapted)

18. Distributors Ltd. own a fleet of lorries which are depreciated on the fixed instalment system at the rate of 25% on the basis that lorries in existence at the end of the financial year are depreciated for a full year irrespective of the date of purchase, depreciation on lorries sold during the year not being brought into account.

The lorries are maintained in the books at cost, the depreciation provision being disposed of in a separate Depreciation Provision Account.

On 1st January, 19.., the total cost of the lorries held and the aggregate sum provided as depreciation thereon were £350 000 and £185 000 respectively. On 1st April, 19.., a new lorry was acquired at a net cost of £25 000 after bringing into account an allowance of £3 000 for the one which it replaced, which latter had been acquired 2 years and 7 months previously at a cost of £20 000.

An addition to the fleet was acquired on 1st November, 19.., at a cost of £22 000. You are required to write up the accounts concerned for the financial year ended 31st December, 19...

London Chamber of Commerce – Intermediate (adapted)

19. The following are the balances of A. Watson, Ltd., on 31st December, 19..:

	Dr.	*Cr.*
	£ thousands	
Capital: Authorised, Issued, and Fully Paid up:		
200 000 5% Preference Shares		200
500 000 Ordinary Shares, £0·20 each		100
General Reserve		285
Profit and Loss Account, 1st Jan., 19..		90
Preference Dividend Account	11	
Trade creditors and accrued charges		48
Customers' unpaid balances	340	
Motor vehicles		2
Furniture, fixtures, and equipment	21	
Premises	99	
Stock in trade	158	
Investments at cost	56	
Dividends received on investments		5
General expenses	118	
Directors' remuneration	22	
Cash in hand and at bank	90	
Gross trading profit for the year ended 31st December, 19..		185
	£915	£915

You are required to prepare Profit and Loss Account for the year ended 31st December, 19.., and Balance Sheet as at that date, taking into account the following:

(*a*) Fixed assets, as shown, are valued at cost less depreciation written off to the end of the previous year of account.

(*b*) The Auditors' fee of £1 000 is outstanding.

(*c*) The Board of Directors decide to (i) write off a further £1 000 from the book value of the motor vehicles and to write down the value of the furniture, fixtures, and equipment to £19 000; (ii) make a provision for doubtful debts equal to 5% of customers' unpaid balances; (iii) appropriate a further £18 000 to the General Reserve; (iv) recommend the payment of a year's dividend on the Ordinary Shares of £0·075 per share.

W.J.E.C. – G.C.E. 'O' Level (adapted)

20. The following are the balances of F. Williams & Co., Ltd., on 31st December, 19...

	Dr.	*Cr.*
	£ thousands	
Capital: Authorised, Issued, and Fully Paid up:		
150 000 6% Preference Shares, £1 each		150
640 000 Ordinary Shares, £0·25 each		160
General Reserve		75
Profit and Loss Account, 31st December (previous year)		59
Trade creditors and accrued charges		273
Freehold property	166	
Plant and equipment	19	
Office furniture and equipment	12	
Motor vehicles	16	
Investment at cost	10	
Stock in hand	405	
Debtors	350	
Bad debts	5	
Bank loan		172
Cash in hand and at bank	3	
Interest on bank loan	9	
Directors' remuneration:		
Fees	5	
Salaries	14	
Gross trading profit for the year ended 31st December, 19..		125
	£1 014	£1 014

You are required to prepare Profit and Loss Account for the year ended 31st December, 19.., and Balance Sheet as at that date, taking account of the following:

(*a*) A dividend of £1 000 on investment received on 31st December, has not been entered in the books.

(*b*) The Auditors' fees for the year amount to £1 000.

(*c*) Fixed assets, as shown, are valued at cost less depreciation written off to 31st December, in previous year.

The Board of Directors decides to (i) write off a further 25% on the book value of the motor vehicles and write down the value of the plant and equipment to £16 000; (ii) make a provision of £10 000 for doubtful debts; (iii) appropriate £20 000 to increase the General Reserve; (iv) recommend the payment of a year's dividend on the Preference Share Capital and one of 20% on the Ordinary Share Capital.

W.J.E.C. – G.C.E. 'O' Level

21. The following list of balances was extracted from the books of Workshops Limited *after* the completion of the Manufacturing Account for the year ended 31st December, 19...

You are required to prepare Trading and Profit and Loss Accounts for the year and Balance Sheet at that date.

	£	£
Cost of goods manufactured	59 800	
Stocks –		
Raw materials, 31st December, 19..	5 650	
Work in progress, 31st December, 19..	1 190	
Finished goods, 1st January, 19..	9 750	
Sundry factory expenses accrued		80
Sundry office and administration charges	7 750	
Sundry selling and distribution charges	13 800	
Interim dividend paid 30th June, 19..	1 500	
Debenture interest, half year to 30th June, 19.., paid	100	
Preference dividend, half year to 30th June, 19.., paid	600	
Plant and machinery at cost	32 500	
Provision for depreciation on plant (1st January, 19..)		10 750
Plant depreciation, provision for current year		3 250
Freehold premises at cost	29 000	
Trade creditors		5 220
Trade debtors	9 100	
Transfer fees		90
Share Capital –		
50 000 Ordinary Shares of £1 each fully paid		50 000
20 000 6% Preference Shares of £1 each fully paid		20 000
5% Debentures		4 000
Reserve		5 000
Provision for bad debts, 1st January, 19..		520
Sales		87 200
Cash in hand and at Bank	16 100	
Bad debts	420	
Profit and Loss Account, 1st January, 19..		1 150
	£187 260	£187 260

In preparing the accounts the following matters are to be brought into account –

(*a*) The company's authorised capital is fully issued.

(*b*) Debenture interest is payable half yearly, the half year to 31st December, 19. ., being due on that date.

(*c*) At 31st December, 19. ., office and administration charges were prepaid £120 and selling and distribution charges due and not yet paid amounted to £350.

(*d*) Provision for bad debts is to be reduced by £60.

(*e*) The directors recommend that the current year's profit be appropriated as follows –

(i) Transfer to Reserve £2 000.

(ii) Payment of half-year's dividend on Preference Shares.

(iii) Payment of a final dividend of 6% on the Ordinary Share Capital.

(*f*) Stock of finished goods at 31st December, 19. ., was valued at £11 950.

Notes.

(i) Income tax to be ignored.

(ii) Candidates are advised to pay particular attention to the set out of assets and of liabilities in the Balance Sheet.

London Chamber of Commerce – Intermediate

22. Summum Bonum Ltd. was formed to take over the business formerly carried on by A. Summum and B. Bonum in partnership, whose Balance Sheet just prior to the take over was as follows:

	£		£	£
Capital –		Premises		50 000
A. Summum	100 000	Plant		75 000
B. Bonum	60 000	Stock and work		
		in progress		40 000
	160 000	Debtors		35 000
Contingency Reserve	15 000	Cash –		
Creditors	31 000	At bank	5 000	
		In hand	1 000	
				6 000
	£206 000			£206 000

The company took over all the partnership assets and assumed responsibility for all the liabilities subject to the following:

(1) It was decided that the contingency in respect of which the reserve was built up would not materialise.

(2) The following revaluations were made –

	£
Premises	80 000
Plant	100 000
Stock	30 000
Debtors	30 000

(3) The purchase price was £250 000 to be discharged by way of an issue at par of ordinary shares of £1 each in the company.

Since it was considered likely that the business would expand, an issue of 100 000 6½% cumulative preference shares of £1 each was made and subscribed for by certain friends of Summum and Bonum at a premium of £0·05 per share payable as follows:

On application	£0·25 per share.
On allotment	£0·55 per share including the premium.
On call	£0·25 per share.
	£1·05

The issue was fully called and paid except for 1 000 shares on which the call moneys have not yet been received.

Record the foregoing by way of Journal entries on the basis that:

(1) The company has carried on with the partnership books.

(2) The ordinary shares have been allotted to the vendors.

London Chamber of Commerce – Intermediate

The following questions have been selected from ***West African Examination Council, School Certificate*** *papers.*

Questions are set in the currencies of The Gambia, Ghana, Nigeria, Sierra Leone and Liberia, but there are no mathematical or accounting differences as all the currencies are now decimal.

TABLE OF CURRENCIES

The Gambia	100 Bututs	=	1 Dalasi (D)
Ghana	100 Pesewas	=	1 Cedi (₵)
Nigeria	100 Kobo	=	1 Naira (₦)
Sierra Leone	100 Cents	=	1 Leone (Le)
Liberia	100 Cents	=	1 Dollar ($)

23. Abiola and Babatunde have been in partnership for many years, sharing profits and losses in the ratio of 3:2 respectively. The following was their Balance Sheet as at 31 December 1976.

	₦		₦
Capital: Abiola	4 000	Goodwill	2 000
Babatunde	3 000	Plant & Machinery	1 800
	7 000	Stock	1 960
		Debtors	2 130
		Cash at Bank	90
Sundry Creditors	980		
	₦7 980		₦7 980

On 1 January 1977, they decided to admit Chike as a partner on the condition that he contributed ₦2 000 as his Capital but that the plant & machinery and stock should be revalued at ₦2 000 and ₦1 900 respectively, the other assets, excepting goodwill, remaining at their present book values. The goodwill was agreed to be valueless.

You are required to show:

(*a*) The ledger entries dealing with the above in the following accounts:

(i) Goodwill Account,

(ii) Revaluation Accounts,

(iii) Capital Accounts;

(*b*) The Balance Sheet of the partnership immediately after the admission of Chike.

W.A.E.C.

24. (*a*) *A* and *B* were in partnership sharing profits and losses in the ratio 2:1. The balance sheet as at 31st December 1977 was as follows:

	₦		₦
Capital *A*	30 000	Plant & Machinery	8 000
,, *B*	20 000	Stock	44 000
Creditors	4 000	Debtors	30 000
Bank overdraft	30 000	Cash in hand	2 000
	₦84 000		₦84 000

On 1st January, 1978 *A* and *B* admitted *C* into partnership upon the following terms:

(i) *C* was to purchase by cheque one quarter of the Goodwill for ₦6 000 and provide ₦20 000 as capital. Profits were to be divided in the ratio 2:1:1 to the partners *A, B* & *C*.

(ii) The capitals of *A* and *B* by additions or withdrawals were to be made proportional to that of *C* on the basis in which profits were to be divisible.

You are required to record the above transactions in:

1. The Bank Account.
2. The Capital Accounts of the partnership.

(*b*) Chike and Dayo formed a partnership on 1st January 1977. The Partnership Agreement of Chike and Dayo contains the following:

(i) The partners' fixed Capitals are Chike ₦10 000 and Dayo ₦8 000.
(ii) Dayo to receive a salary of ₦600 a year.
(iii) Interest on Capital is to be calculated at 5 per cent per annum.
(iv) Chike and Dayo to share profits in the ratio of 3:2.
(v) No interest is to be charged on Drawings on Current Accounts.

During the year to 31st December 1977 drawings were: Chike ₦1 200, Dayo ₦1 000 and the Profit & Loss Account for the year showed a profit of ₦4 500 before charging interest on Capital and Partner's salary.

You are required to show the Current Accounts of Chike and Dayo as at 31st December 1977, after division of the profits.

W.A.E.C.

25. The Thompson Company Ltd. is registered with 100 000 shares of $1 each made up of 40 000 5% Preference Shares and 60 000 Ordinary Shares.

During the year ended 31 December 1978 20 000 6% Preference Shares and 40 000 Ordinary Shares were issued to the public for subscription. All the Shares were taken up and fully paid for by the public with the exception of a holder of 500 Ordinary Shares who could not pay the last and final Call of 50 cents per Share.

At the end of the year the sum of $9 000 was realized as the net profit, and the Directors decided to deal with the net profits as follows:

(*a*) Pay the Preference Shareholders' dividends;
(*b*) Pay a dividend of 5% to the ordinary shareholders only on the fully paid-up Capital;
(*c*) Write off preliminary expenses of $500;
(*d*) Carry the balance forward.

You are required to prepare the Profit & Loss Appropriation Account for the year ended 31 December 1978, and to show how the items should appear in the Balance Sheet as at the end of that year.

NOTE: You are not required to complete the Balance Sheet.

W.A.E.C.

Appendix 4
Examination Questions

THE ROYAL SOCIETY OF ARTS EXAMINATIONS BOARD

SINGLE-SUBJECT EXAMINATIONS

ACCOUNTING

STAGE II (Intermediate)—TUESDAY, 16th MAY, 1978

[TWO AND A HALF HOURS ALLOWED]

You have TEN *minutes to read through this question paper before the start of the examination.*

SECTION A

ALL *questions to be answered.*

1. The following figures relating to the year 1977 have been extracted from the books of Pylon, a trader. All sales and purchases have been entered in the accounts of customers and suppliers.

	£
Sales ledger balances (debit) as at 1st January 1977	15 728
Bought ledger balances (debit) as at 1st January 1977	240
Bought ledger balances (credit) as at 1st January 1977	13 480
Returns outwards	790
Returns inwards	648
Cheques received from customers	164 349
Cheques paid to suppliers	101 440
Discounts allowed	3 942
Discounts received	2 984
Sales	158 423
Purchases	102 481
Cash paid in respect of a credit balance on a sales ledger account	26
Bad debts written off in 1977	2 490
Credit balances on sales ledger accounts as at 31 December 1977	58

You are required to prepare a sales ledger control account and a bought ledger control account for 1977. (22 *marks*)

2. The balance sheet of Crow Ltd. as on 1st January 1977 was as follows:

	£		£	£
Share Capital	200 000	Fixed assets		
Profit and Loss Account	30 400	at cost	230 000	
		less depreciation	118 000	
	230 400			112 000
Creditors	70 600	Current assets		
		Stock	82 000	
		Debtors	64 280	
		Bank	42 720	
				189 000
	£301 000			£301 000

On 1st January 1977, the company issued an additional 50 000 shares of £1 each at a premium of £0·20 per share. Cash was received on the same day.

The net profit for the year to 31st December 1977, after writing off £32 000 for depreciation of fixed assets, was 25% of the capital and profit as at 1st January 1977.

The following additional information is available:

	31st December 1977
	£
Stock	92 400
Debtors	72 800
Creditors	68 400
Bank balance	41 200

You are required to prepare the balance sheet of Crow Ltd. as on 31st December 1977 using the information given above. Make any reasonable assumptions regarding items not specifically mentioned above. (26 *marks*)

3. The following trial balance was extracted from the books of Rail, a trader, as at 31st December 1977:

	£	£
Capital account		36 000
Freehold land and building	19 420	
Furniture and fittings	1 200	
Purchases	88 120	
Sales		106 640
Debtors and creditors	12 400	9 535
Insurances	240	
General expenses	3 100	
Wages and salaries	8 790	
Drawings	4 500	
Bad debts	620	
Balance at bank	2 480	
Provision for doubtful debts at 1st January 1977		275
Discounts allowed	1 100	
Discounts received		820
Stock in trade, 1st January 1977	10 400	
Rates	900	
	£153 270	£153 270

You are given the following information:

(i) Stock in trade, 31st December 1977, £12 470.

(ii) At 31st December 1977, insurances paid in advance amounted to £50.

(iii) Wages and salaries outstanding at 31st December 1977, £410.

(iv) The provision for doubtful debts is to be increased to £300.

(v) On 1st January 1977, Rail purchased a motor van for the business for £2 000 and furniture for the business costing £200. He paid for both the motor van and the furniture with cheques drawn on his private bank account. Rail also took from the business goods costing £250 for his own private use. No entries have been made in the books of the company recording these transactions.

(vi) Provide £140 for depreciation of furniture and fittings and allow for depreciation on the motor van at the rate of 20% per annum on cost.

You are required to prepare a trading and profit and loss account for the year 1977 and a balance sheet at 31st December 1977. (36 *marks*)

SECTION B

Answer EITHER *Question* 4 OR *Question* 5, *not both.*

4. Explain what you understand by (*a*) fixed assets and (*b*) current assets, and outline the way in which stocks are valued. (16 *marks*)

5. What do you understand by the term *working capital* and what is its significance? Illustrate your answer, presenting figures as you would expect to find them in a well-prepared balance sheet. (16 *marks*)

THE ROYAL SOCIETY OF ARTS EXAMINATIONS BOARD

SINGLE-SUBJECT EXAMINATIONS

ACCOUNTING

STAGE II (Intermediate)—FRIDAY, 30th JUNE, 1978

[TWO AND A HALF HOURS ALLOWED]

You have TEN *minutes to read through this question paper before the start of the examination.*

SECTION A

ALL *questions to be answered*

1. What are the terms of the Partnership Act 1890 in relation to the division of profit between the partners in the absence of any agreement between them? (15 *marks*)

2. Ledford Ltd. commenced business on 1st January 1973 and its accounts were made up annually to 31st December. The following figures were extracted from the company's books:

	Sales	Purchases	Increase (+) or decrease (—) in stock during year	Selling expenses	Rent	General expenses
	£	£	£	£	£	£
1973	45 000	48 750	+15 000	1 125	3 750	5 625
1974	67 500	46 875	−3 750	1 687	3 750	6 563
1975	97 500	78 750	+5 625	2 437	3 750	7 500
1976	150 000	135 000	+15 000	4 500	7 500	11 250
1977	187 500	168 750	+18 750	6 563	7 500	14 062

Required:

(*a*) a statement showing the book value of the stock on 31st December each year from 1973 to 1977 inclusive,

(*b*) trading and profit and loss accounts in columnar form for each of the five years to 31st December 1977,

(*c*) a brief discussion of the implication of these figures and the inferences you would draw from them. (35 *marks*)

3. The following trial balance was extracted from the books of Downham Ltd. at 31st December 1977:

	£	£
Share capital		200 000
Freehold land and buildings at cost	125 000	
Motor vans at cost	40 000	
Provision for depreciation of motor vans, 1st January 1977		17 500
Purchases	187 966	
Sales		266 642
Rent and Rates	4 000	
Directors' salaries	21 000	
General salaries	29 348	
Bad debts	726	
Provision for doubtful debts at 1st January 1977		969
General expenses	8 437	
Debtors and creditors	28 328	18 081
Stock in trade, 1st January 1977	36 245	
Bank balance	37 411	
Profit and loss account as at 1st January 1977		15 269
	£518 461	£518 461

You are given the following additional information:

(i) the authorised share capital is 200 000 shares of £1 each, which are all issued and fully paid;

(ii) general salaries outstanding at 31st December 1977 amounted to £367;

(iii) the provision for doubtful debts is to be increased to £1 079;

(iv) stock in trade at 31st December 1977 was £39 176;

(v) rent and rates amounting to £400 were paid in advance at 31st December 1977;

(vi) depreciation on motor vans is to be charged at the rate of 20 per cent per annum on cost;

(vii) it is proposed to pay a dividend on £8 000 for the year 1977.

Required:

a trading profit and loss account for the year 1977 and a balance sheet as at 31st December 1977. (32 *marks*

SECTION B

Answer EITHER *Question 4* OR *Question 5, not both.*

4. What do you understand by the term 'conservatism' in relation to accounting measurement? Discuss the extent to which the use of the convention of conservatism increases the accuracy of the calculation of profit. (18 *marks*)

5. 'Profit is normally calculated by matching costs against revenue.' Discuss this statement and indicate how you would obtain the appropriate figures to complete the matching process. Give your views on the accuracy of the results produced by this procedure. (18 *marks*)

THE ROYAL SOCIETY OF ARTS EXAMINATIONS BOARD

SINGLE-SUBJECT EXAMINATIONS

ACCOUNTING

STAGE II (Intermediate) THURSDAY, 16th NOVEMBER, 1978

[TWO AND A HALF HOURS ALLOWED]

You have TEN *minutes to read through this question paper before the start of the examination.*

SECTION A

ALL *questions to be answered.*

1. Explain why a balance sheet balances and how arithmetical agreement is the inevitable result of the correct application of conventional procedures. Outline the financial and factual relationships recorded in a balance sheet.

(23 *marks*)

2. White is confused and worried and has come to you for advice. He tells you that although he made a bigger profit in 1977 than in 1976 he does not seem to be any better off and is finding difficulty in paying his creditors.

The balance sheets of White's business at the end of 1976 and 1977 are as as shown below:

Balance Sheets

	31st Dec. 1976	31st Dec. 1977		31st Dec. 1976	31st Dec. 1977
	£	£		£	£
Capital account	6 000	5 700	Machines	3 500	8 300
Add Net Profit for year	2 400	4 100	Stock	900	3 500
			Debtors	800	3 000
			Cash	2 000	1 700
	8 400	9 800			
Less drawings	2 700	1 500			
	5 700	8 300			
Creditors	1 500	8 200			
	£7 200	£16 500		£7 200	£16 500

Explain the situation to White and advise him on future policy. Support your advice with numerical statements. (25 *marks*)

3. Swallow Ltd. manufactures nest boxes of one standard type. The following trial balance was extracted from the company's books on 31st December 1977:

Trial Balance

	£	£
Share capital authorised and issued 50 000 shares of £1 each		50 000
Share premium		5 000
Freehold premises at cost	49 000	
Plant and machinery at cost	11 000	
Provision for depreciation of plant and machinery to 1st January 1977		6 600
Debtors and creditors	12 950	7 840
Stock of raw materials, 1st January 1977	4 780	
Stock of completed nest boxes in warehouse (1 000 nest boxes), 1st January 1977	2 000	
Provision for doubtful debts, 1st January 1977		220
Bad debts	620	
Directors' remuneration	8 490	
Balance at bank	3 410	
Manufacturing wages	9 400	
Raw material purchased	14 410	
Sales (12 640 nest boxes)		56 880
Administration expenses	3 450	
Rates	720	
Salaries	5 460	
Selling and distribution costs	3 290	
Profit and loss account balance at 1st January 1977		2 440
	£128 980	£128 980

You are given the following additional information:

(*a*) Stock of raw materials at 31st December 1977, £6 290.

(*b*) During 1977, 12 000 nest boxes were completed and transferred from the factory to the warehouse. The nest boxes transferred and the stocks of completed nest boxes are to be valued at cost.

(*c*) There were no stocks of partly finished nest boxes at 1st January 1977 or at 31st December 1977.

(*d*) The provision for doubtful debts is to be reduced to £200.

(*e*) Provision for depreciation of plant and machinery is to be made at 10% per annum on cost.

(*f*) Manufacturing wages outstanding at 31st December 1977 amounted to £600.

(*g*) There was a payment in advance for rates amounting to £60 at 31st December 1977.

(*h*) A dividend amounting to £5 000 is proposed for 1977.

(*i*) £2 000 is to be transferred to general reserve.

You are required to prepare Manufacturing, Trading and Profit and Loss Accounts for the year 1977 and a Balance Sheet as on 31st December 1977. Ignore taxation. (36 *marks*)

SECTION B

Answer EITHER *Question 4* OR *Question 5, not both.*

4. What is the significance of the balance on a partner's capital account? What events will cause the balance to change over time? (16 *marks*)

5. What is the relationship between net profit and the change in the net assets of a firm during a period of time? (16 *marks*)

THE ROYAL SOCIETY OF ARTS EXAMINATIONS BOARD

SINGLE-SUBJECT EXAMINATIONS

ACCOUNTING

STAGE II (Intermediate)—TUESDAY, 6th MARCH, 1979

[TWO AND A HALF HOURS ALLOWED]

You have TEN *minutes to read through this question paper before the start of the examination.*

SECTION A

ALL *questions to be answered.*

1. The balances on the personal ledger control accounts of Galway Ltd. at 31st December 1977 were as follows:

	Dr.	*Cr.*
Bought Ledger	96	56 900
Sales Ledger	97 550	48

The following transactions take place during 1978:

	£
Purchases	194 720
Sales (including £2 540 cash sales)	251 160
Payments to suppliers	216 100
Allowances made by suppliers	2 880
Interest charged to customers	150
Receipts from credit customers (including £250 cheque dishonoured)	260 090
Bad debts written off (including dishonoured cheque)	1 260
Discounts received	2 520
Discounts allowed	5 860
Refund of customer's overpayment	370

Debit balances on suppliers' accounts at 31st December 1978 amount to £150, and credit balances on customers' accounts are £230.

Required:

Prepare Galway's sales ledger control account and bought ledger control account for 1978: carry down the closing balances. (22 *marks*)

2. The following details are extracted from the books of the Fellowship Club:

I	31.12.77 £	31.12.78 £
Bar stocks	8 200	11 936
Creditors for bar supplies	4 080	4 568
Creditors for expenses	160	248

II Summary bank account for 1978

	£		£
Balance at 1st January 1978	13 280	Bar purchases	80 760
Subscriptions received	12 400	Salaries	16 840
Bar sales	107 600	Rent of club premises	2 800
Interest on investments	4 160	Rates	2 000
		General expenses	5 360
		Cost of new investments	26 000
		Balance 31st December 1978	3 680
	£137 440		£137 440

On 1st January 1978 the club held investments which it had purchased for £49 200 and the furniture in use was valued at £30 400.

The owners of the club premises have offered to sell them to the club for £140 000. The committee has decided to buy with the help of a bank loan of £60 000 repayable at the rate of £20 000 a year, the first repayment due on 31st December 1979 and thereafter at annual intervals. The investments are to be sold and will realise £80 000. The sale will be completed on 1st January 1979.

Depreciation should be charged on the furniture and equipment at the rate of 10 per cent per annum on the opening value.

Required:

(*a*) A bar trading account for 1978.

(*b*) A profit and loss account for 1978.

(*c*) A balance sheet as at 31 December 1978.

(*d*) A brief discussion, supported by appropriate figures, in which you give your views on the prospects of the club meeting its commitment to the bank, on the assumption that the annual surplus is maintained at its 1978 rate for several years.

Note. Ignore bank interest.

There are no subscriptions in arrears or in advance. (32 marks)

3. Bacton Ltd. manufactures a single product. The company's factory is divided into two departments designated department A and department B;

the product must pass, at successive stages, through both departments before it is ready for sale. Each department in the factory is completely independent of the other and each is under separate managerial control. The accommodation in the factory is fully utilised, and all plant is working at maximum capacity.

Bacton's summary revenue account for 1978 is as follows:

	£	£
'Department A' Costs		
Materials and Wages		50 000
Depreciation		12 000
Accommodation		8 000
Transfer to Department B		70 000
'Department B' Costs		
Materials and Wages	50 000	
Depreciation	12 000	
Accommodation	8 000	
		70 000
Cost of production		140 000
General expenses		36 000
Net profit		24 000
Sales (200 000 units)		£200 000

There is a heavy demand for the product and the directors of Bacton are considering the possibilities of expansion. Additional accommodation is available for any of the alternatives discussed below. No changes consequent on the proposed expansion are envisaged at the existing factory, and production will continue there at the current level at 1978 costs and selling prices: the net profit from existing activities is therefore expected to be maintained at its current level of £24 000. The minimum amount by which capacity can be increased in both Department A and Department B will produce a further 200 000 saleable units a year.

The following three proposals for increasing activity are being considered:

(I) Accommodation and plant to be acquired to expand both Department A and Department B at equal levels. The cost of the additional accommodation and the depreciation charge on the new plant will be the same as that for existing production and the materials and wages cost in each department will remain at 25% of total selling price.

(II) The purchase of components for Department A from an outside source at a price of 40p per unit. Expansion of manufacturing capacity in Department B on the same terms and at the same cost as for proposal (I).

(III) The purchase of finished goods from an outside source at 90p per unit and their sale at 100p per unit. No additional capacity would be required.

General expenses will increase in all cases at the rate of £2 000 per 50 000 units sold.

Required:

(i) A financial statement which will guide management in making its choice between the three proposals for increased outputs on sales of (*a*) 50 000 units and (*b*) 100 000 units.

(ii) Brief comments which will help management to understand the significance of the statements prepared.

Note: Current production at 1978 prices will continue unchanged irrespective of the choice that is made. (32 *marks*)

SECTION B

Answer EITHER *Question 4* OR *Question 5, not both.*

4. A company balance sheet shows one account for ordinary share capital irrespective of the number of shareholders: a separate capital account for each partner is reported in the balance sheet of a partnership. Explain the reasons for and advantages of this difference in treatment. (*14 marks*)

5. What do you understand by the term 'entity concept' as used in accounting, and what are the merits of the concept in the context of the recording procedures that have been developed by the accountant? (*14 marks*)

Index

Note: Page numbers shown in *italic type* refer to pages in Part 2 in the Complete Course.